VILLAGE LIFE IN NORTHERN INDIA

VILLAGE LIFE IN NORTHERN INDIA

STUDIES IN A DELHI VILLAGE

BY OSCAR LEWIS

WITH THE ASSISTANCE OF VICTOR BARNOUW

UNIVERSITY OF ILLINOIS PRESS, URBANA, 1958

To my Indian students:

Harvant Singh Dhillon
Indera Paul Singh
Rajpal Singh Rathee
Kamal Prakash
R. N. Bansal
Pulin Garg
Venu Ramdas

Preface

The studies in this volume are intended as a contribution to our under-standing of peasant life in contemporary India. Although peasantry still constitutes almost three-fourths of the world's peoples and makes up the bulk of the population in the underdeveloped countries, it has been rela-tively neglected by social scientists as a special field of study. Anthro-pologists have specialized in primitive or tribal societies, sociologists in urban societies, and rural sociologists in modern rural societies. Thus the great majority of mankind has had no discipline to claim it, and only now is a comparative science of peasantry beginning to take form.[1]

In recent years, following the establishment of Point Four and other action programs dedicated to raising the standard of living in the under-developed countries, there has been an increasing recognition of the need for a better understanding of peasant societies. Anthropologists in particu-lar have been giving more attention to peasant societies in contrast to their earlier almost exclusive concern with tribal societies. This new inter-

[1] This is not to minimize the large number of studies of peasant communities which have been done in Middle and South America, China, Japan, India, and Europe. How-ever, a self-conscious awareness of peasantry as a special subject for cross-cultural analysis is quite recent. The first published book by an anthropologist dealing with peasantry per se is the recent volume by Robert Redfield, *Peasant Society and Cultures,* University of Chicago Press, 1956.

est has been on both the theoretical and practical levels. Anthropologists have begun to re-examine the concept "peasant society," and the folk-urban and other typologies in which it appears, in the light of more recent research experience.[2] Anthropologists have also participated directly in action programs as administrators, consultants, and research workers, and have helped train specialized personnel for foreign assignments.

In 1952 Dr. Douglas Ensminger invited me to become consulting anthropologist for the Ford Foundation in India. I was assigned to work with the Program Evaluation Organization of the Planning Commission to help develop a scheme for the objective evaluation of the rural reconstruction program which was going on in fifty-five pilot community projects in India. Although I had had some experience in the study of peasant cultures in Mexico, Cuba, and Spain, this was my first visit to India, and I felt at a great disadvantage in acting as adviser to my Indian colleagues without firsthand knowledge of Indian village life. The invitation by Professor D. G. Karve, then head of the Program Evaluation Organization, to direct a pilot research project for his organization was therefore especially welcome to me. Indeed, my work in village Rampur stands out as the high light of my year in India. Although I have traveled the length and breadth of India, visiting villages as well as cities and universities, and consulting with Indians in all walks of life, it was not until I had studied one village intensively that I began to learn something about Indian life.

The studies presented in this volume, then, grew out of this pilot research project in Rampur. The broad objectives of the project were: (1) to demonstrate the relevancy of the intimate understanding of village life and organization for the work of the evaluation officers as well as for the multipurpose village workers; (2) to obtain significant baseline data in a village within a community project area prior to the start of the action program, so that some measure of control might be had in the study of the impact of the community development program upon the culture and economy of the village; and (3) to develop some research papers which would reflect modern field-work techniques of cultural anthropology and sociology and which could thereby serve as research models for the evaluation officers.

The research methods used in this study were those of the current anthropological and sociological repertory and included participant-observers, interviews, the use of schedules and questionnaires, autobiographies, case studies, and the use of village records and census data. However, the

---

[2] Numerous articles on the nature of the folk and peasant society have appeared in professional journals within the past few years (Miner, 1952; Foster, 1953; Mintz, 1953; Redfield, 1953b; Lewis, 1955a; Wolf, 1955).

Rampur study was not planned as a traditional community study with systematic ethnographic coverage. Rather, we wanted some understanding of those aspects of village life which would be germane to the problems facing the Community Development Projects and the Program Evaluation Organization. We were especially interested in the social structure, the locus of power, and the nature and meaning of leadership. Our work was problem-oriented from the start. Among the problems we studied intensively were what the villagers felt they needed in housing, in education, in health; land tenure and land fragmentation and the current land consolidation program; and the newly created government-sponsored panchayat. Special reports on some of these problems were prepared for the Planning Commission. However, in this volume I am presenting some of the more general cultural data gathered in the course of the field work.

Our project differed from earlier anthropological community studies in still another way. We were subject to time pressure and the need to justify anthropology and sociology to government administrators at each point in the investigation. Although anthropology has a long and honorable history in India, members of the Planning Commission and other administrators still thought of anthropology as the study of prehistory and the description of esoteric customs of tribal peoples. The development of applied anthropology in the study of contemporary peasantry was still in its infancy in India. Indeed, I suspect some of my colleagues wondered why an anthropologist was a consultant on a rural reconstruction program. Our research project, therefore, had to meet the challenge of coming up with data which would be useful and enlightening to government administrators, some of whom were of village background and all of whom considered themselves experts on village life. Work under these conditions was quite different from that of the traditional anthropologist who goes off to the Arctic or jungles of Borneo to become an unchallenged expert on an unknown people. Our data had to meet the test of the Indians themselves both on the village and government levels. I am glad to report that the Planning Commission has seen fit to publish some of our findings and has also organized parallel studies along similar research lines in other parts of India.[3]

Primarily for reasons of convenience of access to New Delhi, a village in the Community Development Project of Delhi State was selected for this intensive study. After a brief review of some of the characteristics of the 100 villages within the project area, we realized that there were at least fifteen variables which would seem to be significant for a cultural study of a community. These variables included such items as location in the

[3] See Dhillon, 1955.

relatively unhealthy lowland area along the Jumna River as contrasted with location in the higher and drier area known as the *bangar;* population size; the number of separate castes and their occupational distribution within a single village; the relative degree of isolation due to differences in communication facilities; the incidence of disease; the presence or absence of a school in the village; the degree of influence of the Arya Samaj movement; the incidence of tenancy; the extent of irrigation; the proportion of communal lands to privately held lands; and finally the extent to which government programs had been active in the village in past years.

It was apparent that no single village could possibly give us a sample of the total range of diversity found in the project area, much less that of North India as a whole. On the other hand, almost any village would serve our purpose so long as we knew what the village was typical of and what it was not typical of.[4] We therefore decided to select a village that would be about in the middle of the population range of the 100 villages in the project area, and one that would have a good representation of castes and occupations.

Our major objective during the first few weeks of the research was to establish and solidify our rapport with the villagers. Accordingly, the first week was devoted to informal talks in which we discussed village problems, what improvements the villagers felt were needed, the kinds of improvements they thought most feasible both on an individual family basis and on a village basis, the history of past efforts at improvement by the government, the attitudes of the villagers toward the Community Projects Administration, and their knowledge of the Five Year Plan. Most of these sessions were group sessions, as much by necessity as design, since we found it almost impossible to hold a private interview without neighbors and relatives dropping in. This situation must be kept in mind by any student from the West who takes privacy for granted and whose research methods, such as polling, depend upon individual opinions and responses. Only after two months of work in the village did we feel that we could insist upon private interviews when necessary, especially in connection with taking the life histories of villagers. During some of the interviews I used an interpreter who was also an expert in shorthand. He recorded the

---

[4] It must be remembered that the community method is not primarily a matter of studying the community. Rather, it uses the community as a natural setting for the study of human behavior and the interconnections between social and psychological acts and processes. It is assumed that communities give us some cell-like minimal duplication of the basic cultural and structural whole, especially in a peasant country like India. For a lucid and concise statement of the methodology and logic of the community study method see Arensberg, 1954.

interviews verbatim, thereby providing greater accuracy and objectivity of the interview situation as well as capturing some of the flavor of the local idiom.

Our next step was to gather a sufficient amount of basic demographic, economic, and social data which would serve as a background for the analysis of any specific problem. Much of these data were recorded on a household and family basis and an accumulative dossier was built up for each. Every family and household was assigned a number which thereafter was used to identify the family. In addition alphabetical lists of both sexes were drawn up, caste-wise, with the corresponding family and house-site number after each name. In this way we were able to identify all individuals in the village in respect to caste and family membership.

To avoid unnecessary annoyance to the villagers, as many data as possible were obtained from village *patvari* records. Later, as our rapport improved, a house-to-house village census was taken which covered the following items: name, sex, age, clan, and caste of each family member; marital status, age at time of betrothal, age at time of celebration of the *gauna;* village of birth; occupation; employment outside the village; pensions; educational experience and literacy; leadership position in terms of membership in the official panchayat organization. In the case of agriculturists we obtained data on landownership; size of cultivation units; fragmentation in terms of number of separate plots; land self-cultivated; land rented in; land rented out; land mortgaged in; land mortgaged out; ownership of oxen, bullock carts, and agricultural machinery.

With the aid of the above data a socio-economic point scale was developed by which each household was ranked according to the score it received on five separate indexes: housing, landownership, income from outside employment, highest school grade completed by family members, and literacy. In addition a total socio-economic score was obtained for each family. With the aid of this point scale we were able to select a sample of thirty households which was representative of all the major socio-economic variables in the village. These thirty families now became the subjects of special intensive studies of needs in housing, health, and education. In addition other special studies were undertaken, such as an analysis of the village *patvari* records; intercaste relations and the breakdown of the *jajmani* system; a comparison of the old caste panchayat and the new statutory panchayat; a study of the ceremonial cycle and the life cycle; a study of factions, social organization, and leadership; and finally a brief study of the religious and ethical concepts of the villagers.

The field research was carried on by the author over a period of about eight months from October, 1952, to June, 1953, with the assistance of Indian students. I am grateful to Mr. Harvant Singh Dhillon, Mr. Indera Paul Singh, Mr. Kamal Prakash, Mr. Rajpal Singh Rathee, Mr. Pulin Garg, Mr. R. N. Bansal, and Miss Venu Ramdas; working with these young Indians was one of the most satisfying experiences of my year in India. Mr. Dhillon helped gather the data on land tenure and economics for Chapter 3 and the data on factions and other aspects of social organization for Chapter 4. In addition he was my interpreter and general field assistant. Mr. Singh collected the data on the festival cycle for Chapter 6 and contributed many of the photographs which appear in this volume. Mr. Prakash helped gather data on the *jajmani* system for Chapter 2 and data on concepts of disease causation for Chapter 8. Mr. Rathee gathered data on diet, clothing, housing, and panchayats for Chapter 1, supplied the drawings of agricultural implements, and also helped prepare the village maps. Mr. Garg gathered the data on concepts of religion and ethics for Chapter 7. Mr. Bansal collected and translated the songs which appear in Chapter 5, and Miss Ramdas gathered some material on the life cycle. I also wish to express my appreciation to Mr. A. P. Dhariwal for his help in checking the Hindi terms used in this book.

I want to thank Dr. Douglas Ensminger of the Ford Foundation for having made possible my trip to India and for having given me sufficient freedom from my administrative duties in New Delhi to carry on this research. In my opinion Dr. Ensminger and the Ford Foundation have made a contribution of lasting value by their aid and encouragement to the Planning Commission in its establishment of a special Program Evaluation Organization. The creation of this organization at the very highest administrative levels of the Indian government and staffed by Indian social scientists has put India in the forefront of those countries which are attempting to utilize the social sciences in the planning of national programs.

I am also grateful to Professor D. G. Karve, formerly head of the Program Evaluation Organization, and Tarlok Singh, of the Planning Commission, for their continued interest in my research in India and for many personal kindnesses shown to me and my family. Because both men have that rare combination of administrative skill and solid scholarship it was an unusual pleasure and privilege for me to work with them.

My greatest debt in connection with this book is to the villagers of Rampur, who generously and patiently gave of their time to members of our research party. I hope that this volume will in some small measure justify the villagers' faith that a better understanding of their way of life and their problems will facilitate the work of the community development program in India and thereby help the villagers.

Closer to home, I want to thank my colleague, Dr. Victor Barnouw, for his valuable library research and editorial assistance in preparing many of the chapters in this volume. Although Dr. Barnouw was never in Rampur, he has worked in other parts of India. I am grateful to the Graduate Research Board of the University of Illinois for a special grant which made Dr. Barnouw's collaboration possible. Thanks are also due to the Behavioral Sciences Division of the Ford Foundation for a grant-in-aid in 1952 which helped with the field work in India and with expenses incurred in preparing the manuscript.

Thanks are due to the *Scientific Monthly* for permission to reprint the article on "Caste and the *Jajmani* System in a North Indian Village"; to the *Journal of Economic Development and Culture Change* for permission to use portions of my article on "Aspects of Land Tenure and Economics in a North Indian Village"; to the American Philosophical Society for permission to reprint my article on "The Festival Cycle in a North Indian Jat Village"; to the *Economic Weekly* of Bombay for permission to use my article on "Group Dynamics in a North Indian Village: A Study of Factions"; and finally to the University of Chicago Press for permission to reprint the chapter on "Peasant Culture in India and Mexico: A Comparative Analysis." In bringing together these scattered articles and in adding four new chapters, it is hoped that the reader will get a more rounded view of life in an Indian village.

Contents

VILLAGE LIFE IN NORTHERN INDIA

1

The Setting

Rampur, a village with 1095 inhabitants, is located in Delhi State about 15 miles west of the city of Delhi.[1] Delhi (including New Delhi) is the largest inland city of India and Pakistan. Formerly a center of Mughal power and influence and later of British administrative control, it is now the capital of the Republic of India. But despite its closeness to this great urban center, the village of Rampur shares the general cultural traits of most of the villages of the Punjab.

The Punjab, which is adjacent to Delhi State, is a meeting place of Hinduism and Islam. The recent partition of the Punjab between India and Pakistan reflects the greater strength of Islam to the west and of Hinduism to the east. Some writers have stated that the caste system is weaker in the Punjab than in other parts of India, that rules governing untouchability are weakly observed there, and that the influence of Brahmans is slight.[2] But these generalizations apply more particularly to West Punjab,

---

[1] It is a few miles from Gheora and Nangloi, two stations on the Delhi-Ferozpur railway line, and 2 miles from the main Delhi-Fazilka road, with which it is connected by a cart track. The name "Rampur" is fictitious.

[2] O'Malley, 1932:23, 144-45; *Imperial Gazetteer, 20*:287; Ibbetson, 1916:3, 6.

Fig. 1. *Village houses as seen from above. Dung cakes are drying on the roof of the house in the foreground.*

where the numbers of both Brahmans and "untouchables" like the Camars have long been lower than in the eastern part of the region.[3]

Rampur lies on the edge of this zone of transition, in a region known geographically as the Indo-Gangetic Divide and culturally as Sirhind or Hariana.[4] Just to the north of the village, at Panipat and Karnal, crucial battles have often been fought, for this tract is on the route followed by invaders from the northwest—early Aryans, Greeks, Persians, Scythians, Mughals. For 150 years, from the time of Timur to Akbar, armies passed through and clashed in this area. When the Mughal empire declined at the close of the seventeenth century, the Sikhs rose to power and struggled with the Marathas throughout this territory between 1760 and 1805. Then the British seized control.[5] It is striking that in spite of this history, and in spite of Rampur's numerous ties with the world outside the village, it still remains conservative in so many respects.

THE JATS

Rampur and its adjoining villages are dominated by the Jats, the principal landowners and cultivators of the district. It is officially known as a Jat village for this reason. The Jats are the largest cultivating caste in northwestern India, numbering 8,377,819 in 1931.[6] They are an ancient ethnic group believed to be of Indo-Scythian origin and to have entered India at about the beginning of the Christian era. "The Jat is in every respect the most important of the Punjab peoples," writes Ibbetson.[7] Ibbetson also observes: "Socially the Jat occupies a position which is shared by the Ror, the Gujar, and the Ahir, all four eating and smoking together. He is, of course, far below the Rajput, from the simple fact that he practices widow-marriage. The Jat father is made to say, in the rhyming proverbs of the countryside—'come my daughter and be married; if this husband dies there are plenty more.' But among widow-marrying castes he stands first."[8]

Although he places the Jats far below the Rajputs on the social scale, Ibbetson believes that Rajputs and Jats are of the same stock, present-day Rajputs being descendants of those who once attained power, while the Jats are descended from those of lower status, who took to widow mar-

---

[3] Darling, 1934:261-66; see maps, *Punjab Census,* 1911:437.

[4] Spate, 1954:483-84.

[5] Ibbetson, 1883:25-26.

[6] *Encyclopaedia Britannica,* 1954, *12:*970-71.

[7] Ibbetson, 1903:74-75.

[8] Ibbetson, 1903:76. In Rampur widow marriage is limited to the junior levirate.

riage.[9] Local Rampur tradition affirms the connection between the Rajputs and the Jats. Some of the local Jats claim to be descendants of Rajput-Jat marriages. The villagers also say that Rampur was founded about eight hundred years ago by Dabas Jats who came from the town of Chori in Moradabad District, Uttar Pradesh.[10]

There is some evidence for considering the southeastern Punjab near Delhi as the original "homeland" of the Jats. In nearby Bharatpur and Dholpur were founded the only Jat states historically known, centers of power which developed when the Mughal empire decayed. The Jats were among the first Hindu groups to rebel against the persecutions of Muslim rule under Aurangzeb.[11] Perhaps partly because of the unsettled character of the period, they were then known as seminomadic plunderers and looters. Sarkar has characterized them at this stage as follows: "Every Jat peasant was practised in wielding the staff and the sword; they had only to be embodied in regiments, taught to obey their captains and supplied with fire-arms to make them an army. As bases for their operations, refuges for their chiefs in defeat, and storing places for their booty, they built several small forts amidst their almost trackless jungles and strengthened them with mud walls that could defy artillery. Then they began to raid the king's highway and carry their depredations even to the gates of Agra." [12]

With the collapse of the Mughal empire the Jats spread out from the rough marginal areas where they had been living to better and more fertile lands farther north. They thus came to occupy the best farming country in the area, and have remained there ever since. Most of the Jat villages are found in upland regions where the climate is relatively good and malaria relatively scarce. Many of these villages were probably already occupied when the Jats overran the region, which is evidenced, as Mukerji points out, by numerous village names suggesting a Muslim origin—Abupur, Asifpur, Latifpur, Faizpur, etc. In one Jat area as many as 126 villages out of 160 are named after Muslims.[13]

---

[9] Ibbetson, 1903:75.

[10] There is said to have been a palace in the region at that time. When the queen of the palace asked her husband who the newcomers, the Dabas Jats, might be, the king answered jokingly that they were her brothers. Taking him at his word, the queen went to meet the Jats and invited them to stay. But later on quarrels broke out between them and the king, and according to one version of the story the king was killed. Another version has it that he simply died. In any case, the queen committed *sati*, or suicide, and in doing so bequeathed a curse upon the womenfolk of the Dabas Jats, predicting that they would thenceforth lead a hard life—as they have done ever since.

[11] Sarkar, 1937:243.

[12] Sarkar, 1937:305.

[13] Mukerji, 1934:27.

Jat villages are of the type which Enayat Ahmad has designated as "compact" and which he associates with the dry western areas. In such regions the population tends to cluster around the water source, and fear of hostile raids also draws the people together.[14] Jat villages, says Mukerji, are unusually large, both in population and in area, when compared with those of other castes. He attributes this to the success of the Jats in farming. Jat villages are also cleaner and far more prosperous than those of other castes.[15]

One reason for this prosperity, according to Mukerji, is the Jats' effective exploitation of irrigation canals. "It is no strange coincidence to find . . . the fields nearest irrigation channels and wells possessed by the Jats." The nature of the region and its climate demand irrigation for successful farming. "The principal characteristic feature of Jat agriculture," writes Mukerji, "is the widespread system of double cropping, the annual fluctuations of which are mainly due to annual variation and the distribution of rainfall. If the amount of rainfall in the *kharif* [autumn-crop] season is not sufficient then in the absence of artificial irrigation double cropping would be an impossibility. Hence the indispensability of canal irrigation in the year of deficient *kharif* rainfall." [16]

The Jat is famous in India for his skill in farming. According to Ibbetson, the Jats of the southeast Punjab are even better cultivators than the more western Jats because of the help they receive from their womenfolk. "Directly we leave the south-eastern districts and pass into the Sikh tract, women cease to perform the harder kinds of field work, even among the Jats. While in the Musulman districts they do not work at all in the fields." [17]

The Jats, both men and women, are hard workers, as the reports of settlement officers during the British period attest. "From the time he [the Jat] is old enough to wear a piece of string round his middle and drive the cattle to the field, until he is too old to do more than sit in the sunshine and weave a hemp rope, his life is one of unceasing toil, borne patiently and without complaint." Because he is "unremitting in toil, thrifty to the verge of parsimony, self-reliant in adversity, and enterprising in prosperity, the Jat . . . is the ideal cultivator and revenue-payer." [18]

[14] Ahmad, 1952.

[15] Mukerji, 1934:21.

[16] Mukerji, 1934:19.

[17] Ibbetson, 1903:79.

[18] Darling, 1925:38, 94.

Ibbetson has assembled some local proverbs about the Jats which give some idea of their character and reputation: "Though the Jat grows refined, he will still use a mat for a pocket-handkerchief." "An ordinary man's ribs would break at the laugh of a Jat." "The Jat is such a fool that only God can take care of him." "The Jat's baby has a plough-handle for a plaything." [19]

The Jats, then, are energetic and relatively well-to-do peasants. Although they seem very poor to a Westerner, they are well off when compared with peasants in other parts of India. According to Mukerji, they are taller, stronger, and better fed than certain peasant groups farther to the east. Indeed, says Mukerji, even their cows are stronger and sturdier than those in other parts of India—thanks to the relatively favorable climate and to the pre-eminence of the Jats in agriculture. [20]

CLIMATE, SOIL, AND WATER RESOURCES

The statement that the climate is relatively favorable needs some qualification. For the weather can be very taxing, particularly in the hot summer months from April to June, when the temperature may rise to 115 degrees. The area is dry and relatively treeless. Warm winds blow across the area, starting early in April, as precursors of the monsoons, and fill the air with sand and dust. The monsoons come in July and August. More than half the average rainfall of the year comes during these months. Since Rampur is situated on an upland plain it is not exposed to river floods, but it does lie at a slightly lower level than its neighboring villages, and excess surface water drains toward it, turning the village streets into quagmires during the rainy season. The battering of the rain, moreover, threatens the mud walls of the village houses (which have to be constantly replastered and repaired), muddies wells, cripples transportation, and helps to spread sickness throughout the village. The rainy season is therefore a season of disease, particularly malaria and skin diseases. But the weather finally gets cooler and healthier, and a dry wintry period from October to January follows.

Despite its discomforts, however, the upland region where Rampur is situated is comparatively healthy. Malaria is less frequent here than in the more low-lying terrain along the Jumna River. The soil is also quite good and well suited for agriculture. There are three types of soil: loam, clay

---

[19] Ibbetson, 1903:76-78.
[20] Mukerji, 1934:17.

loam, and sandy loam. The clay loam and loam types of soil, which constitute the major part of the irrigated land, are very productive; they are
best suited for wheat cultivation.

The average rainfall for the Delhi district from 1869 to 1879 was 23.1
inches. The rainfall is very irregular from year to year, and this is a serious
matter to the peasants, for while a good monsoon means good crops, a bad
one may mean famine. A report made in 1880 gave the following as years
of drought: 1739, 1770, *1783-84, 1803-4,* 1813-14, 1819, 1825-26, 1827-28,
1832-34, *1837-38, 1860-61,* 1865, 1868, 1877.[21]

As the following figures show, the rainfall in 1950-51 was nearly double
that of 1947-48: 1946-47: 30.42 inches; 1947-48: 16.92 inches; 1948-49:
22.53 inches; 1949-50: 28.80 inches; 1950-51: 32.91 inches.

The monthly variation of rainfall is also uneven, being determined by
the monsoons:

Month	1948-49	1949-50	1950-51
July	6.53	18.77	12.70
August	9.83	1.64	9.67
September	3.89	5.31	6.61
October	0.08	——	——
November	——	——	——
December	——	——	——
January	——	0.35	0.87
February	0.52	0.20	——
March	0.31	0.78	1.50
April	0.05	——	1.06
May	0.51	0.15	——
June	0.81	1.60	0.50
Total	22.53	28.80	32.91

Canals and wells supplement the rainfall. There are eleven Persian
(bucket-and-wheel) wells for irrigating the fields around Rampur, and
there are eighteen hand-lever wells *(dhenkali).* The latter are small pits,
the bases of which are plastered with mulberry sticks. A long beam with a
bucket attached at one end is used as a lever to draw water. These small
wells are prepared by vegetable growers. It is not hard for them to do so,
for the water level is hardly 10 feet from the soil. Due to the presence of
salty, brackish water there is a relative paucity of drinking wells in the
area. Rampur has four—two for lower-caste untouchables and two for the
higher castes.

---

[21] Wood and Maconachi, 1882:19. The worst years are italicized. See also Ibbetson,
1883:4.

Water not used for household purposes or for drinking is obtainable from the village pond where the animals drink. This pond, which is shared with the neighboring village of Rasulpur, is refilled, when required, through the canals.

Fifty years ago about half the cultivable land at Rampur was irrigated by canals. Now only about one-sixth is canal-irrigated, due to the increased demands for water by other communities along the canal system. There has been an increased use, during recent years, of Persian wells, seven of which have been built since 1940.

COMMUNICATIONS OUTSIDE THE VILLAGE

The village cannot be called an isolated community. Most people in Rampur have traveled by train at least once. Just after World War I bus service was started on the highway 2 miles from the village. People with milk or vegetables to sell in Delhi sometimes catch the bus on the main road. The train is cheaper—5 annas for one-way fare as against 6 for the bus. (About 5 cents in American money.) Some people walk to Delhi and back. Most transportation in and out of the village is by bullock cart. One

Fig. 2.   A woman resting under the shade of a bullock cart.

frequently sees such carts go by, loaded with fodder or sugar cane. The villagers trade with the nearby towns of Bahadurgarh and Narela, where they sell their surplus grain and buy various supplies such as timber and brick for their houses. The cart track which connects Rampur with the main road is traversible by car in dry weather (although automobiles seldom go to Rampur), but only a bullock cart can get through during the rainy season. There are thirty-three bullock carts in the village. No one owns an automobile, but there are sixty to seventy bicycles in Rampur, most of which are used by the men who have jobs outside the village and who cycle to work.

Some of the men have traveled long distances in search of work, on pilgrimages, or in army service—some as far east as Burma. Few have gone to the south of India, but many have traveled to northern cities such as Agra, Hardwar, Garh Mukhteshwar, and Benares. Villagers go to one of the latter places when there has been a death, to perform the last ritual of placing the ashes of the deceased in the Jumna or the Ganges. Some villagers go to Delhi during the rainy season or to bathe in the Jumna on festival occasions in July-August and October-November.

More intimate contacts are established with other communities through the provision of village exogamy and the requirement to find wives in places some distance away from Rampur. (This will be discussed in more detail in Chapter 5.)

The village is also tied to other villages through the operations of the multivillage panchayat system to be discussed later. A network of social ties is thus established over a wide area. Nevertheless, most villagers spend most of their time within the village itself. Apart from the occasions itemized above there is very little movement in and out of Rampur, and the bus and the train are not often used.

THE VILLAGE SCENE

Rampur has an area of 784 acres or 3765.5 *bighas*.[22] The inhabited area covers about 16 acres and the village is tightly crowded within this small area. Population has almost doubled in the last fifty years but the land resources have remained the same.[23]

There is no orderly arrangement of streets in Rampur. There is no village

---

[22] *Bigha:* about ⅕ of an acre.

[23] The growth of Rampur's population may be traced in the records of the village *patvari*, or accountant, where the following figures are given: 1901: 636; 1911: 560; 1921: 570; 1925: 570; 1929: 570; 1931: 645; 1940: 645; 1951: 965.

Fig. 3. *A village street.* Note the pakka caupal *in the background.*

center, no temple, and no government or public building (except for the school) for the village as a whole. The village accountant, or keeper of village land records, who is an official of the revenue department, lives with one of the more prosperous families and has no official residence as such. Were a new accountant installed, he would have to make his own lodging arrangements.

There are no stores in Rampur, no police station or post office. There is no doctor, the nearest being at a hospital in Nangloi. (A local schoolmaster serves as village physician.) Significantly, there are no vacant houses in the village. With the increasing population and the scarcity of land, the villagers have begun to build two- and three-story houses, for the traditional village house-site area has been used up.

The village streets are wide enough to accommodate a bullock cart, but all the house drains come out into the street, sometimes making trespass difficult. One main thoroughfare runs east-west through the village, and two or three others run in a roughly north-south direction, on the outer margins of the village. (See Map 1.) There are also numerous small dead-end streets or alleys.

The two principal buildings, which serve communal functions, are the *caupals*, or men's club houses, one for each *pana* division of the Jats. These large, quite imposing buildings are situated on the main transverse road, one to the east and one to the west. There is no wall around the village, as in some North Indian villages.

Also attractive are some of the finer residences. These have handsome wooden doors, pillars of the classic Greek type at entranceways, and Moorish-like arches over the doors. Little effort at decoration is discernible in the mud houses of the poorer folk, although one may see red handprints on the walls of some of the houses. These are made at the time of a wedding, or when a son is born.

Around the village, and also in various open places within the village itself, stand piles of dung cakes. There are two types of such piles, one small, the other large. The latter, known as *bitauras*, are covered with a kind of straw matting. Both types of dung heaps are neatly, even elegantly constructed and receive great care. Other structures in the village which show evidence of artistry are the straw-matted, broad-based conical structures known as *boongas* which are used to store wheat and barley chaff for animal feed.

Outside the village a mechanical cane crusher is operated, and beside the dung heaps and scattered trees one may see a small shrine dedicated to one

Fig. 4. Impressively carved wooden doors of a well-to-do Jat's house. Note the elephants carved on the stone benches and the painting above the arch.

of the village gods. The fields where the men work lie round about, their general color being a muddy brown with patches of green. There is more green, of course, after the rains.

Within the village one rarely sees a solitary figure. Crowds gather easily around the visitor and follow him down the narrow streets and in and out of houses. Children play boisterously in large groups; men chat and smoke hookahs together, while women work wooden spinning wheels at their doors or sit sewing together. Cows and bullocks wander about through the streets among the people.

An attractive sight in the mornings and late afternoons is the files of women, in small family groups, carrying water from the wells. Large water pots are balanced on their heads, usually secured by a cloth ring set beneath the pot. They walk gracefully, often singing as they go. The women wear full wide skirts *(ghaghri)* of coarse cotton cloth. Some are blue with white and red, or yellow, spots, and some are striped blue and red. They also wear a shirt *(kurta)* and a shawl *(orhna)*, and some women still wear a bodice *(angi)* to cover the breasts. Unmarried girls wear a half-sleeved

Fig. 5.   Even Jat and Brahman girls make cow-dung cakes. The structure behind these girls is made of such cakes. The clothing (silver and kamiz) *shows Punjabi influence.*

jacket *(garkhi)* with buttons up to the neck. In the past few years since Independence there has been a change in women's styles due to the incursion of refugees from West Punjab into the Delhi area. Refugee women have now introduced their own types of clothing — baggy pajama-like trousers *(silvar)* and a long collarless blouse *(kamiz)*—now worn to an increasing extent in Rampur. Much of the women's clothing is brightly colored, and sometimes spangled with rhinestones and little mirrors. Women also wear heavy silver jewelry on their arms, necks, and ankles.

The men are dressed more soberly than the women in Western-type shirts, with the shirttails hanging down, and either trousers or cotton *dhotis* (full, draped trousers). They wear turbans *(pagri)* on their heads and sandals on their feet. Sometimes a sheet-like wrapper *(cadar)* is thrown over their shoulders. Army clothing is sometimes seen. In wintertime both men and women may wear underwear, sweaters, and socks to keep warm.

POPULATION CHARACTERISTICS

Twelve castes are represented in the village, with the following distribution: seventy-eight Jat families, fifteen Brahman, twenty Camar (leatherworker), ten Bhangi (sweeper), seven Kumhar (potter), five Jhinvar

Table 1

POPULATION DISTRIBUTION BY AGE, SEX, AND CASTE, RAMPUR, 1953

Age Group	Jats M	Jats F	Brahmans M	Brahmans F	Camars M	Camars F	Bhangis M	Bhangis F	Others M	Others F	Total
0 - 4	52	52	13	9	14	7	5	3	15	14	184
5 - 9	44	49	7	10	6	11	5	5	15	12	164
10 - 14	39	32	11	4	5	7	2	2	14	13	129
15 - 19	37	28	6	5	7	3	5	4	10	6	111
20 - 24	38	37	3	3	2	4	2	2	7	4	102
25 - 29	29	22	3	4	2	1	1	1	2	4	69
30 - 34	24	17	4	5	2	6	1	2	7	10	78
35 - 39	16	12	4	3	6	5	0	2	3	3	54
40 - 44	11	7	2	2	3	5	0	0	2	3	35
45 - 49	16	17	2	2	2	1	3	3	3	3	52
50 - 54	12	10	2	1	4	1	2	0	1	2	35
55 - 59	9	3	1	1	0	0	0	0	4	1	19
60 - 64	11	9	1	2	0	0	1	0	3	1	28
65 - 69	3	7	0	0	0	1	0	0	0	0	11
70—	2	3	0	0	0	2	1	0	0	1	9
Total	343	305	59	51	53	54	28	24	86	77	1080

Table 2

COMPARISON OF AGE DISTRIBUTION OF INDIA AND VILLAGE RAMPUR

Age Group	India	Rampur
0–9	28.4	32.2
10–19	20.7	22.2
20–39	32.0	28.1
40–59	14.9	13.1
60—	4.0	4.4

(water carrier), four Dhobi (washerman), four Khati (carpenter), three Nai (barber), two Chipi (calico printer or tailor), one Lohar (blacksmith), and one Baniya (merchant). There are no Muslims in the village. A few Muslims lived in Rampur some years ago, but left before Partition.

The population distribution by age, sex, and caste is shown in Table 1.

There is a total of 648 Jats, 110 Brahmans, 107 Camars, 52 Bhangis, and 163 members of the remaining eight castes. We find a preponderance of males over females, 569 to 511, for the village as a whole. However, this is mainly accounted for by the single caste of Jats. Although male preponderance has often been noted as a population characteristic for the Jats in the Punjab, and sometimes attributed to the practice of female infanticide, it would be difficult to make use of the latter explanation for our village, because the sexual distribution among the Jats in the early years (0-9) is about equal.

Table 3

SIZE OF HOUSEHOLDS BY CASTE, RAMPUR, 1953

Number of Persons in House Site	Jats	Brahmans	Camars	Bhangis	Others	Total
1–3	9	1	4	1	3	18
4–6	19	7	13	8	11	58
7–9	21	4	3	1	12	41
10–12	18	1	1	0	0	20
13–15	6	2	0	0	0	8
16–18	4	0	0	0	0	4
19	1	0	0	0	0	1
Total	78	15	21	10	26	150

Table 4

DISTRIBUTION OF HOUSEHOLD TYPES BY CASTE, RAMPUR, 1953

Household Type	Jats	Brahmans	Camars	Bhangis	Others	Total
I	23	7	16	6	15	67
II	45	8	3	4	9	69
III	9	0	1	0	2	12
IV	1	0	1	0	0	2

A comparison of the age distribution of village Rampur with India as a whole is shown in Table 2.[24]

A point that deserves mention is the unequal distribution of the aged by caste. It appears that there are more than twice as many persons aged fifty-five and over among the Jats, in proportion to their total number, as there are among either the Bhangis or the Camars. Whereas 7.3 per cent of the Jats are over fifty-five, only 3 per cent of the Bhangis and Camars are fifty-five or older. This suggests that the higher standard of living among the Jats may make for greater longevity.

The age distribution of the village population follows quite closely the figures for India as a whole. (See Table 2.)

Approximately two-thirds of the house sites in the village have four to nine persons per house site. However, the range varies considerably by caste and even within castes. The range for the village is from one to nineteen. The Jat households are by far the largest. The average size of household for Jats is 8.3, for Brahmans, 7.3, for Camars, 5, for Bhangis, 5.2, and for the remaining castes, 6.6. However, the differences by caste are more striking than is revealed by these averages. (See Table 3.)

Table 5

PERCENTAGE DISTRIBUTION OF FAMILY TYPES BY CASTE, RAMPUR, 1953

Family Type	Jats and Brahmans	Other Castes
	per cent	*per cent*
Nuclear	32.2	64.8
Extended	66.7	33.3
Alone	1.0	1.7
Total	99.9	99.8

[24] Davis, 1951:86.

Table 6

DISTRIBUTION OF MARRIED COUPLES BY CASTE AND HOUSE SITE, RAMPUR, 1952

Caste	Total Number of House Sites	Total Number of Married Couples Living Together
Jat	78	156
Brahman	15	22
Camar	20	21
Bhangi	10	13
Kumhar	7	10
Jhinvar	5	5
Khati	4	4
Dhobi	4	5
Nai	3	3
Chipi	2	2
Lohar	1	1
Baniya	1	1
Total	150	243

Twenty-nine out of a total of thirty-three households with ten or more persons are Jat households. Only four non-Jat households in the village have ten people or more, and three of these are Brahman.

An analysis of the kinship composition of each household in the village shows that there are three or four major family constellations. Type I is the simple biological family consisting of father and mother with unmarried children. Types II and III are forms of the extended family. Type II consists of father and mother with or without unmarried children plus one, two, three, or even four married sons and their wives and children. Type III represents a further stage, where the basic unit is a group of brothers and their spouses and children, with only the husband's father or mother. Type IV consists of widows or widowers living alone. The distribution of these types by caste is shown in Table 4.

Again, we find a marked difference in the distribution of family types by caste. Sixty-seven per cent of all house sites with extended families of Types II and III in the village are Jat, and almost 70 per cent of Jat households are of the extended family type. The Brahman family constellations tend to follow the Jat pattern, but among the lower castes the nuclear family predominates. If we group the Jats and Brahmans together as compared with the other castes, the contrast appears very clearly. (See Table 5.)

In order to get some idea of the number of families who live on each house site we can chart the distribution of married couples living together per house site. (See Table 6.)

Again we see that the greatest concentration is among the Jats, 156 couples living on seventy-eight house sites. However, this does not mean that Jat households are more crowded than others, because many Jats, unlike most other castes, have additional living quarters *(baithak)* where the men sleep.

HOUSING

The houses of the Jats, the dominant caste, are clustered together, for the most part, in the center of the village on either side of the east-west thoroughfare, but other Jat homes are found in scattered marginal parts of the village. Some of the Brahmans are situated in the center among the Jat families, but there is also a group of Brahmans in the northern end of the village. The Nais and the single Baniya family are found in the center of the village. Most of the other castes are located in the outskirts. The Camars make up a solid block in the northeastern section near the Kumhars, and the Bhangis form a block in the southwestern end. The Dhobis and Chipis are in the southern part, the Jhinvars and the Lohar in the northern.

Six types of houses are distinguishable according to their functions:

1. *Baithak*—a house or a room used by men only, for social purposes and for sleeping
2. *Baithak*-and-cattle enclosure—a *baithak* in which cattle are also kept
3. *Ghar*—a house in which the women of a family live
4. *Ghar*-and-cattle enclosure—a *ghar* in which cattle are also kept
5. Cattleshed—a shed in which only animals are kept
6. Combination—a house in which *baithak, ghar,* and cattle enclosure are grouped in a single unit

The village houses may also be classified into three types according to the materials used in their construction:

1. *Kacca*—a house made of unbaked mud bricks
2. *Pakka*—a house made of fired bricks
3. *Kacca-pakka*—a house made of both types of bricks [25]

---

[25] Combining these two classifications we may say that the Jats have six *kacca* and seven *pakka baithaks;* fifteen *kacca* and fourteen *pakka baithak*-and-cattle enclosures; thirteen *kacca*, two *kacca-pakka*, and twenty-three *pakka ghars;* ten *kacca*, three *kacca-pakka*, and thirteen *pakka ghar*-and-cattle enclosures; three *kacca*, three *kacca-pakka*, and one *pakka* cattleshed; and three *kacca*, one *kacca-pakka*, and six *pakka* combination houses. There are nineteen two-story houses among the Jats. The Brahmans have two *kacca* and one *pakka baithak*-and-cattle enclosures, and nine *kacca* and four *pakka ghar*-and-cattle enclosures. The Camars have four *kacca* and one *pakka baithak*-and-cattle

In some of the brick houses there are architectural refinements, such as those noted before—impressive studded wooden doors, Moorish arches, and ornamental fretwork. In some of the courtyards there are arch-shaped recesses set in the brick walls for lamps, like those found in old Mughal palaces.

The best *pakka* homes are vastly better than the mud homes of the poor, which have a comparatively shapeless appearance. As a defense against the rain, some mud buildings are equipped with roofs of tin sheeting and some with sloping thatch, but most *kacca* houses have flat mud roofs. These mud homes are quite uncomfortable during the rainy season, when cattle, dung, urine, and mud accumulate, and the houses become hot, smelly, and

enclosures, and twenty-two *kacca ghar*-and-cattle enclosures. The Bhangis have two *kacca baithak*-and-cattle enclosures and ten *ghar*-and-cattle enclosures. The Nais have two *kacca ghar*-and-cattle enclosures and one each of the other types. The Dhobis have one *kacca* and one *kacca-pakka ghar*-and-cattle enclosures. The Jhinvars have five *kacca ghar*-and-cattle enclosures. The Chipis have one *pakka baithak*-and-cattle enclosure and two *kacca ghar*-and-cattle enclosures. The Khatis have two *kacca* and two *pakka baithak*-and-cattle enclosures, and four *kacca ghar*-and-cattle enclosures. The Kumhars have one *kacca baithak*-and-cattle enclosure and six *kacca* and one *kacca-pakka ghar*-and-cattle enclosures. The Lohars have one *kacca ghar*-and-cattle enclosure.

Fig. 6.   Interior of a pakka *house of a well-to-do Jat family.*

full of mosquitoes. Chunks of mud are thrown about by the swishing of the cows' tails. It is understandable that two-story houses are preferred, enabling the occupants to sleep upstairs away from the animals and other disturbances. But only a few can afford this luxury.

The data on the *pakka* and *kacca* homes show that most of the compound-unit *pakka* houses have been built by the Jats, while the lower castes tend to live in one-room mud houses. Great variations may occur within a caste, however, for many of the Jats live in the latter type of dwelling; the differentiation is not simply along caste lines.

Interestingly, we found more complaints about housing conditions and more expression of needs for improvement among those with better housing that among those with the poorest quarters. The absence of financial resources makes improvement seem impossible to the poorer villagers. On the whole, the villagers give higher priority to education than to housing improvements.

We noted what kinds of improvements were most often suggested. Jats who lived in *pakka* houses said that they would like chimneys built (not a single house in the village had one), separate quarters for animals, and a separate room for bathing. Many families said that they would like to

Fig. 7. Interior of a kacca *house of a Camar family.*

have separate shelters for cattle and separate *baithaks* for the men. No houses had latrines, but no one expressed a wish to have one, and many raised objections at the suggestion of having a latrine or toilet within the house. Many wanted a second story and more rooms. Some wanted new wooden beams and a new plastering of the walls.

KINSHIP UNITS AND VILLAGE SUBDIVISIONS

To further understand the social organization of Rampur we must examine the meaning of four basic terms used by the villagers, namely, *kunba, gotra, tholla,* and *pana.*

The term *kunba* is used to refer to any group of relatives who trace their relationship through the male line. It may refer to a father and son, in which case it would be a two-generation *kunba,* or it may refer to all male descendants of a great-great-grandfather, in which case it would be a five-generation *kunba,* and would include many cousins. The term *kunba* tells us little about the size of the group. A small *kunba* may consist of only one or two households, while a large one may consist of as many as ten or more. A *kunba* is therefore a localized patrilineage and will be referred to hereafter simply as lineage. A lineage of small depth (one or two

Fig. 8.   Caupal *of* pana *Dhan Singh.*

generations) will be called a minimal lineage, while one of great depth (three, four, or more generations) will be called a maximal lineage.

The term *gotra* refers to nonlocalized, exogamous, patrilineal, and named kinship units which we will call a clan. In the Jat caste in Rampur there are three clans, Dabas, Deswal, and Kharab. The Dabas clan is the oldest in the village and by far the largest. According to local tradition, Dabas, the founder of the clan, was one of three great-grandsons of the famous ruler Prithvi Raj,[26] the other two being Hudah and Dhiya. It is believed that the three brothers settled in Rampur in about 1200 A.D. However, the Hudah and Dhiya people moved away, leaving only the Dabas group in Rampur. Members of the Kharab and Deswal clans came later, by invitation of the Dabas people to whom they were affinally related.

The Dabas have since spread out and today occupy fifteen more or less contiguous villages, although there are other villages scattered here and there within the area. In addition to these fifteen villages the Dabas people have "adopted" five more villages, whose inhabitants, although not Dabas Jats themselves, accept the latters' leadership. These twenty villages form an exogamous as well as an administrative unit known as a *bisagama*, in which the Dabas panchayat exerts authority. This will be discussed later.

The Jat lineages and clans are grouped within Rampur into units locally known as *thollas* and *panas*. These function as semipolitical units for which we find no equivalent terms in English. The village is divided almost equally into two *panas,* known as Dhan Singh and Harditt, and each of these consists of two *thollas* as follows:

Pana Dhan Singh	*Pana Harditt*
Tholla Dhan Singh	*Tholla* Harditt
Tholla Teka	*Tholla* Jaimel

Each *pana* has one *tholla* with a *pana* name and another *tholla* with a different name. *Tholla* Dhan Singh consists of a large single maximal lineage of the Kharab clan, made up of three sublineages in which all members trace their descent from a common ancestor. Teka *tholla* consists of two maximal lineages, both of the Dabas clan. Thus, *pana* Dhan Singh includes members of two different clans.

Tholla Harditt consists of two maximal lineages, one of Dabas clan, the other of Deswal clan, while *tholla* Jaimel consists of three maximal lineages, all of Dabas clan. Here again, we see that *pana* Harditt includes members of two clans.

Although members of the Dabas clan are found in three of the four *thollas* and therefore in each of the *panas,* the Dabas members of any one *tholla* think of themselves as more closely related to each other than to

---

[26] This tradition is also mentioned in Purser and Fanshawe, 1880:25.

Dabas of a different *tholla*. Similarly, the Dabas members of one *pana* think of themselves as more closely related than to the Dabas of the other *pana*.

The *panas* and *thollas* were named after popular men of Rampur by the British revenue officers in about 1860, in their attempt to enhance the position of the local leaders. Dhan Singh and Harditt, as well as Teka and Jaimel, died about sixty years ago and are remembered by some villagers as leaders of their respective lineages.

The ages of these subdivisions vary considerably. About two hundred years ago there were only two divisions in the village, probably two *panas*, constituted by the ancestors of the present-day Teka and Jaimel *tholla* residents who claim to be descended from the original settlers and trace their ancestry back for about 750 years. On the other hand, the families of Dhan Singh *tholla* can claim only about 150 years' residence in the village, for they were invited in at that time by Teka members as *bhanjas*, or sister's sons. Harditt *tholla* too claims old families in its genealogy, but these have died out. The present Harditt families are relative newcomers, descendants of sister's sons who were invited in to Rampur about one hundred years ago by some Jaimel families.

The *panas* are of approximately equal strength, Dhan Singh having forty families and Harditt thirty-eight. Moreover, each *pana* has an equal amount of land, pays the same revenue, and is represented by a separate *lambardar* or headman. The *tholla* strength varies considerably as follows: Dhan Singh, twenty-eight families, Jaimel, twenty-two, Harditt, sixteen, and Teka, twelve. Teka, the smallest *tholla* and one of the oldest, is the most cohesive, while Dhan Singh, the largest and most recent, is the most disunited. It must be noted that the *pana* and *tholla* divisions, used for revenue purposes, apply only to the Jats and to the Brahmans who are their occupancy tenants. This means that the official social organization of the village, as recorded in the village *patvari* records, is in terms of a single caste, the Jats, which clearly dominates the economic and political life of the village. The other castes are not members of any *pana* or *tholla*. They live on village communal land which is owned collectively by the Jats.

The distribution of village house sites by *panas* and *thollas* is shown on Map 1.

It can be seen that the houses of *thollas* Harditt and Jaimel, which together constitute *pana* Harditt, cluster together in a single area, whereas the houses of *pana* Dhan Singh are more scattered and are divided by Harditt *tholla*. This particular pattern is quite recent. Fifty years ago each of the two *panas* constituted two distinct and cohesive geographical units

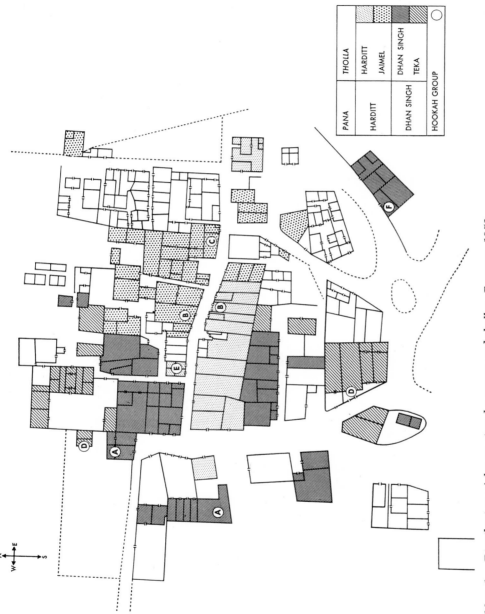

PANA	THOLLA		
HARDITT	HARDITT		
	JAIMEL		
DHAN SINGH	DHAN SINGH		
	TEKA		
HOOKAH GROUP	○		

Map 1. Distribution of house sites by panas and thollas, Rampur, 1953.

of the village. To this day villagers will speak in terms of "our half" of the village rather than in terms of the *pana* names. While clear-cut *pana* division of house sites has suffered, the agricultural lands of each *pana* still form separate units, and it is this which helps to perpetuate *pana* distinctions among the villagers.

PANCHAYATS

A panchayat (literally a council of five) is a group of recognized leaders who meet to pass on judicial cases or problems, or who convene to plan some undertaking or course of procedure in a matter requiring united action. The importance of panchayats in village life has increased in recent years due to the rural reconstruction program associated with India's First Five Year Plan. It seems to be a basic assumption of the Planning Commission that the panchayats are democratic, representative bodies which will forward the objectives of the Plan. This is indicated in the following quotations which set forth the impressive new responsibilities to be assumed by the panchayats:

Panchayats have an indispensable role to play in the rural areas. As representing the best interests of all sections of the community their status is unique. Many activities such as, framing programmes of production for the village, obtaining and utilising governmental assistance for the betterment of the village, such as, the construction of roads, tanks, etc., encouraging villagers to improve the standards of cultivation, organising voluntary labour for community works and generally assisting in the implementation of economic and social reform legislation passed by the States, will naturally fall within the purview of the panchayat. . . . It is . . . very necessary that co-operative agencies in the village should have the closest possible relationship with the principal democratic body namely, the panchayat. . . . it will be possible to build up a structure of democratic management of developmental plans through both the organisations, the panchayats and the co-operative societies.

In relation to land policy the role of the village panchayat becomes an extremely important one, because there are certain problems which none but the panchayat can deal with. . . . the panchayat should become the agency for land management and land reform in the village. In other words in the case of all owners any leasing of land should be done, not directly, but through the village panchayat.[27]

The village panchayat, then, is to safeguard the interests of the landless tenants in the community, to enforce tenancy legislation, and to act as the

---

[27] *The First Five Year Plan*, 1952:165, 195-96.

local agent for land reform. However, as Daniel Thorner has argued,[28] this optimistic faith seems misplaced. In Rampur, as well as in many other such villages, the village panchayat is dominated by the landowning caste—in this case the Jats, who are not likely to abandon their own landed interests. And in the case of judicial disputes, the Jat-dominated panchayat cannot be considered an impartial tribunal. When there are conflicts between the Jats and the lower castes, the latter are not in a good position to defend their interests.

There is some hope, perhaps, in the new statutory multivillage panchayat, which has been functioning since 1949. One purpose underlying the creation of the statutory panchayats was to make a more impartial tribunal available to the lower castes. There is more legal formality associated with the statutory than with the traditional panchayats. Members are elected. (There is a minimum of three and a maximum of seven.) The members, who are to be regarded as government servants, are generally younger men with some education, in contrast with the emphasis on age and seniority in the traditional panchayats. Decisions in the statutory panchayat are arrived at by voting rather than through the traditional method of reaching a unanimous verdict through discussion and majority pressures. There is a schedule of meetings, and records are kept of the proceedings. If anyone wants to have a certified copy of any of the records, he may get one by paying 4 annas per 100 words.

However, despite the greater impartiality of the statutory panchayat and the protection afforded by its legal safeguards, the lower castes have not taken much advantage of it. In fact, the number of cases brought before the statutory panchayat has been going down. In 1949, when sittings were first held, there were forty meetings with a full quorum. In 1950 there were thirty-seven, in 1951, thirty-seven; but in 1952 there were only twenty-two sessions held. During this period the panchayat dealt with eighty-three cases. Only fourteen of these could be called criminal cases, half of which concerned disputes between Jats. Two involved disputes between Camars, and one a dispute between Brahmans. There were, however, some intercaste disputes: two between Camars and Jats, one between Jat and Nai, and one between Nai and Camar. The lower castes may, in time, have more recourse to the statutory panchayat. At present, however, it seems to have become a forum for the airing of rather trivial disputes between individuals. Partly because of the greater familiarity and more traditional procedures, the villagers tend to turn to the traditional rather than to the new statutory panchayats. It is in the caste and village panchayats that the more vital

[28] Thorner, 1953a.

Fig. 9.   *An aged but active and energetic Jat spokesman of the village panchayat.*

issues affecting the people are considered. The establishment of a new school, problems concerning land consolidation, the sending of a delegation to the revenue department — in all these matters the village panchayat played the dominant role in recent years.

The caste panchayats are also to be considered. These are leadership groups for the different castes—Camars, Bhangis, etc.—each of which deals with matters affecting the caste in question. Here again, among these groups the most powerful and important one is the Jat.[29]

The judicial functions of the traditional panchayats and their role in regulating moral conduct are often described in discussions of panchayats, but they have other functions which are less familiar but also important. If an individual wants to give a Kaj feast in honor of a dead ancestor or a feast to celebrate the birth of a son, he informs the caste and village panchayats, in order to secure the cooperation of the community. Or he may wish to distribute sweets in the village on the occasion of a son's marriage. The panchayat may refuse to allow such a distribution. If so, no one will accept the sweets. The panchayat may similarly refuse to sanction the celebration of a Kaj.

The panchayat may also establish certain general standards—for instance in setting limits to dowries, in the number of persons to participate in a marriage party, or in the amount of money spent on wedding gifts. Such regulations may have little effect and may be circumvented by well-to-do families for the sake of family prestige, but they may help to alleviate the difficulties of poor families to some extent. Panchayats may also regulate the customary dues involved in the system of *jajmani* relationships described in Chapter 2.

Panchayats may meet on a multivillage basis, and there is an organizational structure for that purpose. As indicated earlier, Rampur is one of four villages constituting a *caugama,* or four-village unit, which in turn forms part of a twenty-village unit known as a *bisagama.* The constituent villages, offshoots formed in the past due to overcrowding in the parent villages,[30] are tied by kinship bonds and act together on some ceremonial occasions and for panchayat meetings. The *bisagama's* twenty villages are

[29] As another type of panchayat one may also perhaps include the informal hookah-smoking groups of the various factions, for they constitute, in effect, faction panchayats. The term "faction panchayat" is used in Dhillon, 1955:103 ff.

[30] According to Ibbetson, these new settlements always appear on the edge of the drainage line from which their tanks would be filled. "In this way were divided many villages known by the same name with the additions of the words *kalan* and *khurd* (big and little)." Ibbetson, 1883:74.

known as Dabas Jat villages, for they accept Dabas leadership even though some other clans are represented in the area.

Some of the villages are known as *caudhar* or leader villages, some as *dada, dadi,* or *vazir*—grandfather, grandmother, and minister villages respectively. Through kinship bonds, ceremonial occasions, and panchayat meetings, village bonds are maintained.

The fifteen Dabas villages in the twenty-village group are divided into five district units as follows:

1. *Dugama* (two-village unit)
   a) Kanjhawla
   b) Ladpur
2. *Tigama* (three-village unit)
   a) Puth
   b) Sultanpur Dabas
   c) Barwala
3. *Caugama* (four-village unit)
   a) Madanpur
   b) Rampur
   c) Rasulpur
   d) Mubarakpur
4. *Caugama*
   a) Salahpur Majra
   b) Jat Khor
   c) Punjabi Khor
   d) Chandpur
5. *Dugama*
   a) Gheora
   b) Sawda

The first village in each of these units is the leader of the respective units, and Kanjhawla, the first village of the first unit, is the leader of the twenty-village unit.

If a panchayat meeting governing all the villages within the group must be convened, the Kanjhawla panchayat informs the Madanpur *caudhari;* the latter circulates the news about to the other Dabas villages. The villages in this area are very evenly spaced, about ½ to 2 miles apart, and it does not take long for news to travel.

The panchayat organization of the Camars and Bhangis is modeled after that of the Jats, having the same leader villages.

The twenty-village unit belongs to still larger networks culminating in a 360-village unit in which kinship relationships are still traced; but the two-village and four-village units are more significant in Rampur's social relationships. These units are still active and functional in this part of India, although less so than in the past, when they were strong enough to exile families and administer punishment and jail sentences. It has been less than ten years since over 100,000 rupees were collected for the construction of a higher secondary school through the channels of these inter-village organizations.

AGRICULTURE: CROPS

There are two crop seasons in the agricultural year. The first, *samnu* or *savani* (from Savan, July-August), is the autumn or *kharif* crop, which is dependent upon the monsoon rains. The second, *sarhi*, is the dry-season or *rabi* crop, which is dependent upon irrigation.[31] Spate's table for the agricultural cycle in the upper Ganges plains is applicable to Rampur:

mid-June to mid-July.............kharif sowing
August through September........tillage for rabi
early October to early November....kharif harvest, rabi sowing

[31] Ibbetson, 1883:166.

Fig. 10.   Some of the family members rest and others take their turn at the job over the cane crusher.

December to mid-February........weeding and irrigation of rabi
March to mid-April..............rabi harvest
mid-April to mid-May............threshing and sale of rabi
mid-May to mid-June.............culture of cane in irrigated land [32]

Sugar cane is the chief cash crop grown during the first crop season. It grows best in fairly stiff loam and needs abundant rain. Ibbetson says that its cultivation is far more laborious than that of any other staple, for the land must be ploughed at least ten times and well supplied with manure, the more manure being used, the better the yield.[33] The Jat cultivators at Rampur have experimented with several different kinds of sugar-cane seeds and are familiar with their various characteristics. According to Spate, the most striking agricultural development of recent years has been the supplanting of cotton by sugar cane as the chief cash crop.[34] Cotton was formerly grown in the Rampur area, but it no longer is.

Jovar, or *juar,* a millet, is one of the major crops grown in the rainy sea-

[32] Spate, 1954:504. See also the chart on agricultural products in Wood and Maconachi, 1882.

[33] Ibbetson, 1883:180-81.

[34] Spate, 1954:504.

Fig. 11.   A close-up: sugar cane is fed into the cast-iron crusher.

son. It does not require manuring or irrigation. *Jovar* grows best in medium loam and is not grown at all in very sandy soil. Two to five ploughings are required.

Most of the bread eaten during the winter is made of *bajra* flour.[35] *Bajra* is a millet which thrives best in sandy soil. It is generally sown on poorer soil than *jovar*, and is not manured or watered. It is sown as soon as the first rain falls and is usually sown sparsely, along with a pulse.[36]

The pulses include *mung, cana,* and *dhangla. Mung* is a green gram, *cana* a black gram. *Dhangla* is sown for human consumption. *Gavar*, another important crop, is a legume which is unfit for human consumption but excellent fodder for bullocks.

Hemp is sown after *jovar*, being succeeded by wheat, barley, or gram. It is generally sown next to sugar cane. It requires two ploughings but no hoeing or cleaning, and does not need the help of manure or irrigation. Hemp seed is used as feed for the bullocks and the fiber is used in rope-making.

The chief staple crop of the second crop season is wheat. Wheat will

[35] Ibbetson, 1883:187.
[36] Ibbetson, 1883:187.

Fig. 12.   Sugar-cane juice is thickened to make gur *by boiling it in large iron pans.*

grow in almost any soil, except the stiffest, where barley, which is particularly hardy, may be sown instead.[37]

AGRICULTURE: TOOLS AND EQUIPMENT

There are some indispensable tools for dry cultivation owned by every family: an ax and a spade for removing weeds, etc., a lash, made of narrow strips of leather tied to a 2-foot rod of bamboo, for steering oxen, a *khurpa,* an iron blade for cutting grass, and a plough. (See illustration.) Wooden ploughs are more widely used than steel ploughs. The latter are more expensive, more difficult to repair, and require strong bullocks for their operation. More land can be cultivated by the lighter wooden plough. When fields are infested by deep-lying roots, peasants try to borrow a steel plough from some well-to-do cultivator. Like the *khurpa*— and until recently the lash—wooden ploughs are locally manufactured.

[37] Ibbetson, 1883:189-90.

The wooden plow with the yoke.

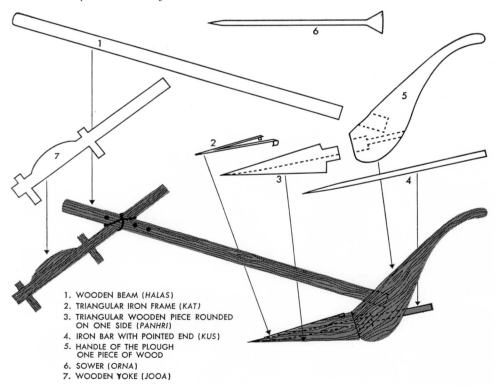

1. WOODEN BEAM (HALAS)
2. TRIANGULAR IRON FRAME (KAT)
3. TRIANGULAR WOODEN PIECE ROUNDED ON ONE SIDE (PANHRI)
4. IRON BAR WITH POINTED END (KUS)
5. HANDLE OF THE PLOUGH ONE PIECE OF WOOD
6. SOWER (ORNA)
7. WOODEN YOKE (JOOA)

Special ploughs are used for sowing. There are forty-seven of the latter type and fifty-five regular ploughs among the seventy-eight Jat families, but only fifteen steel ploughs.

Other items used in dry cultivation are the *maij, kolhari,* and the bullock cart. These are not indispensable, like the tools mentioned above; they may be lent from one household to another. The *maij* is a rectangular log about 4 feet long, 1½ feet wide, and 4 to 6 inches thick, with two pegs for the attachment of ropes. The *kolhari* is a roller made of stone, or sometimes of wood, used for crushing the mud lumps formed in a field after ploughing. The bullock cart has two wheels and is largely made of wood, except for the axles, bearings, iron strips for strengthening the joints, and iron wheels, which have recently replaced the old wooden ones. Of the thirty-three bullock carts in the village, only two have wooden wheels. Thirty of the carts are owned by Jats, the other three by Brahmans.

In addition to the foregoing, some extra tools are required for wet cultivation, particularly for drawing water. There are two methods of drawing water from wells: the Persian well system and the *la-caras* system, for

Fig. 13.   A Persian wheel, one of the main sources of water for irrigation. Its innovation has reduced the demand for the Camar-made leather bag formerly used for drawing water.

which a thick jute rope *(la)* and leather bag *(caras)* are used. In the latter system a bag full of water is drawn over a pulley by two bullocks yoked to the rope. This method is now almost extinct, for the Persian well has superseded it. The first Persian well mechanism at Rampur was installed in 1928; there are now eleven in the village. Camars formerly made and repaired the leather bags used in irrigation; with the change in the well system, however, their work has been reduced, while that of the village Lohar, who has taken over the job of repairing Persian wheels, has been increased. Persian wells are easy to operate; children can run them, supervising the bullocks that turn the wheel and riding on the wheel too, as a kind of sport. The new irrigation system has increased the area of land under wet cultivation and has accordingly given the villagers more work to do.

Another machine used by the villagers is the mechanical chaff cutter. Every cultivating family in Rampur has one. They were introduced into the village in 1929 and have come to be preferred to the older type of hand chaff cutter. There are eighty-three mechanical cutters and forty-three of the older type in the village. The mechanical cutter is a simple machine with easily available replacement parts. The cost ranges from 65 to 100

Fig. 14.   A mechanical chaff cutter. This machine has made the Jat farmers less dependent upon the help of the lower-caste Camars.

rupees,[38] and the average yearly expenditure incurred in operating it is 10 rupees. The new chaff cutter has been a great labor-saving device for the men, but not for the women and children who now sometimes operate it.

There are three iron sugar-cane crushers in the village. Wooden ones were formerly used but have been superseded by the new machines. An iron crusher is worked on a cooperative basis by a number of sugar-cane growers. Another innovation, introduced only two or three years ago, is the iron threshing machine. There is only one in the village.

AGRICULTURE: METHODS

Sowing for the *kharif* crops begins in Cait (March-April)—first *jovar* and then *bajra*. Broadcast sowing is preferred when the ground is moist; when it is dry a drill may be used—especially with *cana*.[39] Sowing for the *rabi* crops begins in the Hindu month of Asauj, the latter part of September, and continues for about three months. The order of sowing is gram, barley, and wheat, although barley may be sown last.

---

[38] A rupee is worth 16 annas, or about 21 American cents.

[39] Wood and Maconachi, 1882.

Fig. 15.   A young Jat hali *weaving a hemp rope during the slack season.*

There is not much preparation of the land for dry crops. Only one ploughing is done during the hot days before the monsoon, when the earth is
parched, dry, and hard to plough. Only heavily weeded fields require any
extra preparation. The field is divided lengthwise into a number of rectangular strips (halai) and is ploughed in one continuous furrow. If the field
has been under cultivation the year before, ploughing is done to make fur-
rows perpendicular to those of the previous year.

In all types of ploughing a yoke of standard size is used, and the oxen
walk on either side of the furrow, with the ploughman following behind
and keeping to the left of the furrow.

Sowing generally begins a few days after the first rainfall, preferably
when the earth's surface is not muddy. If the rains are plentiful, gram seed
may be sown soon after harvesting the jovar and bajra crops. The amount
of seed sown per day depends upon the type of grain and the speed of the
bullocks and the ploughman. The earth turned over by the plough covers
the seeds by about an inch as the plough proceeds.

The first step in harvesting is to cut the plants and to make them into
bundles which are carried away in cartloads. Corn stalks are removed from
the stems, which are set aside as fodder for cattle. If the grain is to be stored
for more than a year, fine sand and nim leaves are mixed with it, and the
whole collection is put into large gunny sacks smeared with cow dung, to
prevent rats from getting in.

Some magical and astrological beliefs enter into the farming practices.
On Monday and Saturday a man should not plough with his face to the
east. He should not travel north on Tuesday and Wednesday, west on Fri-
day and Sunday, or south on Thursday. Wednesday is good for sowing and
Tuesday for cutting the crops.

The Jats cultivate their own fields but sometimes need additional help.
Camars used to provide extra manpower and still do on occasion, although
they no longer help the Jats as they once did. During the kharif season
laborers are given at least a rupee a day plus some bread. The Jat notifies
his men the evening before and calls for them in the early morning. Food is
brought out to the fields by the Jat's son, daughter, or wife, and there is an
occasional break for hookah smoking. Otherwise work continues until sunset. Then the men go home together and receive payment. In the rabi
season the workers prefer to take grain rather than cash.

In planning agricultural innovations it is useful and important to know
what the patterns of change have been before the advent of the community
projects. With this in mind we studied the major innovations in Rampur.
Our findings showed the following: (1) Improved implements and tools of

production, generally involving the substitution of iron for wood. Examples are the iron plow, rollers, the substitution of the iron wheel for the wooden wheel in oxcarts. (2) The gradual introduction of vegetable growing by the low-caste Jhinvars and the adoption of the practice by a few Jat families. (3) The introduction of new and improved seeds, especially in sugar cane and wheat. (4) The substitution of the Persian well for the older leather-bucket system. (5) The substitution of a machine chaff cutter for the hand cutter.

On the whole these changes have been time-saving devices but have not yielded any significant increase in total agricultural production.

LIVESTOCK

Rampur's animal population includes 103 bullocks and bulls, about 100 buffaloes, 38 cows, 23 goats, 7 lambs, 16 donkeys, 1 mule and 1 camel.

Cattle are particularly important in the agricultural economy. According to Ibbetson, an ox begins work when it is almost four and works for ten years. "For a bucket well, eight oxen is the full complement; for a Persian wheel, four. A plough is now always reckoned at two bullocks. It used to

Fig. 16.   Two of the village bullocks.

be reckoned at four; but I think the change is due only to the greater sub-division of land owing to increased population." [40]

Buffaloes are valued more than cows in this region. A cow gives eight to ten calves, one a year; a buffalo will give fifteen or more.[41] Ibbetson says that a buffalo will give 6 to 10 *sirs* of milk daily for eight months, while a cow will yield 3 to 5 *sirs* daily for five or six months. Buffalo milk, moreover, produces more *ghi* (oil of butter). "If a villager loses his cow he only grumbles a little harder than usual; if he loses his buffalo he sits down and cries." [42]

Apart from their value as draft animals and producers of milk, butter, and *ghi*, cattle are of crucial significance in the village because of their dung. The dung is used for two purposes: as fertilizer in the fields and as fuel. Sugar cane requires a lot of manure; some is also used for wheat and other crops.[43] The almost treeless character of the countryside around Rampur makes dung a necessity for fuel. Ibbetson has pointed out that cow dung has just the right kind of properties as a fuel, making it even preferable to wood from the standpoint of a peasant housewife: ". . . the vessels of unglazed pottery in which all who are not rich enough to afford a complete stock of brass vessels cook their food, will not stand well any fire fiercer than the smouldering one given by dung; and in the second place, the wood fire would need constant attendance. What the housewife wants is a fire over which she can put her pot of *dal* [pulse soup] or vege-tables, and go off to the fields, or to the well, or to spin in the alley, feeling sure that the fire will smoulder on and gently simmer the food. And dung gives her exactly what she wants." [44]

The Kumhars also need dung for the firing of their pottery. It is under-standable then that the villagers value dung so highly and that they lavish such artistic care on the *bitauras*, the shapely dung heaps which adorn the village streets.

DIET

Most of the villagers are vegetarians. Until recently the Camars provided an exception, being traditionally eaters of the cattle they skinned for leather.

[40] Ibbetson, 1883:163. Since Ibbetson's time there have been some changes. Nowa-days only four bullocks are required for a bucket well and two for a Persian well.

[41] Wood and Maconachi, 1882.

[42] Ibbetson, 1883: 195-96. A *sir* is a weight of about 2 pounds.

[43] Ibbetson, 1883: 165.

[44] Ibbetson, 1883: 165.

But in the past twenty years, in an effort to raise their status, many Camars have stopped eating meat. However, the Bhangis continue to do so.

Wheat and millet are the major staple foods. Green vegetables and pulses constitute only a minor addition and are regarded as delicacies. In the winter, however, wild greens are gathered in the fields by many families. Milk and milk products are consumed especially among the wealthier families in the village.

Sit, a kind of buttermilk, is usually available for the asking. In the early morning hours poor folk may be seen going to different houses with earthen pitchers, collecting *sit.*

Roti, made of wheat or millet, is eaten every day, with either a vegetable curry, *dal, dahi* (curds), *ghi,* or *sit. Catni,* made of crushed onion, salt, and chili, may be substituted. The poorer people cannot afford butter or *ghi.* To improve the flavor of some dishes, especially those made with wild greens, a hot cow-dung coal dabbed with *ghi* is dropped into the pot during the cooking.

There is almost no variety in the meals served. Day in and day out, with few exceptions, the villagers eat the same food throughout the year. This is one reason why festivals are welcomed with such enthusiasm. On such occasions various delicacies are prepared. But these occasions occur only about twice a month.

Guests are served special foods: wheat *roti,* a vegetable curry or *dal,* sugar, and *ghi. Bajra* is considered inferior, so guests are not served *bajra roti,* if possible. Nor are they served *roti* without *ghi.* The guest sits at meals alone. Members of the family eat their usual fare, but children of the household may be given some of the special food. Some categories of guests are given special foods; a son-in-law, for example, is served a particular kind of wheat *roti,* a vegetable curry or pulse, and *ghi bura* (sugar with *ghi*). A Brahman guest who visits a Jat also receives special treatment, and a Brahman woman is invited to cook for him. The Brahmans smear the hearth and a space around it with cow dung before cooking the meal. Only certain types of food may be given to a Brahman. Food known as *kacca,* cooked in water, may be accepted by a Brahman only from another Brahman; but *pakka* food, cooked in *ghi,* is acceptable from other "clean" castes. Some well-to-do families may honor a guest with such delicacies as *halva, puri,* and *khir.*[45]

During the summer and rainy months three meals are served, but in

---

[45] *Halva* is made by mixing *ghi* with wheat flour and then frying the flour until it turns brown. Boiling sugar syrup is added. *Puris* are fried *rotis* of small size, made of wheat flour and cooked in *ghi. Khir* is a rice-milk pudding.

winter adults have only two, although children generally continue to have three meals. The morning meal in winter is cooked by 8:00 A.M. *Bajra roti* is the main fare. The members of the family eat it hot, sitting near the hearth on the floor. At no meal time do all the family members eat together. Children and elderly persons are generally served first; the others come one by one, eat their meals, and go. The women of the household eat last— never with the men.

The evening meal is cooked at about 7:00 P.M. and consists of the same food. In summer and rainy months wheat *roti* is prepared instead of millet. A midday meal is served, in which *roti* may be combined with *sit, dal, catni,* or *gur* (a crude brown sugar containing molasses). Vegetable curry is only rarely prepared. A thick porridge made of *bajra* may be added at the evening meal.

EDUCATION

Toward the turn of the century the villagers of Rampur, particularly the landowning Jats, became concerned about the educational facilities for their children. They finally persuaded the district officials to establish the first village school for boys in 1908.[46] This school served the four villages of the *caugama* which have always cooperated on educational matters. In 1929 a girls' school (with female teachers) was started in Rasulpur, but it closed down in 1934 and was not reopened until 1943. A new wave of enthusiasm for education came in 1944-45, when another school for girls was opened at Madanpur and, more important still, the Kanjhawla High School was started. The latter was sponsored by a regional patriotic society, the Hariana Shakti Education Society, which represented over a hundred villages in the area. Finally, in 1950, Rampur established its own girls' school, which now includes some students from Rasulpur. Thus the people of Rampur send their children to three local schools: two primary schools within the village, and a high school only a few miles away. The villagers are proud of their schools and claim that their village is ahead of others in this area when it comes to education. "You won't find any of the surrounding villages as advanced educationally as ours," asserted the local headmaster; and many others echoed this statement.

Education is not, however, uniformly distributed. There are sharp variations in school attendance with regard to sex, age, and caste. While 70 per cent of the boys of school age go to school, only 23 per cent of the girls do so. There are 381 children of school-going age (5-19) at Rampur, but only

[46] Before this some children went to school in nearby Mundka and Karala.

187—or about 50 per cent—of these attend school (147 boys, 40 girls). In the case of the girls, education is generally limited to the years between five and fourteen. The percentage of school-going girls in the first age group (5-9) is 30.75 per cent; in the second (10-14) it is lower—25 per cent; and in the 15-19 age group the representation is only 5 per cent. In the case of the boys the percentage of school attendance climbs from about 68 per cent in the 5-9 age group to 85 per cent in the 10-14 bracket, then drops to 49 per cent at 15-19. School education for girls is a fairly recent development in India and is only slowly making headway in the villages. In Rampur it is almost limited to the Jat, Brahman, and Khati castes: 40.2 per cent of the Jat girls aged 6-15 (thirty-one out of seventy-seven), and 30 per cent of the Brahman girls (three out of ten), attend school. Four of the five Khati girls in this age bracket (80 per cent) attend school. But only one of the sixteen Camar girls (6.2 per cent), attends, and none of the other castes has any girls in school at all.

In terms of primary school attendance the castes of the village fall into three groups which cut across the usual caste rankings in some respects. The relatively low-caste Nais and Khatis are grouped with the Jats and Brahmans in the category with highest school attendance; the Camars and Jhinvars form an intermediate group, while the Chipis, Lohars, Kumhars, Dhobis, and Bhangis (mostly low castes) make up the group with lowest school attendance. (See Table 7.) As part of the national effort to raise the lot of untouchables, Harijan (low-caste) students are not only exempt from the 2-annas-per-month school fee but may apply for special scholarships of 1 or 2 rupees per month. But only some Camar families have taken advantage of this opening. Although the Bhangis and Dhobis make up fourteen of the village's 150 families, they have no children in the primary school, and the Kumhars, with seven families, have contributed only one student. Economic and occupational factors seem to be involved here. The group with highest school attendance includes those with the most economic security, especially in the case of the Jats, who are the landowners of the village. It also includes occupational groups (Nai and Khati) whose work does not demand the help of children in the 5-14 age bracket. There is no great demand at present for the services of the barber and carpenter, and in their work children can be of use primarily after twelve years of age. In the case of the Kumhars, however, children can be put to work at various unskilled or semiskilled tasks: carrying clay, breaking the clods, adding water, taking care of the donkeys. The same may be said of the Bhangis. Since the struggle for livelihood is serious, it may be hard to spare children in the 5-14 age group when their work is of real assistance to the family.

Table 7

SCHOOL ATTENDANCE, AGES 6-15, RAMPUR, 1953

	Boys	Girls	Boys and Girls
Jat			
total	87	77	164
school attendance	80	31	111
per cent	91.9	40.2	67.6
Brahman			
total	19	10	29
school attendance	16	3	19
per cent	84.2	30.0	65.5
Camar			
total	14	16	30
school attendance	12	1	13
per cent	85.7	6.2	43.3
Bhangi			
total	6	7	13
school attendance	0	0	0
per cent	0	0	0
Kumhar			
total	4	6	10
school attendance	1	0	1
per cent	25.0	0	10.0
Jhinvar			
total	9	4	13
school attendance	6	0	6
per cent	66.6	0	46.1
Khati			
total	4	5	9
school attendance	4	4	8
per cent	100.0	80.0	88.8
Dhobi			
total	4	1	5
school attendance	0	0	0
per cent	0	0	0
Nai			
total	3	1	4
school attendance	3	0	3
per cent	100.0	0	75.0
Chipi			
total	1	3	4
school attendance	1	0	1
per cent	100.0	0	25.0
Lohar			
total	2	1	3
school attendance	1	0	1
per cent	50.0	0	33.3
General			
percentage	81.0	29.7	57.3

Some lower-caste informants also said that untouchables are discriminated against to some extent at the schools and are not treated so well as the higher-caste children. Moreover, education is not always seen as an asset. When there are educated villagers without jobs, the value of such training may be called into question.

When it comes to higher education the Brahmans and Jats are again in the lead. Fifty-seven students from Rampur attend the higher secondary school at Kanjhawla. Jats, Brahmans, and Camars are principally represented, with thirty-seven, nine, and six students respectively. Jhinvars and Chipis each have two, Khatis one. About fifteen students in the village have matriculated, and six students from Rampur (all Jats) are in college at Delhi. Apart from the teachers and matriculated students at Rampur, there are about thirty-five villagers who may be called "educated"—mostly members of the higher castes.

Unfortunately, higher education does not seem to bring practical returns to the villagers. Of the seven boys who passed the higher secondary school in 1950-52 two are now unemployed, while three have gone on to college and two are employed. Altogether, there are nineteen "educated" unemployed persons at Rampur. Higher education tends to make the individual unsuited to farm work but does not necessarily prepare him for other occupations, especially not at a time when unemployment among the educated in India is so high and the competition for available jobs so great. Many students used to become teachers after matriculation, but opportunities in this field have been reduced through the institution of a new government requirement that only students trained in basic education at Ajmer College may become teachers in this area, and unfortunately admission to Ajmer College is becoming increasingly difficult. However, education is still associated with high status and prestige.

One more point may be made about the schools here. Quite apart from its formal educational functions, the school system has played a significant role in social solidarity. The public-spirited efforts made by many people to establish schools in the four-village and still larger units have helped to knit the different villages together. It is noteworthy that membership on committees for this purpose cuts across caste, village, and faction lines; this is a hopeful indication for the future.

LIFE CYCLE

According to the traditional Hindu views which are often cited in the literature about India, an individual's life is conceived to be divided into

Fig. 17.   A Jat boy from the village, student in a Delhi college.

four stages *(asrama)*. In the first stage, the individual is in the status of pupil and maintains submissive obedience toward his *guru* (teacher), as well as strict chastity *(brahmacarya)*. In the next stage the individual is a householder, a responsible family man *(grhastha)*. In the third stage he begins to break away from the world of social obligations. He and his wife retire to the forest to cultivate the life of meditation. In the fourth and final stage the individual becomes a wandering mendicant with no settled home or occupation *(bhiksu)*.[47]

These ideal stages bear little resemblance to the present-day life cycle in Rampur, where one finds neither the strict chastity of the *brahmacarya* stage among the young men nor an ascetic withdrawal from life among the old people. The following is a very brief account of the characteristic life cycle, which touches on only a few main points.

Certain ceremonies *(sanskara)* mark stages in the life cycle of the individual, some even being performed before and after the actual life span. To celebrate a forthcoming birth, a *sanskara* is held when a woman is pregnant. Another is performed after the individual has died. Most of these ceremonies, however, take place during childhood. The most important and lavishly celebrated is that of marriage. A Brahman is usually present to perform ritual acts at a *sanskara*, a fire *(havana)* is lighted, *mantras* (incantations) are recited by the Brahman, and there is distribution of food.

What might be called the first of these ceremonies in the life cycle, the *garbha sanskara*, is performed at pregnancy, and relatives and friends are invited. The Brahman officiates and receives from 2 to 10 rupees.

During pregnancy the woman is generally given somewhat better food than usual and perhaps lighter work to do, although she ordinarily continues working until the time of delivery. The husband is discouraged from having sexual relations with her at about the sixth month.

At the time of labor a *dai*, or Bhangi midwife, is called in to help in the delivery. The mother and newborn child are secluded in a corner of the house. If the family has only one room, a cloth curtain is put up to separate them from the others. The mother does not leave this corner for ten days. During this time her only attendant is the midwife, who bathes her and cleans up the corner. It is the midwife who cuts the umbilical cord —with any sharp instrument that happens to be at hand. No medicines are applied. The cord is buried in a hole at the foot of the mother's cot, for it is believed that if it were disposed of outside, some animal might eat it, and then the child would die.

During the ten-day period of seclusion the mother may lie on the cot

[47] Zimmer, 1951:155-57.

without clothes, if the weather is warm, or covered by a blanket. The baby is not swaddled, as this is not practiced in Rampur. Nobody visits the mother during these ten days, because she is believed to be polluted by the birth. The midwife throws her unclean bath water out at some distance from the house. The midwife receives from 2 annas (about 4 cents) to 1¼ rupees (about 25 cents) for her services. She may also be given the discarded clothes worn by the mother, but these are often ragged and almost useless. The mother may be more generous to the midwife if the baby is a boy than if it is a girl.

The baby is not placed at the breast right after birth. If it is born in the morning, it may not suckle until evening, but in the meantime it is given some sugared water with the help of cotton wool or soft cloths dipped in water. As soon as the sun has set, the mother's sister-in-law brings a small brass tray *(thali)* and a bunch of grass with which she washes the mother's nipples. The mother squeezes some of her first milk onto the *thali*. She may also throw some jewelry onto it. Then the baby may be suckled. It is rare for a woman to lack milk. If this should happen, goat's milk may be given, or a wet-nurse resorted to.

A Brahman associated with the family may designate a day for the first official bath for the baby and mother. This is usually on the day of the birth or the following day. Many people do not bother to consult a Brahman. Friends and relatives come to the house on this day, bringing grain. This is given to a female Nai, or Nain, who takes over the job of attendant from the midwife a few days after the birth. As mother and child are bathed, the women stand about singing songs. Food is distributed among them. Then the Nain makes palm marks on both sides of the door. More grain is given and there is more rejoicing when a son is born than when the baby is a girl. A *thali* is beaten and other loud noises are made to celebrate the birth of a son, but not that of a daughter.

About ten days after the birth the Brahman officiates at another *sanskara*. The mother is bathed by the Nain beforehand, and the floor is given a new coating of dung in preparation. Three principals must take part in the ceremony — the mother, the child, and a male representative of the family (father, uncle, or grandfather, etc.). The Brahman lights a small fire, to which he adds incense and *ghi*. Then he reads aloud some Sanskrit verses, at the conclusion of which he ties arm bands *(ponchi)* to the wrists of the mother, the child, and the man of the household. The Brahman receives about 1 rupee and some flour for these services. At this time the Brahman may also suggest four names for the child, one of which is chosen by the family.

A big feast is the climax of the celebration. All the members of the family's *pana* may be invited—even the whole village—and bands may play all day long, if the family is well-to-do. The *neota* system, which is described in the chapter on marriage (pp. 176-77), may be resorted to in order to help finance the celebration.

After the purificatory fire ceremony, the mother may go out of her home, but usually she continues to rest for another twenty or thirty days, doing very little work. She is given a lot of flour and *ghi* to eat, if possible.

In Rampur a woman usually gives birth to a child in her husband's home, not in that of her parents, as is the case in Maharastra.[48] However, she usually takes the baby to her parents' home about a month after the child is born and stays there for a while, nursing it. It is said that this trip is taken to avoid conceiving again too soon.

The next ceremonial step in the life cycle of a boy comes when the child has his first haircut. Jats and Brahmans generally have this done in the month of Baisakh (April-May) at the shrine of Ghantal Deo, one of the village gods.[49] This usually takes place within the first year after the child's birth. Members of the lower castes—Camars, Kumhars, etc.—generally go to Beri or Gurgaon for the first haircut, especially if a vow has been made to one of the Matas (goddesses) to do so.[50] Some of the hair, together with 1¼ rupees, is offered at the shrine of the goddess. A feast may or may not be given in connection with this ceremony. These customs do not concern girls, whose hair is not cut.

During the first nine months a child is given no food other than its mother's milk. After that buffalo milk and a little porridge may be given. The child is usually weaned while the mother is pregnant with the next one—perhaps in the fourth month of pregnancy. Weaning may be accomplished by applying the bitter paste of *nim* leaves to the nipples.

There is little fuss about toilet training. After the child can understand instructions, the mother repeatedly tells him not to soil the bed. He may be beaten if he does so. The mother takes the child out into the fields as he grows older, until he learns to go there for the purpose of excretion.

As has been noted in the section on education, about 70 per cent of the boys of school age and 23 per cent of the girls go to school. When a boy first goes to school, a special *sanskara* may be performed to mark the occasion, with the usual fire ceremony and a feast.

The principal ritual experience in an individual's life is that of marriage.

---

[48] Karve, 1953.

[49] See pp. 204-5.

[50] See p. 205.

This is not a brief ceremony performed in one afternoon but consists of a series of rituals stretching over a period of two or three years. Boys are married at fourteen or fifteen, girls at twelve or thirteen, but cohabitation starts a few years later. When one compares the marriage ceremonialism here with that in some other peasant cultures, such as Mexico, one is struck by the enormous amount of elaboration lavished on this *rite de passage* with respect to the time and money spent on it, the number of ritual steps taken, their degree of elaboration, and the number of individuals and communities involved. (Marriage ceremonies are described in detail in Chapter 5.)

Observances at death ceremonies have changed in recent years in some respects due to the influence of the Arya Samaj movement. Formerly the son or younger brother of a dead man shaved his head and mustache on this occasion. He slept on the floor instead of on a cot. He wore special clothing, told beads, and sang devotional songs. It was the duty of the son or younger brother to light the crematory fire and to carry the bones of the deceased to the Ganges two or three days after the cremation. Various taboos attended this trip. The man was not supposed to urinate until he had cast the remains into the river. Then he would go to the toilet, bathe, offer money to a Brahman priest, and have the priest write the dead man's name in a record book. On the way home the man would carry a pot of Ganges water, and from time to time he would sprinkle some of the water along the way. While the main outlines of these patterns have been preserved, some features are no longer followed.

Thirteen days after a death a ceremony is held at which Brahmans and children are feasted.

Then, two or three months later, or sometimes a year later, a feast called Kaj may be given to honor the dead man. People from many villages are invited to some of the more elaborate Kaj celebrations.

THE DAILY ROUND

The men of Rampur work hard and so do the women. A Jat housewife arises at about 4:00 A.M. and grinds grain for the day. This may take about two hours. There is never much flour stored ahead of time, although when a woman is expecting a baby and has no one to grind for her, she may lay up a store beforehand. Theoretically a girl is not required to grind at her parents' home, but children generally work with their parents if they are not attending school. The boy works with his father, the girl with her mother. At dawn the housewife sweeps her house and perhaps collects cow dung from the cattleshed, which she makes into cakes for fuel. Then she goes to get water from the well, carrying two large pitchers on her head, for she has to bring enough water to last until her afternoon trip.

The woman may go to work in the fields, but if there are children to look after she stays at home. Food cooked the night before and freshly prepared *roti* are taken out to the men in the fields. After that the housewife has some time to herself. She may do some sewing or gossiping with neighbors. Then she prepares food for the next meal. By 1:00 P.M. she is free for an hour or two, unless the children demand attention. At about 3:00 she begins to work at various household jobs: beats *bajra* for *rabri* (curds and flour), makes the fire, and sets water to boil. If there are cows and bullocks at the house, the woman gives them fodder. Then she goes on her second trip to the well.

At around sunset the men come home and have their meal. Cows and bullocks which have been let out to pasture also return, shepherded by little boys. The first and the last sound heard in the day is the jingling of cow bells; now the cattle are put into their sheds, and the men eat their dinner.

The members of the family sit about in the dim light of an earthenware

Fig. 18.   Interior of a Jat house showing grindstones for flour, pots and pores.

lamp containing oil and a cotton wick. (Usually there is only one such lamp.) After dinner cots are pulled out for sleeping. Now that it is dark, women may go out into the fields to defecate, and some members of the family may wash themselves in the dark, although this is not a daily habit.

Men are seldom seen in the home; during the day they work in the fields, and any spare time is spent in the *baithak*, or men's quarters, where the men meet to chat and smoke the hookah. The men sleep in the *baithak* too, visiting their wives only briefly at night for sexual purposes. The *baithak* is sometimes located in the same compound as the women's *ghar*, but often it is in a completely separate place, many streets away.

After food has been eaten, lights put out, and the front door bolted, everyone goes to sleep. There is little noise at night—only a few voices talking, some children crying. For a while a few dim lights flicker in the dark, then go out. And the village sleeps.

2

Caste and the *Jajmani* System*

Although there is a great deal of literature about the caste system of India, very little attention has been paid to its economic aspects.[1] Most books and articles on caste have concerned themselves with the problems of its historical origin and development, with the rules and sanctions governing endogamy, food taboos, ritual purity, caste ranking, and the more dramatic injustices of untouchability. It is common in works about caste for the author to list the castes of a particular region with some account of the traditional occupation of each; but it is a curious fact that the author generally avoids what might logically seem to be a next step—an analysis of how these groups interact with one another in the production and exchange of goods and services. William H. Wiser, in a book called *The Hindu Jajmani System*, was the first to describe in detail how such goods and services are exchanged in a rural Indian village. It is greatly to Wiser's

* Appeared originally as an article written in collaboration with Victor Barnouw (*Scientific Monthly*, 83:66-81).

[1] A caste is an endogamous social unit, membership in which is determined by birth; it is often associated with a particular occupation and with restrictions about the acceptance of food and water from other caste groups. Castes tend to be ranked, with the Brahmans being traditionally assigned the highest status and "untouchable" castes like the Bhangi (sweeper) the lowest.

Fig. 19.   A Nai's son giving a weekly shave to his Jat jajman in the main street of Rampur.

credit that he was able to characterize *jajmani* relations *as a system*. Some knowledge of this system is crucial for an understanding of the economic aspects of caste in rural India.[2]

Under this system each caste group within a village is expected to give certain standardized services to the families of other castes. A Khati (carpenter) repairs tools, for example, a Nai (barber) cuts hair; but they do not necessarily perform these services for everyone. Each man works for a particular family or group of families with which he has hereditary ties. His father worked for the same families before him, and his son will continue to work for them, the occupation or service being determined by caste. The family or family head served by an individual is known as his *jajman*,[3] while the man who performs service is known as the *jajman's kamin* or *kam karne-wala* (literally, worker). These are the terms used in northwestern India; in other parts of India where the system prevails other terms may be used.

It is a characteristic of this system to operate without much exchange of money. For it is not an open-market economy, and the ties between *jajman* and *kamin* are not like those of employer and employee in a capital-

---

[2] Wiser, 1936. There have been a few other works dealing with the relationships between caste and economics, notably Nehru, 1932. Kumar Goshal has emphasized the economic basis for the caste system in the following words: "Hindu reformers failed to make any headway against the caste system because it was rooted in the economy of India, and only a change in that economy could bring about a change in the social structure. The economic system was stabilized at a low level, based upon more or less self-sufficient village communities which combined agriculture and handicrafts. Production was on a small scale, and for consumption rather than exchange. Everything moved in narrow, well-worn grooves fixed by custom. It was a pre-capitalist economic system, whose static quality could have been altered only by an expanding dynamic market for exchange of commodities. As long as this was lacking, the social relationships of the people could not possibly be altered." Goshal, 1944:59. O. C. Cox was also aware of the importance of economic factors, as the following quotation shows: "The caste structure is fundamentally a labor structure, a system of interrelated services originating in specialized groups and traditionalized in a religious matrix." Cox quotes Pramathanath Bannerjea as follows: "'The chief economic significance of the system is that it fixes absolutely the supply of any kind of labor. The scope given for the play of competition thus becomes limited, and consequently the law of demand and supply is rendered inoperative or oppressive in its operation. When any change takes place in the economic world, labor is unable to adjust itself. . . . Wages and prices have very often to be regulated by custom or some artificial means.'" Cox, 1948:62, 67.

An awareness of the relationship between caste and economy, however, seems to be missing in even such a standard book as J. H. Hutton's *Caste in India*, in the revised edition of which (1951) there is no reference to the *jajmani* system or to Wiser's work.

[3] *Webster's Dictionary* (1950) defines *jajman* as "a person by whom a Brahman is hired to perform religious services; hence a patron, client." The word derives from the Sanskrit *yajamana*, the present participle of *yaj*, to sacrifice. The term ultimately came to be used for anyone standing in the relationship of employer.

istic system. The *jajman* compensates his *kamins* for their work through periodic payments in cash or grain, made throughout the year on a daily, monthly, or biyearly basis. *Kamins* may also receive benefits such as free food, clothing, and residence site, the use of certain tools and raw materials, etc. To Wiser these concessions represent the strength of the system and are more important than the monetary payments.[4] Despite the increased use of money in recent years, the peasants nowadays tend to prefer grain payments to cash, since grain prices have risen so enormously in the past decade.[5]

When Wiser wrote his book he did not know how general or widespread this system might be, although he referred to some passages in the works of other writers which suggested that it had a wide range of diffusion. This conclusion is supported by more recent studies, which give evidence for much the same kind of system in eastern Uttar Pradesh,[6] parts of Malabar and Cochin,[7] Mysore District,[8] Tanjore,[9] Hyderabad,[10] Gujarat,[11] and the Punjab.[12] Regional differences of course appear.

A major function of the *jajmani* system is to assure a stable labor supply for the dominant agricultural caste in a particular region by limiting the mobility of the lower castes, especially those who assist in agricultural work. If a *kamin* leaves the village, he must get someone to take his place—usually a member of the same joint family. This does not usually involve sale, and the *jajman* is not likely to object, so long as the position is filled. But such transfers are rare.[13] The *kamins* have valued rights and advantages which make them hesitate to move. We get a picture of this from the autobiography of a sweeper:

. . . my father's family have been serving a certain number of houses for the last few hundred years, from generation to generation. It was an unwritten law that if my family wanted to move out of the town to go somewhere else, they would have to find someone else in their place. In this matter the high castes have no choice as to who would work for them. If my people wanted to sell the work of

---

[4] Wiser, 1936:6-11.

[5] See Eames, 1954:19.

[6] Opler and Singh, 1948; Reddy, 1955.

[7] Miller, 1952.

[8] Srinivas, 1955a; Beals, 1955.

[9] Gough, 1955.

[10] Dube, 1955.

[11] Steed, 1953.

[12] Darling, 1934.

[13] See Eames, 1954:21. According to Singh (1947:98) Bhangis can sell their *jajmani* rights for as much as 200 rupees. See also Reddy, 1955:135.

the street in which they were working they could do so to another family of our own caste. The sale was only effected on condition that in that particular area no others of our community had any claim, and also that the people who bought it were satisfied that our family had been working there for at least two generations; the price would be fixed according to the income of the area. . . . But sales of this nature very rarely take place, as it means losing one's birthright and the family reputation. Also, this is the only means of livelihood open to us, and the richer the landlord we serve, the more prestige and honor we have. . . .[14]

Moreover, the community may put pressure on an individual to make him stay. Nehru cites the case of a village which instituted legal proceedings in a criminal court, seeking to insure that the village Lohar (blacksmith) not migrate to another community, as he had threatened to do,[15] and Wiser describes the efforts of the people of Karimpur to keep a restless Dhobi (washerman) within the village.[16] Even if a *jajman* should be dissatisfied with his *kamin's* work, he would find it hard to replace him.

It is not easy for an agriculturist to remove a family attached to his household and secure the services of another. For example, A, a barber, is attached to the family of B, an agriculturist. If for any reason B is greatly dissatisfied with the services of A and wants those of another, he cannot abruptly dismiss A. His difficulty will not be in dismissing him, but in finding a substitute. Each of these castes has its own inter-village council. Occupational castes have a developed trade unionism. . . . No one else would be willing to act as a substitute, for fear of being penalized by the caste panchayat. It may even be difficult for a number of families to join together and import a family belonging to that occupational caste from a different village. First, under these conditions of tension, an outside family would not come for fear of social pressure and ultimate ostracism for such an action. And if they do come, the caste fellows already in the village would make things very difficult, even unbearable, for them.[17]

Not every village has a full complement of specialists. In a survey of fifty-four villages in the mid-Gangetic valley S. S. Nehru found that no single caste occurred in all the villages surveyed. Camars (leatherworkers) were found in only 64 per cent of the villages; Ahirs (herders) in 60 per cent; Brahmans, Nais, Lohars, and Telis (oilworkers) in 40 per cent; Dhobis and Kurmis (weavers) in 36 per cent; Kumhars (potters) in 30 per cent; and Baniyas (merchants) in 16 per cent.[18] Nehru gives various reasons for the unexpectedly low figures of these caste groups. The Nai (barber),

---

[14] Hazari, 1951:12-13.

[15] Nehru, 1932:27.

[16] Wiser, 1936:123.

[17] Dube, 1955:60.

[18] Nehru, 1932:23-29.

for instance, is a journeyman who goes from door to door and village to village. "No client needs him more than once a week and less than once a month. Also, the various festivals and ceremonies when his services are in urgent demand do not figure all too frequently in the village calendar. Hence alone or through a relation, one Nai can minister to the needs of more than one village; if the figures are an index, more than two villages." [19] The Dhobi (washerman), on the other hand, has a small representation because he serves primarily upper-caste or upper-class patrons. The women-folk of most lower-class families do the family wash. According to Singh, one seldom finds more than three Dhobi families in a village, and often only one, catering to a group of villages.[20] Singh also says that the Bhangis (sweepers) are as sparsely scattered as the Dhobis, with their largest concentration in the towns.[21] Nehru explains that a single Baniya (merchant) can finance operations in villages within a radius of 10 to 20 miles or more; hence one need not expect to find Baniyas in every village.[22] The supply and demand factor suggests that there must be some mobility, despite the localizing function of the *jajmani* system.

Jajmani rights, however, which link one to certain families, may be regarded as a form of property passing from father to son. Like land property, it is equally apportioned among brothers when they separate.[23] Certain problems eventuate from this: "When a Lohar family multiplies and divides the work, each share comes to compass the work of fewer agriculturists unless they also multiply at the same rate. Of course when the latter multiply faster, the Lohars become responsible to a greater number of agricultural families, even though the extent of work may remain the same." [24] The apportionment of *jajmani* rights may prove to be very unequal, as Reddy has shown. From a table giving the number of *jajmans* served by ten Lohar families in Senapur, it appears that one Lohar family serves only seven *jajman* families, while another serves thirty-seven.[25] The rewards in grain and other benefits are of course proportionate. The *jajmani* system, then, provides some security in assuring one a position in society, but also gives rise to economic insecurity for some of the *kamins*.

In his pioneer work Wiser summed up what seemed to him to be the

---

[19] Nehru, 1932:24-25.
[20] Singh, 1947:93.
[21] Singh, 1947:95.
[22] Nehru, 1932:26, 27.
[23] Reddy, 1955:133.
[24] Reddy, 1955:130.
[25] Reddy, 1955:133.

advantages and disadvantages of the *jajmani* system in relation to the nation, the village community, the caste group, and the individual. On the whole, he emphasized the integrating and security-giving aspects of the system and described how it provided "peace and contentment" for the villagers.[26] Yet at other times, as we shall see, Wiser emphasized its attendant injustices. How the *jajmani* system affects the villagers who live by it, and what the future of the system may be in a developing money economy, are subjects that will be discussed toward the end of this chapter. First we will describe how the *jajmani* system functions at present in Rampur.

THE *JAJMANI* SYSTEM IN RAMPUR

In Wiser's terms the Jats are the principal *jajmans* for the other caste groups in Rampur.[27] According to the traditional mode of ranking, the Brahmans are superior to the Jats. The Brahmans do have the dominant position in Wiser's village of Karimpur, where they are the landowners and number forty-one families in a population of 754.[28] But in Rampur the Brahmans are occupancy tenants of the Jats and are subservient to them.

The caste groups of Rampur have traditionally been related to one another through the mutual obligations of the *jajmani* system, the rules of which have been codified. Table 8 is an extract from the *wajib-ul'-arz*, the customary law of Rampur, which specifies the kinds of work to be done by the different caste groups and the rates of compensation. The provisions of the *wajib-ul'-arz* have legal effect, for British legislation continued to support these customary rules under civil law.[29]

It may be noted in this table that various rights and duties are specified in connection with weddings. Marriages are the high points in the social life of a village and represent a great expenditure of wealth by the families concerned. All the castes, or most of them, are brought into some connection with a wedding, in which the importance of the family and the village are demonstrated, and in which a *jajman's* ties with his *kamins* may be strengthened. The same is true, to a lesser extent, of funerals and other *rites de passage*, as well as of village festivals. The service ties of the various caste groups are indicated in Table 9.[30]

[26] Wiser, 1936:187.

[27] For Rampur's caste distribution, see pp. 15-16.

[28] Wiser, 1936:19.

[29] Wiser, 1936:14-15.

[30] See Wiser, 1936:70 ff.; Hazari, 1951:13-15. Shridhar Misra (1951:98) gives a list of payments at marriage and sacred-thread ceremonies to different "village servants" in a village in Uttar Pradesh.

Table 8

RULES OF SERVICE, RAMPUR

Caste	Type of Service	Rights Earned Through Service
Khati (carpenter)	To repair agricultural tools.	One *maund* of grain per year along with *ori* rights (2½ *sirs* of grain twice a year at each sowing season).[31]
Lohar (blacksmith)	As above.	As above.
Kumhar (potter)	To supply earthenware vessels and to render services of light nature at weddings.	Grain to the value of the vessels. Additional grain at the son's or daughter's marriage, according to status and capacity.
Hajjam or Nai (barber)	To shave and cut hair; to attend to guests on their arrival and to render other services of light nature at weddings.	At each harvest as much grain as the man can lift by himself. Additional grain at the son's or daughter's marriage, according to status and capacity.
Khakrul or Bhangi (sweeper)	To prepare cow-dung cakes; to gather sweepings, to remove dead mules and donkeys; to collect cots for extraordinary needs, and to render services at weddings.	Meals and *rabri* twice a day; at each harvest as much grain as the man can lift by himself and also at the son's or daughter's marriage, according to status and capacity.
Camar (leather-worker)	If a man assists in agriculture and gives all kinds of light services	he gets one-twentieth of the produce.
	If he does *begar* (compulsory labor), renders ordinary service, and removes dead cattle	he gets one-fourth of the produce and the skins of dead cattle.

Thirty or forty years ago a Khati at Rampur worked for his *jajman* all the year round. His work consisted in making plows and repairing them in the fields, making plow yokes, three-legged stools, legs for string cots, and various farming implements. The wood was supplied by his *jajman*.[32]

The traditional payments for this work are specified in Table 8, but informants gave a somewhat different itemization as follows:

1. Forty-five *sirs* of grain from the wheat crop (in the dry season).

[31] *Maund:* a unit of weight containing 40 *sirs*, or about 80 pounds.

[32] For a fuller list of items made by village carpenters, see Wiser, 1936:35-36.

2. As much wheat fodder as one person can carry (in the dry season).

3. As much *jovar* fodder as one person can carry (in the rainy season).

4. One or two *maunds* of green fodder (gram or peas).

A common form of payment, as specified in items 2 and 3 above and in the barber's list of rights in Table 8, is the provision that a man may take home from the crop as much grain as he can carry by himself. This is, of course, an elastic amount. A generation ago the village Lohar carried such a heavy load that he vomited blood on reaching home, and died instantly.

In addition to the grain payments received from each *jajman*, a Khati also gets payment in cash or kind for noncustomary services such as the making of wheels, planks, handles of milling stones, etc. Daily meals are provided while the Khati is working at wedding preparations for a *jajman's* family, cutting the wood for fuel, etc., and he is feasted at the wedding itself and given 1 rupee thereafter. Interservice relationships exist between the Khati and Nai, Dhobi, and Kumhar families. Each of the Khati families acts as *jajman* toward one Camar and one Bhangi family, which provide services for them and work at their weddings, when both families are feasted.

While *jajmani* services are still exchanged, cash payments for carpentry are increasing and *jajmani* ties have weakened. The Khatis have fewer *jajmans* than formerly. They seldom repair plows in the fields nowadays, and they are slow in completing jobs required by their *jajmani* obligations. The *jajmans* find that if they want to get work done on time, it is better to pay something in cash as well.

The famine of 1944-45 damaged the *jajmani* relationships between the

Table 9

JAJMANI RELATIONSHIPS AMONG DIFFERENT CASTES, RAMPUR

Number	Caste	Serves	Is Served by
1	Brahman	2, 3, 4, 5, 6, 7, 8, 9, 10	3, 4, 6, 7, 8, 10, 11, 12
2	Jat		1, 3, 4, 6, 7, 8, 10, 11, 12
3	Baniya	all	1, 4, 8, 10, 11, 12
4	Nai	1, 2, 3, 5, 6, 7, 8, 9, 10	1, 3, 8, 10, 11, 12
5	Chipi	1, 4, 10	1, 3, 4, 8, 10, 11, 12
6	Khati	1, 2, 3, 4	1, 3, 4, 8, 10, 11, 12
7	Lohar	1, 2, 3, 4	1, 3, 4, 8, 10, 11, 12
8	Kumhar	all	1, 4, 10, 11, 12
9	Jhinvar	cash relationships	cash relationships
10	Dhobi	all	1, 3, 4, 8, 11, 12
11	Camar	1, 2, 3, 4, 5, 6, 7, 8, 9, 10	8, 12
12	Bhangi	all	8, 10

Khatis and the Jats. Since grain was scarce, the Jats decided to reduce the customary dues. The village panchayat accordingly announced that the grain payments would be half the traditional amount that year. The Rampur Khatis and Lohars did not agree to these conditions and said that they would not work for their *jajmans* if they insisted on such terms. Six Jat families then broke off *jajmani* relationships with the Khatis and now do their own work, or else get it done by cash payments. Three of the Jat families have taken up carpentry. One of these families is dependent upon it as a full-time profession, while the other two are on a near-professional basis. The full-time Jat carpenter learned his trade while he was employed at the civil ordnance depot at the Delhi cantonment. The others learned the trade by themselves.

Only two of the four Khati families at Rampur now carry on the traditional trade. Two Khatis are teachers; one of these supplements his income by prescribing medicines. The trade of carpentry has seen some reverses in recent years. Bullock carts formerly had wooden wheels, which used to last for a year or two, and thus provided the Khati with a dependable source of income. But now iron wheels have taken their place. Out of

Fig. 20.   A Khati repairing the axle of a cart. Note the iron wheels now in use.

thirty-three bullock carts now at Rampur, thirty-one have iron wheels. Plankmaking has also declined; people from Rampur now prefer to have their wood cut in Delhi by a buzz saw. The two Khati carpenters at Rampur are in debt. One of them has two employed sons who help to ease his burden; the other Khati has some part-time work as a mason and also sells milk, but he is still in debt. The decline of the carpenter's importance in this village may be seen from the fact that whereas Rampur's 1100 inhabitants are served by two or three underemployed carpenters, Wiser's village of Karimpur, with 754 inhabitants, had eight carpenter families whom Wiser described as being "constantly occupied." [33]

The single Lohar in Rampur is also in debt. He formerly made and repaired his *jajman*'s agricultural implements (axes, knives, and chopping tools) and during the harvest sharpened their sickles daily. In return his *jajmans* paid him according to the schedule given in Table 8. The sale of tools was a supplementary source of income.[34]

Technological change is not responsible for the Rampur Lohar's poverty. He does not have the money to buy tools and equipment. His difficulties seem to stem largely from having too large a family; he married twice and had three children (all daughters) by his first wife and seven children (four sons, three daughters) by the second. The marriages of his daughters put him in debt. The efforts of this man to support himself and his family show the difficulties of making ends meet in a village like Rampur. In order to pay off his debts, the Lohar decided to make some extra money by plying a horse-*tonga* (two-wheeled passenger cart) between Mundka and Rampur. So he borrowed 300 rupees at 15 per cent interest and bought a *tonga*. But then the Lohar fell sick and had to sell the *tonga* again for 150 rupees in order to pay for his treatment. Harassed by his creditors, the Lohar left the village after handing over the charge of his *jajmans* to a Lohar from a neighboring village. A year later, when he returned to Rampur, the Lohar found it hard to get his *jajmans* back. He had also lost some of his land in the meantime, and the income from supplementary sources had been insig-

---

[33] Wiser, 1936:40.

[34] Reddy gives some details about the Lohar's work and payments in eastern Uttar Pradesh. This includes carpentry, which in Rampur would be done by the carpenter. "The carpentry that is needed in the construction of houses, major repairs of mechanical chaff-cutter and sugar-cane press and making of carts are outside the Jajmani system. Small repairs in the house or minor adjustments of the chaff-cutter and sugar-cane press are generally done by one's own Lohar *Parjan [kamin]*. If the work takes less than an hour, the Lohar does not get any payment. If such work, however, extends over a few hours, he gets a nominal payment in grain that is sufficient for one meal. If the work outside the Jajmani system takes a whole day or more, he gets fixed wages." Reddy, 1955:136.

nificant. His debts are still mounting, for the Lohar has to support his wife, four sons, two daughters, and two daughters-in-law. His oldest son, who is sixteen years old, helps him in his work, but there are no other earning members in the family.

The "mixed" nature of the *jajmani* system at Rampur is illustrated in the cases of the Chipi and Dhobi. Two generations ago there were no tailors in Rampur, but a Chipi from Gheora came from time to time to stitch clothes. Then the villagers urged him to move in and stay. He did so, and his descendants (two families) still carry on the trade. The Chipis charge fixed rates in cash or kind for their work when dealing with Jat, Baniya, Khati, Lohar, or Jhinvar (water carrier) families. However, in the case of the Nais and Dhobis they stitch clothes free of charge in return for the latters' services. For services at weddings the Chipis receive from 15 to 30 rupees. They are supplied with earthenware by a Kumhar, who receives so much grain per vessel; a Dhobi washes their clothes without charge; a Bhangi does all their sweeping in exchange for one *capati* (wheat cake) a day with leftover food and an occasional present of old clothes. These families

Fig. 21.   *The Chipi charges a fixed rate for his work except in the case of the Nais and Dhobis, whose clothes he stitches free of charge in return for their services.*

are feasted and given money at Chipi weddings—5 rupees for the Kumhar and 1 each for the Dhobi and Bhangi. A Camar is given 1 rupee at the weddings at which he assists, but there have never been interservice relationships between the Chipis and Camars.

There are four Dhobi families in the village, but two of the family heads have turned to other occupations—agricultural labor in one case and work in an ordnance plant in the other. The two remaining Dhobi families have twenty-one *jajmans* in Rampur between them and from ten to fifteen in a neighboring village. They receive from 10 to 20 *sirs* of grain from each *jajman*. They also have interservice relationships with Nai, Chipi, and Kumhar families, while some Bhangis do their sweeping at the *capati*-per-day rate. Formerly the Dhobis depended completely upon their local *jajmans* for a living, but nowadays they have customers in Delhi as well.

Both social and technological changes have affected the position of the Nais, or barbers, in Rampur. The Nais used to cut the hair, toenails and fingernails of their *jajmans*, while their wives shampooed the women's hair.[35] On harvest days the Nai at Rampur shaved his *jajmans* in the fields and received one sheaf from each one. After the harvest the Nai was invited to take a load of as many sheaves as he could carry, or else he was given from 20 *sirs* to 1 *maund* of grain. The Nai also served as marriage go-between. A barber was often commissioned by a girl's parents to find a suitable match for the daughter. When the barber had found a boy with the right qualifications, he was sent to the youth's home along with a Brahman to offer *tika*, the ceremonial placing of a forehead mark. The Nai received *neg jog* from the boy's parents, a gift consisting of 15 rupees in cash and a double cotton sheet, while the Brahman received 9 rupees and a single sheet. It was the Nai who arranged the match; the Brahman's role was secondary. The Nai was thus a man of importance in the village. According to Wiser, the Nai and his wife were among the few people at Karimpur who devoted all of their time to their *jajmans*. They had no time for farming.[36]

In recent years the Nai's position at Rampur has changed for the worse. About twenty-five years ago a Jat panchayat at Bawana ruled that a Nai would thenceforth receive only 6 rupees as *neg jog*. The Bawana Nais re-

[35] "Shaving under the arms weekly, finger-nail cutting weekly, and toe-nail cutting fortnightly, are added to the tonsorial duties of the barber. Ordinarily hair is cut monthly except when his clients have their heads shaved for religious purposes or through choice. . . . At the time of a wedding he not only shaves the men in his own jajman's household, but he also shaves the guests from other villages—relatives of his jajmans." Wiser, 1936: 38-39.

[36] Wiser, 1936:38-39.

fused to accept this ruling. The Jats then decided to dispense with Nais as go-betweens and to arrange their daughters' marriages themselves. In protest the Nais stopped shaving and cutting their *jajmans'* hair, hoping that this would lead the Jats to resume the old system. Instead, it led some of the Jats to buy razors and to shave themselves, so that when the barbers took up their trade again, they found that they had lost some of their *jajmans.*

Meanwhile changes in women's hair styles have adversely affected the Nain, or barber's wife. Formerly hair was set above the head; the barber's wife, who was expert in setting it after a shampoo, received 1 *sir* of grain for dressing it. The present hair style is simpler; any woman can now arrange her own. Thus she is apt to shampoo and dress it herself and seldom calls in a Nain.

One of the three Nais from Rampur is now working as a barber in Delhi; the second is a teacher, and the third a truck driver in Delhi. But they all come back to Rampur on Sundays and give shaves and haircuts to their remaining *jajmans.*

Another group affected by recent panchayat rulings is the Kumhars (potters), of whom there are seven families at Rampur. Except for one

Fig. 22.   A Jhinvar pauses for a moment during the performance of his duty.

family whose head man is working in Delhi, each of the Kumhar families has a fixed number of *jajmans* to whom it supplies clay vessels in exchange for specified amounts of grain.[37] The *jajman* must take earthenware from his own Kumhar and from none other. No other Kumhar would supply such vessels in any case, unless the *jajman's* own Kumhar lacked them. The Kumhars keep donkeys which are needed for hauling clay from the river banks. These donkeys are lent out to *jajmans* when needed. This adds to the grain supplied by the latter—from 20 *sirs* to 1 *maund* of grain plus one bundle of dry fodder. A bundle of green fodder is also given from the *kharif* crop. Still more grain may be obtained from weaving, a supplementary trade engaged in by Kumhars. There are also, of course, opportunities at weddings, when *jajmans* require many clay vessels for their guests, and when the Kumhars are feasted. On these occasions they receive about 2½ rupees and about 5¼ *sirs* of grain.

[37] "The Kumhar makes for village use, large round-bellied water jars, various types of jars used for milking, boiling, churning, etc., lids for water and milk jars, funnel-shaped tobacco pipe bowls, saucers which are used for the mustard oil lights, saucers for serving liquid foods at weddings, cups without handles, jars for storing grain, smaller jars for preserving spices and chutneys, feeding jars for cattle, and various other types of clay vessels." Wiser, 1936:45-46.

Fig. 23.   A Kumhar at his work.

A commodity much needed by the Kumhars—and by all the other villagers as well—is cow dung. Since there are only thirty-seven trees in the whole village (each privately owned and having a fixed monetary value), wood cannot be used for burning, and cow dung is the only available fuel. Everyone needs it for that purpose, but the Kumhars need more than others, for they must have plenty of fuel to fire their pottery. Firing takes place about seven times a year, and enough cow dung must be acquired each time. The competive scramble for cow dung among the villagers has deprived the fields of manure for fertilizer. Faced with this problem, the village panchayat passed a ruling three years ago prohibiting its collection and imposing a fine of 5 rupees upon anyone who violated the rule. Much clandestine collecting no doubt takes place, but the Kumhars have now been compelled to buy much of their fuel. For each firing about 9 rupees' worth of cow-dung cakes must be obtained. All the Kumhars are now heavily in debt and can hardly afford the extra costs. One Kumhar owes a debt of over 500 rupees but cannot pay a single pie toward either the principal or interest.

The handling of cow dung is traditionally the Bhangi's job. There are ten

Fig. 24.   The Kumhar has a fixed number of families whom he supplies with clay vessels.

Bhangi (sweeper) families in Rampur, about half of which have found employment in Delhi or elsewhere. The remaining families still work for their *jajmans*. Bhangis used to receive a *capati* a day from the latter and from 20 *sirs* to 1 *maund* of grain at harvest time. They were feasted at weddings and received 1 rupee in cash, together with the leftovers of the meal. For playing drums on the occasion of the birth of a son to a *jajman*, the Bhangis were given some *gur* and wheat; while at a Bhangi wedding the *jajman* of the family presented a rupee and from 2½ to 5 *sirs* of grain. These obligations are no longer adhered to with regularity. Only a few *jajmans* give grain annually nowadays. Some do so if the Bhangi helps with the harvest, but the payment is small. One Bhangi who had sixteen Jat families as *jajmans* helped nine of the families at harvest time. Three families gave him only 5 *sirs* of grain; the other six gave from 15 to 20 *sirs*. The women in most of the Jat and Brahman families at Rampur now handle cow dung and make cow-dung cakes themselves. However, the Bhangis are still indispensable as sweepers and removers of refuse from the home. So the *jajmani* relationship persists, although at a low rate of return for the Bhangis.

All the Bhangis at Rampur are heavily in debt and owe money to the

Fig. 25.   A Jat woman making cow-dung cakes for fuel.

Jats. In the past they used to borrow money from their *jajmans*, either interest-free or at very low rates, but now they must pay from 12 to 18 per cent a year. Moreover, it is not easy to get loans. If a Bhangi approaches one of the Jats for this purpose, he may be told sarcastically to seek help from the Congress Party or from one of the politicians the Bhangi voted for on election day.

It is not surprising that the Bhangis have become hostile toward the Jats, as have the Camars, who will be discussed later. This hostility has been fanned by some restrictive measures which have cut down the Bhangis' sources of income. The Bhangis formerly kept poultry. But the Jats were annoyed when the chickens made tracks over their freshly made cow-dung cakes, and they expressed their displeasure by manhandling some of the Bhangis. No chickens are kept nowadays. The Bhangis also used to keep pigs. But the pigs, like the chickens, were apt to stray and spoil somebody's crops. The Jats told the Bhangis that the pigs would not be allowed to drink at the village pond. Fines were imposed if pigs were found drinking there. The Bhangis therefore had to sell their pigs or else take them away to relatives in other villages. The loss of chickens and pigs meant a loss of supplementary income—not a small matter to people so deeply in debt.[38]

The greatest break with the *jajmani* system at Rampur has come from the Camars, traditionally the leatherworkers of India. They formerly removed their *jajmans'* dead cattle, repaired their shoes and other leather objects, and helped them in agricultural work. George Briggs, writing as long ago as 1920, affirmed that the special role of the Camar in India's rural villages was doomed:

With the rise of the large-scale tanning industry in certain large centers, the village tanner's enterprise is being reduced to smaller dimensions. There is little likelihood that the rural industry will survive. In this connection it is interesting to note that during the decade ending in 1911 there was a very marked decrease (36.9 per cent.) in the number engaged in tanning, currying, dressing, and dyeing leather. At the same time the Chamar population increased. Furthermore one of the results of the war has been a very great advance in large-scale tanning. The demand for village tanned leather is gradually being reduced to that of water-buckets and thongs. The former will be supplied more and more from chrome tanned leather, which is not a rural product at all, and finally, cheaper fabrics made from vegetable fibres will supplant leather for irrigation purposes.

---

[38] According to Mukerjee, however, some low-caste groups have deliberately abandoned the raising of pigs and poultry in order to raise their status. See Mukerjee and others, 1951:14.

Slowly factory tanned leather will supplant village tanned leather in the village shoemaking industry.[39]

However, leatherworking is only one of the Camar's traditional tasks. Ibbetson has described some of their duties in the Karnal tract, not far from Rampur: "The Chamars are the coolies of the tract. They cut grass, carry wood, put up tents, carry bundles, act as watchmen and the like for officials; and this work is shared by all the Chamars in the village. They also plaster the houses with mud when needed. They take the skins of all the animals which die in the village except those which die on Saturday or Sunday, or the first which dies of cattle plague. They generally give one pair of boots per ox and two pairs per buffalo skin so taken to the owner." [40]

Table 10 gives some of the traditional obligations and payments for the Camars at Rampur.

Camars were formerly required to perform *begar,* including compulsory service for government officials who visited the village. In general, their position has always been a very low one, but recently they have been making efforts to raise their status, and have discontinued some of their traditional *jajmani* obligations and services. They have developed mutual feelings of hostility with the Jats in consequence. During the past twenty years or so the Camars seem to have been losing some of the sense of inferiority associated with their low-caste status and untouchability. This has partly been due to the efforts of organizations like the Arya Samaj, the Congress Party, and some of the other political parties in India. The Arya Samaj, a Hindu religious reform movement, has long campaigned against caste restrictions in this area, apparently with some effect. At an Arya Samaj conference in Rampur in 1910 some non-Brahman groups, principally the Jats, were persuaded to wear the sacred thread, formerly reserved for the use of Brahmans. The Jats were urged not to feast Brahmans on ceremonial occasions, for this custom merely developed greediness in the latter caste. Besides, the speakers pointed out, village Brahmans are mostly illiterate, being Brahmans only by birth, and have no real knowledge of the Vedas. In 1933 a second Arya Samaj conference was held at Rampur, this time directed against untouchability. The speakers told the Camars in the audience that unpaid *begar* service had no legal basis and that they should refuse to perform it. The speakers promised the Camars assistance if they got into trouble for refusing *begar* service. As a result, the Camars stopped rendering *begar.*

---

[39] Briggs, 1920:227. The increasing use of Persian wells has cut down on the demand for leather buckets.

[40] Ibbetson, 1883:116-17.

Table 10

SERVICES RENDERED AND PAYMENTS RECEIVED BY CAMARS, RAMPUR

Occasion	Service Rendered	Payment Received
Boy's marriage	1. Felling trees, cutting wood for fuel. 2. Providing a watch at the house after the wedding party has left. 3. Accompanying the wedding party; attending to the bullocks at the bride's home.	1. Meals given when cutting wood. 2. One rupee at departure of the wedding party. 3. One rupee at departure of the wedding party from the bride's home. 4. One rupee and some grain (usually 5 to 10 *sirs* of wheat).
Girl's marriage	1. Cutting wood for fuel. 2. Assistance in reception of wedding party. 3. Feeding their bullocks. 4. Keeping watch where party camps. 5. Making repairs in the house.	1. Meals given to the whole family four times during the three-day stay. 2. One rupee at wedding party's departure. 3. One rupee, wheat (usually 5 to 10 *sirs*), and clothes after the wedding.
Ordinary service	1. Work without payment for officials (*begar*). 2. Repairs of *jajman*'s shoes. 3. Work in extraordinary situations (illness or death, etc.). 4. Help in harvesting. 5. Removal of dead cattle.	1. Meals on days of work for *jajman*. 2. One *sir* of grain at harvest time. 3. Grain left over on the threshing floor. 4. Animal carcasses taken. 5. One-fortieth of the grain produced (minimum 2 to 5 *maunds*).
Extraordinary service	1. Full-time work in harvesting *rabi* crop. 2. Full-time work in harvesting *kharif* crops.	1. One-twentieth of the produce. 2. One-tenth of the produce if 100 *maunds* or over: more if the *kharif* crop is less. 3. Meals given on workdays.

The Camars who carried away the dead animals of their *jajmans* used to eat the flesh of these animals. When previous attempts had been made to remove untouchability, the Jats had objected on the grounds that the Camars ate carrion. At the 1933 conference the Arya Samaj speakers exhorted the Camars to give up eating the flesh of dead animals and to keep themselves and their homes clean, so that untouchability could be removed. The Camars took a vow to do so. Most of the Jats at the conference then drank water at the hands of the Camars. These Jats were subsequently boycotted by the Brahmans for this violation of caste rules.

Despite this gesture on the part of some of the Jats, tensions developed between the Jats and the Camars which had been manifest before the 1933 conference. In 1926 the Camars refused to pay the traditional house tax (*kudhi-tarif*) of 2 rupees per year to the Jats. The Camars of the few surrounding villages raised 450 rupees, a tremendous sum at that time, and took the case to the court. However, the other non-Jats of the village, still dependent upon the Jats as their *kamins*, did not support the Camars. All the Jat factions united in opposing the Camars. The case dragged on for two years, and the Jats finally won. However, the Camars still refused to pay the tax, and a court decree was obtained by the Jats for the auction of the Camars' property. Both the *lambardars* of the village and other Jats, led by the court-appointed officer, went to the house of the leader of the Camars and forcibly confiscated some brass vessels, *ghi*, and cotton, all of which were taken to a Jat's house where they were held until the tax was paid.

A few years later the Camars and Jats fought another court case. This time the Camars brought criminal proceedings against some Jats who had beaten them for carrying meat in their pots. Then, in 1938, the house-tax question came up again. During the preceding ten years the Jats had failed to collect the house tax, which they now demanded in a lump sum. When the Camars pleaded inability to pay, the taxes during this ten-year period were forgiven. But the Camars went on to pay taxes from 1938 to 1947. There were three other court cases between the Camars and Jats from 1930 to 1947. In one case the Jats asked the Camars to assign a man each day to keep a day watch to guard Jat harvests against animals and thieves. When the Camars refused, the Jats took the case to court. A compromise was reached in which the Camars agreed to a night watch rather than a day watch. The Camars interpreted this as a victory and they became more aggressive, severing all their occupational and ceremonial relations with the Jats including the burial of dead animals. After about six months, however, they resumed the removal of dead animals and maintained this service until the time of Independence. During World War II many Camars from Rampur were employed in a nearby ordnance depot and in other military jobs, which gave them an opportunity to take an independent stand.

With the coming of Independence, the position of the Camars was strengthened both legally and ideologically. Now the Jats could no longer enforce the provisions of the *wajib-ul'-arz*, which specified the traditional village duties. The Camars stopped payment of the house tax and the handling of dead animals. However, with the more limited opportunities for employment after the war the Camars once again became dependent upon the Jats. This put them in a difficult position vis-à-vis the Jats, because they had openly opposed the latter in the panchayat and had supported the Congress Party candidate who was opposed by most of the Jats.[41]

Giving up the practice of removing dead animals was a gradual process. For a while the Camars removed only those dead animals which had died a lingering death from foul-smelling body wounds. The Jats disposed of other carcasses by burial. This violated provisions laid down in the *wajib-ul'-arz*. Previously, when a Jat had buried a dead bullock, the Camars had reported the matter to the police, who then had the carcass dug up and turned over to them. If the skin were decomposed, the Jat was made to pay the cost of the skin to his Camar.

The burial of animals by the Jats, however, was not without precedent. A mass burial of animals used to take place at *akta* ceremonies, when there was a cattle epidemic. On these occasions a curer was brought to the village, and all the livestock was brought together in one place. The curer performed some ritual actions and burned incense near the animals, all of which were driven beneath a sacred stick. Ganges water was sprinkled about in all the houses. No outsiders were admitted into the village on this day, nor could any of the villagers leave. Various taboos prevailed: no iron utensils were used, flour was not milled, *capatis* were not cooked, and houses remained unswept. The ceremony began on a Saturday and lasted until Sunday evening. At these times the Jats used to seek the Camars' permission to kill and bury the cattle, but this permission was readily granted, for the Camars also wanted the epidemic to end. Gradually, however, the Jats began to perpetuate the practice of burying dead cattle.

In 1934-35 the Camars temporarily gave up removing dead animals, partly due to objections raised by a doctor, who claimed that they were skinned too near the villagers' homes. Two years later, when a different place was set aside for the skinning, the removal of dead animals was resumed rather halfheartedly by the Camars. In 1947, on the eve of Indian independence, the Camars at Rampur gave up the practice altogether and have not resumed it since.

After the 1933 Arya Samaj conference, when the Camars gave up rendering *begar* service, the Jats began to cut down on the amounts of grain given them, claiming that the stipulations in the *wajib-ul'-arz* had been violated by the Camars. Some of the latter say that this was a mere excuse on the part of the Jats. The main factor, according to them, was the increased price of grain.

Another factor must have been the increasing fragmentation of land.

[41] For a similar dilemma, see Cohn, 1955:68 ff.

When landholdings were large and could not be managed without out-side help, the traditional assistance of the Camars was sought and welcomed by the Jats; but as landholdings became smaller and families larger, and as pressure on the land brought about further fragmentation, the assistance of the Camars became less crucial. This was, of course, a gradual process; it did not happen overnight.

Technological changes have also had their effect. A mechanical iron cane crusher has now supplanted the old wooden type of crusher and obviated the large work crew that managed the old machine. Chaff-cutting machines have supplanted the old tools used for that purpose. The Jat landowners are now less dependent upon the Camars in these areas.

Meanwhile the Camars have been trying to raise their socio-religious status by following higher-caste practices and giving up the consumption of dead animal flesh. The ties to their *jajmans* have weakened. Gradually they have given up repairing the latters' shoes, another of their traditional *jajmani* obligations.

The opportunity to enter schools is a new channel to higher status. None of the older Camars at Rampur can read or write, but 85 per cent of their boys aged six to fifteen are attending school. In Kanjhawla High School the

Fig. 26.   One of the three Camar weavers at his loom.

untouchables and higher-caste boys eat together, while in the local school young Camars and Jats sit side by side. Since 1949 a Camar has been elected to the newly constituted four-village council.

During World War II new kinds of employment were made available to the Camars, and some went to Delhi to work. Although there has been a postwar contraction of employment, four of the twenty-one Camar families at Rampur have found employment outside the village. Two work as agricultural laborers for one or two months a year at daily wages. Some work as occasional day laborers. Three Camar families do weaving, four have taken up a guava garden on a contract basis, and four have started vegetable growing. Some raise cattle to supplement their income. Only two Camars in the village are shoemakers.

One of the Camars was asked why the other Camars did not also make shoes to supplement their income. He answered that capital is needed to buy cured hides, which cost from 50 to 60 rupees. Even if they somehow managed to buy a hide, they would have to sell shoes on credit and in most cases receive only grain in return. The problem of getting funds for another hide would remain as before. The informant was questioned as follows:

Q. "How did you manage it before?"
A. "We used to remove the dead cattle and tan the hides ourselves."
Q. "Couldn't that system be revived?"
A. "Most of us don't want to skin leather any more."
Q. "But couldn't you find just one man who would agree to do it for the others?"
A. "Well . . . that's a good idea. But all the other villagers would have to agree."

As it is, under the present system all the hides at Rampur are going to waste, buried in the earth year after year. If cured hides cost from 50 to 60 rupees, this represents an enormous loss to the villagers.

It is not only low-caste groups which have abandoned their *jajmani* obligations at Rampur. The Brahmans have also done so. They formerly used to officiate at marriages and other ceremonies at the homes of their *jajmans*, at which times they received from 20 *sirs* to 2 *maunds* of grain and fodder. Every day during the cane-crushing season a farmer would set aside from 1½ to 2 *sirs* of *gur* for his Brahman. Brahmans had traditional roles to play at festivals such as Kanagat and Makar Sankrant, at which they were feasted, and also in the event of a Kaj, a celebration in honor of the dead. The Arya Samaj, as has been noted, has expressed opposition to the feasting of Brahmans, and the Jats have been influenced by this point of view. Partly for this reason—perhaps also for the sake of economy—they have stopped feasting Brahmans. A Kaj has not been given for several years, and at festival times the Brahmans are seldom fed. (Cows or young girls are sometimes fed instead.) The Rampur Brahmans, for their part, claim to regard the acceptance of food and charity as demeaning and prefer not to receive it. The Brahmans no longer settle marriage agreements, cook food at weddings, or carry on priestly functions. Four of the Rampur Brahmans are now cultivators, although only two make this their sole means of support. One of the Brahmans is a tailor, another sells silk.

There is one Baniya (merchant) family in the village which owns a shop. According to Wiser, the Vaisyas, who are absent in Karimpur, do not form an essential part of the Hindu *jajmani* system. This grouping would include the Baniya. Wiser quotes Sir Henry Maine to the effect that "the grain dealer (Vaisya) is never a hereditary trader incorporated with the village group." [42] The villagers at Rampur, however, speak of the Baniya as if he took part in the *jajmani* system. He has *jajmani*-type relationships, at least, with the Brahman families in Rampur and is served by Nais, Dhobis, Kumhars, Camars, and Bhangis. Besides selling grain and other commodities the Baniya enters certain records in an account book for the benefit of some Rampur families. The gift of money *(neota)* presented at a wedding is recorded in this book, for double that sum must be paid back when there is a marriage in the donor's household. The Baniya receives 2 rupees for this service. He also keeps records without charge of loans made by one man to another. The Baniya was formerly paid for weighing grain, but most people weigh it themselves nowadays, and he has lost this source of income. According to Ibbetson, the Baniyas in the Karnal tract give a ball of *gur* on the day after Holi and some parched rice or sweets on Divali to the proprietors "in recognition of the subordinate position which they occupy in the village." [43]

To sum up the present situation of the *jajmani* system: The system is still functioning in Rampur, a village close to Delhi, the nation's capital. Despite modern improvements, technological changes, India's five-year plans, the influence of reformist movements and political ideologies, the system is not yet dead. However, changes are taking place. The Camars have stopped fulfilling some of their *jajmani* obligations toward the Jats, who have reciprocated in turn. There are also indications of tension between the Jats and the Bhangis, although the latter continue to serve their *jajmans*. The Brahmans have lost their priestly functions. The Dhobis, who formerly depended completely upon their local *jajmans,* now have customers in Delhi

[42] Wiser, 1936:143.
[43] Ibbetson, 1883:118.

as well. The Khatis and the Lohars are abandoning their traditional trades. The Nais have lost their roles as marriage go-betweens as well as some of their opportunities as barbers. Some of their former *jajmans* shave themselves; their wives shampoo their own hair.

Most of the lower-caste villagers—and many of the Jats—are in debt. Some have been led to change their occupations and have gone to Delhi to look for work. Technological changes and the increasing land fragmentation have reduced the need for help in agriculture among the Jat families. Meanwhile, the Arya Samaj and some of the political parties have preached, with some effect, against caste restrictions. All these factors have led to a loosening of *jajmani* ties and obligations.

DISCUSSION

In a chapter in which he weighed the advantages and disadvantages of the *jajmani* system, Wiser drew an essentially benevolent picture of how it provided "peace and contentment" for the villagers.[44] The account by Opler and Singh has a similar emphasis: "Not only does everyone have some place within the Hindu system, but it is significant that every group, from the Brahman to the Chamar caste, has been somehow integrated into the social and ceremonial round of the community and has been given some opportunity to feel indispensable and proud."[45]

Our picture of Rampur, however, leads to a quite different assessment, for it seems evident that the relationship between *jajman* and *kamin* lends itself to the exploitation of the latter. Landownership is the basis of power in Rampur. All the village land, including the house sites, is owned by the Jats; the other castes are thus living there more or less at the sufferance of the Jats. It was this crucial relationship to the land, with the attendant power of eviction, which made it possible for the Jats to exact *begar* service from the Camars in the past, and still enables them to dominate the other

[44] Wiser, 1936:187.

[45] Opler and Singh, 1948:496. The institution of caste has, of course, been lauded and attacked by various writers both in India and the West. Sir Henry Maine described it as "the most disastrous and blighting of all institutions," and Rabindranath Tagore called it "a gigantic system of cold-blooded repression." O'Malley, 1932:vii. But Abbe Dubois, who was often critical of Indian customs, referred to caste as "the happiest effort of Hindu legislation." Dubois, 1947:28. Gandhi expressed both points of view at different times. "Historically speaking," he once averred, "caste may be regarded as man's experiment of social adjustment in the laboratory of Indian society. If we can prove it to be a success, it can be offered to the world as a leaven and as the best remedy against heartless competition and social disintegration born of avarice and greed." But Gandhi also wrote: "Caste has nothing to do with religion. It is harmful both to spiritual and national growth." Bose, 1948:232, 234.

caste groups. Moreover, some of the latter, like the Bhangis, are deeply in debt to their *jajmans.* This gives the Jats an additional hold over their *kamins.*

This exploitative situation can be shown to exist in other areas where the *jajmani* system is found. Writing of a village near Lucknow, Majumdar and his colleagues write that the higher-caste people always try to humiliate the lower castes. "The Thakurs dictate the most ruthless terms to the Chamars who take their fields as share croppers." [46] Reddy notes that a Lohar receives much less for his work from his Thakur *jajmans* than he gets from other castes.[47] Even Wiser, despite his favorable assessment, saw the harsh realities of the power relationship.

The leaders of our village are so sure of their power that they make no effort to display it. The casual visitor finds little to distinguish them from other farmers. . . . And yet when one of them appears among men of serving caste, the latter express respect and fear in every guarded word and gesture. The serving ones have learned that as long as their subservience is unquestioned, the hand which directs them rests lightly. But let there be any move toward independence or even indifference among them, and the paternal touch becomes a strangle-hold. . . . in every detail of life have the leaders bound the villagers to themselves. Their favour may bring about a man's prosperity and their disfavour may cause him to fall, or may make life so unbearable for him that he will leave the village.[48]

It is also evident from Wiser's data that the upper castes receive much more than the lower castes do in goods and services.[49]

That the ownership of land, including house sites, is the crucial factor, appears in other areas as well. "In the old days," writes Darling of the Punjab, "village servants were in complete subjection to their 'masters,' and this is still largely the case in the feudal north and west. There the fear of ejection from the village is a yoke which keeps the head bowed, and only those who own their own house and courtyard dare assert themselves." [50] An informant told Gittel Steed: "You have seen the whole Bakrana, every house probably. Have you seen any house that can be called a good house? This is because everyone is frightened of being driven out at any time. No one wants to build a good house here." [51] "That the *zemindar* [land-

---

[46] Majumdar, Pradhan, Sen, and Misra, 1955:211.

[47] Reddy, 1955:137. Reddy also mentions that Lohars get beaten by their *jajmans* for delinquencies in their obligations, pp. 139-40.

[48] Wiser and Wiser, 1951:18-19. See also Cohn, 1955:61.

[49] Wiser, 1936:70-71. See also Misra, 1951:98.

[50] Darling, 1934:272.

[51] Steed, 1953.

owner] is all-powerful in such places need hardly be stressed," writes Mohinder Singh. "The threat of demolishing a man's dwelling or ejecting him
therefrom are powerful weapons in his hand for extorting *begar*. Till recently the cultivators did not have any rights in their house sites." [52] Miriam
Young presents a striking passage in relation to *begar:* "The Jats said [to
the Camars] 'You'll do no more forced labor for us? Very well, then you
shall no longer have any rights or privileges in this village.' They were not
allowed to graze their cattle on common land, not allowed to bring in fuel
from the fields or the jungle. If they got out of their own quarters into
neighboring fields or jungle it was by stealth. Access to wells which they
had regarded as their own was denied them, debts of long standing were
suddenly foreclosed, land which they were renting was seized from them,
individuals were beaten and their property looted." [53]

While the landowners are generally of higher caste in Indian villages, it
is their position as landowners, rather than caste membership per se, which
gives them status and power. In Karimpur, where the Brahmans are the
landowners, the traditional cast hierarchy prevails. But in Rampur the
Jats own the land and the Brahmans are subservient to them. Majumdar
and his colleagues present a similar picture in their description of the village near Lucknow: "The respect which the Brahmins enjoy is merely conventional; in daily life, however, the Brahmins are treated on an equal
footing with the other castes. . . . The Thakurs are the most influential group
of people in the village because they are economically better off. They own
most of the agricultural land in the village. They are the landlords who give
employment to the other caste-people. The various other castes serve the
Thakurs as their dependents." [54] Opler and Singh also report that in Madhopur the Brahmans, "in spite of their top position in the orthodox social
scale, are not influential. The reason is that they are economically dependent on others." [55] In Madhopur it is the Thakurs who own the land, over
82 per cent of it, and it is they who form the dominant caste, as in the study
just cited. In another village described by Opler and Singh a lower-caste
Ahir is headman of the village and leader of the village panchayat. He owns
50 acres—"the only villager who has actual ownership of any substantial
portion of village land." [56] In an early work by Russell and Hira Lal an area
is discussed where Kunbis have higher than usual status. "The only reason-

[52] Singh, 1947:35.
[53] Young, 1931:152.
[54] Majumdar, Pradhan, Sen, and Misra, 1955:193.
[55] Opler and Singh, 1952:180.
[56] Opler and Singh, 1952:187.

able explanation of this rise in status appears to be that the Kunbi has taken possession of the land and has obtained the rank which from time immemorial belongs to the hereditary cultivator as a member and citizen of the village community." [57]

Since the passing of *zamindari* abolition bills, the key power of landowners may have been curtailed in certain areas. Majumdar and his colleagues, for example, report that in the village they studied near Lucknow, where *zamindari* abolition has taken place, Camars now refuse to perform *begar*, while the barbers refuse to draw water for the Thakurs and will not wash their utensils or remove their leaf plates any more.[58] However, the occurrence of *begar* since Independence has been noted in some areas—by Gittel Steed, for example,[59] and by Shridhar Misra.[60]

A qualification may be suggested, that while a landowner may have both tenants and *kamins*, the two groups need not be identical. He may have *kamins* who are not his tenants. This point is made by Opler and Singh, who also note that when there are disputes between Thakurs, tenants align themselves with their landlords.[61] Perhaps a more crucial consideration, however, is that the Thakurs in Senapur, like the Jats in Rampur, form a caste group which may (despite factional cleavages and differences in wealth) join ranks in solidarity against the lower castes in crucial issues. All the Jat factions in Rampur, for example, united in opposing the Camars over the house-tax matter.

The lower castes, theoretically at least, have a potential retaliatory weapon in the boycott, or withdrawal of their services. Thus, when the Nais of Rampur were informed of a decision of the Jats to reduce the *neg jog* paid at weddings, they stopped shaving and cutting their *jajmans'* hair in protest. But the sequel is instructive: The Jats retaliated by buying razors and shaving themselves. This shows that such protests may prove self-defeating. It also indicates that the *jajmani* system may be disrupted by action of either the *jajmans* or the *kamins*, or by the cumulative effect of both.

As the *jajmani* system declines, a great deal of tension is bound to de-

---

[57] Russell and Hira Lal, 1916, 4:22.

[58] Majumdar, Pradhan, Sen, and Misra, 1955:191-92.

[59] Steed, 1953.

[60] Shridhar Misra in Mukerjee and others, 1951:58. In a rural survey conducted by Misra, eleven out of forty persons examined on the subject of *begar* admitted that they had to do *begar* at the instance of *zamindars*. Such *begar* usually takes the form of ploughing without payment once a year. For some striking descriptions of *begar* during the period of British rule, see Emerson, 1944:28, 173.

[61] Opler and Singh, 1948:495.

velop between the landed and the landless, between the upper and lower castes, particularly since the system's decline is concomitant with a great increase in population and a decrease in the size of landholdings. Although the dominant position of the Jats is not yet in jeopardy in Rampur, their influence over the lower castes has been much reduced, and the demands of the lower castes have increased. It would therefore seem that the *jajmani* system contains some explosive potentialities and that, as the system continues to weaken, we may expect to see a heightening of the conflict between the dominant and subordinate castes in villages like Rampur.

Meanwhile, despite the weakening of the *jajmani* system and the inroads of a money economy in Rampur, the social aspects of the caste system have changed very little. The rules of endogamy are not questioned.[62] In spite of the influence of the Arya Samaj, the traditional caste rules governing interdining and the taking of water still prevail. The Jats will not share their hookahs with Camars or sit on the same string cots with them.[63] When community project speakers address the people of Rampur in would-be democratic assemblages, the Camars remain on the outskirts of the crowd. Patterns of hierarchy and social distance persist, and the psychology of caste still permeates interpersonal relationships.

In some ways caste identifications have even strengthened in Rampur. Among the Jats the emphasis on caste loyalty may represent a defensive reaction to the weakening of the *jajmani* system, while among the Camars it signifies a united stand against the higher-caste landowners. A similar point, on a broader scale, has been made by Srinivas, who discusses the ways in which the modern political system, including universal adult franchise, has strengthened caste.

The principle of caste is so firmly entrenched in our political and social life that everyone including the leaders have accepted tacitly the principle that, in the provincial cabinets at any rate, each major caste should have a minister. (And this principle has travelled from our provincial capitals back to our village *panchayats*—nowadays the latter give representation on the *panchayat* to each caste including Harijans.) In the first popular cabinet in Mysore State, headed by Shri K. C. Reedy, not only were the ministers chosen on a caste basis, but each had a secretary from his own sub-sub-sub-caste. And today in Mysore this principle is followed not only in every appointment, but also in the allotment of seats in schools and colleges. . . . voting is on a caste basis, and voters do not

[62] Caste endogamy is still the rule even in large cities, as was shown in a study by Noel P. Gist. "Out of some two thousand married Hindu household heads who supplied information," writes Gist, "only nine stated that they and their wives belong to different castes." These surveys were made in Mysore and Bangalore. Gist, 1954:128.

[63] See also Cohn, 1955:61.

understand that it is immoral to demand that the elected minister help his caste-folk and village folk. . . . no explanation of provincial politics in any part of India is possible without reference to caste. . . . In general, it may be said that the last hundred years have seen a great increase in caste solidarity and the concomitant decrease of a sense of interdependence between the different castes living in a region.[64]

While this may perhaps be overstating the case, it is a necessary corrective to the more widely held assumption that caste is crumbling rapidly. The decline of the *jajmani* system then will not necessarily be followed by an automatic or speedy disintegration of the caste system. Instead, caste may continue to take on new functions and manifestations.

[64] Srinivas, 1955b, 1231-32. For some other discussions of the new functions of castes, see Gadgil, 1952:187; Ryan, 1953:321; Davis, 1951:175.

3

Land Tenure and Economics

In this chapter we will be concerned with land tenure, population pressure, and economics, and their relationship to the social organization of Rampur. To be sure, land tenure is generally considered to be the province of an economist rather than of an anthropologist. But since the latter generally works on a more microscopic scale within a particular village community than does the economist (who proceeds for the most part on a nation-wide, regional, or municipal basis), the anthropologist may be able to reveal relationships between local social patterns and the land tenure system which might perhaps escape those who work on a larger scale. We tend, for example, to think of castes as forming rather homogeneous units, and they are so described, at least by implication, in much of the literature. But our study shows that even in a small village dominated by a single proprietary agricultural caste (the Jats) there is a great range of variation within the caste with regard to socio-economic status, landholdings, etc.

Land is greatly valued in Rampur, for the village is predominantly agricultural. The Jats and Brahmans are the principal agriculturists here, for it is only members of these two castes who cultivate with oxen and plow and have the status of permanent cultivators in the village. Until recently

Fig. 27.   Outskirts of the village. Note the bitauras *in the foreground and the* boongas *in the background.*

Table 11

AVERAGE MONTHLY OUTSIDE INCOME BY CASTE AND NUMBER OF FAMILIES, RAMPUR, 1953

Caste	Total Number of Families	Number of Families With Outside Income	Average Monthly Income per Family	Total Outside Income
Jat	78	42	145	6077
Brahman	15	10	142	1421
Camar	20	5	53	265
Bhangi	10	4	72	289
Kumhar	7	2	45	90
Jhinvar	5	0	0	0
Khati	4	2	250	498
Dhobi	4	1	80	80
Nai	3	2	115	230
Chipi	2	0	0	0
Lohar	1	0	0	0
Baniya	1	1	100	100
Total	150	69		9050

none of the Jats grew vegetables, for that was considered a low-caste occupation. In 1925, however, under the influence of Arya Samaj preaching, one of the Jats began to grow melons. Today there are thirty Jats who grow melons and nine Jat families which have taken to raising potatoes. Vegetable gardening is also carried on by five Jhinvar and four Camar families, one Kumhar and one Brahman family. The lower-caste vegetable growers have no plows or oxen but practice hoe cultivation, irrigating their lands from shallow pit wells. Lower-caste men, particularly the Camars, also work as occasional day laborers for the Jats.

Although all Jats own land, twelve Jat families do not cultivate, and ten Brahman families do not do so. This leaves sixty-six Jat families engaged in agriculture, plus five Brahman, five Jhinvar, four Camar, and one Kumhar: a total of eighty-one families directly dependent upon the land.

We estimate that thirty-eight out of sixty-nine noncultivating families still depend, at least to some extent, upon the grain payments made through the *jajmani* system: sixteen Camar, eight Bhangi, six Kumhar, three Nai, two Khati, two Dhobi, one Lohar. Some of these families have *jajmans* in neighboring villages. This makes it difficult to determine accurately how the villagers are supported, for we cannot consider Rampur in isolation. Rampur *jajmans* also have *kamins* from neighboring villages.

Many families have sources of outside income. Among the Jats this applies to fifty-seven men from forty-two households. These forty-two households, therefore, are not solely dependent upon agriculture. Twelve Jats are teachers, fifteen are in the army or police service, fifteen are working as clerks, drivers, or peons in the post office, or in mills or factories, and ten work in a nearby ordnance plant. Five receive regular pensions. It is interesting to note that of the fifteen Brahman households, as many as ten have sources of outside income. Five Brahmans are teachers, seven work at jobs in mills, ordnance plants, etc., one is a tailor, and one sells milk. (The latter two are not included in Table 11, since they do not have regular incomes.)

Four of the Camar families have work outside Rampur. One has a regular income as village *caukidar* (watchman). Three Camar families do weaving, four have taken up guava gardening on a contract basis, and some raise cattle to supplement their incomes. Most of the rest work as occasional day laborers in the fields. Two Khatis are teachers. Four Bhangis are employed. Two Bhangis and two Kumhars have jobs in Delhi. Some Kumhar families do weaving and keep donkeys to supplement their income. One Dhobi has a job in the ordnance plant. Two Nais are employed, one as a teacher, the other as a truck driver. The Baniya in Rampur has a military pension.

Sixty-nine of the 150 families in the village have a total average monthly income of over 9000 rupees. The distribution of this income by caste is shown in Table 11.

It can be seen that over 80 per cent of the total outside income of the villagers is earned by two castes—the Jats and the Brahmans. They have a higher proportion of employed families and a higher average monthly income than do the lower castes. The only exceptions to this general trend are the Khatis and Nais. The difference between the average monthly income of the Jats and Brahmans as compared with that of the Camars, Bhangis, and Kumhars is striking.

The fact that over 50 per cent of the Jat landholding households have at least one family member employed outside the village suggests the inability of the limited land base to support the Jats adequately, much less

Table 12

PERCENTAGE DISTRIBUTION OF JATS AND NON-JATS IN SOCIO-ECONOMIC GROUPS, RAMPUR, 1953

Group	Jats	Non-Jats	Total for the Village
Ia	0	41.66	20
Ib	56.4	56.95	56.6
II	37.17	1.38	20
III	6.41	0	3.3

Table 13

DISTRIBUTION OF AVERAGE MONTHLY OUTSIDE INCOME AND LANDHOLDINGS BY SOCIO-ECONOMIC GROUPS AMONG JATS, RAMPUR, 1953

Socio-Economic Group	Number of Families	Number of Families With Outside Income	Total Average Outside Income (rupees)	Average Income per Family Employed	Total Land Owned (acres)	Average Land per Family Employed (acres)
Ib	44	14	1283	94.5	257.2	3.3
II	29	24	3793	156	319.2	9.7
III	5	4	1001	250	141.5	20.4
Total	78	42	6077		717.9	

all of the villagers. Most of the employed Jats come from cultivating families; only eight of the twelve noncultivating Jats are employed. The range in income per family among the Jats is great—from 15 to 600 rupees per month, the latter being earned by three members of a single household.

The relationship between outside income, landholding, and other socio-economic indexes was analyzed with the aid of a socio-economic point scale devised for the qualification of each of the following traits: landownership, land cultivated, housing, outside income, highest school grade completed, and school attendance. Each family received a point score for each trait and also a total score. It was found that the families clustered into three socio-economic groups which we have designated, from lowest to highest,

Table 14

SIZE OF LANDHOLDINGS AND AVERAGE MONTHLY OUTSIDE INCOME AMONG JATS, RAMPUR, 1953

Size of Holding (*bighas*)	Number of Families Without Outside Income	Number of Families With Outside Income	Average Monthly Outside Income per Family (rupees)
less than 10	3	4	262
10–29	12	17	118
30–49	8	6	126
50–69	7	7	101
70–89	4	2	196
90–109	1	2	140
110–129	0	3	252
130–149	0	1	125
230–249	1	0	0
Total	36	42	

as Group I, with subgroups Ia (1-3 points) and Ib (4-15 points), Group II (16-24 points), and Group III (25-33 points). (See Table 12.)

In Table 13 we see that size of landholding and amount of outside income are positively correlated with the total socio-economic score as measured by our scale. Whereas 80 per cent of the families in Groups II and III are employed, only 32 per cent of those in Group Ib are employed.

The relationship between size of holding and outside income is analyzed in Table 14. We find that both small and large landholdings are distributed among those with outside income as well as among those without outside income. Some trend is suggested, however, by the fact that approximately 60 per cent of the thirty-six families with the smallest holdings have outside jobs.

PAYMENT OF THE REVENUE

The definition of property rights in an Indian village is largely determined by who pays the revenue in it. Rampur is known officially as a "modified *pattidari*" village, which means that part of the village land is owned in common and part by individuals whose rights can be traced genealogically. Baden-Powell coined the term "joint village" for a type of North Indian village in which the land is assessed by the government as though it were one estate, the entire village being held accountable for the revenue payment in a lump sum. Rampur is a "joint village" of this type, having, among other characteristics of the ideal "joint village," an area of wasteland owned in common by the proprietary group.[1]

Taxes are fixed at a certain period and remain the same until the next "settlement." (The last such settlement for Rampur took place in 1909, when the village revenue was fixed at 1397 rupees; but the land consolidation program now in progress will soon bring about a new settlement.) The Jats pay the revenue through the *pana* subdivisions described before.[2] Each *pana* owns approximately 12 *hals*[3] or 375 acres of land, and each pays the same amount of revenue. Each *pana* has a headman, through whom revenue matters are handled.[4]

The 784 acres of Rampur appear on the revenue books as one estate with a single tax. The tax is paid in two parts, one by each of the headmen. According to the law, the headmen are responsible for the taxes of their

[1] Baden-Powell, 1899:15.

[2] See pp. 22-26.

[3] *Hal* (literally plough): a measurement of land, about 31.25 acres.

[4] This function of the *lambardar* existed before the establishment of British rule, according to Ibbetson, who spent more than eight years investigating the revenue system of the Karnal district near Rampur. See Ibbetson, 1883:92.

pana. Theoretically, it is the headman who pays the entire tax for the *pana* of which he is titular head. However, the villagers have a different concept of the tax system. They see it as a purely individual matter, each man paying the tax on the land he individually owns and which is his through inheritance. The villagers do not acknowledge the headman's responsibility for any taxes but his own. In practice, each landowner feels himself responsible for the tax on his plots, and he pays the annual revenue to the headman, who in turn pays the total sum of his *pana's* taxes to the government. So far there has been no opportunity to test the villagers' concept of the tax system at Rampur. As yet no individual landowner has refused to pay his tax.

There are two principal types of landholding in Rampur: common lands and private lands. Both of these terms require some qualification. The common lands *(samilat)* are held in common only by the Jats and not by the other castes in the village. Moreover, rights in the use of these lands are portioned out in certain ways, as will be seen below. Common lands, which are nontaxable, cover only about 5 per cent of the village lands.

The second main type of landholding at Rampur is private agricultural

Fig. 28.   Seated left is one of the two lambardars *of the village smoking hookah in front of his house as he discusses politics with another Jat leader.*

lands, rights to which are traced genealogically and recorded in the books of the village *patvari*. These records contain the size, name, and location of the lands owned by each individual and the amount of the tax due. About 95 per cent of the village land is private. But "private" should perhaps be put in quotation marks, for Indian peasant attitudes toward private agricultural lands are not quite the same as a Westerner's. Ibbetson has discussed this difficulty:

The villages of the Tract have, for the purposes of settlement, been classified as follows:—64 held wholly in common by the body of owners (*zamindari*); 22 divided among the several branches of the community according to ancestral shares (*pattidari*); and 250 held in severalty by the individual households, the holding of each being quite independent of any fixed scale (*bhayachara*). But this classification is practically meaningless. . . . it is, as a rule, impossible to describe the tenure of a village in a word, or to classify it satisfactorily under the recognized headings. . . . [I believe] property in severalty, based solely upon actual possession, to have been entirely a creation of our own; that before our times the breaking up of land gave the cultivator a right to hold that land undisturbed so long as he paid the revenue on it, but gave him no further rights; and that it gave him this much whether he was an owner or not. In old days, members of the proprietary body returning to the village after an absence of even half a century or more were admitted to their rights without question; and there is still a strong feeling against rights being extinguished by absence from the village.[5]

COMMON LAND

In North Indian villages the common lands have a traditional function. They serve primarily collective purposes such as the grazing of cattle and the provision of wood, for they generally contain a wooded area. However, the common in Rampur is small, comprising only 5 per cent or 41.25 acres of the total area of the village. This is not unusual, although in nearby Mundka almost 50 per cent of the village land is in the common. Most of the land in Rampur is cultivable, and the demand for land is great, which may help to explain the smallness of the common. The common lands in Rampur are too limited for grazing, and there are only thirty-seven trees in the whole village, each of which is privately owned and has a definite monetary value affixed to it, which is recorded in the *patvari* records. Thus the common is now something of an anachronism, having collective tenure without collective functions. The absence of a communal grazing area and sources of wood adds to the burdens of the villagers. The lack of a wood supply has forced them to use cow dung for fuel; hence they can return

[5] Ibbetson, 1883:95-97.

little of it to the soil as fertilizer. Enough fodder must be raised to support the cattle, which are needed for agricultural purposes.

Rights to the use of common lands are based upon the amount of private land each Jat holds. One might expect the common to be a source of village unity, but here the rights of so many people in so little land have led to bitter quarrels which have been a source of dissension. A distinct departure from the traditional functions of the common has been the cultivation of small sections by those Jats whose private lands border upon it. This has annoyed those who were not located where they could extend their plots.

Despite their deficiencies, however, the common lands do provide what little room there is for expansion in Rampur, primarily for the building of new houses and roads. Although the major part of the common consists of uncultivable wastes which cannot serve for agriculture nor for grazing, the genealogically traced rights of each of the Jats in the common lands are carefully guarded. Despite their small size, the latter are divided into several types as follows: (1) the village common *(samilat dhe)*, (2) *pana* common lands, (3) *tholla* common lands, (4) the village habitation area *(abadi dhe)*.

The Village Common

This comprises the largest of the communally held lands, consisting of 37.1 acres, or 178 *bighas* and 8 *bisvas*.[6] All the Jats of Rampur have rights in the use of this village land, which lies scattered throughout the area outside the central habitation site. It is further subdivided as follows:

1. Cultivable land
   - *a*) Canal-irrigated . . . . 4.6 acres
   - *b*) Unirrigated . . . . 3.5 acres

   Total . . . . 8.1 acres
2. Uncultivable land
   - *a*) Land left fallow for four harvests . . . . 1.25 acres
   - *b*) Land left fallow for more than four harvests . . . . 6.5 acres
   - *c*) Waste and grazing land . . . . 22.5 acres

   Total . . . . .30.25 acres

---

[6] For the convenience of the Western reader we have converted the local Indian measures of *bighas* and *bisvas* into acres. We have used 4.8 *bighas* for an acre in accord with the local *patvari* records in this village. Most land records are in *bighas* and *bisvas*. The latter is ¹⁄₂₀ of a *bigha*. The conversion of *bisvas* into our acres gives us only tenths or hundredths of an acre and seems too small to be worth handling. However, from the point of view of the villagers each *bisva* is precious. The very act of converting *bighas* and *bisvas* into our acres does some violence to the psychology of the villagers.

The cultivable lands were never divided among the people as were the habitation area and the *pana* and *tholla* lands. However, the Jats whose private plots bordered on the common expanded their cultivation plots onto the latter, even to the extent of filling in some of the water pools and the banks of the village pond. Some years ago the families which were not able to expand onto the common brought this problem to the courts, specifying who had appropriated land and the amounts taken. They won the case and forced the others to cease their illegal cultivation. For some time this land lay fallow, but after five or six years the former transgressors began to inch onto it again. Altogether 8.1 acres have been brought under cultivation in this way.

The noncultivable lands of the village common consist of the following: (1) the village pond, (2) small pools or tanks, (3) the land occupied by the school and school grounds, (4) the land occupied by two *pana caupals*, or men's houses, (5) the land occupied by four houses other than the *caupals*, (6) the roads which pass through the village, (7) sandy or muddy spots which cannot be worked, (8) land near the village used for the storage of manure.

These lands cover the larger part of the village common, 30 acres out of a total of 37. None of this land has been officially distributed among the Jats. The only case of this sort occurred some fifteen years ago, when the Jats, through the village panchayat, decided to distribute what they thought to be 2.5 acres of the village common. This small portion lay on the border of the village habitation area, and was used exclusively by the people of *pana* Harditt as a storage place for manure. However, when the *patvari* record was examined, it was discovered that at the time of the settlement of 1909 one of the Jats, with the connivance of the *patvari*, had managed to have .6 of an acre of the section of 2.5 acres registered in his own name. Therefore there remained only 1.9 acres for distribution. These plots were never, however, officially registered, because the *patvari* wanted 30 rupees for the registration, which the villagers refused to pay. As has been noted, some houses have been built on the village common. In one of these cases, a Jat who built a new house on his own private land managed to use a small piece of common land also. The villagers did not realize it at the time, but now suspect that the Jat bribed the *patvari*.

Pana Common Land

Each *pana* has some land of its own, and so has each *tholla*. *Pana* Dhan Singh, whose members hold 375 acres of land, has 1.5 acres of common land. This is in addition to their rights in the village common. The *pana* land is some distance away from the village habitation area, and only .4 of an acre is cultivable. This small piece, which was once part of a pool, is now cultivated by three separate families whose private holdings adjoin it.

Tholla Common Land

The two *thollas* of *pana* Dhan Singh each possess their own special *tholla* land in addition to their *pana* land. Members of Teka *tholla*, for example, have .6 of an acre. Although this land is referred to in the *patvari* records as common land, and is therefore exempt from taxes, the village panchayat divided it among the members of Teka *tholla*, each member receiving about .1 of an acre (11 *bisvas*).

There is an interesting case concerning the rights of one member of Teka *tholla* in this land. After the distribution, Jat Ram allowed two carpenters to build their houses on his share of the land and accepted money from them. However, since no land may legally be sold to non-Jats, it could not be transferred as having been sold. Instead, Jat Ram tried to have it transferred as *hebah,* or charity. His appeal for this action was accepted by the court officer *(tehsildar)* but turned down by the Deputy Commissioner. Nevertheless, the two carpenters had already built their houses on the land, and after having given money to Jat Ram they continued to live there.

The members of Dhan Singh *tholla* have a larger area of common land than those of Teka *tholla*. *Tholla* Dhan Singh has 1.9 acres, which were divided among members of the *tholla* before the settlement of 1909. It is generally used as a threshing area, although .1 of an acre is occupied by the house of one member of the *tholla*.

The Village Habitation Area

At each settlement the limits of the habitation area are fixed. The habitation area or residential section of the village is excluded from the revenue system, and is therefore tax free, in distinct contrast to the house-site tax found throughout much of the world. Since the area is tax free, there is no necessity for the *patvari* to maintain a record of the individual site holders. It is said that the individual sites were plotted on a map during the settlement of 1880, but at present there is no exact record of these holdings. The habitation area now consists of 15.8 acres. However, settlement records show that it has steadily increased in size since 1842. Traditionally, it is a type of common land which differs from the others in that houses are constructed on it, as well as courtyards and other enclosures. In 1917 the reality of common holdings was put to the test in a court case, which the members of Teka *tholla* brought against all the other Jats in the village, demanding

partition of the entire area. The court ruled against them, stating that although the residence area was land traditionally held in common by the
landowners of the village, it was in fact held in severalty by the same landowners, who had occupied certain sites for generations. To partition the
land on which their houses were built, the court officer said, would constitute a hardship for the inhabitants of the village, many of whom had
occupied the same sites since its foundation. However, the court ruled
that all the land which had become part of the habitation area since the
settlement of 1880 was available for partition. Thus the members of Teka
tholla received a small area lying just outside the former (1880) limits.
This area, used for dung storage, was just what Teka *tholla* wanted. About
fifteen years ago the remainder of the land which fell between the limits
of 1880 and 1909 was divided among the remaining three *thollas* through
action of the village panchayat.

All the non-Jats of the village live on land made available by the Jats and
have only occupancy rights to their house sites. Many of the non-Jats have
resided in Rampur as long as have the Jats themselves. But they cannot
sell the land if they want to leave the village, as many are now doing, to
seek employment in the cities. Recently, when a Camar wanted to leave
the village, he pawned his house to a Khati for 1500 rupees, so as not to
take a complete loss on its value.

Thus common land, which should traditionally be used for grazing,
wood collecting, etc., appears to have undergone the same divisions for
private purposes as have the rest of the village lands. Officially, the four
types of common land are still held in common and are not taxed. But the
village common land not covered by water has been unofficially divided,
at least in part, into individually worked agricultural land. The *pana* and
tholla lands have also suffered divisions and are also used almost entirely for
private ends. Finally, the village habitation site has been declared officially,
in a court decision, to be land held in severalty, since it was divided by the
simple fact of housebuilding, and therefore is used exclusively for private
purposes. Even the non-Jats who live on land made available to them by
the Jats have occupancy rights to their house sites, and although they cannot sell their sites, they can pawn them.

PRIVATE LAND

The total number of acres of private land, on which revenue must be
paid, is 717.4; with the exception of 4.2 acres, all of this is cultivable.[7]

---

[7] According to the village *patvari* records, half of the cultivable land (340.2 acres)
is canal-irrigated, but in reality only one-sixth of this land is canal-irrigated now, for

Table 15

DISTRIBUTION OF PRIVATE AND COMMUNAL LANDHOLDINGS BY CULTIVATED AND UNCULTIVATED AREAS (ACRES), RAMPUR, 1952

Type of Land	Total Area	Cultivated Area					Uncultivated Area		
		Unirri-gated	Canal	Well	Well and Canal	Total	Fallow	Waste	Total
Private holdings	716.8	339.9	340.3	16.5	16.5	712.2	3.1	1.5	4.6
Communal holdings									
1. Village	37.2	3.5	4.6			8.1	6.6	22.6	29.1
2. *Pana*	1.4		.4			.4	.3	.7	1.0
3. *Tholla*	2.6						2.4	.2	2.6
Village habitation area	15.8							15.8	15.8
Area covered by canals	4.7							4.7	4.7
Government area	5.1							5.1	5.1
Total village land	784.0	343.0	345.0	16.5	16.5	721.0	12.0	51.0	63.0

Changes have been taking place in the land-use patterns stemming from land pressure and other factors. There has been an increase in the number of individual holdings and a decrease in their size.[8] Moreover, landholders are afraid to rent out their land, because of the occupancy rights which may be gained by the renter.

There are two categories of privately owned land. The first is known as *malik kamil,* or perfect ownership. Holders of this type of land have rights in the village common proportional to their private holdings. The second category is known as *malik kabza,* which entails possession of land without any rights in the common. The distinction between the two categories lies only in the question of communal rights. In both cases the owner is responsible for the revenue assessed on his land and is entitled to enjoy the full fruits of the land. In Rampur the majority of landownership is of the perfect ownership type.

the water supply has been reduced to about one-third of what it was at the time of the settlement of 1909, due to the greatly increased demand for water along the canal system.

[8] See Table 19, p. 105.

The basic division of land in Rampur, however, is that of family ownership. Traditionally, the villagers have held land as joint families, married
brothers and their families living together and working their inherited land
jointly. However, during times of economic stress or depression there seems
to be a tendency for members of the joint family to split up their land into
separate holdings.[9]

All the Jat families in Rampur own land, but although the village lands
are divided equally *pana*-wise, they are somewhat unequal *tholla*-wise and
very unequal family-wise, as may be seen in Table 16. Teka *tholla* is the
group that is best off as far as landownership is concerned, with only twelve
families dividing 173.5 acres, giving an average of 14.4 acres per family.
Tholla Dhan Singh is the worst off, with the largest number of families in
Rampur (twenty-eight) dividing 176.2 acres, and therefore having an
average of only 6.3 acres per family. These averages are misleading, however, for there is great variation in the size of the individual family holdings within each *tholla,* as shown in Table 17.

In Teka *tholla* only one family has less than 4.2 acres, as compared with
twenty-four families in the other three *thollas* who have less than that.
Moreover, the largest landholding family of the village belongs to Teka
tholla. This family owns 52.1 acres of land, although two married brothers
and their families own half the land individually. Teka *tholla* seems to be
the most conservative of the four *thollas,* and adheres more strongly to the
traditional joint family pattern, a factor which helps to keep down the
total number of families and the increasing division into smaller plots
which has taken place among the other *thollas.*

It is also apparent from Tables 16 and 17 that *tholla* Dhan Singh is the

Table 16

**LAND DISTRIBUTION BY VILLAGE SUBDIVISION (PANAS AND THOLLAS) AND
BY FAMILIES, RAMPUR, 1953**

Village Subdivision	Number of Families		Number of Acres		Average Number of Acres per Family	
Pana Dhan Singh	40		349.7		8.7	
Tholla Teka		12		173.5		14.4
Tholla Dhan Singh		28		176.2		6.3
Pana Harditt	38		362.4		9.5	
Tholla Jaimel		22		219.2		9.9
Tholla Harditt		16		143.2		8.9

[9] For a later discussion of this point, see "Land Fragmentation."

Table 17

SIZE OF LANDHOLDINGS BY FAMILIES WITHIN THOLLAS, RAMPUR, 1953

Size of Holding (acres)	Number of Families				Total Number of Holdings
	Teka	Dhan Singh	Jaimel	Harditt	
less than 1	0	3	0	0	3
1–4	1	12	4	5	22
4–10	4	8	9	8	29
10–20	4	3	8	2	17
20–40	2	2	0	2	6
over 40	1	0	0	0	1

least well off. It is the only *tholla* in which there are members holding less than 1 acre. In fact, twenty-three of its twenty-eight families hold less than 10.8 acres per family, fifteen of which have less than 4.2 acres.

Jaimel *tholla,* which has the greatest amount of land, is close behind Dhan Singh with fourteen of its twenty-two families holding less than 10.8 acres of land. Harditt *tholla* has only thirteen families with less than 10.8 acres. Therefore, *tholla*-wise, we can rate the families of Teka, Harditt, Jaimel, and Dhan Singh from best to worst off in that order, with respect to landholdings. The number of families in each *tholla* of course influences the amount of land each family can hold, and it must be remembered that the number of families per *tholla* differs greatly.

Some other aspects of landownership may be pointed out: twenty-five of Rampur's families own less than 4 acres, while twenty-nine families own between 4 and 10 acres per family. In other words: 69 per cent of the families own less than 10 acres, 21.6 per cent own between 10 and 20 acres, and 8.8 per cent own more than 20 acres. This last 8.8 per cent of the families own 27.7 per cent of the total village lands.[10] Forty-four families, or 57 per cent of the Jats, own less than 12.5 acres. This is considered substandard, not enough to support an average family with a team of oxen. Only fifteen families (19.23 per cent) cultivate what is considered to be a

[10] To put it in still another way: 72 per cent of the Jat landholding families own less than 12.5 acres, while 57 per cent cultivate less than 12.5 acres; 20 per cent own and cultivate between 12.5 and 18.7 acres; and 8.8 per cent own and cultivate over 18.7 acres, or more land than is considered ideal for one team of oxen; 15.38 per cent of the Jats either rent out their land, because they have so little that it is not worth while to cultivate it, or else they have outside occupations. Four families cultivate less than 1 acre. While all the Jats own land, twelve families, or 15 per cent, cultivate none; 72 per cent own between .2 and 12.5 acres, but only 57 per cent cultivate between .2 and 12.5 acres.

good amount of land (13 to 18 acres), while seven families (8.96 per cent) cultivate more land than is considered good for one team of oxen.

OXEN

The range in wealth within the Jat caste may also be studied in connection with the ownership of oxen. Oxen are necessary in cultivation and also represent items of prestige for their owners. However, only forty-six of the Jat families have a team of oxen; ten families have one ox, and twenty-two have none. Of the latter twelve are noncultivators, renting out land, four cultivate less than 1 acre, and six cultivate between 2 and 4 acres.[11]

There has been a decrease in the number of oxen at Rampur. In 1909 the number of bulls and bullocks was 119; it rose to 125 in 1914 and then fell off to 109 in 1953. The decrease in the number of oxen may be related to the decrease in the number of cultivating families.

The term *hal* is used for a team of oxen. *Hal* means plow, so a team is

[11] In addition to the Jats, four Brahman families at Rampur have oxen. Three of these families have a pair, and one has a single ox.

Fig. 29.   A scene outside the village during sugar-cane-crushing season. Special feed is given to the oxen at this time.

Table 18

DISTRIBUTION OF OXEN AMONG JATS AND BRAHMANS BY SIZE OF CULTIVATING UNIT, RAMPUR, 1953

Size of Cultivating Unit (acres)	Number of Families With No Oxen	Number of Families With One Ox	Number of Families With a Pair of Oxen	Total Number of Families With Oxen
0	12	0	0	0
less than 10	10	2	15	17
10–12	0	0	11	11
13–18	0	6	16	22
19–22	0	3	4	7
25–38	0	0	3	3
Total	22	11	49	60

equated with a plow. Those who have only one ox speak of having half a plow. Most of the agricultural work requires a team, so that the eleven families who have only one ox must borrow another from a relative or a friend to do their work properly. Since it is felt that the proper amount of land necessary to cultivate with a pair of oxen is from 13 to 18 acres, it is clear from Table 18 that only sixteen families with a pair cultivate this amount of land. Surprisingly enough, fifteen families with a pair and two with one ox are families who are cultivating less than 10 acres. In other words, about 28 per cent of the families who own oxen have oxen which theoretically should be a burden.

TENANCY

There are two types of tenancy at Rampur: occupancy tenancy and tenancy at will. In both cases the land measurements are exact, regardless of how small the land parcel may be, and the rights to the land are jealously guarded. Occupancy tenancy is applied only to the Brahmans who were invited into the village many years ago. There are fifteen Brahman families in Rampur. Four of these, as has already been noted, have oxen; eleven do not. Of the second group only one family has contact with the soil. This is a "non-*marusi*" (occupancy tenancy) family which engages in hoe culture. The latter represents an even greater departure from the traditional pursuits of the Brahman caste than does the plough agriculture pursued by the other four families.

Occupancy tenancy breaks down into three categories. The first includes all the Brahmans who are occupancy tenants of Teka *tholla*. They pay only the revenue on the land they occupy to the owner of that piece of land. They do not pay any additional fee *(malikana)* to the owner. Only 14 acres of land come under this type of tenancy. The second category includes all the Brahmans who are tenants of Jaimel *tholla*. They must pay the land-owners a fee of 2 annas for every rupee of revenue due on the land, in addition to paying the revenue. This involves 11.2 acres. The third category is known as "old possession" *(kabza kadim* or *darinah)*. This type of occupancy does not even require the occupant to pay revenue to the Jat owner. However, if the owner wants to, he can take his case to court and have this type of occupancy changed to one of the other two forms (known as *marusi)*. Four Jat families hold 4 *bighas,* and two Brahman families hold 3.3 *bighas* in this fashion (.4 of an acre). The occupants of these 26 acres have practically all the rights over the land they occupy except the right to sell it. All the Brahman families in Rampur are occupancy tenants, even though they do not all cultivate land. Recently the consolidation committee asked the Brahmans to become owners of their land, after coming to terms with the Jats. However, this solution involved the Brahmans receiving less land than they now hold in occupancy; so they refused.

Tenants at will are of two types: those who are tenant owners, or who have land of their own, and landless tenants. Most of the land rented out by the owners is rented to relatives, generally members of their own faction, who are tenant owners. Only 4.6 acres of land are cultivated by the eleven nonlandowning cultivating families. The only Brahman who rents land rents it from his own brother, from outside the village.

The rental arrangement has always been verbal, and the share which the renters pay is now 50 per cent of all the produce. However, the non-Jat hoe cultivators make cash payments of 40 to 45 rupees per *bigha*.

There is only one Jat family which now pays a one-third share to the owner, because that family supplies water from its own well. However, the number which paid one-third was previously greater.

In 1947-48, according to the *patvari* records, .6 of an acre of well-irrigated land, 15.4 acres of canal-irrigated land, and 19 acres of unirrigated land were rented, all at the rate of one-half of the grain produced on it.

There is little land for rent in Rampur, although the demand for it is great. There is great competition for the little bit which is for rent, and those who are able to rent out land gain prestige by doing so. Thirty-one Jat families are able to rent out land, and only twenty-one Jat families rent in land, as does one Brahman family and eleven lower-caste families. However, the total amount of rented land in Rampur is only 100 acres. Ten families of Jaimel *tholla* rent out 42.1 acres, eleven families of Dhan Singh *tholla,* 32.2 acres, two families of Teka *tholla,* 12.7 acres, and eight families of Harditt *tholla,* 13.3 acres.

There is some difficulty in determining the exact amount of land that is cultivated on a rental basis in Rampur. A comparison of the data on rentals as given in the village *patvari* records with our data based on interviews of landowners and tenants reveals a considerable discrepancy and suggests that the *patvari* records are unreliable on this particular score. According to the *patvari* records for 1952 there were only seven landowners renting out a total of 28.3 acres of land. This was the figure recently given to the Community Projects Administration in their survey of the village. But according to our data there were over thirty families renting out 100 acres of land. It appears that the *patvari* records give us only about one-third of the total rentals. It is also interesting to note that the seven individuals listed as renting out land all had small holdings of about 5.2 acres. The fact that landowners with large holdings are not mentioned may reflect their power position vis-à-vis the *patvari.*

In recent years many rentals have not been listed as such because of the peasants' fear of land reforms whereby tenants may be given permanent or occupancy rights in the land. Landowners will therefore rent to relatives but will list the plot as being self-cultivated. Similarly, there is a tendency for landowners to shift tenants from one plot to another to guard against tenant occupancy claims. Finally, the *patvari* often lists brothers as being owner-cultivators even though they may have separate households with only one brother actually cultivating the land while the other brothers work at outside jobs.

LAND FRAGMENTATION

Land fragmentation, which is one of India's great problems, is in evidence at Rampur. A distinction should be made between decrease in the size of landholdings and fragmentation of cultivation units, although both processes have been occurring simultaneously. Table 19 shows the extent of decrease in size of landholdings over a forty-three-year period in Rampur. In 1910 there was not a single household with a holding of less than 6.25 acres. But by 1953 thirty-six households, or 46 per cent of all landowning households, had holdings of 6.25 acres or less. At the other end of the scale we find that whereas ten households, or nearly 40 per cent, had holdings of over 18 acres in 1910, only six households, or about 8 per cent, had such holdings in 1953. (See Table 19.)

With the limited land available, the continued breakup of land parcels

Table 19

DISTRIBUTION OF LANDHOLDINGS BY SIZE OF HOLDING AND BY NUMBER OF HOUSEHOLDS, RAMPUR, 1910 AND 1953

Size of Holding		Number of Households	
Bighas	Acres	1910	1953
1 – 10		—	9
11 – 20		—	17
21 – 30	4.6 – 6.25	—	10
31 – 40		5	12
41 – 50		5	4
51 – 60	10.6 – 12.5	1	5
61 – 70		—	9
71 – 80		17	6
81 – 90	16.9 – 18.75	—	—
91 – 100		6	1
101 – 150		3	4
151 – 250	31.5 – 52.2	0	1
251 – 500		1	—
Total		38	78

by inheritance can only lead to smaller and smaller holdings. The number of individual owners has been rising steadily at Rampur since the settlement of 1909. In 1909 there were 1214 separate agricultural plots. In 1948 there were 1572 plots, an increase of 358. Table 20 shows the fragmentation of plots from 1908 to 1948. It will be seen that the highest incidence occurred during the depression years. This breakup is apparently due to several factors such as population pressure, urbanization, increased dependence on a market economy, and inheritance patterns. The traditional inheritance pattern in Rampur is for all the sons of a man to inherit equal shares in his land, regardless of their age at the time of his death. Formerly the pattern was for the brothers—unless they had had some violent quarrel —to maintain the land and work it in the form in which they had received it from their father. However, this traditional type of joint family holding seems to break up in times of economic hardship and at times when individuals wish to leave the village to seek work in factories, the army, or other fields.

A man who is leaving the village for work often wants to make an official separation of his own inherited share of the land from that of his brothers, so that while he is away there will be no quarrels over the land. By going to the *patvari* a man can have his share of the land registered as separate plots. Then his share can be rented to his brothers, if they want it, or to

Table 20

FREQUENCY OF PLOT FRAGMENTATION, RAMPUR, 1908-9 TO 1947-48

Years	Total of New Plot Numbers
1908–9 to 1911–12	18
1912–15	11
1916–19	9
1920–23	12
1924–27	2
1928–31	68
1932–35	55
1936–39	14
1940–43	31
1944 to 1947–48	6

someone else. When the man is away, therefore, the land is rented out; thus he feels that he is protected against encroachment, and the bases for quarrels are lessened. In other cases an heir may apply to the *patvari* to divide his inherited land, because as time goes on the shares may become too small to be worked profitably, and he may therefore prefer to rent out his inherited share.

The entire village lands are divided into twenty-four *caks,* as the land units are called, according to their relative value. Eleven of the *caks* belong to *pana* Dhan Singh and nine to *pana* Harditt; the remaining four *caks* are shared by the members of each *pana*. Each *cak* is named, the name generally indicating its major characteristic or its location. The purpose of the *cak* divisions is to delimit the good, bad, and indifferent land for apportioning. The private holdings of each family are divided as equally as possible among the various *caks,* so that each owner has a small amount of each type of land. The result is that nearly every family has landholdings scattered in from ten to twelve sections of land. The advantage of this system is that nearly every landholder has equal shares of all the types of land—canal-irrigated, well-irrigated, nonirrigated, sandy and loamy soils. The disadvantage of the system is the extreme fragmentation to which it leads. When a joint family splits up and the members start to cultivate individually instead of as a joint family, they not only split up the family lands in each *cak* but also split up many of the distinct plots in each *cak,* so as to get as even a qualitative division of land as possible.[12] As a result, 80 per cent of the plots in Rampur have an area of less than 1 acre, the average

---

[12] This points out nicely the basic equality of rights within the joint family which is traditional in North Indian villages.

falling between .2 and .6 of an acre. The present government plan for the consolidation of land will probably be unable to overcome this extreme fragmentation of landholdings, and its rather moderate aim is to bring the average size of plots to about 1 acre. This consolidation will constitute the new settlement for the village.

The small cultivating units can become economic only if a good number of families rent out their land, so that those families which have their own oxen and are in need of land to cultivate can get it. However, renting out land is feasible only if those with small areas can get work outside of agriculture. Apparently this has been possible for some in recent times. Before 1940 the cultivating units were even more uneconomical, for most of the Jats were trying to earn a living from their land, as they could not find outside work. The possibility of renting in land was lessened. The other alternative to renting, that of mortgaging the land, increased, but the amount of mortgaged land was small. In 1929 it was only 30.2 acres, but in 1939-40 it had risen to 81.25 acres. Some of the families who were forced either to rent out part of their land or to mortgage part of it became even poorer, to the extent of having to give up their oxen.

LAND TRANSFER

The transfer of land through means other than inheritance may be effected through: (1) sale, (2) mortgaging out, (3) receiving back mortgaged land, (4) gift. The total number of land transfers during the last forty-four years in Rampur has been 570. With the exception of two cases of sale, all of these transfers were due to mortgaging. Again, exactness of measure is important, regardless of the smallness of the land parcel to be mortgaged. As has already been stated, sale almost never takes place, since all the males in a family have rights in the land, and since a man's sons inherit equally. If a man has no sons he is apt to adopt one, preferably a sister's son, to whom he can will his land. Gifts of land almost never take place, as land is much too precious.

Mortgaging, however, has become a way of making money from one's land without actually losing title to it by sale or possibly through occupancy rights in the case of a long-term rental. But mortgaging takes place only under great stress, since it is a blow to a Jat's social prestige if he has to mortgage his land, for it is a clear indication of poverty, and inability to use the land for production. A man whose land is mortgaged out can hardly make good marriages for his sons and daughters.

There are many reasons for mortgaging land: (1) The death of one or more of the working members of the family, reducing the family to a small size. In such a case, a small family which cannot work all its land rents out part of it. Renting, however, decreases its profits, and through renting a small family may become poor and eventually have to mortgage at least part of its land. (2) The death of a few animals within a short period can lead to the poverty of a family and the enforced mortgaging of part of the land to get new animals. (3) Legal quarrels among the villagers are a frequent cause of impoverization and of mortgaging out land. (4) Sometimes the inability of a poor Jat family to marry off its sons forces a mortgaging out of lands in order to bring in girls.

Obviously, mortgaging is basically a method of receiving a large lump sum of money on one's capital goods. The money can be used for some important purpose such as a wedding or a legal case. Most Jats mortgage their land with the expectation of being able to reclaim it eventually. Formerly, however, they often mortgaged it to a Baniya, or moneylender, who often foreclosed. But some years ago legislation was passed in Delhi State making it impossible for non-Jats to take land in mortgage, to buy land, or even to buy animals. As a result, land is now sold or mortgaged only between Jats in this state.

During and immediately after World War I and World War II the rate of mortgaging out land decreased, and the rate of reclaiming mortgaged land increased, as the Jats had opportunities to earn money by outside employment. Their first move was to buy back their mortgaged land. However, during the depression years of 1927-39 the trend was in the opposite direction. Much more land was mortgaged out than was taken back. During the war years almost no land was mortgaged out.

The thing that stands out in Table 21 is the increase in the mortgaging out of land during the depression years of the thirties and the rapid recovery of land in the war years of the forties. Between 1929 and 1934 forty-four persons mortgaged out 61 acres of land, and seven persons recovered 11 acres of mortgaged land. But between 1941 and 1951 thirty-nine persons mortgaged out 47 acres, while eighty-two persons recovered 117 acres! Note also the tremendous increase in the value of land as reflected by the mortgage figures. The average value of land mortgaged between 1910 and 1919 was about 450 rupees per acre, as compared to 1000 rupees per acre between 1941 and 1951.

At the present time there are only six families in Rampur which have land mortgaged out. Three are from *tholla* Dhan Singh and three from Jaimel. They have only 10.7 acres between them. On the other hand, ten families from the same *thollas* have mortgaged in 25.3 acres. This includes

Table 21

LAND MORTGAGES AND RECOVERY OF MORTGAGED LAND, RAMPUR, 1919-51

Years	Mortgaged Out			Mortgage Recovery		
	Number of Cases	Area (acres)	Mortgage Value (rupees)	Number of Cases	Area (acres)	Mortgage Value (rupees)
1909–11	2	2	100	2	5	1,318
1911–13	3	5	1,455	2	3	849
1913–15	10	19	7,705	5	8	2,150
1915–17	10	17	2,476	6	12	4,194
1917–19	5	7	3,200	5	6	1,615
1919–21	3	6	2,200	13	21	6,895
1921–23	3	7	3,590	7	8	3,083
1923–25	6	16	12,273	5	17	6,250
1925–27	0	0	0	0	0	0
1927–29	4	4	1,447	1	1	215
1929–31	6	11	3,850	1	1	150
1931–33	13	22	10,032	1	3	600
1933–35	12	13	4,853	0	0	0
1935–37	9	12	3,975	4	5	1,725
1937–39	4	3	695	1	2	1,025
1939–41	2	2	180	2	2	475
1941–43	3	6	4,250	3	13	5,717
1943–45	22	31	24,209	52	78	33,531
1945–47	5	4	5,087	14	14	9,471
1947–49	6	3	8,350	11	10	12,224
1949–51	3	3	5,000	2	2	3,500

land mortgaged in from another village. One of the villagers of Rampur has mortgaged out land to a man from the neighboring village of Rasulpur. The period of the mortgage is sometimes quite long. One family moved away from the village sixty-five years ago, mortgaging out land in the village. They held onto it, however, until recently, when they finally sold it after having become firmly entrenched in another village.

One of the most outstanding aspects of land tenure in Rampur is the remarkable stability of landholding. Although there has been much juggling about of small plots of land, the over-all picture has remained very steady.

DISCUSSION

Despite the differences in landholding, wealth, and power within the village, the main problem in Rampur is not one of excessive concentration of land in the hands of a few. While there may be a tendency in that direction, the situation is not comparable with that in certain *zamindari* areas, where the exploitation is greater. There is no absentee landownership in Rampur, and there are no large landholdings, to the extent found elsewhere. The main problem in the village seems to be simply an inadequacy of land resources. The point is worth stressing, for the current emphasis in agrarian reform measures in India is on the abolition of intermediary ownership rights in land and the attempt to settle land rights on the cultivators themselves.[13]

Rampur, however, presents the picture of a village in which such a state of affairs already exists. Yet the majority of the people are still poor and ill-fed. A more egalitarian distribution of land among the cultivators would only further the already excessive land fragmentation. There are 721 acres of cultivable land at Rampur. Hence only 4.88 acres of land are available for the support of each of Rampur's 150 families, or ⅔ of an acre per person. This is not enough to provide a good standard of living for the people.

One solution to the problem would be more irrigation facilities. This is the most prominent "felt need" expressed by the villagers. They seem to feel that if the new community projects cannot increase canal irrigation, they will not have much of value to offer the village. About one-third more land might be irrigated, which would greatly increase the agricultural yield.

Apart from this, the greatest need is for more outside income. If India's new Five Year Plan should succeed in fostering industrial output and in creating new jobs on a large scale, overpopulated villages like Rampur might be relieved of land pressure. This, combined with the effects of the current land consolidation program, should make larger cultivating units possible; then modern farm machinery and modern agrarian techniques might profitably be introduced. One difficulty at present is the slow development of industrialization and the scarcity of available jobs. The cities are already crowded with the unemployed. Moreover, most of the villagers are not trained for factory work.

In some discussions of India's economic development, it is assumed or stated that the present caste inequalities will automatically be reduced as the lower castes—especially the landless villagers—obtain jobs in the cities. These are the groups which would presumably be the first to seek urban employment, since they are the worst off under present conditions.

The growing class of landless rural laborers are the first to feel the pinch of agricultural distress, and improved means of communication enable them to leave the villages in search of work and higher wages. . . . Sometimes the agri-

---

[13] See Moore, 1955: 124-28.

culturist may seek employment in the towns to evade the village moneylender or to earn enough for buying cattle or more land. Sometimes again the village menials and drudges belonging to the depressed classes migrate to towns in the hope of bettering their prospects. Distress and not ambition being the chief spur, we may hazard the statement that those who migrate to the cities are more often than not the least competent and the most helpless of the village population.[14]

While our Rampur data do not deal with migration, but rather with people who work outside and continue to live in the village, a different picture emerges from this study. As we have seen, it is the higher-caste Jats and Brahmans at Rampur who have taken the greatest initiative in getting outside work, who have the best-paid jobs and the greatest number of them. A similar state of affairs has been described by Eames for a village in eastern Uttar Pradesh, where the Thakurs are the landowners, holding 82 per cent of the village land. More migrants are from the Thakur caste than from any other group, although they are second in terms of population. Members of this upper-caste group go to a greater variety of places to find employment, get better positions than lower-caste men, and earn and remit more money than do the lower castes.[15] If such conditions are prevalent in other Indian villages, it might mean that the inequalities of the caste system will be perpetuated, for the members of the higher castes would be the ones to benefit most in an industralized India.

It is evident, in any case, that Rampur's problems cannot be considered in isolation. Whether the solution comes through industrialization or a reorganization of agriculture or both, it will have to depend upon long-term changes in the larger economy of India.

---

[14] Jathar and Beri, 1949:64-65. See also the authors' quotation from the report of the Royal Commission on Labour of 1931, *ibid.*, and the brilliant essay by D. R. Gadgil in Madan, 1953:77-112.

[15] Eames, 1954:25.

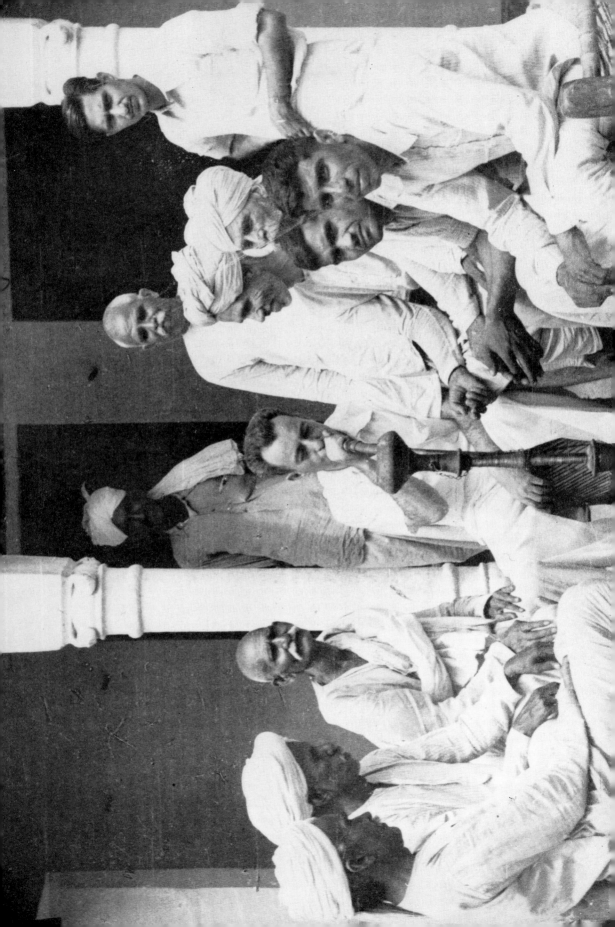

4

Group Dynamics: A Study of Factions Within Castes

Most discussions of Indian village social organization have emphasized the importance of caste, kinship, intervillage networks, and occasional alliances between castes which have been called factions or parties. In our study of Rampur we discovered still another dimension of the social structure, and one which has received insufficient attention in the past; namely, the existence of small cohesive groups within castes which are the locus of power and decision making and contribute to the compartmentalized and segmented nature of village social organization. The study of these small groups takes us to the very heart of village life. It provides us with the key to the communications channels of the society and also reflects many of the values of the people. In this chapter, then, we will systematically examine the nature of these small groups, their number, size, age, composition, economic and social characteristics, internal structure and leadership, the processes by which they are formed, and, finally, some of the practical implications of these findings for community development programs in India.

After intensive study in Rampur, we found twelve small groups locally

Fig. 30. Author with a Jat hookah group.

known as *dhars*. The word *dhar* literally means the upper part of the body and the use of this term for groups of people carries out the idea of physical unity, that is, members of the same *dhar* are all of one body. The *Hindustani Dictionary* of J. T. Platts (1925) defines *dhar* as "bodies" but adds that in North India the common meaning is "parties." In Rampur, however, the word parties refers to larger political groupings and to more temporary alliances than is denoted by the term *dhar*. I have therefore translated *dhar* as faction, for this seems to me the nearest equivalent in English for the sense in which the villagers themselves use the term. However, it must be emphasized at the outset that the term faction as here used does not denote only opposition or hostile relations between groups, nor is discord and dissension necessarily the predominant quality in interfaction relations. The small groups which we have delineated are held together primarily by cooperative economic, social, and ceremonial relations. Dhillon has put it well in his recent comparative analysis of a similar phenomenon in the South Indian village of Haripura. He writes: "While hostility towards other groups is a common attribute of factions and new factions are often formed as a result of quarrels and disputes, this is seldom the only or even the major force which holds factions together." [1]

While most villagers in Rampur are perfectly aware of the existence of these factions both in their own and other castes, it is not an easy task to delineate them, because of the complexity of interfaction relations and the reluctance of villagers to talk with outsiders about the intimate details of village life. The factions are generally referred to by the names of their leaders or in some instances by the nickname of a lineage, that is, when the faction and the lineage are synonymous. For example, many years ago a number of Jat families who were expelled by a village panchayat decree sought refuge in a village called Dhamar. Later, when they returned to Rampur, they became known as the Dhamariyas and now all belong to a single faction.

As indicated above, the factions follow caste lines. However, factions from different castes may and do form alliances or blocs, which in effect are factions on a different level from those discussed here.

The distribution of factions by caste is as follows: six among the seventy-eight Jat families; one among the fifteen Brahman families; two among the twenty-one Camar families; two among the ten Bhangi families; and one among the seven Kumhar families. Of these, the Jat factions are by far the most powerful and dominate the political life of the village. Because of the

[1] See Dhillon, 1955:30. Whether or not we define the term *dhar* as "faction" does not materially alter the analysis.

small number and economic dependence of most of the lower castes they do not have the strength to act as independent factions. As a matter of fact the Camar factions are relatively recent and their emergence is closely related to the increase in jobs outside the village and the gradual breakdown of the old *jajmani* system. It is noteworthy that both the Jats and the lower castes are split among themselves. However, the Brahmans form more or less of a cohesive group, although they are in many ways subservient to Jat interests. In short, we can think of the factions in the village in terms of three sets, Jats, Brahmans, and Harijans (lower castes).

The functions of factions differ somewhat by caste. All factions operate as more or less cohesive units on ceremonial occasions, particularly births, betrothals, and marriages; in court litigations; in the operation of the traditional caste panchayats; and in recent years in district board, state, and national elections.[2] Moreover, all of the factions have one or more of their own hookah-smoking groups which serve as social centers where there is daily face-to-face contact. Jat factions have a few special functions. They act as units in cooperative economic undertakings such as moneylending and the renting of land, and also in quarrels over land, especially village communal lands.

For a faction to operate successfully over an extended period of time it must meet three conditions: (1) It must be sufficiently cohesive to act as a unit. (2) It must be large enough to act as a self-sufficient ceremonial group, for example, it must be able to summon an impressive number of relatives for a marriage party. (3) It must have sufficient economic resources to be independent of other groups. This means that it must have some well-to-do families that can rent out land or act as moneylenders for its poorer members. It must also have sufficient resources to fight expensive and lengthy court cases. If we examine our twelve factions in terms of these criteria it at once becomes apparent that the Jats come much closer to approaching these conditions than the non-Jats and are therefore stronger and truer factions. Four of the six non-Jat factions can not meet the economic criteria and therefore can hardly be considered as independent factions of the same order as the Jats.

In interfaction relations members of friendly groups will share most of the functions we have described above for each faction, except that it is done on a lesser scale and the relationship is much less stable than within a single faction. For example, on ceremonial occasions it is expected that

[2] Prior to 1947 and Independence the franchise for district board elections was based on possession of property. This meant a practical exclusion of all non-Jats from the voters' list in Rampur.

all the members of a single faction will be invited, including the women. But in relations between friendly factions it is obligatory to invite only one male representative from each of the lineages of the faction. Thus, if there are four married brothers living in separate households only one need be invited, although more may be. However, their wives are generally not invited and this cutting out of the women is one of the major differences between intrafaction and interfaction relations. Similarly, there is much less informal visiting among the women of separate though friendly factions than among women of the same faction.

Members of hostile factions will not attend each other's ceremonial celebrations, will not visit each other's homes, and as a rule will not smoke the hookah together, except at the home of a member of a neutral faction. In panchayat meetings the representatives of hostile factions can be counted upon to marshal vicious gossip about rivals. However, direct attack in public is rare. Instead, indirection is developed to a fine art. It is to be noted that members of hostile factions generally do not cease talking to one another, and are polite. This allows for the possibility of improving relations or at least joining up temporarily with one hostile group to fight another. Factions which enjoy the reputation of being relatively neutral and of having friendly relations with all groups are the most influential in the village.

There are some occasions, though these are relatively few and far between, when members of different factions come together despite their differences and unite for some common action. The major occasions are funerals, the building of village wells, the cleaning of the village pond (twice in the past forty years), the repair of subcanals for irrigation, and certain holidays such as Holi and Tij. Moreover, there is a tradition of presenting an appearance of unity to the outside. For example, if two men of hostile factions have married daughters living in the same village, whenever one of the men visits that village he must visit the daughter of the hostile faction and pay the customary 1 rupee to symbolize the fact that she, like his own daughter, is a daughter of the village.

SPATIAL DISTRIBUTION WITHIN THE VILLAGE

The distribution pattern of the houses of the various faction members is shown in Map 2.

It can be seen that the houses of C are clustered together and form a a single neighborhood. This is also true of E, all of whose houses are on a single street. The houses of D form two separate neighborhoods while those of B are on three separate streets and can be said to form three

FACTION A
FACTION B
FACTION C
FACTION D
FACTION E
FACTION F

THOLLA BOUNDARIES:
HARDITT —·—·—·—
JAIMEL —··—··—··—
DHAN SINGH ------------
TEKA ———————

N
W—E
S

Map 2. *Distribution of house sites by Jat factions, Rampur, 1953.*

Table 22

POPULATION CHARACTERISTICS OF JAT FACTIONS, RAMPUR, 1953

Faction	Total Number of Families	Total Number of Family Members	Average Size of Family	Number of Adult Males
B	21	166	7.9	49
A	14	121	8.6	32
D	14	141	10.7	37
F	13	93	7.1	28
E	9	77	8.0	17
C	7	50	7.1	14

adjoining neighborhoods. However, the houses of *A* and *F* are scattered all over the village, with the scattering greatest in *F*, the least cohesive of all the factions. It is interesting to note that *C* and *E*, geographically the most compact, are also the two most cohesive factions in the village. This will be discussed in detail later.

NUMERICAL STRENGTH

The size of factions in terms of numbers and families, total population, and total number of adult males is shown in Table 22.

We see that there are four large factions and two small ones. The largest, *B*, is three times the size of the smallest, *C*. There is also considerable range in average size of family within each faction. *D* has the largest families with an average of 10.7 members per family, followed by *A* and *E*. *B*, *F*, and *C* have the smallest, with *C* showing 7 as the average size.

The larger families in *D* reflect the stability of the joint family in this group. Seven out of fourteen families in *D* have from ten to nineteen members and seven out of fourteen families in *A* have from ten to eighteen members.

There appears to be no relationship between the influence of factions and their size. *F*, which is the least influential, has thirteen families while *D*, the most influential, has fourteen. There appears to be an inverse relationship between size and cohesiveness, that is, the smaller factions are the most cohesive. However, there are other factors involved which will be discussed later.

FACTIONS AND KINSHIP

The role of kinship in the composition of factions is extremely important.

Table 23

DISTRIBUTION OF JAT LINEAGES AND CLANS BY FACTION, RAMPUR, 1953

Faction	Number of Families	Number of Lineages	Number of Clans
C	7	1	1
E	9	2	2
A	14	3	2
D	14	4	2
B	21	3	2
F	13	3	1

In questioning informants about the membership of their particular faction they tend to equate their faction with their kinship group, even when they are aware that the two may not entirely coincide. This is particularly true when kin belong to separate but friendly factions. There is a strong reticence, however, to volunteer the information that close kin belong to hostile factions. But when the question is put directly it will be admitted. There is not a single case of brothers belonging to separate factions, only one case of first and second cousins, and only four cases (out of fourteen) of third cousins.

Of the six Jat factions, one consists of members of a single lineage, another consists of members of two lineages, each of a different clan, three consist of three lineages, again representing more than one clan, and one consists of four lineages representing two clans.

It is clear that the lineage and the faction are not synonymous. However, they seem to have been so about a hundred years ago when only two factions existed, each a lineage of a single clan. At present, however, members of as many as four lineages are joined together in a single faction because of common interests. The present composition of factions therefore represents different historic levels of faction development. Apparently new factions developed when members of new clans came into the village. This will be discussed later.

FACTIONS AND *PANAS*

There are three factions in each *pana*: A, F, and D in Dhan Singh, and B, C, and E in Harditt. (See Chart 1.)

It can be seen that in each *pana* two of the factions are hostile to each other and one is neutral. The hostile factions within each *pana* combine with one of the groups in the opposite *pana* so that each hostile faction is

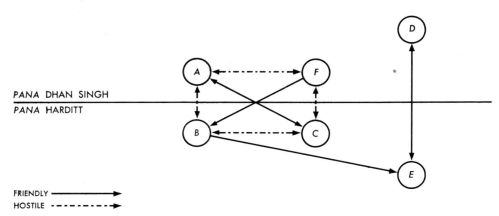

PANA DHAN SINGH

PANA HARDITT

FRIENDLY ———————→
HOSTILE ------→

*Chart 1.   Sociogram showing inter- and intra-*pana *faction relations, Rampur, 1953.*

hostile to two groups (one in each *pana*) and friendly to a third. This pattern is in accord with the well-known Indian proverb which says, "The enemy of your enemy is your friend."

The hostility between factions of the same *pana* is generally more bitter than between factions of opposite *panas*, for it represents a violation of the ideal pattern whereby relatives are supposed to get along. But by the same token the closer kinship bonds between factions of the same *pana* imply a greater potential for some future rapprochement. The traditional obligations to family members on ceremonial occasions act as a constant pull for unity.

FACTIONS AND *THOLLAS*

As has been indicated earlier, each *pana* is divided into two subgroups known as *thollas*. (See p. 23.) The number of factions within the *thollas* increases progressively as we go from the smallest to the largest *tholla*. Teka *tholla*, the smallest, has one faction; Harditt *tholla* has two, Jaimel *tholla* has three, and Dhan Singh *tholla* has four. In terms of the *tholla* composition of factions, we find that three factions consist of families from one *tholla* each and three consist of families from two *thollas*.

ECONOMIC AND SOCIAL CHARACTERISTICS

The factions show significant differences in a number of important economic and social characteristics. The study of these differences has been greatly facilitated by our earlier determination of the relative socioeconomic position of all families in the village with the aid of various point scales. (See pp. 90-91.) We can establish the ranking of the Jat factions by adding up the total number of points obtained on all of the scores by the families in each faction and dividing by the number of families per faction. The ranking is shown in Table 24.

Beginning with the total socio-economic scores we see that A, D, and C rank highest and E, B, and F lowest. The correlation between the total scores and the separate scores is very high in housing and quite high in most of the other indexes with only a few exceptions. In short, A, D, and C are clearly the wealthiest groups. It is noteworthy, however, that the basis of the faction socio-economic strength differs considerably. A, which ranks first on total score, ranks sixth or last on land owned and land cultivated. But it ranks first in outside income and second in education. This negative correlation is significant and reflects a widespread trend whereby the smaller landowners seek outside employment and rely more heavily upon the education of their children. The converse of this proposition is shown strikingly in the case of D.

A more detailed examination of the landownership picture reveals that D, C, and E own the most land per family, and B, F, and A the least. The total land of each faction and the average per family are given in Table 25.

It can be noted that the rank order of factions for land owned and land cultivated per family is almost identical. In A, which ranks lowest, six out of fourteen families do not cultivate land, while in D, C, and E all but one family (in E) are cultivators.

In comparing Tables 25 and 26 we are struck by the inverse relationship between landholding and amount of outside income on a faction basis. We have no specific information which would fully explain why the families in A have so much higher incomes than those in D. However, we know that the educational level of A is considerably higher than that of D. Moreover,

Table 24

RANK ORDER OF JAT FACTIONS ON SOCIO-ECONOMIC INDEXES, RAMPUR, 1953

Faction	Total Socio-Economic Score	Housing	Land Owned	Land Cultivated	Outside Income	Highest Grade Completed
A	1	1	6	6	1	2
D	2	2	1	1	5	5
C	3	3	2	2	6	1
E	4	4	3	3	4	4
B	5	6	4	4	2	3
F	6	5	5	5	3	6

Table 25

DISTRIBUTION OF LANDOWNERSHIP BY FACTION, RAMPUR, 1953

Faction	Number of Families	Land Owned (acres)	Average per Family (acres)
D	14	181.47	12.96
C	7	86.04	12.29
E	9	87.29	9.69
B	21	173.33	8.25
F	13	102.27	7.86
A	14	85.42	6.10

we have seen that the bulk of the noncultivating Jat families are in *A*, and five out of six of these families have outside income.

Perhaps the most dramatic evidence for the socio-economic basis of the factions emerges from a study of the renting and mortgaging of land. In five of the six factions not a single individual rents land out to other factions. *D*, the only exception, has a surplus of land and rents out to *B* and *E* as well as to Brahmans and Camars. However, in principle no faction will rent out land outside of its own faction if there is anyone within the faction who needs land. In the case of mortgaging, faction solidarity is even more striking, for there has not been a single case in the last five years of land mortgaged outside of one's own faction. This is all the more significant in the face of the demand and competition for land.

Turning from a comparison of the factions to a consideration of the wealth distribution within the factions we find that each faction tends to reflect a cross section of the wealth distribution pattern of the village. Each has at least one well-to-do family which acts as moneylender and has

Table 26

AVERAGE MONTHLY OUTSIDE INCOME BY JAT FACTION, RAMPUR, 1953

Faction	Number of Families	Number of Employed Families	Income (rupees)	Average Income per Employed Family
A	14	9	1843	205
B	21	10	1781	178
E	9	4	602	150
F	13	9	940	104
C	7	2	195	98
D	14	8	716	89

sufficient land to rent out to poorer members of the faction. Each faction also has one or more strong and dynamic figures who tend to keep the faction united. An analysis of the socio-economic position of the families within each faction shows that five out of the six factions have one member in the highest group or Group III. D and A both have a preponderance of Group II families. B, which has the largest percentage of poor (Group I) families, is also the least cohesive of all the factions.

COHESIVENESS

The varying degree of cohesiveness of the factions appears to be a function of the size of the group, geographical compactness, closeness of kinship ties, the degree of economic self-sufficiency, the past history of factionalism, and the age of the group. When all these factors are considered together we find that the factions fall into three groups: C and E the most cohesive, A and D less so, and B and F the least cohesive. Now let us examine each group in more detail, beginning with the most cohesive and ending with the least cohesive.

Faction C—seven families—is united by close kinship bonds. Its members are of a single lineage of Dabas clan and are descendants of a common great-great-grandfather. The houses of C form a compact neighborhood. This faction in its present form is about thirty-five years old. However, none of the present members or their ancestors, for a period of 125 years, have belonged to a separate or opposing faction. At no time has there been a quarrel among the present members. The sense of unity and distinctness of this faction is reflected by the popular saying of the villagers that this group, known as Dhamariyas, forms an independent village within a village, or a fifth village within the four-village unit. C has a tradition of strong and popular leaders known for their aggressiveness. This has tended to isolate this faction from the rest of the village, thereby strengthening its internal cohesiveness. The members of C never rent land to or from the members of other groups nor do they take loans from any of the factions within the village. They prefer to deal with moneylenders in other villages to maintain their independence in their own village.

Faction E—nine families—consists of members of two lineages which, though not closely related (one is of Dabas clan and the other of Dahya clan), have been together in a single faction for many years. The age of the present faction composition is twelve years. However, the present members acted as a unit for the past thirty-five years when they were part of a larger faction. Still earlier there was a history of some conflict between some of the families of the same lineage. The houses of *E* form a single cluster and are on one street. Because the group is small it tends to act as one large family. The members sit and smoke together often and consult with each other even on small matters. They constitute a single hookah group. Unlike *C*, the leaders of *E* have a reputation of being quiet and humble men who are secure in their wealth and exert a great deal of influence by their relative neutrality. They are closely tied with *D*, from which they rent land.

Faction *A*—fourteen families—consists of three lineages, two of which are closely related (both are Kharab clan), one with eleven and one with two families. The third (Dabas clan) of one family is unrelated. The heads of nine of the eleven families have the same grandfather and constitute the core of the faction. The houses of *A* are scattered all over the village and there are two separate hookah groups. The present members or their ancestors have been in a single faction for over one hundred years. During this time there has been some splintering off of some families and this has hurt the reputation of the group. However, the history of factions indicates that during crisis periods the families who left the faction reunited with it. Because of this, *A* is considered tricky and unpredictable. Like *C*, *A* has a tradition of aggressive leadership and is relatively isolated from the rest of the factions.

Faction *D*—fourteen families—is made up of four lineages. Three of these, consisting of twelve families of Dabas clan, are closely related. The fourth, consisting of two families of Kharab clan, is unrelated. The houses of *D* form two separate neighborhoods and have two hookah groups. The members of *D* are proud of the fact that no one from the three core lineages belonged to other factions. Between thirty-five and fifty years ago, however, some of the present members or their predecessors belonged to opposing factions but never fought court cases against one another. The leaders of *D* are also proud that their group represents the oldest genealogical lineage in this and three other surrounding villages. The members of *D*, along with those of *A* and *C*, can also boast of being direct descendants of some of the most popular and traditional leaders of the village.

Faction *B*—twenty-one families—consists of three lineages, two of which, made up of families of Dabas clan, are closely related, while the third, consisting of seven families of Deswal clan, are unrelated and belong to a different *tholla*. The houses of *B* are somewhat scattered and constitute three adjoining neighborhoods. One of the elements of strength of *B* is that both headmen of the village belong to this faction. In fact this means that most of the official contacts from the outside are established through members of this faction.

Faction F—thirteen families—consists of three closely related lineages of Kharab clan. The houses are widely scattered as in A. This is the youngest of the factions. It was formed about four years ago and some of its members joined only two years ago. All of the members formerly belonged to A. Moreover they did not all split as a unit but left one or two at a time, more because of their hostile relations within A than because of any great pull of F; that is, they were pushed out rather than pulled in. Most of the families who recently left A were poor and may therefore be tempted to rejoin their relatives in A.

In summary, the factors which make for greater cohesiveness are the small size of the group, the compact residence pattern within one neighborhood and few hookah groups, the internal structural homogeneity of lineage and clan membership, economic self-sufficiency, a long history of internal peace and unity, and strong leadership.

INTERNAL STRUCTURE AND LEADERSHIP

The internal structure of each of the six Jat factions shows many interesting differences. This structure is represented graphically in Chart 2.

The first thing to note is the rather large number of men who are considered spokesmen or leaders—twenty for seventy-eight families—indicating the tendency to spread leadership roles. The greatest spread is in D, the smallest in F. The large squares within the circles represent primary leaders, the smaller squares, secondary leaders. It will be seen that five of the six groups recognize more than a single man as leader. In A, D, C, and E any one of the leaders may speak for the group as a whole and in critical situations may make independent decisions, although the practice of delegating authority to individuals is frowned upon and the leaders themselves are not in the habit of making independent decisions. In C the major leader is an aggressive and dominating figure and in his absence there is no able spokesman for the group. In B and F the leaders are much more dependent upon constant consultation with other members of their respective factions because these factions are much less cohesive than the other four. The four more cohesive groups are conscious of this weakness of B and F and will sometimes deride them on this score.

In A, D, and B there is a division of labor among the leaders. The older men act as ceremonial leaders, the younger and more educated men as

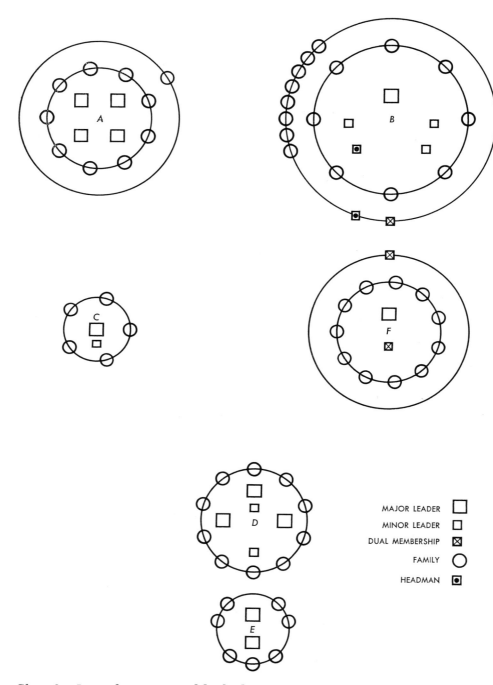

Chart 2.   Internal structure and leadership of Jat factions, Rampur, 1953.

representatives of the group on secular committees. In E both leaders are of about equal age and play interchangeable roles.

It will be seen that A, F, and B are shown in Chart 2 with outer circles. This is intended to indicate that there are families in each of these factions which show the beginnings of dual loyalties. B has the largest number of such families. However, only in F is there a clear-cut case of dual allegiance. This is the case of the headman who belongs to both B and F.

An analysis of the personal and socio-economic characteristics of Jat leaders reveals that leadership depends upon the following factors in order of importance: wealth, family reputation, age and genealogical position, personality traits, state of retirement, education, connections and influence with outsiders, and, finally, numerical strength of the family and lineage.

Wealth is a basic criterion for leadership. Although leaders are found among all three socio-economic classes, they clearly come from the upper levels of each and the correlation between wealth and leadership is highest as we move up the scale. (See Table 27.)

Four of the five families or 80 per cent of the families in Group III are represented among faction leaders, whereas only approximately 47 per cent of Group II families and only 2 per cent of Group Ib families are represented.

The social reputation of a family plays a very important role in leadership position and is dependent upon the giving of Kaj (death feast), Desotan (birth feast), and elaborate marriages. The Kaj and Desotan feasts have to be given for the entire village, including all castes, and some are given for a four-village or twenty-village unit. These occasions are remembered for generations. Seven of the primary leaders and one of the secondary leaders have given at least one Kaj ceremony each; in addition one has given four and another three. The last Kaj feast was given about twenty-five years ago but is still talked about.

Family reputation is also judged in terms of the charity given to the

Table 27

DISTRIBUTION OF JAT LEADERS BY SOCIO-ECONOMIC POSITION, RAMPUR, 1953

Socio-Economic Group	Number of Leaders	Total Number of Families in Village
III	4	5
II	14	30
Ib	1	43

Table 28

AGE DISTRIBUTION OF JAT LEADERS, RAMPUR, 1953

Age Group		Number of Leaders	Total
Over 50	57-65	8	12
	51-56	4	
Below 50	40-50	6	6
Below 40	30-40	0	2
	20-30	2	
Below 20		0	0

Gaushala (charitable organization for the support of cows), and to schools. In the recent campaign for funds to build the Kanjhawla secondary school twelve of the fifteen families which contributed over 100 rupees each were from among Rampur's leaders. Families which have held official positions as revenue officials or headmen or who have been money-lenders are also popular. Among the things which hurt family reputation are the mortgaging out of land, sexual misdemeanors, and being jailed. However, families which have the reputation of being aggressive and fighters are feared and may become leaders.

Age is another clear-cut criterion of leadership. (See Table 28.)

Only one primary or major faction leader is below the age of fifty; eight of the twelve leaders over fifty are between fifty-seven and sixty-five years of age. However, of these only two leaders, those of E and F, are the sole representatives of their groups. The remaining six are essentially ceremonial leaders and are leaders by virtue of the respect for their seniority of age and genealogical position in the lineage. They are relatively inactive and delegate their powers to younger secondary leaders, particularly in activities which require education, such as membership on the school committees and official panchayats. The four leaders still in their early fifties are all active leaders and spokesmen for their factions. Only the leader of B consults with his faction members on matters relating to E.

All leaders below fifty are secondary leaders. They act as advisers and carry out the activities delegated to them by the primary leader. The presence of two leaders in their twenties points to a new trend and shows the great value placed upon education.

A fundamental requisite for leadership in this village is humility, self-abnegation, and hospitality, especially within the in-group. The importance given to these values is reflected in everyday life by the use of conventional expressions and behaviors such as respectful kinship terminology, the kneeling of women before older people to ask for blessings, and the use of phrases such as "Come and sit in my humble home," or "Please partake of our poor food," etc. In answering inquiries concerning the ownership of land or houses, they will always say, "This is your land." Similarly, in replying to questions about the relationship of family members they will say, "This is your son," "This is your daughter," etc. Leaders will never refer to themselves as such and will make a point of attributing leadership qualities to the others who are present.

Other traits which are highly valued include unquestioning loyalty to the group, keeping promises, and speaking ability, especially at panchayats. Aggressiveness is valued if it is expressed against an out-group in defense of the in-group. However, as we have seen, the most influential leaders are the nonaggressive men.

The next important factor for leadership is the need to have sufficient time at one's disposal to devote to the various activities which leaders must carry on, particularly in attending panchayats, in fighting court cases, in collecting contributions for various causes, in arranging marriages, and in other ceremonial activities. Thus traditionally most leaders have been retired or semiretired men. Eight of Rampur's leaders are fully retired and five are semiretired, doing agricultural work. All of the eight leaders are primary leaders. Another group of five leaders are middle-aged men with jobs. Still another group of leaders is emerging from among the young, educated men in the village who are unemployed. Although there are still only two in this group, one a primary leader, the other a secondary leader, this is a trend that will probably increase.

Of the twenty leaders, eleven, or over 50 per cent, have some school education, four are literate but with no formal schooling, and five are illiterate. All five illiterate leaders are in their late fifties and with one exception are ceremonial leaders only. The four literate but uneducated leaders are secondary leaders. Of the eleven educated leaders, five are secondary leaders but all are in their forties. Thus we see that education is an important factor in achieving primary leadership, though once jobs are obtained the role becomes that of secondary leader.

Families with good connections on the outside either through marriage into important families or through personal friendships with officials or other important people enhance their leadership position in the village. These connections are utilized by the leaders to help the members of their respective factions in the marriage of sons, in getting jobs, and in court cases.

We now come to the final factor in leadership—family size and the size of the lineage. We find a significant correlation between leadership and family size. Seventeen out of the twenty families of Rampur's leaders have the largest families in their respective factions. Moreover the families of the primary leaders are generally larger than those of secondary leaders. There are only four families among the Jats which are as large as the leaders' families but do not have a leadership role. In the case of the three leaders with small families we find that they have the support of very large lineages.

In summary, we see that in the traditional pattern of leadership the older men were both the ceremonial and panchayat leaders. With the coming of education and outside employment, however, middle-aged educated people are being given opportunities by the older people to represent them in official panchayats, school committees, and deputations outside the village. Moreover, youth leadership, particularly of the educated unemployed, is developing and represents a threat to the traditional values of the villagers.

INTERFACTION RELATIONS

A study of the present-day behaviors and the history of relationships between members of the various factions in the village enables us to distinguish three broad types of relationships: positive or friendly, negative or hostile, and neutral. The strength and quality of each of these relations differ considerably. Moreover, the positive relations can further be classified into four orders of preference which reflect differences in the quality of the relationship. Preference can be defined in terms of the intensity of the relationship and the number of people who interact in any two groups. For example, when two groups have primary reciprocal preferences it signifies that more members from each group have active friendly relations with one another than with members of any other groups. As the order of preference between any two groups decreases the intensity of the relationship decreases and fewer people interact.

To facilitate an analysis of these varied relationships we have constructed a sociogram indicating the relationships between the factions by various symbols. It should be noted that most groups give or have preferences, and are the objects of preferences by others. We will begin our analysis of the major Jat factions and then go on to examine the relations between the Jats and non-Jats.

Fig. 31. A youth leader in native attire: an educated young man, a threat to the traditional values of the village.

Chart 3 shows three major sets of factions among the Jats consisting of two groups each, namely, A and C, B and F, and D and E. The first two sets have hostile relations as indicated by the fact that no lines connect them. However, neutral set D-E is more closely related to B and F than to A and C. If we examine each order of preference between the groups the relationship pattern will become clear. Only two of the three sets have a primary reciprocal relationship, that is, A and C, and D and E. F owes its primary relationship to B, and B in turn to E.

In tracing the secondary preferences we see that the lines are essentially from both sets of hostile factions to the neutral ones, D and E. However, the ties between sets B-F and D-E are obviously much stronger than the ties between sets A-C and D-E, for in the latter case D and E receive secondary preferences but do not reciprocate. The third preferences show that A and C are now receiving some support from D and E, and F is showing some support toward D. However, it is not until we come to the fourth or weakest preferences that F receives allegiance from D and E. It is clear that F is in the weakest position in its relationship to D and E, followed only by C.

In an attempt to quantify the relative influence of each group in relation

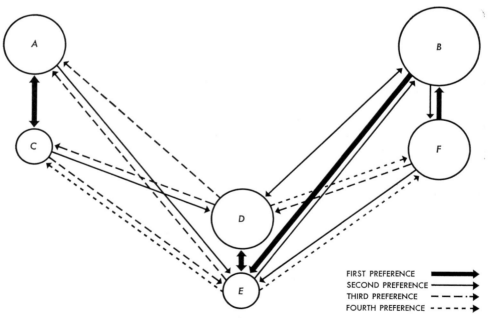

FIRST PREFERENCE
SECOND PREFERENCE
THIRD PREFERENCE
FOURTH PREFERENCE

Chart 3.   Sociogram showing all preferences in interfaction relations among Jats.

to the others, we can examine the number of arrows of various orders of preferences directed toward each group. The influence of a faction can be seen from the number and type of preference which it receives from other groups. (See Table 29.)

From this point of view we see that E is the most influential group since two factions representing about 50 per cent of the Jat families owe primary allegiance to it. Moreover, two other factions give it secondary preference and the third gives it tertiary preference. It can be seen that D ranks second in influence. It receives preference from all groups, one primary, two secondary, and two tertiary. B ranks third, receiving one primary and two secondary. A and C come next, both receiving one primary each, A receiving two tertiary preferences and C one tertiary and one quaternary preference. F is by far the most isolated group, receiving no first preference, only one secondary, and two fourth preferences.

In order to illustrate the meaning and content of interfaction relations and convey something of their flavor and complexity, we will present the relations of a single faction, E, with each of the other factions.

Relationships of Faction E

The closest ties of E are with members of D. E invites the members of D to attend all important ceremonies, including the birth of a son, the ceremonial first bath of the mother after birth, the ceremony symbolizing the purification of the mother ten days after the birth, and all the various ceremonies involved in marriage, beginning with the betrothal and ending with the receiving of the marriage party. The close unity between the two factions is most clearly reflected in the practice by the members of both factions of extending a *chulah neota,* whereby one entire family is fed for

Table 29

INTERFACTION RELATIONS SHOWING NUMBER AND TYPE OF PREFERENCE RECEIVED BY EACH JAT FACTION, RAMPUR, 1953

Faction	First Preference	Second Preference	Third Preference	Fourth Preference	Total Number of Preferences Received
E	2	2	1	–	5
D	1	2	2	–	5
B	1	2	–	–	3
A	1	–	2	–	3
C	1	–	1	1	3
F	–	1	–	2	3

a day. *E* and *D* have had these close relations for at least thirty-five years and have supported each other in numerous court cases and other quarrels. There is not a single case in which they have opposed one another. However, in two cases *D* remained neutral while *E* opposed *B*.

The relationship of *E* to *B* is weaker than to *D*, primarily because *E* has differentiated relations with some of the lineages in *B*.[3] The members of *E* have consistently been on intimate terms with a Dabas lineage of seven families in *B*, with whom they exchange the traditional ceremonial invitations and visit frequently. With another Deswal lineage of seven families of *B* who are of the same *tholla* as *E*, the members of *E* continue their ceremonial relations despite one serious court case between them about fifty years ago. They also smoke together frequently at each other's hookah groups, which are just across the street from one another. With a third lineage of seven families in *B* the members of *E* have severed all ceremonial relations though they do not abuse each other, and will sometimes smoke together at the hookah group of some of the other families in

[3] It should be noted that until twelve years ago, for a period of eight years, the present members of *B* and *E*, along with half the members of *D*, were the members of a single large faction.

Fig. 32.   Members of a faction smoking hookah in a baithak.

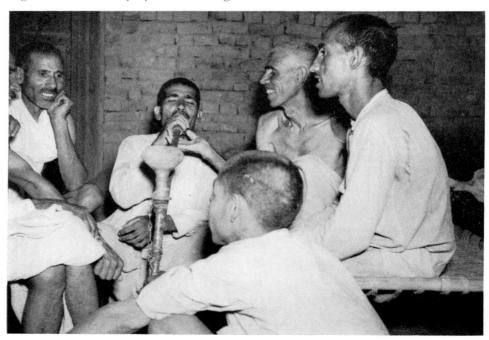

B. There have been three serious court cases between the members of *E* and these seven families of *B*.

In the first case, which occurred about sixty years ago, the headman who belonged to *E* was implicated as an accomplice in a murder case. A Jat of *E* killed his wife by tying her in a room with smoking cow dung. With the help of the headman of his own faction he then attempted to cremate her and thereby cover up any evidence of murder. The story goes that while the dead body was being taken to the cremation ground with the help of the headman, some members of *B*, with the help of *C*, stopped the cremation, called the police, and arranged for an autopsy. The case went to court, the man was convicted, and the headman lost his post, which was taken over by a member of *B*. The second case involved a quarrel over irrigation rights. It went to court and lasted for several years. *E* finally won. The third case occurred in 1947 when the headman took possession of a house vacated by Muslims who had left the village. The headman claimed that he took the house in place of payment of a debt owed by the Muslims. The members of *E*, with the help of *A*, took the case to court on the ground that the property of a non-Jat belonged to the village and so could not be sold to a private individual. *B* won the case, which was then taken up by *A* and *C* without the help of *E*.

As we have indicated earlier, *E* also had a serious court case about fifty years ago with the Deswal lineage of *B* over the inheritance of land. An adopted member of *E*, who came to the village with his brother, died issueless and 200 *bighas* of his land were claimed by the families of *B*. The case went to court and dragged on for many years. *B* finally won. However, a Dabas panchayat was called and *B* returned 100 *bighas* to assuage *E*.

The relationship between *E* and *A*, which we have designated as the third preference of *E*, is considerably weaker than those described earlier. Seven of the nine families of *E* visit very rarely and only occasionally smoke hookah together with the members of *A*; the women have no ceremonial relations with one another except for one ceremony of the exhibition of the dowry at marriage. However, the seven families of *E* still send the traditional invitation to marriage ceremonies to one male member of each of several families in *A*. Two families of *E* are close neighbors of one of the leading lineages of *A*. They visit each other's houses, smoke together, will act as host for each other's guests, and invite each other, including the women, to all ceremonies.

E has fought a number of cases against *A* in recent years, as well as many years ago. The last case occurred about fifteen years ago, when *E* supported members of *D* and *E* against *A*, and in another case when *A* remained neutral while *B* was fighting *E*. This mutual neutrality tended to reduce the earlier hostility. Finally, in 1947 *E* and *A* united together, in the Muslim house case mentioned earlier, against the headman's lineage within *B*. But when *B* won the case, *E* dropped out and refused to renew it as desired by *A* because of the pressure of the Deswal lineage of *B*.

The relationship between *E* and *C* is rather complicated. Here we find a combination of hostile and friendly relations which on the whole tend to cancel each other and thereby make for a neutral quality. Indeed, most of the fourth preference relationships approximate neutrality. None of the families of *E* and *C* invite one another to traditional ceremonies, nor do they have any economic relations at present. Two of the families of *E* who smoke at the hookah group of *A* have developed quite friendly relations with it. Only rarely do members of *E* and *C* smoke at each other's hookah groups. Because of the aggressive nature of the leaders of *C* they sometimes attempt to establish their superiority over *E*, boasting that they have helped them in the past.

The undercurrent of hostility between these two factions is expressed by their attitudes toward each other. Members of *C* boast that they have given loans to *E* to help them marry their daughters as well as to help them in a court case. They will also sometimes remind listeners that about twenty years ago *C* saved members of *E* from a beating by members of *B* who were outraged because of allegations of some illicit sexual relations between a married man of *E* and a woman of *B*. Similarly, they will boast of having helped members of *E* redirect the flow of water in one of the subcanals which had been forcibly blocked off by members of the adjoining village of Rasulpur, in the knowledge that members of *E* were too weak to oppose them. On the other hand they also boast of having successfully fought a case against *E* about sixty years ago, which cost *E* its *lambardari*.

For its part, the members of *E* are also quite critical of members of *C*, claiming that they are aggressive, boastful, and deceitful. However, the attitudes of *E* toward *C* are much milder than those of *B* and *F* toward *C*.

The relations of *E* to *F* are similar to those of *E* to *C*, for *F*, like *C*, is the most isolated group. Except for occasional visiting and smoking together, there are no ceremonial, economic, or political relations between the two. The fact that the leader of *F* is a close friend of the headman's lineage of *B*, which is hostile to *E*, does not improve the relationship between *F* and *E*. However, this potentially hostile influence is partially canceled by the fact that *F* also has friendly relations with the Deswal lineage of *B*, which in turn has close relations with *E*.

There have been neither quarrels nor collaboration between E and F in the four years since F has emerged as a faction. It is significant, however, that the two groups do not use abusive language against each other, thereby making for a kind of stable neutrality.

It is interesting to note that in terms of sociogram analysis the preference of E for F is fourth while that of F for E is second. This indicates how much more isolated F is than E in relationship to the other factions.

Jat and Non-Jat Faction Relations

The non-Jats in the village are split into a number of factions along caste lines and within castes. The number and strength of these factions is shown in Table 30.

It will be seen that the average size of family of most of the non-Jats is much smaller than that of the Jats, in some cases less than half as large. Camar b and the two Bhangi factions are so weak in total numbers and in adult males that they are quite ineffective as independent factions both from a social and economic point of view. But they think of themselves as separate factions. On the whole the non-Jats depend much more heavily upon intervillage relations for their ceremonial life than do the Jats. Moreover, all except the Camars are still occupationally dependent upon the Jats.

In terms of our socio-economic scale the Brahmans are clearly at the top and the Bhangis at the bottom of the ladder. The Brahmans are twice as well off as the Camars and the Camars twice as well off as the Bhangis. (See Table 31.)

A comparison of the distribution of Jats and non-Jats on our socio-economic scale was given earlier in Table 12, p. 89. There we saw that approxi-

Table 30

POPULATION CHARACTERISTICS OF NON-JAT FACTIONS, RAMPUR, 1953

Caste	Faction	Total Number of Families	Total Number of Family Members	Average Size of Family	Number of Adult Males
Camar	a	16	81	5.06	16
Camar	b	5	26	5.2	6
Brahman		15	110	7.33	23
Bhangi	a	5	30	6	5
Bhangi	b	5	22	4.4	6
Kumhar		7	39	5.57	10

Table 31

AVERAGE SOCIO-ECONOMIC SCORE PER FAMILY OF NON-JAT FACTIONS, RAMPUR, 1953

Caste	Average Socio-Economic Score
Brahman	9.53
Camar *b*	4.66
Camar *a*	4.17
Kumhar	2.18
Bhangi *a*	2.46
Bhangi *b*	1.50

mately 41 per cent were in the lowest group, Ia, 56 per cent in Ib, 1 per cent in II, and 0 per cent in the top group, III.

In examining the distribution pattern of wealth within each faction we find that only among the Brahmans is there a single family with sufficient wealth to keep the group united. Moreover, twelve out of the fifteen Brahman families are in the upper-lower group whereas most of the non-Jats are in the lower-lower. However, the Camars rank next to the Brahmans in their distribution in the upper-lower or Group Ib. This reflects the tendency toward upward mobility of the Camar group in the village resulting primarily from the large number of jobs they have had outside of the village. Since 1943 they have attained complete occupational independence from the Jats and this has increased the tension between the Camars and the Jats. Only the Camars and the Brahmans feel strong enough to take an independent stand on some issues in their relations with the Jats.

The pattern of leadership within the non-Jats follows the older traditional lines in which the older members are the spokesmen of the various groups. Only among the Camars is education beginning to enter as a new factor in leadership.

Interfaction Relations Among the Non-Jats

The split within the Camar group dates back to the twenties when the families in Camar *b* were accused by the other Camars in the village of betraying the Harijan struggle against the payment of the house tax to the Jats. Later in the thirties the split was intensified when the Camars of a neighboring village, aided by Camar *b*, abducted a relative of the leader of Camar *a*. The Camars of Rampur held a panchayat to persuade the members of Camar *b* to return the girl. When this failed a panchayat of a few hundred villagers was called. Again no agreement was arrived at. The case finally went to court and three of the five members of Camar *b* were arrested. They were released with the help of the Jat headman who posted a bond for them. The case was finally won by Camar *a*, but it resulted in the emergence of two clear-cut factions among Camars, not only in Rampur but in most of the villages of the area. Since the watchman of the village is from Camar *b*, the group feels more closely tied to the Jats, especially to *D* and *F*, than to their fellow Camars.

The split within the Bhangis took place about thirty-five years ago over the question of the inheritance of leadership after the death of the Bhangi leader. The son of the dead leader was challenged in his assumption of leadership by a Bhangi of a different lineage who was much older and claimed to be a "brother" of the dead leader. However, since the mother of this man had two husbands, one of whom was not of this village, some of the Bhangis claimed that the man's father was not of their clan and had no rights to ceremonial or secular leadership. As a result of this quarrel a split developed, after which they stopped attending each other's marriage ceremonies. In 1944, while most of the adult males from Bhangi *a* were away in military service, the members of Bhangi *b* constructed a wall encroaching upon the house sites of *a* and thereby took possession of the trees. The case was reported to the police by Jat *A*. Again the headman of Jat *B* sided with Bhangi *b* while Jat *A* sided with Bhangi *a*, but the latter lost out.

The Brahmans, consisting of two lineages, are united within the village and attend each other's ceremonies. They have very close relations with Jat *D* whose land they hold as occupancy tenants. Unlike other non-Jat factions they have been acting as an independent unit for many years, both because of their economic independence as occupancy tenants and because of the mutual dependence of Brahmans and Jats upon one another on ceremonial occasions.[4] The houses of the Brahmans are found in two groups, one a compact unit on the outskirts of the village and the other a unit inside the village. Both groups visit each other frequently.

The Kumhars, who live together in a compact unit, are the descendants of families who have lived for hundreds of years in this village. The Kumhars are all related to one another and are generally consulted on village-wide matters by Jats, with whom they still maintain their traditional occupational relations.

In Chart 4 we see that each of the Camar groups gives its allegiance to separate Jat factions which are hostile to each other and also to two factions which are neutral. The relationship between Camar *a* and Jat *D* has been

---

[4] It should be noted that while Brahmans in the village of Rampur have not been acting as priests for many years they still rank quite high socially and are invited to various ceremonies as a token of respect.

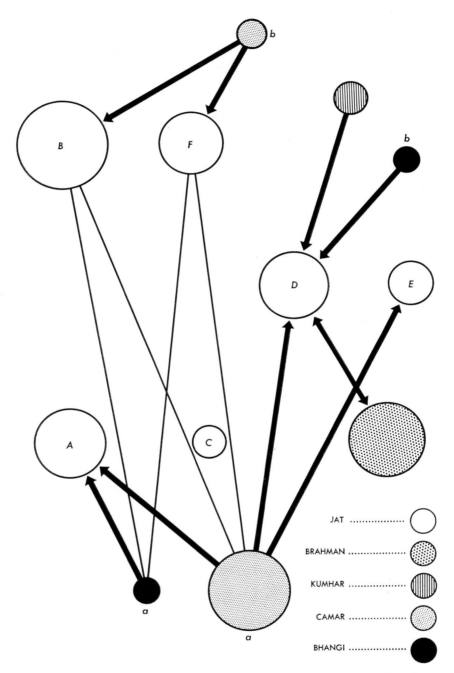

JAT .... ○

BRAHMAN .... ◉

KUMHAR .... ◉

CAMAR .... ◉

BHANGI .... ●

Chart 4. Sociogram of village factions showing primary and hostile relations of non-Jats to Jats.

quite friendly for many years. This was expressed in 1932 during an Arya Samaj conference in the village when one family from *D*, alone among all the Jats in the village, acceded to the Arya Samaj request to take water with the Camars. Similarly, in the 1943 quarrel between Jats and non-Jats one of the lineages of Jat *D* supported the Camars. Again, only a few years ago one of the Jats of *D* gave 100 rupees to a Camar *a* family to help them marry their daughter. In 1949, during a quarrel of Camars with one of the leaders of Jat *B* over the ownership of land, *D* was inclined toward the Camars, though it did not support them as openly and actively as did Jat Factions *A* and *E*.

The friendship between Camar *a* and Jat *A* is based upon their common hostility toward Jat Factions *B* and *F*. During the 1949 quarrel between the Camars and Jat *B*, the members of Jat *A*, along with *E*, supported the Camars in their court fight. It should also be noted that during the boycott of Camars by Jats in 1943, one of the leading families of Jat *A* gave milk to the Camars, for which it was fined by the Jat panchayat. *A* also gave some support to the Camars in a house-tax case of 1938, which will be described later.

The friendship between Camar *b* and Jat Factions *B* and *F* developed in 1935 as a result of Jat *B*'s aid to Camar *b* during their quarrels with Camar *a*. The friendship was strengthened in 1947 when the headmen of Jat *B* were instrumental in getting a man from Camar *b* appointed as village watchman.

One Bhangi faction owes its preference to Jat *A* and the other to *D*. While Bhangi *b* has no hostile relations with any of the Jat factions, Bhangi *a* is hostile to Jat Factions *B* and *F*, the very groups to which Camar *b* is most closely attached. This has the effect of weakening the unity of Bhangis and Camars. On the other hand, Bhangi *a* and Camar *a* have close relations and their loyalties and hostilities with respect to the Jats follow similar patterns. Both of these Harijan factions accuse Bhangi *b* and Camar *b* of betraying Harijan unity and being dominated by the Jats.

The Camars appear to be the only low-caste group in the village who have attempted to take an independent stand against the traditions of Jat domination and to champion the cause of the Harijans in this and the surrounding villages.[5] Four factors have combined to make this possible: (1) increased occupational independence; (2) the refusal of the Jats to employ Camars as agricultural laborers on the traditional grain-share basis because of the high price of grain; (3) the increased educational oppor-

---

[5] See pp. 71-79.

tunity for the Harijans; (4) the encouragement and support received from the Congress, and, much earlier, the Arya Samaj.

These trends began at least as early as the first world war when some Camars found outside employment. After the war, when the Camars faced unemployment, they found that the Jats had begun to do agricultural labor themselves due to the high price of grain, and no longer wanted them as field hands. Of course a contributing factor was the increased population among the Jats.

There is a growing sense of Harijan solidarity despite the existence of splits among them. This solidarity has been encouraged by the special consideration given to the Harijans in education and in employment opportunities. These special privileges have increased the hostility of the Jats, who somewhat ironically demand equal treatment and opportunity for Jats on the ground that some of them are just as poor as Harijans.

The interfaction relations of both Jats and non-Jats extend across village lines. There is a group of about twenty-five villages which are the most actively connected in this faction network. In intervillage relations the faction picture is considerably simplified, since as a rule there are only two major factions per caste in each village. In all but one of the past eight district board elections which we have studied there were never more than two candidates, each backed by a faction, from the constituency.

THE PROCESS OF FACTION FORMATION

To better understand the process of the formation, splitting, and reformation of factions, we must examine the history of factions in the village. This history can be divided into five periods which reveal four separate stages in faction development. These stages are presented graphically in Chart 5.

In Stage 1 we find two hostile factions along *pana* lines. In Stage 2 there are still only two major factions along *pana* lines but some of the membership shifts back and forth. It should be noted that Stage 2 sometimes reverted back to Stage 1 since there was always the pull of kinship bonds. In Stage 3 a new faction develops, drawing members from each of the two earlier factions, and all three are hostile to one another. In Stage 4 the present stage is reached. Here we see the pattern described earlier whereby each *pana* has three factions, two of which are hostile to each other and the third neutral, with the strongest friendly relations across *pana* lines. Now let us turn to an examination of the outline of events in each of the historical periods we have delineated. It will be helpful to the reader to refer back to Chart 5 as the discussion develops.

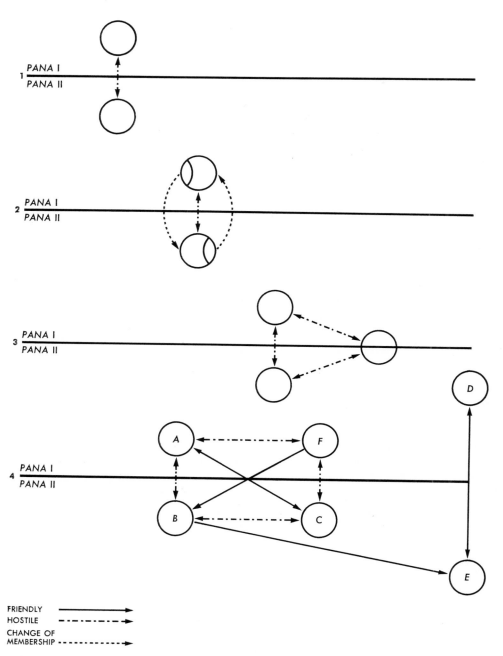

Chart 5. Stages in the development of Jat factions, 1800-1953.

First Period

The earliest horizons in social organization that can be reconstructed with the aid of informants date back to a period about 120 to 150 years ago when the ancestors of the present-day members of Teka *tholla* (Faction *D*) invited in their sister's sons who were naturally of a different clan than the Dabas (Kharabs), and gave them a part of their 900 *bighas* of land. During this period the Kharabs and members of Teka *tholla* constituted one *pana* (which we shall call *Pana* I) and one faction. Ancestors of present-day Jaimel and Harditt formed another faction and *pana* (which we shall call *Pana* II). Thus we see that in this first stage the faction and *pana* were synonymous.

Second Period, 1835-90

About twenty years before the Mutiny of 1857 the Dabas members of Teka *tholla* quarreled with their *bhanjas* or sister's sons, who were trying to grab more and more land, and joined the Dabas of the opposite faction against the Kharabs. However, the Dabas had been seriously weakened somewhat earlier when one of their own panchayats had expelled a strong group of Dabas families who were accused of murdering the person who had brought in the Kharabs.[6] After these families were expelled, the Kharabs took possession of the greater part of Teka *tholla* land and drove most of the remaining Dabas out of the village. A few years before the Mutiny of 1857 a large multivillage Dabas panchayat was called and it was decided to bring the Dabas back to Rampur. Most of the Dabas regained their land, but the lineage of Teka *tholla* which had originally invited the Kharabs could not get their land. Again, a Dabas panchayat was called and a tax of 8 annas per family was assessed to raise funds to fight the case in court against the Kharabs. The case continued for four years and the Dabas finally won the decision. However, the leader of the victorious family was poisoned on the very day of the court decision and the court documents which he carried were stolen by the Kharabs. The Mutiny of 1857 occurred in the same month, and with the ensuing confusion in the years that followed the case could not be pursued and the Kharabs remained in possession of the land thereafter.

During the four years that the above case was in the courts there were other violent struggles between the Kharabs and Dabas factions in the village; the most serious involved the abduction by one of the Kharabs of a

---

[6] Most informants claim that the Kharabs killed this man but managed to cast suspicion on the Dabas.

Dabas girl from a neighboring village.[7] This led to physical violence in which fifteen men were wounded and a Kharab killed. Some Dabas were arrested but were freed with the breakdown of law and order during the period of the mutiny.

Still another quarrel during this period takes us back to the Teka lineage. When this lineage returned to the village they invited in another group of *bhanjas* locally remembered as "Bhupenwallias," who, following the example of the Kharabs and with their help, took away most of Teka *tholla* land. A Dabas multivillage panchayat was again called, funds were raised, the case was successfully fought in the courts, and the "Bhupenwallias" were ousted from the village.

Third Period, 1890-1915

In the beginning of this period we find that Teka *tholla* left their Dabas brethren and allies and realigned themselves with the Kharabs. However, after years a split developed within Teka *tholla* and one important lineage headed by a strong and popular leader left the group and joined the opposing faction. A number of events combined to bring about this realignment. In 1890 a serious quarrel arose over land boundaries between the Brahmans and the Dhamariya group of Jats which led to the death of one Brahman and the infliction of critical injuries on another four. When the case went to court the Brahmans were supported by the Kharabs as well as by Teka *tholla,* the latter because it felt responsible for the Brahmans, having brought them to the village, the former because of their enmity to the Dhamariyas, who had killed one of their members. The case went through a few courts and the Dhamariyas were finally freed.[8] This common action of the Kharabs with Teka *tholla* brought them together.

The next shift in group membership involved a split within one *pana* which occurred as a result of the headman case described earlier, whereby a family in Harditt *tholla* lost its headman to Jaimel *tholla* due to the efforts of Jaimel. This family left its lineage and joined the Teka-Harditt group of *Pana* I.

About five years later a difference within Teka *tholla* developed over an issue of land inheritance. One of the family heads in Teka *tholla* gave half of the land of his issueless deceased brother to the sons of his paternal cross-cousin whose wife he had married. After his death his sons were

[7] The family which suffered this dishonor is locally referred to as Muc-kate, or "Those who lost their mustaches," i.e., their honor.

[8] Because the leaders of a nearby five-village unit helped the Dhamariyas in this case they have remained close friends and have been supporting each other's candidates in elections.

instigated by members of the opposite *pana* (II) to take the case to court. However, the case was dropped and Teka *tholla* split, half of the members aligning themselves with the opposite *pana*.

Still another change of membership across *pana* lines occurred in about 1900 when a member of Jaimel lineage was murdered by someone of another lineage of Jaimel, leading the first lineage to join the opposite *pana*.

Thus at the end of this period there were still only two major factions in the village. One faction, primarily of *pana* Dhan Singh (*Pana* I), consisted of the following: all of the Kharabs, one-half of Teka families, one lineage of Jaimel, and one family of Harditt. The second faction, primarily of Jaimel, consisted of the rest of the families. There was hostility between these two factions and they fought a bitter court case against one another during the preparation of one of the village men's houses in 1910.

Fourth Period, 1915-39

During this period a new faction developed, drawing its members partly from each of the two former factions. This third group, hostile to the other two, was formed when the Teka families who were divided, half in *Pana* I and half in *Pana* II, joined together and took along with them

Fig. 33.   An old man smoking a native pipe.

some members from each of the two earlier groups, thus forming a hetero-geneous unit. The three groups now became a triangle of hostility and fought famous court cases against one another, most of which have been mentioned earlier in our discussion of interfaction relations.

It should be noted that these twenty-four years were a transition period during which the bases for new patterns of leadership and factionalism were prepared as a result of the many economic and educational changes which followed World War I. These new forces led to considerable shifting about of faction membership and finally resulted in the emergence of our present-day factions.

Fifth Period, 1939-53

During this period the Kharab faction of *Pana* I split in two, forming the present-day Factions *A* and *F*, while the mixed faction split three ways into the present-day Factions *D*, *B*, and *E*. The third group remained stable and is our Faction *C*. The specific causes for these splits have already been discussed. However, from a broader point of view the increase in numbers of factions can be seen as the result of forces which had been growing in the third period but which received their expression later. This will be discussed on the following pages.

CONCLUSIONS

By way of conclusion let us attempt some answers to two sets of ques-tions which have implications for both theoretical and practical purposes. First, what are the causes of factions? How stable are they? Under what conditions do they develop and break down? Second, what does the study of factions reveal about the nature of village social organization, leadership patterns, and value systems? What are the implications of this data for practical programs of rural reconstruction?

It is clear from our data that factions are an old, ingrained pattern in village life and need to be considered as a basic aspect of traditional village social organization along with castes, *tholla, panas,* clans, lineages, and other groupings. Moreover, in view of a common misconception, it is im-portant to note that they are not political groupings, or temporary alliances of individuals to fight court cases, although some of them do take on political functions and become involved in power politics. Rather, they are primarily kinship groupings which carry on important social, economic, and ceremonial functions in addition to their factional struggles against one another. It is these positive functions which account for the remark-able stability of these groups over the years. When changes in faction membership do occur it is the family and sometimes the large extended family rather than individuals which shifts allegiance from one faction to another.

Viewed broadly, one of the fundamental causes of factions is the insecurity of village life with its scarcity of land and limited resources. More specifically, we have found that new factions developed as a result of (1) quarrels over the inheritance of land; (2) quarrels over the adoption of sons (the presence of an only son in a family makes a potentially charged situation because of the threat from the *hakikis* or inheritance claimants; (3) quarrels over house sites and irrigation rights; (4) quarrels over sexual offenses; (5) murders; and finally (6) quarrels between the castes. The villagers sum this all up by a popular saying that both factions and quarrels revolve around wealth, women, and land.

The sharp increase in the number of factions since 1939 seems to be related to the gradual accumulation and culmination of forces which had been at work in the previous fifty years. Chief among these forces were the rapid rise in population, the gradual weakening of the joint family, increased vertical economic mobility with some families going up and others down, and increased education. Whereas earlier quarrels had led to minor shiftings of members from one faction to another, quarrels in this later period, when families were larger and had increased sources of income, led to the splitting off of larger units which were strong enough both socially and economically to form independent factions.

However, in the long run these same forces which have led to the mushrooming of factions may bring about the elimination of factions based on kinship. This trend can already be sensed, although only faintly, in Rampur, where we find increasing instances of members of one joint family joining up with opposite factions. Moreover, education is beginning to provide a new basis for unity between individuals on a non-kinship level. For example, the children of opposing village factions who have been to a higher school together are developing bonds which in the future may affect faction alignments. The elimination of poverty and ignorance, the raising of living standards, the continued increase in education, and the gradual incorporation of the peasants into the mainstream of national life may in the future weaken or eliminate factions based on kinship.

Our findings in Rampur suggest that the community in the sense of a cohesive and united village community or in the sense of the American neighborhood, village, or trading center community hardly exists. Caste and kinship still form the core of village social organization and this splits the village into separate communities which have their close affiliations across village lines. As we have seen earlier, there are occasions when the village acts as a unit. However, these are relatively infrequent and with the weakening of the old and traditional *jajmani* system the segmentation within the village is all the more striking, nor has it been replaced by any new uniting forms of social organization.

However, the weakness of the village community is partially compensated for by the strength of intervillage networks. The persistence of these traditional large-scale intervillage networks for ceremonial and panchayat purposes provides a natural grouping of villages and ready-made channels of communication which might be effectively utilized by the Community Projects Administration in its organization of village circles and in other aspects of its work. Moreover, the fact that the village in northern India is not a self-sufficient isolate for social and economic purposes suggests that the process of diffusion of new knowledge and practices may occur in India at a more rapid rate than in other countries where the village is a highly isolated, integrated, and cohesive unit. For example, our study of innovations in agriculture over the past thirty years showed that new seeds and practices came in from villages which formed part of the panchayat and kinship network.

The kinship basis of village social organization, whereby an individual's primary loyalties are to his own family and lineage, shows the difficulties ahead in building a modern secular democratic system based upon voting and the delegation of authority to selected individuals to represent large masses of people. The theoretical assumption behind the democratic system based on voting is that the individual is an independent, thinking being capable and ready to make his own decision. However, in a kinship-organized society such as village Rampur, it is the large extended family which is the basic unit for most decision making. At best, voting becomes an extended family process which violates the spirit of individuality inherent in the Western electoral system.

Leadership in Rampur is limited to faction leadership and is primarily of a protective and defensive nature in which each faction or combination of factions defends its family interests. The leader is essentially a spokesman for a family or a group of related families and has little authority to make independent decisions or to exercise power over the group.

Village-wide leadership does not yet exist and the idea of positive constructive leadership in the public interest is only now gradually beginning, particularly in connection with the establishment of village schools. As yet there are no village heroes or outstanding citizens who are popular for their contribution to village welfare as a whole.

The outstanding characteristics of Jat leaders are the possession of wealth, good family background, a reputation for being charitable and giving elaborate feasts, advanced age, education, influence with towns-people, free time to pursue the interests of the group, humility, hospitality, trustworthiness, speaking ability, and the support of a large extended family.

The fact that leadership is spread out rather than concentrated is a great advantage to the village-level worker. Since one out of every four or five heads of families holds some leadership position, the village-level worker is bound to come into contact with leaders even in a random sampling of cooperators.

Other important and perhaps distinctive aspects of leadership patterns include the following:

1. The effort to minimize rank and status differences within the castes. For example, it was difficult to find out who the leaders were by direct questioning. A typical response to the question "Who are the leaders?" was "Every Jat is a leader." This playing down of individual differences is one of the crucial values in this culture.

2. The reticence to delegate authority or leadership functions to any single individual over a period of time without provision for frequent consultation with his faction members in decision making. This is one of the main reasons for the lack of popularity of the new official panchayat which is based upon elections. Since the three official panchayat members from Rampur represent only three of the twelve factions, the villagers do not consider this body as truly representative of their interests. Consequently, the old traditional caste and village panchayats enjoy much more prestige and authority than the official panchayat. When village-wide public issues, such as land consolidation and the building of a school, arose in the past few years, they were entrusted to the caste panchayat rather than to the official panchayat which has already become a court for personal litigations.

3. The almost complete absence of youth leadership. That age is still very important can be seen from the fact that most leaders are over forty. However, youth leadership is slowly beginning to emerge with increased education. Younger educated men who live in the village are acting as representatives in school and panchayat matters, and are coming forward in village discussions of public issues.

4. Women have no direct role in leadership. They do not attend panchayats.

The implications of our findings for community development work are many-faceted. The existence of factions, the persistence of kinship loyalties, the absence of village-wide leadership, and the limited identification with larger groups, present some hurdles for community development. It is essential that all those connected with village work understand the complexity of village social organization so that they can utilize that organization most effectively in the attainment of their goals. If those sponsoring community development work desire to encourage the breakdown of factions and the development of village-wide and nation-wide loyalties, the first step must be to become aware of the existing factions, their nature and dynamics. To ignore these factions or, just as bad, to admit that they exist and then forget about them will simply help to perpetuate rather than eliminate them. It is only in action programs around common goals that factionalism can be reduced and perhaps eventually eliminated.

However, it must be emphasized that the small groups which we have called factions have their positive aspects for community development work: (1) They provide ready-made communication channels to the people. If a village-level worker reaches even a single leader in each faction, his message is sure to reach all the families of the village. (2) They provide ready-made cooperative groups for community projects, and thereby obviate the greater amount of work that would be necessary in a less organized and more individualistic type of society. (3) The organization of leadership on a faction basis provides for a much closer representation of the people than is possible in that more sophisticated and monolithic type of political democracy of some modern Western nations which is based on delegated authority. In view of this, it may be desirable to build upon the present faction organization a sense of wider community loyalties rather than to destroy the traditional organization.

Our data underlines the well-known dangers of working only or primarily through the official headmen of a village. If one followed this approach in the case of Rampur he would find it difficult to reach all the villagers, and even worse, he might offend and estrange a large portion of them. As we have seen earlier, both of the official headmen happen to belong to a single Jat faction, B, which along with F is hostile to A and C. Our own field research experience illustrates what might readily happen to an action program. We first established contact with the villagers through the aid of a native of the village who happened to be an agricultural government officer. His family belonged to B so our early contacts were with the members of that faction, including the two headmen. We worked in the village for over six weeks before we could break out of this small circle without offending our friends who, it seems, consciously or unconsciously were keeping us away from the group toward which they were hostile.

Our contacts slowly spread from members of *B* to *F*, *D*, and *E*, but it was not until we systematically set out to study the social organization of the village that we realized the importance of *A* and *C*, which represent over 30 per cent of all the Jat families. Moreover, the leaders of these groups knew we were working in the village but did not approach us. And when on a few occasions we asked the official headmen to call the villagers together, they avoided contacting members of *C* and *A*.

In terms of the interfaction relationships in this village it is clear that *D* and *E* would be the crucial ones for village-level workers to work through since most of the communication between the villagers becomes channelized through these two relatively neutral and very influential groups.

Knowledge of the social organization of the village might also enable one to successfully channelize the hostility between groups into positive and constructive directions by encouraging their competition toward village-wide goals. The possibilities of this approach received dramatic confirmation in an experimental meeting called by our staff for the purpose of checking, in a relatively controlled situation, the findings of our study. If our findings were accurate we might expect that a meeting of all the faction leaders would result in the expression of aggression between the hostile groups. A meeting was called and each of the members of the field staff kept careful notes on the content and sequence of all that transpired. Less than half an hour after the meeting began the factional groupings became glaringly apparent with open attacks one against another. The purpose of the meeting had been explained in terms of asking the leaders to decide upon some priority among the things they would like to do themselves to improve their village, as part of their participation in the community development scheme. After much discussion and some controversy, the leaders agreed that the most urgent need of the village which might feasibly be carried out with the aid of the Community Projects Administration was the cleaning of the village pond. However, they emphasized that while they were willing to contribute labor they could not pay a single pie. Indeed, they sounded as if they were doing a favor to the community projects by agreeing to do something for their own village. Finally, one of the more aggressive and sophisticated faction leaders stood up and said that some money could be collected if it were done on a group basis and that his group would contribute 100 rupees more than any other group in the village. This started the ball rolling, and soon the leader of an opposing faction stood up and said their group would also contribute.

Another incident which occurred a few days later showed the importance of understanding the faction relations across village lines. The project executive officer came into the village accompanied by a friend who was the principal of a nearby secondary school and an outstanding leader of one of the two factions active in this area on an intervillage level. He asked the headmen to call the villagers together, and a few of the leaders and villagers of B, F, D, and E were called. Interviews with members of A and C later revealed that they suspected the neutrality and motives of the project officer because he traveled in the company of an opposite faction leader. Moreover, the absence of representatives from opposing factions in the village made the meeting dull and the officer left feeling that these villagers were apathetic. Two days later he returned to the village, this time calling together the leaders of all factions. The villagers showed considerably more enthusiasm and arrangements were made to begin work on the pond.

It should be emphasized that both the theoretical and practical findings of this study would be considerably enhanced by additional comparative studies of village social organization in other parts of India. Studies of social organization are particularly crucial for any evaluation effort which attempts to understand the effects of the community development program upon the culture and psychology of the people.

In the past few years a great deal has been written and spoken about the meaning and goals of the community development program and its crucial importance for the future of India. Throughout this discussion two dominant themes have appeared—one economic, the other psychological. On the economic side the stress has been upon the goals of improved technology, increased production, and higher standard of living. On the psychological side the goals have been stated in terms of enhancing the spiritual values of the villagers, developing initiative and respect for the dignity of labor, and changing the total world outlook.

Between these two levels of description or analysis, the economic and the psychological or spiritual, there has been a gaping abyss which many have been trying to bridge by the simple statement that economics and psychology are related. In some quarters it has been assumed that economic development would almost automatically change the psychology of the people. Indeed, I have heard speakers state categorically that it is difficult to measure progress toward the spiritual goals since they are imponderables, but that the clearest evidence of change in individual psychology is increased production. Such thinking agrees neither with the findings of modern social science nor with the philosophical traditions of India.

Our study suggests that a crucially important middle term in the economic-psychological equation needs to receive more attention and can help to resolve the dilemma created by the above dichotomy. This term is social organization. The middle ground of social organization is the framework within which the economic and psychological factors operate and interact and must be clearly understood. On the village level the so-called imponderables or psychological factors can be studied most effectively in terms of what happens to the social organization (the family structure, the caste system, the class system, factions), voluntary local organizations, and local government. Certainly, for sponsors of community development programs this sociological approach would seem to be more practical than the approach of individual psychology which, if applied scientifically, would mean the administration of psychological tests to villagers to determine whether their mentality has been changed by the program.

The relative emphasis upon economics and psychology rather than sociology in India is probably a passing phase. The very term social organization still seems to carry abstract and negative connotations to administrators. In part this is due to the inherent difficulties in studying social relations, which are subtle and complex and have to be inferred from behavior rather than studied directly. Economics seems much more practical and concrete, and psychology, too, has a stronger ideological basis in traditional Indian culture because of the Hindu philosophical emphasis upon introspection and salvation through individual effort and self-improvement rather than through planned changes in the very structure of the society.

It is through the integration of all three disciplines of economics, sociology-anthropology, and psychology that the social scientists can make their most effective contribution both to the study of society and action programs.

5

The Marriage Cycle

In Rampur, as in other parts of India, the process from betrothal to the consummation of marriage may cover many years. Five phases may be singled out. The first is *the search for a suitable bridegroom,* conducted by the girl's father, and *the conclusion of the engagement.* The second is *the preparations for the wedding,* consisting of the sending of formal letters by the girl's father to the boy's father announcing the wedding date, as well as the sending of invitations to relatives and friends; the taking of ceremonial baths by the prospective bride and groom; the preparation of clothes, ornaments, and foodstuffs for the wedding; the collection of money by the two fathers; and some ceremonies at the boy's village prior to the departure of the wedding party. The third phase is *the wedding* itself: a two- or three-day affair including the reception of the wedding party at the girl's village, the wedding ceremony, presentation of the dowry, and formal farewells. The fourth stage is *the ceremonial reception of the girl in the boy's village.* The fifth includes *the consummation of the marriage* and the beginning of cohabitation.

A total of twenty ceremonial steps may be singled out within these five phases as follows:

Fig. 34. *A young bride with all her ornaments. Women married into the village have to wear veils over their faces.*

I. The Search for a Bridegroom and the Engagement
   1. The *sagai* (engagement) ceremony
II. Preparations for the Wedding
   2. Notification of the wedding day
   3. *Lagan* (a formal reminder)
   4. The *bans* (ceremonial oil baths)
   5. Presentation of the *bhat* (wedding clothes and money) by the mother's brother
   6. Erection of the *mandha* (marriage pole)
   7. *Ghur charhi* (the boy's ride on horseback to the village shrines)
   8. *Johari* (ceremonial sucking of the mother's breast)
III. The Wedding
   9. *Milni* (reception of the wedding party)
   10. *Barat lena* (honoring of the groom by the Brahman of the bride's family)
   11. *Barauthi* (honoring of the groom by members of the bride's family)
   12. *Chunri* (presentation of gifts to the bride's family)
   13. *Phera* (the taking of marriage vows and circumambulation of the fire)
   14. *Kannya dan* (the girl's father's bestowal of his daughter and the dowry)
   15. *Mur khulai* (joking between the groom and the bride's female relatives)
   16. *Bida* (farewell ceremony)
IV. Reception of the Bride in the Groom's Village
   17. The blocking of the doorway by the groom's sister
   18. *Mukh dikhana* (viewing the bride's face)
   19. *Kangna khelna* (playing games)
   20. Trip to the village shrines
V. *Gauna,* Consummation of the Marriage

After a general discussion, the various phases and ceremonies will be described with numbers corresponding to those in the outline. The description will refer primarily to Jat marriages, but those of lower castes will also be included.

AGE AT MARRIAGE AND *GAUNA*

It is a vital obligation for a man to get his daughters married. His salvation in the other world and his peace of mind in this one depend on it. In

Rampur there are two unmarried girls aged sixteen, but none older than that, although there are two girls of eighteen and one of seventeen who have gone through only the early stages of marriage and not the final consummation. There is one Jat girl in Rampur who was married as late as twenty.

The proposal must come from the girl's side.[1] Hence it is the males who are more apt to remain unmarried. Some do not receive proposals. All the same, most boys are married by the time they are sixteen. There are six unmarried boys of sixteen in Rampur, and one each for the following ages: seventeen, eighteen, nineteen, twenty-one, twenty-two, twenty-five, twenty-seven, twenty-nine, thirty. There are two men who married at twenty-five, one who married at thirty, and one who married at twelve but whose marriage was never consummated, and who is now a widower at thirty-two.[2]

There is usually an interval of about three years between the wedding and the ceremony of *gauna* (or *gavana*), when cohabitation begins. Most girls are married at twelve or thirteen and have the *gauna* at fifteen or sixteen. Most boys are married at fourteen or fifteen and have the *gauna* at seventeen or eighteen.[3] The marriage age seems to have been going down in most caste groups at Rampur, but it has been going up slightly in the case of the Jats. Among the Jats, moreover, the interval between marriage and *gauna* has been getting shorter. Among Jats over thirty-five years of age we find that there was an interval of six years between wedding and *gauna*, but among those under twenty-one the interval is only two years.[4]

---

[1] This seems to be the general pattern in North India. However, Ibbetson, writing in 1880 about the Karnal district, not far from Rampur, stated that it was possible for the proposal to come from the boy's side, in which case the boy sent his sister's necklace; if the girl kept it, his proposal was accepted. But this was done only when the families were acquainted. Ibbetson, 1883:126.

[2] J. Planalp writes of Senapur village in eastern Uttar Pradesh: "Sometimes, if a boy reaches the age of 25 or so without having been sought after in marriage, some respected elders of the village may use their influence to try to make him a match. But even so, there are in Senapur six or eight adult men who are not married, simply because for some reason no match-making parties came to their family, or, if they did, were unwilling to conclude a marriage." Planalp, 1955:28.

[3] According to Ibbetson (1883:127) the Jats in the Karnal district in the 1870's married at five and seven.

[4] To present the data in more detail: Among a group of thirty-four Jats over fifty years of age the average age at marriage was 12.3, at *gauna*, 18.4. Twenty-five female Jats in the same age group had an average age at marriage of 11.1, at *gauna*, 15.7. Thirty-four male Jats in the 35-49 age group had an average marriage age of 12.0 and an average *gauna* age of 17.5. Twenty-nine female Jats in the latter group had an aver-

The Brahmans show no particular change in different generations. The marriages of Brahman boys have taken place at an average age of fourteen, their *gaunas* at seventeen. Among Brahman girls the ages are thirteen at marriage and fifteen or sixteen at *gauna*. At the lower end of the caste hierarchy the Bhangis also show stability, with boys tending to marry at fourteen and having the *gauna* at sixteen, while girls are married between eight and thirteen and have the *gauna* by the time they are sixteen.

Camar boys are married at an average age of sixteen and have the *gauna* at twenty. This is a relatively late age for the beginning of cohabitation; the figure is based upon four informants in the 21-34 age group and six in the 35-49 age group. The only informant in the over 50 age group was married at twenty-four and had the *gauna* at twenty-five; the only Camar in the below 21 age group was married at the age of thirteen and had the *gauna* at eighteen. If the latter is not simply an aberrant case, it may suggest a tendency toward earlier marriages. Otherwise, late marriage seems to be characteristic of male Camars. Camar girls are married on the average at about thirteen with the *gauna* at fifteen or sixteen (based on twelve cases in the 21-49 age group).[5]

RULES OF ENDOGAMY AND EXOGAMY

The search for a bridegroom is complicated by involved rules relating to caste, locality, and clan. The main feature of these rules, except with regard to caste, is the requirement of exogamy. Caste rules demand that all members marry within the caste. A Jat must marry a Jat, a Brahman a Brahman, and so on. These endogamous rules are adhered to without exception in Rampur. There are no cases of intercaste marriage. Close intermarriage within the caste is also prevented by the exogamous rules for village and clan.

A bridegroom must never be chosen from the same village in which the prospective bride lives. This rule is extended further to include any village whose lands touch the lands of the bride's village, or the lands of the four-village unit of which Rampur is a part. Moreover, any village in

age marriage age of 9.8 and an average *gauna* age of 15.6. The largest number of cases fall in the 21-34 age group, where seventy-two male Jats had an average age at marriage of 15.2, at *gauna*, 18.4, while fifty-two females had an average age at marriage of 12.6, at *gauna*, 16.0. In the 20 and under age group there were twelve males with an average age at marriage of 14.3, at *gauna*, 16.2, and there were twenty-nine females with an average age at marriage of 13.6, at *gauna*, 15.7.

[5] According to Cohn (1954:222) the age at marriage among Camars has been going down markedly. Thirty years ago the bride and groom were twelve and sixteen years of age. Now they are five and seven.

which one's own clan is well represented must also be avoided. One should even shun villages in which the other clans of one's own village are well represented. In effect this means that villagers of Rampur cannot marry into any of the twenty nearby villages which are either predominantly peopled by Dabas Jats or have accepted Dabas leadership for panchayat purposes. (See p. 29.) In addition, one cannot marry into one's father's clan, mother's clan, father's mother's clan, or mother's mother's clan. (Recently the prohibition against marriage into the mother's mother's clan has been relaxed.) These rules eliminate many villages for marriage purposes.

In villages like Rampur kinship terms are generally applied within the caste. A girl may call all the boys and girls of the village in her own generation "brother" and "sister" and all the men of her grandfather's generation "grandfather," etc. This practice is even extended to other castes, from the highest to lowest, thus giving an at least verbal manifestation of village unity. This custom may inhibit further marriage possibilities, for if one has a relative in a village who calls all the men and women there "brother," "sister," etc., one would not be apt to marry into that village. For example, Ram Swarup, a Bhangi from Rampur, rejected a proposal for his son, because his father's first wife came from the same village as the would-be daughter-in-law. All the people of that village would thus be his *mamas,* or mother's brothers, and hence ineligible for marriage to his son.

The non-Jat castes in Rampur, recognizing the social superiority of the Jats, try to follow Jat marriage regulations. Although there are representatives of more than one clan for each of the lower castes in Rampur and in the larger twenty-village unit, the lower castes observe the Dabas twenty-village unit as an exogamous area.

According to a census taken in the village, the 266 married women in Rampur came from about two hundred different villages at distances of up to 40 miles, with the average distances falling between 12 and 24 miles. It is interesting to note that the lower castes travel farther in search of brides than do the upper castes. Jats and Brahmans travel only 12 to 13 miles; Nais go about 24 miles, and the Camars average 20 miles.[6] In the case of daughters who marry out of the village we find that over 220 girls from Rampur married out into about two hundred villages. This small village of 150 households may therefore be seen as forming the locus of affinal kinship ties with over four hundred other villages. In contrasting this picture with that of Mexican peasant life, the phrase "rural cosmo-

[6] Concerning Camar marriages Cohn writes: ". . . the greater the distance from which the bride comes, the greater the prestige." Cohn, 1954:12.

politanism" was applied in a previous publication.[7] This rural cosmopolitan-ism provides a striking contrast with the characteristic village isolation found in rural Mexico.

ECONOMIC EXCHANGES AT WEDDINGS

It is customary to spend large sums of money on weddings, even at the risk of going deeply into debt. For example, a Rampur Camar who was already in debt tried to get a loan of 500 rupees for his son's marriage; when asked why he should spend so much, he said that he could not con-ceive of spending less. The average wedding seems to cost somewhere between 1000 and 2000 rupees, although it may run as high as 10,000.

The groom's father must pay for the transportation of the wedding party and for the band, but his main expenses are usually for ornaments for his daughter-in-law. A Bhangi informant at Rampur said that he had bought three pounds of silver and eleven ornaments for his daughter-in-law—six ornaments for her feet, three for her neck, and two for her hands. He bought a set of clothing for the bride and one for his son, 2 *maunds* of sugar, from 18 to 20 *sirs* of *ghi*, 1 *maund* of gram, and 3 *maunds* of wheat. New clothes were purchased for every member of his family, and wedding invitations were sent to the following: three of the man's maternal uncles and one paternal uncle, two husbands of his wife's sisters, one of his son's maternal uncles, four sisters, eight daughters and nieces, and the daughter of one of his cousins. Five singers and a band were hired. Here the Bhangi was able to share expenses with a man whose son was marrying the younger sister of the bride-to-be. His share was 70 rupees. This does not represent a complete itemization of wedding expenditures, for there are many in-cidental expenses, presents, and so forth.

The father of the bride spends more money than does the groom's father. He must provide food for the groom's party and money for the dowry, al-though some of his expenses may be shared by his brothers, at whose homes the oil-bath ceremonies are celebrated.

Various relatives must also spend money at weddings. The fathers' brothers and mothers' brothers of the bride and groom give clothing and ornaments, but these obligations are ultimately reciprocal; equivalent re-turns are made by the recipients on the occasion of marriages in the donors' families.

The main recipient of gifts at marriage is the bride. She receives orna-ments from her father-in-law, dresses and money from her father, and

[7] Lewis, 1955a:163.

dresses from her father's sisters and father's brothers' wives. Five ornaments are usually given: one for the ankles, one for the wrists, one for the
nose, one for the neck, and one for the ears. Well-to-do families give from
ten to twenty pairs of such jewelry. The bride also receives money at the
ceremonial unveiling of the bride's face.

The groom may receive up to about 100 rupees, a bicycle, or a ring
from his father-in-law. He gets some clothing from his maternal uncle,
and he is also given a few rupees in the course of the wedding.

The sisters of the bride's father receive dresses when they return to
their households after the wedding. The husbands of women of the family
also receive gifts—at least a rupee each. This group includes the husbands
of daughters, of sisters, and of father's sisters. Daughters, sisters, father's
sisters, and father's father's sisters receive a dress each, together with some
sweets to take home. If the father of the bride is well-to-do he may give a
rupee and a tumbler to all the members of the groom's party.

While the latter are staying at the bride's village, they visit the female
members of their own caste who have married into that village from their
own village, and present each one with a rupee. Various relatives receive
a rupee or so at different stages of the wedding.

Other recipients at weddings include the *kamins* connected with the
household through the *jajmani* system. How much each caste group receives on such occasions is prescribed in the provisions of the *wajib-ul-arz*.[8]
The Khati, Jhinvar, Camar, and Bhangi get about a rupee each, while the
Lohar receives about 8 annas. The Brahman gets 8 or 10 rupees. Food and
grain may be given to some of the caste groups, as stipulated in the *wajib-
ul-arz*. At an upper-caste wedding each guest leaves half a *laddu* (sweetmeat) and a *puri* (fried cake) on his leaf plate for the Bhangis. Upper-
caste families give a dress and sometimes money to a *kamin* whose
daughter is getting married.

Weddings are occasions for making new clothes for all the members of
the family. The tailors are always busy at this time. There is a lot of visiting in different homes and much preparation of special foods.

I. THE SEARCH FOR A BRIDEGROOM AND THE ENGAGEMENT

It was formerly the custom for Nais (barbers) to act as go-betweens in
the arrangement of Jat marriages. The Nai generally received about 4
rupees from both sides, or more if the families were wealthy. For the
Karnal district Ibbetson reported that the barber put a ring or 1 rupee into
the boy's hand; "if the boy's father returns Re. 1-4, called *bidagi*, to the

---

[8] See pp. 60-61, 73.

barber to take to the girl's father, he thereby accepts the offer and clinches the engagement." [9]

Nais seem to have arranged marriages for upper-caste patrons but not for lower-caste groups whose hair they would not have been willing to cut. Briggs says that Camars do not normally employ barbers as go-betweens. Fuchs has no reference to such intermediaries in his study of the Balahis. Both authors, however, refer to low-caste barbers—Camars or Balahis, not Nais—who play a role in the negotiations.[10]

Planalp writes that the head of the girl's family used to be accompanied on his mission by a Brahman, a Nai, a Bari, a Kahar, and one or two respected men of his own caste. Nowadays, however, only a Brahman and a Nai accompany the party. According to Planalp, the Nai's role is very important: "While the Thakurs and Brahman, being honored guests, may not enter the house or inquire directly about the family, the Nai is under no such restrictions. He is free to wander about the village, to talk to his fellow Nais or to other low-caste men of the village and thus to gather information about the family of the prospective bridegroom. However, he must be very skillful at this, for hardly anyone will reveal the bad qualities of a boy of the village—all the boy's fellow-villagers will want to see him married." [11]

As we noted in Chapter 2, until about twenty years ago a pattern similar to that described by Planalp was followed in Rampur. A barber and a Brahman were sent to the youth's home to offer *tika*, the ceremonial placing of a forehead mark. The Nai received 15 rupees in cash and a double cotton sheet, while the Brahman received 9 rupees and a single sheet. Elsewhere we have described how panchayat rulings concerning a reduction of the Nai's fees led to a protest strike on the part of the Nais and a decision by the Jats to make their own marriage arrangements for their daughters.[12] At present, then, although the Nais still perform some functions at weddings, it is the father of the girl who makes the initial arrangements, or rather, it is the head of the girl's family who does so—it may be a grandfather or paternal uncle. As Planalp has pointed out, "There is no point in the marriage process at which the *biological* father or mother is expected to play a part." [13]

Usually it is the girl's mother who sets the machinery in motion. As the

[9] Ibbetson, 1883:126.
[10] Briggs, 1920:72; Fuchs, 1951:128.
[11] Planalp, 1955:31.
[12] See pp. 66-67.
[13] Planalp, 1955:28.

daughter approaches puberty, the mother puts increasing pressure on her husband to get busy and look for a suitable match for the girl, and she may upbraid him for not showing enough concern about his daughter's future. The marriage is talked about first in the family circle, but gradually everyone in the village learns that so-and-so's daughter is of marriageable age and that her parents are anxious to betroth her.

The father talks to his friends in the village and asks them to let him know if they hear of a boy who might make a suitable match. If someone mentions a name, the father asks careful questions about the boy's family history and other matters. In this way he starts upon a campaign which comes to occupy most of his leisure time. If these efforts bring no concrete results within a year, he intensifies the search and makes it a full-time job until a match has been arranged.

He may, in consequence, have to do a good deal of traveling from village to village, often taking along his father, brother, elder son, or a friend or two, staying with relatives along the way, if possible. For example, Mam Chand, a Dabas Jat, took two friends, Kishan Chand and Rup Chand, in the search for a groom for his daughter Maro. They spent the first night of their journey in the village of Mam Chand's father's sister, smoking hookah and making inquiries about eligible boys. Here they learned about two boys in Disor Kheri, a village which was satisfactory for their purposes, for Rup Chand's mother belonged to it, and they could therefore expect some help in the search. When they arrived at Disor Kheri the next day, they sought out Rup Chand's maternal uncle. The latter showed Mam Chand a number of boys in the village and introduced him to their parents. An engagement eventually resulted.

Such arrangements are not concluded hastily. There may have to be many family consultations first, after three or four likely boys have been picked out. Each of these cases is carefully discussed in the girl's family circle, with full consideration of such qualifications as appearance, personal qualities, degree of education, and economic prospects. A handsome, light-skinned boy is generally preferred, especially if the girl is beautiful. Some effort is made to match couples with regard to looks, even to the extent of mating an ugly girl with an ugly boy. Phuli, who found himself married to an unattractive girl when he was sixteen, complained to his father about her appearance, whereupon the father pointed out that Phuli himself was short of stature and not handsome.

The boy must belong to a good family, one with as much land as possible. The Jats are particular about this, for they gain their livelihood from the land. If possible, a father will marry his daughter into a large family, so that her work will not be too heavy, for where there are many daughters and daughters-in-law the work will be divided among many hands. A father always tries to marry his daughter into a family which is better than his own. There is thus an element of hypergamy in Jat marriages, but it has not been developed so far as it has among the Rajputs.

The boy must be a "nice person," well brought up and not a potential wife beater. The degree of his education is also considered. Among the lower castes an educated boy has a much better "market value," to use the words of one informant. Jats value education too, but the amount of land owned by the boy's family is perhaps more important.

The qualifications of the different boys are discussed by the girl's family. Other male members of the family besides the father share in the responsibility of getting her married—her father's father (dada), her paternal uncle (tavu), and her elder brother (bhai) if she has one. The mother (ma) and the father's mother (dadi) are consulted only in the home, and they never take part in the discussions with the boy's father, as the males may do. However, their vetoes may be decisive. As Fuchs has said of the Balahi, "Many a clever woman is able to carry her point during the discussions of the men though she remains entirely in the background." [14]

The two principals in the impending marriage, the boy and the girl, are not consulted about it and do not meet or see each other. Although some of the girl's male relatives may see the boy, none of the boy's relatives, either male or female, see the girl. However, they try to find out if she is good-looking and obedient, and whether she belongs to a good family, these being the principal qualities looked for in a bride. Sometimes a photograph of the girl is made available to them.

The examination of horoscopes is a widespread custom in India, to see whether or not the boy and girl will be mutually compatible. Our data do not have much reference to horoscopes. This may perhaps be due to the influence of the Arya Samaj movement. According to Planalp, at least, Arya Samaj influence has led to a decrease in the use of horoscopes in Senapur, where there is a growing skepticism about their reliability.[15]

After the girl's family has decided upon a particular boy, the father of the girl goes to visit the boy's father. If the latter is amenable, serious discussions are initiated. The first consideration concerns the family clans, to make sure that they are compatible and permit marriage. If such is not the case, discussions end at this point. Otherwise, the next matter to be dealt with is the amount of dowry which the girl's father is prepared to give and

[14] Fuchs, 1951:127.
[15] Planalp, 1955:32.

the type of wedding feast which he can afford. Sometimes the boy's father will press for a large wedding feast. This was the case with Phuli, mentioned before, who wanted to have an expensive marriage for his son as a way of raising his status in the village. Phuli demanded that the wedding feast be for a hundred persons, and he rejected many proposals before someone was able to meet his terms.[16]

The father of the girl wants his daughter to be in comfortable circumstances and to have less work to do, ideally, than she has had to do at home. He will sometimes pay more for a wedding than he can afford, in order to marry his daughter into a good family. The wedding feast is an extremely important part of the negotiations, for both families want to have as large a feast as possible for prestige purposes.

Even though the discussions may have been protracted, a rejection is still possible at this point. Mention has already been made of the Bhangi, Ram Swarup, who rejected a proposal because it came from the village of his father's first wife. A second proposal for the same son reached the discussion stage, when it was found that the parents of the girl worshipped Sikh path-ki-wali Mata and would require their son-in-law and his family to join the cult of this goddess. It is believed by followers of the cult that if the husband's family does not join in this worship, the wives of the family will become barren. Rather than get involved with such problems, Ram Swarup rejected the proposal. A third proposal was also turned down because the girl turned out to be of the same clan as the boy's mother.

1. THE *Sagai* CEREMONY

If all conditions are met, and if both families are agreed, the scene is set for the ceremony of *sagai*, "reservation" or engagement, the first official move in the marriage process. Marriages used to be arranged among the Jats when the prospective bride was around ten or twelve years of age, and the interval between marriage and *gauna* was formerly about six years. The "reservation" meant that the parents of the girl were formally reserving a certain boy for their daughter and that during the next six or seven years they would not have to fear that she would remain unmarried. *Sagai* marks a commitment which is seldom repudiated. Only in case both sides agree

---

[16] It happened that after the *sagai*, or engagement ceremony, the girl's father died. Phuli was afraid that the wedding would not be carried out with the same pomp, reasoning that the girl's uncles would not take the same interest in the wedding as her father had done. Therefore he tried to break off the engagement. The girl's family was angered by this and called in their village panchayat. Five elders from the panchayat went to Rampur and argued the case with the village elders, who then went to Phuli and insisted that the marriage be held. The girl's uncles, in turn, promised to carry out all the agreements made by the girl's father. So the wedding took place.

to do so may it be nullified in a prescribed manner. If one side wants to break the engagement while the other does not, the panchayat may be called in for counsel.[17]

If the *sagai* ceremony takes place right after the talks between the two fathers, it is a very simple affair. The father of the girl puts 1, 11, or 21 rupees (always 1 rupee above a round sum) into the hand of the boy. That is all that need be done, although the girl's father may also give a rupee to all the girls from Rampur who have married into the boy's village.

If the *sagai* is performed at a later time, as the Jats prefer, the ceremony is more complicated. On the day before the ceremony the women of the boy's house clean the entire home and smear the floors with cow dung. A large room is prepared for the ceremony. Some cots are placed along the wall for the use of older guests from the village (others squat on the floor). A cot spread with a carpet is made ready for the men of the girl's family. A sitting-board (*patra*) with a carpet is placed in the middle of the room for the boy who is to be betrothed, and opposite it a similar seat for the Brahman pundit who performs the ceremony. The main feature of the ceremony, as in the simpler version, is the gift of money from the girl's father to the boy. This money is placed in the boy's shirt, when he holds up its sides to form an apron-like receptacle known as a *jholi*.[18] After putting the money there, the girl's father places a turmeric mark (*tika*) on the boy's forehead and affixes a few grains of rice to it. The Brahman then recites some Sanskrit verses and ties a cotton thread to the boy's wrist. This completes the ceremony. The boy is then allowed to go to his mother's quarters. The mother eagerly awaits this moment, for she wants to know how much money her son has received. The other women watch as she counts it. Then the boy is told to leave, and he goes to join his friends who are waiting in the street.

There is a custom peculiar to the Jats which is observed at this time.

---

[17] Briggs writes that this ceremony is all but irrevocable. But he adds: "Either party, however, may break an engagement, with the consent of the council (panchayat) by paying twenty-two rupees, or some such sum, part of which goes to the chaudhari, and the rest to the other party. . . . The causes for which such a betrothal may be broken are strife between the families concerned, or the discovery of an incurable disease or of an infirmity in either the boy or the girl." Briggs, 1920:74.

[18] According to Ibbetson, the money consists of a rupee which has been all night in the milk set for butter. It is carried by the Brahman and barber along with a loincloth and a coconut, which are placed in the boy's lap. "Ordinarily *no* relation of the girl *may* take any part in the embassy (*lagi*) of betrothal; but Brahmans send the girl's brother-in-law or relation by marriage." Ibbetson, 1883:127. This represents the earlier pattern now superseded at Rampur, where the girl's father or other relative has taken over the Nai's functions in this sphere.

The girl's father gives a rupee each to the nearest male relatives of the prospective groom, thus acknowledging his relationship to them. He may also give a rupee each to the girls of his own clan who have married into the village.

A feast sometimes follows, to which perhaps only members of the boy's family or clan are invited, or—if the family is a wealthy one—all the people in the village. Brown sugar, rice, *ghi,* and *dal* are served. Lower-caste people stand outside the house to receive sugar. A group of Bhangis may play drums, for which they are given 7 or 8 *sirs* of grain. The girl's father and other relatives do not stay for this feast. They may not eat while in the boy's village, and hence leave as soon as the *sagai* ceremony is over. Meanwhile the boy's family and friends may continue the party all day. The women sing songs on this occasion, as they do at most of the other stages in the marriage process. Here is a song which is sung in the women's quarters, while the men are together in the men's quarters. It expresses curiosity about the prospective bride, whom none of the women have seen.

> Whence comes the coconut and the *tika*
> For our pretty pretty bridegroom?
> The coconut comes from Bagan village,
> The *tika* comes from Badhi village
> For our pretty pretty bridegroom.

> What is done with the coconut and the *tika?*
> Of our pretty pretty bridegroom?
> The coconut is put into his cloth,
> The *tika* is placed on the forehead
> Of our pretty pretty bridegroom.

> His mother inquires about his in-laws' place.
> He has seven brothers-in-law,
> A hundred and fifty sisters-in-law.
> The bride has big beautiful eyes and she is very pretty.
> She has very long hair.
> But oh! Her sisters-in-law have dirty faces,
> And their heads are bald.
> But she is for our pretty pretty bridegroom.

II. PREPARATIONS FOR THE WEDDING

2. NOTIFICATION OF THE WEDDING DAY

A few years generally elapse before the wedding takes place. It is up to the girl's family to end this waiting period by stating that it wants the marriage to be held. The boy's family never makes this request, for it is always the girl's family which takes the initiative in wedding preparations. The time is decided upon on the basis of various factors—the ages of the boy and girl, the finances available, etc. However, the season of the year is generally predetermined, for most marriages take place in May and June, after the harvest. At this time it is difficult to hire bands, carts, and automobiles, or the services of goldsmiths and silversmiths, which are all booked long in advance. The specific date for the wedding may be selected by a Brahman pundit on the basis of astrological reckoning. He is consulted by the girl's family for this purpose. After he has chosen a day, the Brahman writes out his calculations on a piece of paper which is signed by four or five elders of the girl's family and village. A turmeric mark and a few grains of rice are affixed to the letter, which is then tied with a yellow thread and given by the girl's father to a Nai, or some other messenger, for delivery to the boy's family.

The boy's father assembles four or five elders of the family, together with the family Brahman. The latter checks the calculations in the letter, and if he agrees with them, the date set in the letter is officially confirmed. The messenger from the girl's family is given a rupee, and he returns to his village with the formal acceptance of the wedding date. Usually this takes place about two months before the date set for the actual marriage.

3. *Lagan*

Lagan is a sort of reminder about the wedding drawn up by a Brahman for the girl's family. It consists of a few Sanskrit verses, followed by the date of the wedding, the number of persons invited to it (as previously agreed upon by the two fathers), the type of conveyance to be used by the wedding party on its trips to and from the bride's village, and the number of ceremonial oil baths to be taken by the bride and groom. The term *lagan* also refers to ceremonies performed in the two homes at the time of the sending and receiving of this notice.

The ceremony at the girl's house is as follows: The girl sits in front of a *cauk*, a square of flour made on an area recently plastered with dung. The Brahman sits opposite her, reading *mantras* and giving worship to the gods of marriage. Presents are always sent to the boy's family with the *lagan*, and these are held in the girl's lap—such items as a *tiel* (dress) for the boy's mother, two *piths* (long pieces of cloth dyed yellow at the corners), a coconut, a Ganesa (elephant-headed god) made of a lump of earth covered by a red cloth, and a pair of shoes for the mother-in-law.

After the *mantras* have been recited, the girl is asked to stand and place the gifts in her mother's *jholi*. The mother cannot take them if she is pregnant, or if she is a widow; in such cases her husband's brother's wife or some other substitute (always a married woman) may take her place. The *lagan* and the gifts are then handed over to a Nai, or some other messenger, for presentation to the boy's family. Sugar and sweetmeats are distributed among those present, and the women sing songs. Here is a song sung at various occasions, but particularly at marriages, which might be sung at this time. The women are divided into two groups representing the male and female respectively. New words may be improvised for the occasion.

He: I will carry you away. Yes, I'll carry you away.
     I with hair in modern style will carry you away.
She: I won't go. I won't go. You are said to have a bald head.
     I won't go.
He: I will carry you away. Yes, I'll carry you away.
     With a sock I will carry you away.
She: I won't go. I won't go. You have rotten old shoes.
     I won't go.
He: I will carry you away. Yes, I'll carry you away.
     With a blouse I'll carry you away.
She: I won't go. I won't go. You have a torn old loincloth.
     I won't go.
He: I will carry you away. Yes, I'll carry you away.
     With a pretty skirt I'll carry you away.
She: I won't go. I won't go. Your house is a wreck.
     I won't go.

Ceremonies similar to those at the girl's home take place at the home of the boy when the *lagan* is delivered. The elders of the village gather in the *baithak* of the father, and the boy is made to sit is front of a *cauk* while the *lagan* is read aloud. The presents are placed in his *jholi*. Then the boy goes to the women's quarters and gives the gifts to his mother. Here again the women sing songs. They also examine the presents carefully and evaluate their quality, especially the material of the dress; for these may provide indications of the attitudes and intentions of the bride's family. For example, when the *lagan* was received for the marriage of Phuli's son Anand, no shoes were included for his mother. This was considered a bad sign. However, Phuli sent back a generous collection of presents by the Nai messenger: a shawl of artificial silk, nine *nalas* (colored cotton skeins), 2 *sirs* of *mehndi* (henna stain) for the coloring of hands and feet, a comb, and a bottle of oil for the bride.

4. The *Bans*

The *bans* are ceremonial oil baths taken by the boy and girl in their respective villages. The number to be taken is determined by the Brahman of the girl's family and is specified in the *lagan*. According to Ibbetson, the number must be five, seven, nine, or eleven, and the girl must have two less than the boy. They are so arranged that the boy's will end on the night before the wedding procession starts, and the girl's on the night before the wedding.[19]

During the period of the ceremonial oil baths the boy and girl are not expected to work in the fields but are confined to their homes where they rest and relax during the day. At night they are bathed and massaged with *ubtan,* a lubricant paste which gives smoothness and luster to the skin. The girl's oil baths are performed in the homes of her father's brothers—in a different home each night, if possible. The family is treated to a good dinner; then the women bathe the girl. On the first of these occasions, according to Ibbetson, red handprints are made on the walls. Ibbetson's account is worth quoting:

The day of the first *ban* is called *haladhat,* or "red hand." Seven women with living husbands husk 5¼ seers of rice and make sweets with it. The Brahman comes and sticks up two small round saucers, bottom downwards against the wall with flour, and in front of them a floor lamp is kept alight in honor of ancestors. On either side he makes five marks of a bloody hand on the wall. This is done in each house. In the girl's village the street turnings all the way from the village gate to the bride's house, and the house itself, are also marked with red or red and white marks. After the first *ban* the boy has the *rakri* or black woolen thread, with a small iron ring *(chhalla)* and some yellow cloth and betel-nut, tied round his left ankle. The girl has her small gold nosering put on; for up to that time she can wear only a silver one; and she must not wear a large one till she goes to live with her husband. She also takes off her silver wristlets *(chara)* which no married woman may wear; and substitutes for them at least five of glass on each arm. These glass wristlets and her nosering form her *sohag;* and a woman who has a husband living *(sohagan)* must always wear them.[20]

In Rampur the boy is bathed and massaged by women chosen from among his married sisters, brothers' wives, and aunts. He sits on a stool. Four earthenware saucers containing turmeric *(haldi),* henna stain, oil, and milk are placed at his feet. A tray is prepared with the articles for performing *arati:* four lighted wicks with oil, turmeric, henna stain, rice, and a *patka* (piece of cloth). The first step is the anointing with oil *(tel chad-*

---

[19] Ibbetson, 1883:127.

[20] Ibbetson, 1883:127-28.

hana), the boy's feet, knees, and head being touched seven times to the accompaniment of singing by the women. A piece of *gur* is placed at his feet. Then the women rub his body with *ubtan.* Milk is poured over the boy's head from a pitcher *(karva),* and water is poured on his body. Soot from an oil lamp is applied to the boy's eyelashes by means of a flat iron spoon *(palta).* A neckpiece *(hansli)* is placed around his neck. On his ankles are tied a black strand made of his mother's hair, a small iron ring, a piece of red cloth, and a shell. A woman selected as the leader performs *arati,* applying a *tika* mark with turmeric to his forehead and rotating the tray before him seven times. Then she briefly places the sash on his head, covered by the tray. At the conclusion, after a dinner in which sugar and *ghi* are served, the boy's hands are dyed with henna stain and the party breaks up.

The customs associated with the ceremonial oil baths have a rather wide distribution in India. They have been described by Planalp for Senapur in eastern Uttar Pradesh. Here, unlike the case in Rampur, the women who give the oil baths are unmarried girls, which is also the case among the Camars described by Briggs (1920:80). Planalp's account is as follows:

The massaging is done by five young unmarried girls of his *patti [pana].* First each of the girls performs *cumna* ("kissing"). Taking some *dub* grass and rice in each hand, a girl touches him on the feet, knees, chest, and shoulders, ending by making a circle around his head with the right hand. She repeats the process five times. After all the girls have done this they apply a paste made of mustard seed and turmeric to the boy's arms, legs and shoulders, rubbing it into the skin. He has his *dhoti* tucked up short for the massaging. At each massaging the boy is seated on the stool at the west side of the marriage pole and he holds a *dhurhi* (ball of parched rice with sugar syrup), made by his paternal aunt, in his hand. This massaging is a time of light talk and high merriment for the girls and women, although the groom may feel a little sheepish.[21]

Ram Ratan also refers to this kind of joking in his account of the Bhangis of Delhi. Among the Bhangis it is the older brother's wife who performs the massage. "Rubbing the boy's body with the mixture of oil, turmeric, and peameal, she may remark, 'Oh, you have become quite weak. What has happened to you? Where have you lost your energy? What will you do when the girl [comes] to you?' The boy may say, 'Don't worry; at least I am quite strong for you.'"[22]

While the boy and girl are being bathed in their respective homes, the

[21] Planalp, 1955:36-37.
[22] Ratan, 1955:131.

women of each household sing songs. The following, addressed to the bridegroom, are examples of the songs sung in Rampur:

Why is there oil in the bowl?
It is for our darling who sits for the *ban.*
There is beauty paste in the golden bowl.
There is oil in another pretty bowl.
The oil gives beauty to his body.
The beauty paste makes his limbs look bright.
Come, O Grandmother! Look how it becomes him to be a bridegroom!
Come, O Mother! Look and be happy!
Come, O Father's Sister! See how it becomes him to be a bridegroom!
Come, O Sister! See how it becomes him to be a bridegroom!
Why is there oil in the bowl?
It is for our darling who sits for the *ban.*

O bridegroom! Who taught you to talk so sweetly?
Your talk is so sweet and so lovely that it charms our hearts.
O bridegroom! How can we describe your coat?
It is so precious and pretty that it cannot be priced.
Your jacket is so precious and pretty that it cannot be priced.
Your turban border is so precious and pretty that it cannot be priced.
O bridegroom! Who taught you to talk so sweetly?
The red wedding thread around your wrist is so precious and pretty
That a watch stands no chance before it.
O bridegroom! Who taught you to talk so sweetly?
Your turban over your head is so precious that I would give my life for it.
O bridegroom! Who taught you to talk so sweetly?

In addition to the praise of the bridegroom, there may also be abusive references to the prospective in-laws. Such is the case in the following song:

Go and ask the carpenter's son
To bring a wooden stool for our darling son,
For our Ratan Singh, our Badan Singh.
Go and ask the potter's son
To bring an earthen bowl for our darling son,
For our Ratan Singh, our Badan Singh.
Go and ask the shoemaker's son
To bring shoes for our darling son,
For our Ratan Singh, our Badan Singh.
Go and ask the tailor's son
To bring clothes for our darling son,
For our Ratan Singh, our Badan Singh.
Go and ask his dear maternal uncle
To bring garments for our darling son,

For our Ratan Singh, our Badan Singh.
Go and ask his father-in-law,
Who mates with his own mother,
To wed his female monkey to our darling son,
Our Ratan Singh, our Badan Singh.

5. PRESENTATION OF THE *Bhat*

The mother's brother (*mama*) plays an important role in the wedding. In both families it is the mother's brother (of the bride or groom) who provides the *bhat*, the clothing required for the wedding. In the case of the girl her mother's brother may also bring a ring.[23] In the case of the boy, his mother's brother buys a crown to be worn in the marriage procession. Money is also provided by these men. It is the mother's brother who puts the bride into the cart after the wedding for her trip to her husband's home. If the mother's brother has died, these duties fall to his son. If the mother has no brother, the responsibility falls on the man who inherited her father's property. In some cases the mother's brother of the father (of either bride or groom) also brings clothing, which is called *barabhat* (big *bhat*). Ibbetson writes that the girl may be provided with two wedding dresses, one by her own mother's brother and one by the boy's mother's brother. In that case she wears *both* dresses at the wedding.[24]

During the whole period of the oil baths the prospective groom wears the same clothes, which get to smell strongly of oil. These are removed on the day of the wedding procession, when the groom is given a final bath. Cleansed of oil, he puts on the clean clothes brought by his maternal uncles. Before the *bhat* is presented, however, the mother's brother must be honored by an *arati* performed by his sister. According to Ibbetson, she may also perform *sewal*, which consists in picking up her petticoat and touching his body all over with it.[25]

Here is an account of the ceremony as followed in the case of a Bhangi wedding at Rampur: When the mother's brother arrived, he was made to stand on a plank before the threshold, in front of which was a square drawn with wheat flour and embellished with swastikas. The groom's mother came from the house with a large brass plate on which were 5 *sirs* of rice, a *gur* cake, a lamp, and a jug of water. (After the wedding the mother's brother takes home the rice and the *gur* cake.) While women stood behind her singing songs, the mother greeted her brother and placed a vermilion mark on his forehead. Then she moved the brass plate before him with a circular

---

[23] See Ratan, 1955:134; Ibbetson, 1883:129.

[24] Ibbetson, 1883:129.

[25] Ibbetson, 1883:129.

motion, performing the *arati*. The mother's brother then placed two silver rupees in the water jug. The *bhat* in this case consisted of the following: (1) a complete suit of clothing for the groom, (2) a crown *(maur)* for the groom, (3) two shawls or head shawls *(orhnas, chunris)*, (4) fifty-one rupees in cash, (5) one rupee for each of the groom's paternal uncles, (6) one rupee for the leaders of the communal panchayat. These gifts were passed about and shown to those assembled, who looked at them carefully, estimated their prices, and compared them with gifts they had seen at other weddings. Then the mother's brother was given food; before this he was not permitted to eat at his sister's house.

All this time the women continue singing. Here is a song sung in Rampur at this time, which celebrates the generosity of the mother's brother, comparing him favorably with some other relatives.

> My husband's elder brother's wife has five brothers,
> But my own mother has only one.
> The other five came and brought only fifty rupees,
> And they brought a borrowed *chunri* for their sister.
> But my uncle came and brought a *lakh* [hundred thousand] of rupees
> And a gold-embroidered *chunri* for his sister.
> They all began returning to their homes.
> When those five went back,
> Their *chunri* was returned to them by the sister.
> But when my uncle returned,
> I put on his *chunri* and showed them all.

At the time of the presentation of the *bhat*, the *neota* may also be collected. Irawati Karve has given an account of the *neota* system as follows:

The portion of expenses which cannot be borne by the family is made good by the village community. At a particular time in the wedding ceremony all the invited guests give money presents to the groom or the bride. The money is given in cash and received in a big metal dish and a village dignitary keeps careful record of the cash given by each guest. The family who thus receives cash gifts must return them to the respective families when a similar occasion arises. This gift is called the Neota. The Neota registers are kept for generations. The people who pay these gifts need not belong to the caste of a man. They represent most of the families of a village. A new-comer can enter the Neota-circle by starting to make a gift. The Neota account can be closed by giving the dues against one's name plus a little something added to it. A man knows almost to a rupee as to how much Neota money he can expect. Members of the patri-family outside the joint family bring gifts, but they are not Neota gifts. These also must be returned at some future date.[26]

---

[26] Karve, 1953:125-26.

In Rampur the *neota* seems to be kept within the caste. Moreover, the tendency has developed to pay back twice as much *neota* as one has received from a particular person. To take a hypothetical case: A attends a wedding in B's family and gives 2 rupees for *neota*. Later, A's son is married and he invites B. B then contributes 4 rupees. A "potlatching" tendency is discernible here. Fairly sizeable sums may be involved. In the case of the Bhangi marriage discussed above, the *neota* amounted to 225 rupees.

In the marriages of Bhangis and other lower-caste groups, the groom, accompanied by some relatives, may also go to the homes of his *jajmans*, to get donations of money and clothing from them. The wedding band goes along on these occasions, while some people who join the parade may provide entertainment by making obscene gestures. The Bhangi groom in the wedding just discussed received 19 rupees and some grain and clothing from his father's *jajmans*. Jats do not collect money in this fashion.

6. ERECTION OF THE *Mandha*

After the reception of the mother's brother, the women may go to offer worship to the potter's wheel, accompanied, if possible, by a band with a drum. They return with some earthenware dishes in which holes have been

Fig. 35. *A higher-caste married girl at her father's home working embroidery on a veil for her trousseau. Her* gauna *took place a year ago.*

bored in the bottom. A plough pole is now set up at the threshold of the house, and a triangle made of wheat stems is tied to its top. A thin cord of homespun thread colored with turmeric is put through the holes in the dishes, which are then hung from the triangle. Two of the dishes are fixed together to form a cup, into which some rice and pice are placed. The structure, known as a *mandha* or *mandap*, must be made by seven married people. The same thing is done at both the boy's and the girl's homes, but somewhat different structures may be made, and they may be differently placed in the household enclosure.[27]

7. *Ghur Charhi*

The day of the marriage procession has now arrived. The groom is dressed in his wedding clothes and crown, and he gets on horseback to perform the ceremony of *ghur charhi* or *ghora charhi* (horse riding), which consists of a ride around the village on a mare, stopping at village shrines to offer worship. Sometimes the boy rides in a car nowadays, or even on a motorcycle, but this is a departure from the proper tradition. The groom's face may be veiled by silvery threads hanging from his headdress. He carries an iron stick provided by the village Lohar. The groom's *bhabhi* (elder brother's wife) puts some collyrium around his eyes, for which she is given a rupee. His sister's husband ties on his crown—and gets a rupee for that.

The boy is accompanied by a group of women and some drummers. The men do not usually go along. The boy's sister follows him, throwing rice from a dish which she carries. As the procession moves about the village, the women sing songs. Here is one which is sung at this time in Rampur. It gives expression to the tensions involved in the boy's change of status and his reassurance of his mother and father's sister, as he tells them that he will bring his wife home to serve them.

> Mother: O my son! I carried your burden in my womb for ten months. Now settle the debt before you go.
>
> Bridegroom: O my mother! I will bring a maid to serve you, Who is the daughter of that big man—my wife.
>
> Father's sister: O my nephew! I carried your burden in my lap for ten months. Now settle the debt before you go.
>
> Bridegroom: O my father's sister! I will bring pretty garments for you, From that big man's daughter, my wife.

8. *Johari*

After touring the village and visiting the various shrines, the procession moves to the edge of the village, where a carpet is spread for the boy to sit

---

[27] For some descriptions of marriage poles and pavilions, see Briggs, 1920:77-79; Ibbetson, 1883:128; Fuchs, 1951:140.

on. At this point *johari* is performed. This consists in the boy's ceremonially sucking his mother's breast, or, if she is dead, that of his father's brother's wife. At this time his paper crown is removed by his sister's husband or by the Brahman or Nai, who have helped with the marriage arrangements and who are now given 1 or 2 rupees. The wives of the boy's brothers and of his father's brothers put turmeric marks on his forehead.[28]

As soon as the *ghur charhi* and *johari* ceremonies have been performed, the wedding procession *(barat)*, composed solely of males and usually accompanied by the band, sets off for the girl's village. Automobiles and buses may be hired for the occasion. The women pour water over the wheels of the lead car as a send-off. The female members of the boy's family stay at home after the departure of the wedding party and make preparations for the later reception of the bride.

III. THE WEDDING

9. *Milni*

When the wedding party arrives at the girl's village, a messenger, traditionally a Nai, is sent to the girl's house to let her family know that the groom and his party have arrived. The latter wait on the outskirts of the village, where they are formally received by the girl's father and his brothers and uncles *(milni)*. As the bride's father and the groom's father exchange greetings, the former gives the latter some money—from 2 to 5 rupees. However, it is not obligatory for the two fathers to meet. Any elderly males in the respective families may perform these roles.

The wedding party is conducted to the village men's house, where cots have been prepared. The members of the girl's family have seen to it that there are plenty of cots in readiness, just as they have taken pains to have plenty of food on hand. They are anxious to give a good impression, so that members of the boy's party will later comment on the fact that they never had to ask for anything—everything was ready for them. In the men's house the members of the wedding party may be served cold drinks, while those who want baths are given water and oil.

10. *Barat Lena*

An hour or so later some members of the girl's family, accompanied by a Nai and a Brahman, approach the men's house to perform the ceremony

---

[28] Briggs refers to the ceremonial sucking of the mother's breast, as well as a related custom. The mother sits on the edge of the village well, as if she were going to destroy herself—for her son may now neglect her and fail to support her. The son walks around the well seven times and daubs it with turmeric and rice flour. Then he takes his mother home, comforts her, and promises that he will support her and bring his wife home to serve her. See Briggs, 1920:84.

of *barat lena.* As the groom sits on a ceremonial board, a *tika* of turmeric and rice is affixed to his forehead by the Brahman of the girl's family. The Brahman gives the boy some sweets, which he puts into a cloth he is carrying.

11. *Barauthi*

The groom now mounts a mare, if one is available. His crown is tied on his head. Accompanied by his maternal uncle, sister's husband, and a few other men, he approaches the bride's house. There the womenfolk of the girl's family stand, singing songs. Somewhere behind them the bride may be watching. When the singing stops, she may come to the doorway and throw two handfuls of rice at the boy's crown. Then she comes forward with a garland and puts it around the groom's neck. As soon as this is done, the girl runs back into the house. This is the groom's first glimpse of his bride. Now *arati* is performed for the groom, as he stands on a ceremonial board before the door. It is usually done by the bride's mother or some other female relative of the bride.[29] The groom is given a *tika* of rice and turmeric, and he may be sprinkled with a *nim* branch dipped in water by a sister of the bride. He also receives some money—a rupee or so. The women who stand around singing may throw some rice at him.[30]

12. *Chunri*

The boy's father now gives some presents to the bride's family for the girl—ornaments, ribbons for her hair, a veil, some yarn, henna and sugar, and four wooden pegs to be used in the *phera* ceremony. These gifts may be offered ceremonially on a brass tray. After this presentation the wedding party returns to the village men's house. Here the men lounge about, playing cards and smoking hookah. The groom may eat here, for until he is married he cannot accept meals in the girl's house. But the other members of the wedding party may do so and may be invited to lunch if they have arrived early enough for that. The girl's relatives, like the groom, may not eat until after the wedding ceremony is over.

13. *Phera*

We come now to the actual marriage ceremony, the ritual climax, marked by circumambulation of the fire and the recitation of marriage vows by

---

[29] According to Ibbetson (1883:130) it should be the bride's elder married sister or her brother's married daughter.

[30] Briggs (1920:86) writes that among the Camars, while the *barat* is waiting for the wedding ceremony, the female relatives of the bride sing obscene songs in which abuse is directed toward the groom, his relatives and friends; and cow dung, mud, and unclean things are thrown.

bride and groom. This ceremony, known as *phera*, takes place by the marriage pole in the girl's courtyard, where a pavilion has been built, consisting of four upright bamboo poles covered by a sheet. Beneath it is a fire hole (*havan*), on one side of which are two ceremonial sitting-boards. The relatives of the bride and groom sit opposite each other. A Brahman is in charge of this ceremony. He asks the groom to sit on one of the boards, facing east. Then he lights the fire with a piece of burning cow dung. This signalizes the beginning of the ritual. After reciting a few *mantras* the Brahman requests that the girl be brought in. The bride's maternal uncle comes carrying the girl as if she were a child, and places her on the other board. The bride is veiled, dressed in clothes provided by her maternal uncle and ornaments, ribbons, etc., given by the boy's family. The Brahman recites some more *mantras* and then asks the bride and groom to repeat seven vows after him. The groom holds the bride's thumb as he does so. He promises to consult his wife in all things, to take her wishes into account, and not to speak gruffly to her in the presence of her friends. The bride, for her part, vows to be an obedient wife. After making these promises the boy and girl are asked to walk slowly around the fire seven times. The bride goes first, three times, the groom four times. As they circumambulate the fire, the women in the assembly sing as follows:

> Here she takes the first round,
> Her grandfather's granddaughter.
>
> Here she takes the second round,
> Her maternal uncle's maternal niece.
>
> Here she takes the third round,
> Her father's elder brother's daughter.
>
> Here she takes the fourth round,
> Her father's own daughter.
>
> Here she takes the fifth round,
> Her father's younger brother's niece.
>
> Here she takes the sixth round,
> Her brother's sister.
>
> Here she takes the seventh round,
> And, lo! the darling becomes alien.

When the young couple is seated again, the Brahman recites some more *mantras* and applies a *tika* to both bride and groom. Then the bride is lifted up again by her mother's brother and carried into the house.

14. *Kannya Dan*

At the time of the *phera,* or else later on at *bida,* the girl's father hands over his daughter to the groom with the words, "I give my daughter to you." On this occasion the dowry may be given, together with some money for the bride's bangles, for the groom's family cannot supply her with these.

The amount of dowry varies in different families, but the sum is usually between 51 and 101 rupees. The largest amount paid in recent years at Rampur was at a Jat wedding, where 650 rupees were handed over. From five to seven dresses and five utensils (a plate, a brass pitcher, a cooking pot, a large dish, and a spoon) are also given. The dresses go to the mother of the groom, who gives them to her daughters and her husband's sisters. Some sweets are sent along with the bride for distribution in the groom's village.

15. *Mur Khulai*

After the *phera* the bride is carried into the house by her mother's brother. Then the groom is invited to come and eat some sweets in the bride's house. The bride and groom may also make some handprints on the walls *(thapa lana).* But the main feature of this visit is the joking that takes place between the groom and the bride's female relatives. Needles may be stuck in the wall, so that when the groom places his palm there, he will get hurt. The women may push and strike the groom with their fists. He is expected to hit back. The women try to make the groom eat henna and offer worship to a winnowing basket.

These customs are evidently widespread. Planalp has provided an account of this joking in Senapur: "Some of the women are singing, and others laugh and tease him, giving him pushes along the way. If he should happen to fall down they ridicule him unmercifully. They tease him about his appearance and behavior. . . . They tease him about his elder brother's wife, asking him if he has any fun with her, etc. There is at least an undertone of stereotyped abuse or insult in their comments about the female members of his family."[31]

Ram Ratan gives a similar description for the Bhangis of Delhi:

After the *phera* ceremony is over, the bride and bride-groom are taken into the bride's house where the bride's mother unties the bride-groom's head dress. . . . Here the bridge-groom is surrounded by girls and other females of the bride's family who joke with him. One of them pointing towards the bride-groom may remark, "He seems to be foolish and senseless. See, how he gazes at us as if he will eat us." Some other girl may laugh loudly at the groom's stature. Amidst loud

---

[31] Planalp, 1955:52-53.

noise and laughter, the bride-groom is asked to bow down before an old shoe of the bride, wrapped in red cloth which is represented to him as a goddess. If the groom bows down, all [the] women clap and jump and make a roar, all the time hitting with some obscene remarks. But generally the groom does not submit to this as he has been warned by his mother, sisters, and other female relatives against such "traps." [32]

The women may also steal the boy's shoes; he may have to give them money to get them back.

Some time later the wedding party is invited to dinner. This, the second of four meals given to the wedding party, is supposed to be the best of the meals provided by the girl's family.

16. Bida

On the following day the wedding party returns to the boy's village. A farewell ceremony (bida) is held, in which some money may be given by the girl's family to all the members of the wedding party. The women sing songs as the bride is lifted by her mother's brother into her palanquin, oxcart, or automobile, which will take her on her first trip to the groom's family. Some of these songs are full of pathos and help to bring tears to the eyes of those assembled. References to tears are numerous in the songs themselves, as the following examples, collected in Rampur, illustrate:

O Sathan! you are going away!
My eyes are brimming with tears.
I would sew a shirt for my own Sathan.
I would place two lines of buttons on either side.

O Sathan! you are going away!
My eyes are brimming with tears.
I would stitch a skirt for my own Sathan.
I would place two lines of lace on either side.

O Sathan! you are going away!
My eyes are brimming with tears.
I would escort my Sathan to her palanquin.
I would send my brother along.

O Sathan! you are going away!
My eyes are brimming with tears.
I will soon send for my Sathan
By sending her younger brother.

O Sathan! you are going away!
My eyes are brimming with tears.

[32] Ratan, 1955:141.

Here is another song, in which the bride is described as being reluctant to go. She makes excuses to her father, giving reasons for staying a little longer, but he is firm, replies to her objections, and persuades her to leave.

Daughter: O Father! My palanquin stumbles at the threshold of your house.
  Father: O Daughter! We will move the bricks there.
          Now go to your husband's home.
Daughter: O Father! I forgot my doll in the wall shelf of your house.
  Father: O Daughter! My son's daughter will play with it.
          Now go to your husband's home.
Daughter: O Father! The courtyard of your house has so much rubbish to clear.
  Father: O Daughter! I will get a sweeperwoman to clean it. Now go to your husband's home.
Daughter: O Father! My mother weeps without her daughter.
  Father: O Daughter! Your sisters are here.
          Now go to your husband's home.
Daughter: O Father! Your well is deserted without your daughter.
  Father: O Daughter! My son's wife will go to the well.
          Now go to your husband's home.
Daughter: O Father! My playmates weep without your daughter.
  Father: O Daughter! My son's daughter will play with them.
          Now go to your husband's home.
Daughter: O Father! My brother weeps without his sister.
  Father: O Daughter! He will have his own daughter soon.
          Now go to your husband's home.

Here is another song sung at this time:

O darling! Where do you go and how do you hasten?
You leave behind your doll.
You leave behind your playmates.
So forgetful are you, as you go from your father's house!

O bridegroom! Halt the palanquin.
Her grandfather comes running behind.
O bridegroom! Halt the palanquin.
Her grandfather comes running behind.
O bridegroom! Halt the palanquin.
Her father's elder brother comes running behind.
O bridegroom! Halt the palanquin.
Her maternal uncle comes running behind.

O darling! Who wins and who loses?
My grandfather loses and my grandfather-in-law wins.
My father loses and my father-in-law wins.

According to Planalp, the bride's departure is always accompanied by contagious weeping, starting the night before she leaves. The men as well as the women are emotionally moved. "So affecting is this sharp sorrow of separation that there are adult men who try to keep away whenever a girl of the village is leaving home, for fear of being overcome by emotion. When the palanquin moves forward the women follow it a little ways, and at the final farewell the bride's cries become anguished screams." [33] Despite these lamentations the bride will only stay for two or three days at the groom's home on this occasion. Soon she will be home again with her parents—perhaps for several years—until the *gauna* ceremony.[34]

On her trip to the groom's home the bride is not accompanied by any members of her family, with the possible exception of a younger brother, but a female Nai associated with her family may go along.

IV. RECEPTION OF THE BRIDE IN THE GROOM'S VILLAGE

Various ceremonies may be held to welcome the bride and groom in the latter's village. According to Ibbetson, a *sewal* ceremony is performed for them by the boy's mother upon their arrival.[35] Briggs writes that when a Camar bridal party reaches the groom's home, the bride worships the feet of her mother-in-law, and sometimes his brothers and sisters worship her feet.[36] Planalp and Cohn describe a *parcaran* (touching of the feet) ceremony and other rituals held in Senapur at this time.[37]

17. THE BLOCKING OF THE DOORWAY

A custom that is followed in Rampur, as well as elsewhere, is the blocking of the doorway by the groom's sister. As the couple approaches the house the groom's sister blocks the way and will not allow the bride inside until she or the groom hands over some money. However, this does not imply any debasement of the bride, for the following song, sung in Rampur at this time by the women of the boy's household, exalts the importance of the new bride over her parents-in-law.

---

[33] Planalp, 1955:60.

[34] In case a girl marries late, that is, at about twenty, an additional ceremony known as *patra pher* (exchange of the wooden stools) is performed at the time of the *bida* ceremony in order to dispense with the *gauna* ceremony which would involve a delay of another few years. The gifts normally given by the girl's parents to the bridegroom and his relatives are now given, thereby allowing the groom to take his wife to his own village as early as one week after the ceremony.

[35] Ibbetson, 1883:132.

[36] Briggs, 1920:91.

[37] Planalp, 1955:61; Cohn, 1954:216.

Bridegroom's sister: The way is closed, the way is closed.
Mother-in-law is insignificant before our charming bride.

Bride: O Mother-in-law! Why do you strut about
And pretend that you love me so much?
I will not get down from my palanquin
Unless you give me a separate fireplace.
O Father-in-law! Why do you jingle your moneybag?
I will not get down from my palanquin
Unless you build a separate big house for me.

18. *Mukh Dikhana*

The next ceremony to be held is that of viewing the bride's face, a privilege for which those present pay a rupee or so. The bride is supposed to look down modestly as they examine her. Then bride and groom may place palmprints on the walls of his house.

19. *Kangna Khelna*

Next, some ceremonial games are played by the bride and groom in front of the female members of the groom's family. The boy's elder brother's wife *(bhabhi)* is always the referee and receives 10 rupees from the boy's mother as a fee for this service. The boy has to remove a ring from the girl's finger after she has closed her fist tight. The ring is also thrown seven times into a brass vessel filled with *dub* grass, and the bride and groom vie to see who will be the first to take it out. Other games are also played. Bride and groom, for instance, have to untie each other's wrist bands *(kangna)*, while the women watch them, singing songs. According to Ram Ratan, the elder brother's wife engages in sexual joking with the groom at this time.[38] Ibbetson, who also gives an account of *kangna*, describes a curious custom concerning the elder brother's wife: "Then the boy's elder brother's wife (his *bhabhi*) sits down, opens her legs, and takes the boy between her thighs. The girl sits similarly between the boy's thighs, and takes a little boy into her lap. The girl or his mother gives him two *laddus;* and he says 'a son for my sister-in-law and two *laddus* for me.' "[39]

A somewhat similar custom prevails in Rampur. A younger brother or nephew of the husband sits in the lap of the bride and says, "Give me a *laddu,* and God may give you a son." The bride gives him a *laddu* and then pushes him away. These seem to be fertility practices. It is interesting to note the way in which the tie between the elder brother's wife and the groom is brought into prominence at the time of marriage.

---

[38] Ratan, 1955:145.

[39] Ibbetson, 1883:133.

20. Trip to the Village Shrines

The bride and groom make a joint tour of the village shrines, as the groom did before setting out on the wedding procession. When they reach the shrine of Ghantal Deo, the groom beats his elder brother's wife with a stick, and she beats him in return. Then the bride and groom beat each other. This is called *chokain khelna* (playing with sticks). In the evening the bride, accompanied by women of the groom's family, goes to the village pond and sets a little earthen lamp afloat.

On the next day the girl's brother comes to visit the bride in her new home, and on the following day he takes her home. There is no ceremony connected with this, although sometimes the mother-in-law gives the girl a dress and sends some clothes to the girl's sisters and brothers. The girl is now home to stay for two or three years or more, until the time of *gauna*. During this intervening period her life at home continues just as it was before the wedding.

V. *GAUNA*, CONSUMMATION OF THE MARRIAGE

When the girl's parents feel that she is mature enough for married life, they notify the groom's family to that effect. The groom and his Nai then pay a two-day visit to the bride's home, but during this time husband and wife do not speak to one another, and he returns to his village without her. He may even pay a second such visit. But eventually, on a date set by the bride's parents, the bride does go with him for a short stay. The groom's brother generally accompanies them on this trip.

As soon as the groom arrives at the girl's village on this occasion, the girl is made ready for the trip. Her hair is washed and she is bathed and dressed in her best clothes and jewelry. At this time she may be given a trousseau which is first shown to friends and neighbors invited by the family Nai. It may consist of twenty or more articles of clothing, ten or fifteen pieces of jewelry, a spinning wheel, a *mudha* (village chair or stool) to sit on, a cot, a mattress, a quilt, pillows, a mat, and a huge trunk.

The groom has also brought a set of clothing for the bride, but she is not obliged to wear it. Her mother is expected to send gifts to the groom's family—clothing for the women and *cadars* (sheets) for the men, together with a basket of grain to be distributed among the neighbors in the groom's village.

When everything is ready, the girl gets into the vehicle brought by the groom. The women sing farewell songs. The mother, brother, and other relatives may walk along behind the cart or automobile for the first mile or so. Then the mother caresses the girl, says good-bye, and places a rupee in the hands of both bride and groom. Now, for the first time, bride and groom are left alone.

There is no ceremony of greeting at the boy's village, although some women may gather to sing songs while the trousseau is opened and displayed. If the boy has a sister, she opens the bride's trunk, and she may choose whatever she likes from among the bride's possessions.

The bride and groom do not share a separate room during her visit. He continues to sleep in the men's quarters, but he visits her at night, having learned where to find her cot in the women's quarters. The other women will try to let them have some privacy.

Within a few days the bride's brother comes for her again and takes her home. When the girl reaches her house she may be greeted by women singing songs. The following is a song sung in Rampur on this occasion:

> O my friend! My in-laws' house is a wretched place.
> My mother-in-law is a very bad woman.
> She always struts about full of anger.
>
> O my friend! My in-laws' house is a wretched place.
> My husband's elder brother is a very bad man.
> He always slips off to the threshing at his hayrack.
>
> O my friend! My in-laws' house is a wretched place.
> My husband's sister is a very bad girl.
> She takes her doll and runs to her playmates, jeering at me.
>
> O my friend! My in-laws' house is a wretched place.
> My husband's younger brother is a very bad boy.
> He takes his stick and slips off to the men's quarters, joking at me.
>
> O my friend! My in-laws' house is a wretched place.
> The she-buffalo of that house is very bad.
> When I milk it, it urinates, but when Father-in-law milks it, it gives milk.
>
> O my friend! My in-laws' house is a wretched place.
> The buffalo calf of that house is very bad.
> If I untie it, it frets and kicks, but when Mother-in-law unties it, it talks.
>
> O my friend! My in-laws' house is a wretched place!

At the end of a year the bride again returns to her husband's home, and stays for a longer time on this occasion. But she goes back to her village again after a few months. Thus the marriage is entered upon in easy stages, with the bride spending progessively more time in her husband's home. Only her brother may visit her there, except when she is ill, at which time others may call. At certain festival times she returns home or receives presents from her parents.[40] Ibbetson writes: "The village into which his

---

[40] See pp. 207, 208, 218, 222, 227, 233.

daughter is married is utterly tabooed for the father and her elder brothers, and all near elder relations. They may not go to it, even drink water from a well in that village; for it is shameful to take anything from one's daughter or her belongings. On the other hand, the father is continually giving things to his daughter and her husband as long as he lives. Even the more distant elder relatives will not eat or drink from the house into which the girl is married, though they do not taboo the whole village. The boy's father can go to the girl's village by leave of her father, but not without." [41]

A girl has various chores to do in her new home. An unmarried girl is never allowed to grind wheat in her parents' home, but she must do this in the home of her parents-in-law. She must also cook, if she is the oldest daughter-in-law. She must run errands for her mother-in-law, wash her clothes, and perhaps massage her legs. She has a rather distant respect relationship with her father-in-law and covers her face when in his presence. They rarely speak together. A similar relationship prevails with her husband's elder brother (*jeth*), and generally with older males of her husband's family. In the presence of others a woman should show reserved behavior toward her husband. [42]

A woman has a friendly joking relationship with her *devar* (husband's younger brother). Sexual relations may take place between a girl and her *devar*. If this happens, it is not considered reprehensible, although fidelity to the husband is deemed a virtue. The husband's younger brother is a potential husband, if the woman's husband dies. Teasing of a sexual nature often occurs between these two, and the relationship between them, with its sexual implications, is often referred to in songs sung by the women. One Rampur informant said that he believed that nine out of ten men and women in the village had had extramarital relations at one time or another. Such relationships, if they do take place, would most frequently involve *bhabhi* and *devar*.

If the husband dies, the woman's bangles are broken by the members of his family, and the dress which she was wearing at the time of the death is discarded and thrown into the Jumna or the Ganges. Becoming a widow

---

[41] Ibbetson, 1883:134.

[42] Planalp has an interesting passage relating to this matter: "The theme of almost conscious, determined repression of the husband-wife relationship in favor of the greater good and stability of the joint family is one which can be seen in operation in many specific patterns of family behavior. I asked a number of villagers whether, if an elder man of the family were blind, a bride would have to observe purdah before him. Most asserted that she would not, but all agreed without hesitation that even though her husband were blind, a bride would have to keep strict purdah before him if his mother, aunt, or even older sister were present." Planalp, 1955:78.

is believed to be a punishment for sins in a past life. If the woman remains a widow she can never again wear glass bangles, apply *kajal* (soot) to her eyes, or put a *tika* on her forehead, and she is not supposed to wear fine clothes. But a woman does not have to remain a widow, unless she is a Brahman. After the passage of a year or so she may marry one of her husband's brothers. A widower usually remarries—perhaps one of his dead wife's sisters.

REMARRIAGE AND OTHER TYPES OF MARRIAGE

A few other matters relating to marriage may be touched on here. If a man refuses to take a wife home at the time of *gauna*, the wife's family can bring pressure to bear through the panchayat. There was a case of this in a village near Rampur. The man did not want his wife and refused to bring her home. Her family complained to the panchayat, which ordered him to go and get her. He still refused, and the panchayat therefore excommunicated the man and his family from caste. This meant that no one would smoke hookah with him, and that no more marriages could take place with this family. A year later the man went to the panchayat, begged for reinstatement, and promised to take back his wife.

A somewhat different case is the story of Phuli. When Phuli was married, he did not like his wife and considered her ugly. But he brought her home anyway. However, he started to have a romance with the beautiful young wife of his cousin, who lived in another village. This cousin was ill and was not expected to live long. Phuli invited the cousin and his wife to visit him for a while. At this time everyone knew that Phuli was interested in his cousin's wife. The cousin eventually died, and Phuli openly declared that the widow would remain with him as his wife. He also took the woman's young son as his own son. Phuli's first wife died shortly thereafter. Phuli and his second wife lived together for many years.

A few words about other forms of marriage: The *jhar phuna* form of marriage is used by lovers and people who are too poor for a regular marriage ceremony. The man and woman leave the village and build a fire of dry grass and twigs. Then they return and live together as man and wife. No examples of this type of marriage could be cited by Rampur informants, but it was said to have occurred in other villages.

There is also marriage by purchase, generally resorted to by older men. The purchase money may be used to pay off some debt of the girl's father, or else it may be spent on the wedding feast. The price varies between 500 and 1000 rupees.

Occasionally a woman who has been deserted by her husband is remarried. In case of desertion, the first husband may be obliged by the panchayat to pay the woman a fixed sum every six months. If the woman is twenty-five years old or younger she is generally remarried before long, and continues to receive the six monthly payments.

RELATIONS WITH IN-LAWS AS EXPRESSED IN SONGS

Despite the gradualness of the marriage process, the numerous songs sung by the women frequently contain expressions of homesickness, longing for one's own village, and expressions of annoyance at the husband's family. Some of the songs sung at Rampur are given below for the insights that they provide into the characteristic interpersonal relationships within the family.

In the first song a girl asks her mother-in-law to release her from housework and to let her swing beneath the trees. Such songs are sung at the time of the Tij festival.[43]

Daughter-in-law:	Mother-in-law, the month of Savan has come.
	Get me strings of yellow thread for my swing.
	Mother-in-law, the month of Savan has come.
	Get me a plank of sweet sandalwood.
Mother-in-law:	Daughter-in-law, let it come, let it come.
	The plank and strings are ready at home.
Daughter-in-law:	To others, your own, you have already given them.
	Before me you have placed corn to grind.
	I shall break the grindstone into eighteen pieces.
	I will spread this *pisna* [grain] throughout the bazaar.
	Let the *hali-pali* people [ploughmen and cowherds] come.
	Let them pick it up from the floor and eat it.
Mother-in-law:	Listen, son, how this foolish girl talks!
Daughter-in-law:	Mother-in-law, I must go to my father's home tomorrow.
Mother-in-law:	Daughter-in-law, we have work to do in the month of Katik.
	You may go to your father's home after Katik.
Daughter-in-law:	My younger brother's wedding is to be celebrated.
	By that time I will have been back twice, O Mother-in-law!

The girl does have some allies within her husband's family. Although they are strangers at first, she may develop an emotional bond with her husband, and she has the friendly quasi-sexual joking relationship with his younger brother. In some of the songs complaints are voiced over the immaturity of husband or *devar*. In the following this concerns the husband:

---

[43] See pp. 205-7.

There is a banana tree in the courtyard of my home.
I feed it with milk and curd.
I go to my neighbor, sad at heart.
My husband's sister knows the secret of my heart.
She asks, "Why do you stand so sad and still?"
I say, "Your brother is young and still a babe.
He does not know the longings of my heart."
She says, "Take a bath and adorn yourself.
Make a wish from your heart and come with me.
I will make my brother meet you.
Even doors of stone would fall open
And iron bolts fall
Before your beauty, love, and charm."

The potential sexual relationship with the husband's younger brother is hinted at in the following song:

O Mother-in-law, where should I sleep?
It is so cold.
My man has gone away to the army.
He is the guardian of the country.
O Mother-in-law, where should I sleep?
It is so cold.
My *devar* is very young and innocent.
O Mother-in-law, where should I sleep?
It is so cold.
My *jeth* has gone to the fields.
He is the guardian of the fields.
O Mother-in-law, where should I sleep?
It is so cold.

In some of the songs the husband is addressed as an ally, and the complaints about his family are directed to him. He appears in the role of a savior in the following song:

I always kept fetching water from the well.
My hands never rested, and I never sang.
My mother-in-law quarreled day and night.
Nobody loved me—neither my *nanand* [husband's sister] nor my *devar*.
My *jeth* quarreled, and my *devar* threatened me with his stick.
I wish that no woman had to be without her man close by!
She is jostled like a stick by everyone.
Oh, my whole body ached!
Then I sent a letter to my beloved husband,
Saying that the seed which he had sown in the garden

Was ready to be tasted by others.
Then my husband came and asked,
"Fair one, tell me everything truly.
How did your heart suffer?"
I said that I only wished
That no woman had to be without her man close by.
She is jostled like a stick by everyone.
But now my husband has come on leave,
And I have someone on my side.
I feel like a chimney that smokes out briskly.
I feel like a brick which is red-hot.
He has a pistol lying in the corner.
He says that he would kill anyone who made me suffer.
I say "No, my beloved! Forgive them this time.
But if they do it again, hang them all!"

In the two foregoing songs the husband is represented as being in the army. Here is one told from the man's point of view, with the same theme.

In my dream my wife came and passed close by my cot.
She clasped my hand while I was asleep
And then slyly escaped, thus waking me up.
In my dream I had come home on ten days' leave.
Seeing me coming, my wife stood up quickly.
She had two rings on her golden fingers.
She placed pillows under my head and feet on the cot.
She pressed my hands.
Then we spent an eternity together in an embrace.
She clasped my hand while I was asleep
And then slyly escaped, thus waking me up.
She said in the dream, "My *devar* is very naughty and a rogue.
Every day he calls me inside,
But inside I die of perspiration.
He may come outside to me if he wishes.
I am not to blame, dear.
I am stricken with a sinful love.
Either you come home and leave the army
Or I will die by jumping into the well."
She clasped my hand while I was asleep
And then slyly escaped, thus waking me up.
I heard my wife's story.
I have not been good to her,
For I have not taken good care of her.
Such a dream I had this night!

I wish the dawn would break.
She clasped my hand while I was asleep,
And then slyly escaped, thus waking me up.
Any young man who saw my wife would fall in love with her.
But how far is Ambala from the village of Birona?
My heart starts up as I think of her while I sleep here.
She clasped my hand while I was asleep
And then slyly escaped, thus waking me up.

The following is a song of reproach, supposedly sung by a woman who has been raped by her sister's husband:

O sister's husband! I die of shame because of you.
My sister's husband said that he would work at our plough,
And I was to bring his food to the fields.
O sister's husband! I die of shame because of you.

My sister's husband said that I should come quietly
With no one seeing me.
I said that big thorns would prick my feet.
O sister's husband! I die of shame because of you.

They worked at the plough on one side.
The cattle grazed at the other side.
I was lain prostrate between the two bullocks.
O sister's husband! I die of shame because of you.

I came home weeping and crying.
I told my sister that her husband had brought about my death.
She asked what had happened, and whether I had been beaten
With plough wood or plough iron.
I said that I had been beaten with neither.
O sister's husband! I die of shame because of you.

I was lain prostrate between the two bullocks.
They worked at the plough on one side.
The cattle grazed on the other side.
O sister's husband! I die of shame because of you.

Then my sister's husband came home.
My sister asked him why he made his sister suffer.
He said who was she to intervene.
He said that he was my brother-in-law
And I was his sister-in-law.
O sister's husband! I die of shame because of you.

My sister said that he had not given me even
A small piece of bread when I was a babe.
And now he is willing to give the whole plate of food to me!

She said that he did not take me into his lap when I was a babe.
But now he is willing to carry me into the upper apartments!
O sister's husband! I die of shame because of you.

I said that his loincloth was torn, and I could see the inside of it.
He said that my skirt was torn, and he could see the inside of it.

In these songs it is the woman's view of things which finds expression.
The men do not have comparable songs. The following is a girl's complaint
at male dominance:

Vidya said, "Listen, O Sukhma, what a tradition has started!
That one should remain blank without an education!
While brother is sent to study, I am sent to look after the cattle."

Vidya said, "Listen, O Sukhma, what a tradition has started!
The boy is given coats and pants to wear,
But I am given only a tattered head cloth,
And that has been stolen by someone."

Vidya said, "Listen, O Sukhma, what a tradition has started!
Drums are played upon the birth of a boy,
But at my birth only a brass plate is beaten."

Vidya said, "Listen, O Sukhma, what a tradition has started!"

A woman's status improves at the birth of her first son. At this time the
husband's sister has a right to ask for a gift from her sister-in-law. The
following is a song sung at the birth of a son, in which the mother expresses
disinclination to give anything of value.

Ask for a present, husband's sister.
It is your right to ask.
But don't ask for my *chunri,*
My head shawl.

Ask for a present, husband's sister.
It is your right to ask.
But don't ask for my earrings,
The adornment of my face.

Ask for a present, husband's sister.
It is your right to ask.
But don't ask for my skirt,
The adornment of my legs.

Ask for a present, husband's sister.
It is your right to ask.

O, dear husband, just give her the buffalo calf
Which has no tail.

6

The Festival Cycle

Despite the abundant literature available on Hindu festivals and ceremonial life, there are relatively few systematic accounts of the festival
cycle followed in a specific community. The authors of most works on the
subject have tried to be inclusive and cast a wide net, listing and describing
the festivals observed in different parts of India, or within a particular
region.[1] There are also studies like those of Briggs [2] and Fuchs [3] which
describe the festivals observed by a particular caste, but here again the
region covered is wide, and the cycle is not pinned to a specific town or
village. Local differences are widespread in a broad area like Uttar Pradesh
or Maharastra. In considering a particular community one would like to
know which festivals are absent and what local festivals have developed
there; over-all surveys do not supply this information.

   Any analysis of Indian festivals, whether it be historical or functional,

---

[1] Stevenson, 1920; Gupte, 1919; Underhill, 1921; Mukerji, 1918; "An Alphabetical
List . . . ," 1914. The latter deals largely with Bengal. Stevenson's focus is on Kathiawar
and Gujarat, while Underhill gives some emphasis to Maharastra. Gupte's data come
principally from Bengal, Bombay, and Central India, while Mukerji's seem to come from
Bengal and Uttar Pradesh.

[2] Briggs, 1920.

[3] Fuchs, 1951.

*Fig. 36.   A Brahman girl and friend in front of a shrine they built for worship during
the Naurtha (Niortha) festival in Kishan Garhi (courtesy of McKim Marriott
and Robert Redfield).*

should be based upon descriptions of the ceremonial cycle followed in a variety of specific communities. Until we have such data, it will not be possible to assess the role of the Hindu festivals in Indian life and the varying degrees of integration in different localities between the "great" and "little" traditions of Hinduism. McKim Marriott has recently dealt with this theme in a paper which does focus on a specific community—the village of Kishan Garhi in Aligarh District, Uttar Pradesh;[4] but while this is an excellent work of scholarship and analysis it does not supply a systematic detailed account of the festival cycle as a whole. In another recent work S. C. Dube has described the festival cycle of the village Shamirpet in Hyderabad, but his description, although valuable, is necessarily brief; the author disclaims the attempt to give minute ethnographic details concerning the festivals.[5]

The present chapter is devoted to the description and analysis of the yearly festival cycle in Rampur. Rampur has much in common with the village described by Marriott and shares in the great Hindu tradition found throughout India. An analysis of Rampur religious practices also shows the persistence of many elements that are not derived from the Sanskritic Hindu tradition and that are not Muslim. This may seem surprising in view of Rampur's proximity to the capital, but it reflects a characteristic of the Punjab that was singled out by Rose in 1919:

In the earliest days of Hinduism the people of the Punjab proper were a bye-word in the mouths of the worshippers of Brahma, and Brahmaism has always been weaker there than perhaps in any other part of India. Neither Islam nor the Hindu religion has ever been able to expel from the lives of the people the customs and superstitions which they brought with them from the homes of their ancestors; and the worship of godlings unknown to the Hindu pantheon, the social customs which still survive in full force among the majority of the nominal adherents of either religion, and the peculiar cults of the inferior and outcast races, offer for investigation an almost virgin field full of the richest promise.[6]

There are no temples in Rampur, although there are some small local shrines in honor of such deities as Bhuiyan, Gurgaon-wali Mata, and Guga *pir*. There is, however, a temple to Siva (built fifty years ago by a Baniya moneylender) in the nearby village of Rasulpur.

In our discussion of the festival cycle in this village we will be concerned with questions such as these: What is the general role of the festi-

---

[4] Marriott, 1955a.

[5] Dube, 1955:98.

[6] Rose, 1919, *1*:3.

vals in village social life? To what extent do they act as integrating factors and how much community participation takes place across caste and class lines? Is social distance lessened, or do caste distinctions persist in the festivals? Do certain castes have private festivals of their own? Do men and women participate equally in the ceremonial cycle? How may differential participation be interpreted? How are the festivals related to the economic and agricultural cycle? May they be said to act as inhibiting forces in economic production, as some writers have suggested? Do they swallow up capital for conspicuous consumption and take up time which might otherwise be spent in the fields? To what extent does the festival cycle at Rampur reflect the great Hindu tradition? Which elements are local, regional, national? Are the festivals stable or undergoing change? What types of change are taking place, and to what may they be attributed? Does the religious life of the villagers seem to be influenced by latter-day cults or isms coming from the outer world? What may one expect of future adherence to the ceremonial cycle? Some of these are difficult questions to answer, and our data are not always complete enough to provide full answers. But some generalizations may be drawn from the accounts that follow. Here, to begin with, is a list of the festivals observed at Rampur:

Festival	*Month*
Basora	Cait (March-April)
Devi-ki Karahi	Cait
Ghantal Deo	Baisakh (April-May)
Jaith-ka Dasahra	Jaith (May-June)
Tij	Savan (July-August)
Silono	Bhadon (August-September)
Janam Astami	Bhadon
Guga Naumi	Bhadon
Kanagat	Asauj (September-October)
Niortha-Dasahra	Asauj
Karva Cauth	Katik (October-November)
Hoi	Katik
Girdi-Divali-Gobardhan	Katik
Devuthani Gias	Katik
Ganga-Jumna Nahan	Katik
Makar Sankrant	Poh (December-January)
Basant Pancami	Magh (January-February)
Siv Ratri	Phagun (February-March)
Holi-Dulhendi	Phagun

BASORA

The ceremonial cycle begins on the seventh day of the Hindu month of Cait (March-April) with the Basora or Stale *(basi)* Bread Festival.[7] The festival is also known in Rampur as Sidhi (cold) Satain (seven), because the seventh day of Cait is supposed to mark the end of the cold season. People now stop keeping cooked food overnight, lest it go bad with the coming of warm weather. This is a time, too, when diseases are common. Some families therefore travel to Gurgaon, 30 miles from Rampur, to get help from Gurgaon-wali Mata, a goddess concerned with smallpox. Others visit a small shrine to this deity on the outskirts of Rampur.

On the evening of the sixth of Cait, wheat porridge sweetened with brown sugar is cooked by women of the Jat, Brahman, Baniya, and Camar castes. This food is set aside uneaten. Early the next morning, having bathed and dressed in their best clothes, the women carry the porridge, some rice, gram, and water to the goddess' shrine. They go in extended family groups, women of the same caste walking together with their youngest children, singing songs in praise of Gurgaon-wali Mata. "O Mata, you gave us children; now protect them from disease!"[8]

The shrine to the goddess is rather tumbledown, little more than a pile of bricks. Here the Rampur womenfolk pray, facing toward Gurgaon, and pour some water onto a brick slab which represents the goddess. To this they add some porridge, rice, gram, and a smear of turmeric. After repeating their prayers the women move on to a shrine dedicated to Kainthi-wali Mata, a goddess of typhoid. Here the ritual is repeated, with a turmeric mark being placed on the forehead of each child by the mother. Some of the women make vows to present a veil to the goddess or to distribute candy to all the children, if their own child recovers from sickness. This is an occasion, then, for the distribution of brown sugar and sweets to the boys and girls. A Bhangi (sweeper) may bring a cock and hold it over a child's head. To have the cock flutter its wings over a child in this way is considered auspicious, conducive to long life. The Bhangi is given a small tip (1 pice to 1 anna) for this service.

[7] Marriott calls it "leftover food worship" (1955a: 192-93, 212).

[8] Some songs to Gurgaon-wali Mata sung by the Bhangis of Delhi are given in Ratan, 1955. Here is an example:
"I go to worship Gurgaon-wali.
Oh mother, have mercy on me.
I touch your feet and stand before you with joined hands.
Lota [brass jug] is in my hand.
Dhoti is on my back."

Sweepers get some free food as well; their empty bowls set beside the shrine are filled with porridge by the worshippers. If a veil is left behind for the goddess, it is taken by a female sweeper attached to the woman who made the vow. Sometimes small pigs are left as offerings to the goddess, and these are also taken home by the Bhangis. So the sweeper caste derives some benefits from the festival. The Kumhars (potters) are also given porridge on this occasion.

On the way home the women leave some more porridge at the crossroads for the crossroads goddess, Chaurahe-wali Mata, who has power over ghosts. Porridge and turmeric are also left at the shrine of Bhuiyan, the first old man to die in the village after its founding; for in this region it is the custom to worship such a man as a village god.[9] When they reach home at last, each woman pours out some water on either side of her door—a symbol of purification. Then porridge is eaten; no other food is cooked until evening.[10]

Trips to Gurgaon to honor the goddess are not made on Basora day itself but on any Monday that follows during the month of Cait. Here the goddess is given sweets (laddus and patasas) rather than porridge. The trip to Gurgaon may be made to honor a pledge to the goddess in gratitude for the birth or recovery of a child or the contraction of a satisfactory marriage. Such pilgrimages have declined in recent years. Arya Samaj influence is given by villagers as the cause of this. The men, in general, are skeptical of Mata worship and frequently cite an Arya Samaj argument against it: "If you put food on Mata's shrine, a dog comes along and eats it. He also makes

---

[9] See Rose, 1919, 1:374.

[10] According to Abhay Charan Mukerji, cooked food is offered only to the smallpox goddess (also known as Sitala) and not to other deities. "The rule is that cooked food, carried out of the bounds of the chowka or cooking place, becomes ipso facto unclean, and unfit even for respectable mortal taste; hence no cooked food is ever offered in worship at any public temple, the priests alone having the privilege of supplying the deity with his usual meals at the usual hours, during which the public are shut out from the temple and visits are disallowed. But in the case of the goddess Sitala this rule, which is rigidly enforced in other cases, is relaxed, and cooked food from the hands of all castes is freely allowed to come within the sanctum of the temple." Mukerji, 1918: 62. Ibbetson's data disagree with this: "Offerings of cooked food may be divided into two classes. To the benevolent gods, or to ancestors, only pakki roti, that is cakes or sweets fried in ghi, may be offered; while to the malevolent and impure gods, kachhi roti, generally consisting of churma, or stale bread broken up and rolled into balls with gur and ghi is offered. Brahmans will not take the latter class of offerings." Ibbetson, 1883:145. According to Dube (1955:106) cooked sweet potatoes are offered to Siva at his shrine in Shamirpet. Apparently cooked food was offered to demons in ancient times. In the Arthasastra of Kautilya, dated as c. 300 B.C., appears the statement: "In all kinds of dangers from demons, the incantation 'we offer thee cooked rice' shall be performed."

water there. Mata can't stop him. If she had any power, she should kill that dog, but she does not." "Our ancestors were stupid, and we are getting educated," said one villager. "We're learning that all such beliefs are false."

Such attitudes do not particularly seem to influence the women, who still visit the local shrine. However, here too there are some signs of change. It is commonly claimed that more porridge was given to the Bhangis and Kumhars in the past. The attitudes of both donors and recipients are said to have altered. The Jats complain that the Bhangis no longer carry out their *jajmani* obligations. Why, then, should they be fed? The Bhangis, for their part, say that the porridge left in their bowls is both scanty and poor in quality. "Why should I eat it?" asked one. "It won't keep my belly full for a year." Some Bhangis and Kumhars feed the porridge to their animals, which may reflect Arya Samaj teachings directed against the acceptance of leftover food. The custom of holding a cock fluttering its wings above the head of a child is also being discontinued.

Not all villagers approve of the new tendencies. One remarked, "There is no *dharma* [duty] left in the world; nobody works for us, and so we don't do what we should." A Kumhar observed that formerly even animals had enough to eat; nowadays people starve. This Kumhar attributed the decline in Mata worship to the increase in population. "Formerly one went to worship Mata to get more children or to keep those that one had healthy and well, but now every family has five or six children. We don't want any more. My house used to be big enough, but now we have six families in it."

The festival does not involve much expenditure; in fact one saves money on Basora through fasting and eating bread and porridge. The more expensive items—sweets, veils, or pigs given to Mata—are being dispensed with nowadays, according to some informants. But even these items would affect only some of the villagers—those who had made vows to Mata.

The festival of Basora seems to show a cleavage at Rampur between the men and women, with the former expressing skepticism and the latter remaining faithful to the goddess. The men attribute their own attitudes to recent changes and to the influence of the Arya Samaj. However, this interpretation is open to question, for men in this part of India have traditionally avoided involvement in certain religious ceremonies regarded as the province of the women.[11] Worship of the smallpox goddess belongs in this category. Both Rose and Mukerji claim that it is exclusively female in nature.[12]

---

[11] Ibbetson, 1882:101; O'Malley, 1935:104.

[12] Mukerji also claims that it is largely a lower-caste practice: "It must be pointed out that Mother-worship in these rather gross forms is confined exclusively to the female

Rose's account is worth quoting, since it agrees in so many respects with our own data:

These deities are never worshipped by men but only by women and children, enormous numbers of whom attend the shrines of renown on Sitala's *saptami*, the seventh of the light half of Sawan, when only light food is eaten. Every village has its local shrine also, at which the offerings are all impure. Sitala rides upon a donkey, and gram is given to the donkey and to his master, the potter at the shrine, after having been waved over the head of the child. Fowls, pigs, goats and cocoanuts are offered, black dogs are fed, and white cocks are waved and let loose. An adult, who has recovered from small-pox, should let a pig loose to Sitala, or he will again be attacked. During an attack no offerings are made; and if the epidemic has once seized upon the village all worship is discontinued, till the disease has disappeared. But so long as she keeps her hands off it, nothing is too good for the goddess. . . .[13]

DEVI-KI KARAHI

This festival is observed by the Kumhars, Camars, and other low-caste groups, but by only about half of the Jats. The first celebration is on the eighth day of Sudi (latter part)-Cait (March-April), the second on the eighth of Sudi-Asauj (September-October). The main local center of the goddess Devi is in Beri, in Rohtak District. She also has a small shrine near Rampur. During the period of these celebrations harvests are in progress—mustard seed in March-April and millet in September-October. Worship of the goddess is limited to the mornings and evenings. The hearth is given a new coat of plaster, a *ghi* lamp is lit, and a dish of sweets *(halva* or *lapsi)* [14] is placed before the hearth. The mother or grandmother of the family prays, "Oh Devi, keep my children healthy!" Some of the candy is given to a cow; some is set before a Brahman before the family partakes of it. Foods prepared for the holiday are exchanged with different families of

folk of the lower castes. These Mother-goddesses are the most popular deities of Northern India, in the sense that they are publicly worshipped oftener than any other gods or goddesses." Mukerji, 1918:63.

In Rampur, Jat, Brahman, and Baniya women take part in the worship of these deities. One Jat informant, however, said that higher-caste women worship Mata only if they have made vows to do so during the preceding year, at the time of a smallpox epidemic. Under normal circumstances, according to this informant, no higher-caste family would visit the Mata shrine at Gurgaon.

[13] Rose, 1919, *1*:350. See also Ibbetson, 1882:149, for a similar passage from which Rose has probably drawn.

[14] Jat families generally prepare *halva,* made of sugar, flour, and *ghi,* while lower castes and poor Jat families make *lapsi,* consisting of toasted flour, brown sugar, and water.

the lineage. Among the Camars all families prepare a small quantity of *lapsi*, but there is apt to be one Camar family which will cook a large amount of it, about 5¼ *sirs* in weight, for distribution among the other Camar families, including those from the four adjoining villages. This obligation is undertaken because of a pledge to the goddess, if a wish (generally for a son or a fortunate marriage) is fulfilled.

A few families from Rampur attend the annual fair at Beri. Devi's shrine is near a pond whose mud is believed to be sacred. Everyone who goes to worship there digs up some mud from the bed of the pond. Offerings of sweets *(laddus* and *patasas)* are made at the shrine, and a *ghi* lamp is lit there. Those who have made a vow to the goddess, and whose wishes have been granted, offer from 1 to 5 rupees' worth of *laddus*. Five of the sweets are left at the shrine; the rest are eaten by the worshipper or distributed among relatives.

Children born subsequent to a vow made to Devi are taken by their parents to Beri for their first haircut. The first lock of hair cut off is buried in the pond; a few hairs are placed in the shrine. This does not apply to all families, for different clans honor different gods and goddesses. The Dabas Jats prefer to offer the first-cut hair of a child to Ghantal Deo and to celebrate on the latter's festival day instead of on Devi's. Camars and Kumhars flock to Beri because of the trade in leather and donkeys there, and because of the opportunity to meet relatives from the surrounding country. There are wrestling matches, merry-go-rounds, and other such attractions.

In the past most families placed a lighted *ghi* lamp at the small local shrine in Rampur, but now only about twenty-five families do so. However, the women of the village generally light a lamp at home. Special foods are cooked on this day by some of the families, and as one man put it, "It's all done in the name of the goddess, but anyway our children get some good food."

GHANTAL DEO

Ghantal Deo was a bygone leader of the Dabas villagers who was cremated in Rampur. He has now become a god and is worshipped on the ninth of Baisakh (April-May). There is a well-kept, whitewashed monument dedicated to Ghantal Deo near the primary school where Dabas from other villages also come to worship. This festival occurs at a time when the wheat crop has been harvested and the threshing has begun. Women make sweets and pancakes on this day and, singing, carry them to the shrine. Here they dig up some earth from a small pond nearby and then place a lighted earthen lamp and a food offering before the Brahman who sits at the shrine. (He takes the food home later.)

The newborn children of most Jats and Brahmans in the village get their first haircut at the shrine on this occasion, so one or two barbers may be found there. After the haircut, the parents distribute sweets among the bystanders. If a child can't be brought to the shrine, some of the hair is sent along with the offering. Some Jats, however, prefer to have the first haircut done at Beri or Jharoda.

There is no special food exchange on this day, nor are any food gifts presented to the lower castes, who take no part in this holiday. Until seven or eight years ago there used to be a fair in the village on this occasion, and people would come from many villages roundabout. But now only those from the four adjoining villages come to honor Ghantal Deo.

JAITH-KA DASAHRA

On the tenth day of the Sudi fortnight of Jaith (May-June) some families from Rampur go to bathe in the Jumna River near Delhi, to honor the river, which is conceived of as a virgin. The weather is very hot at this time. At the river, leaves bearing small coins and flowers are floated downstream, and bread and gram are distributed to beggars. The Jumna is believed to wash away sins incurred in agricultural work—the beating of oxen, killing of ants, etc. Since the threshing and winnowing of crops are now over, it is a good occasion for such a purificatory bath. Informants say that this ceremonial bathing is not so widely observed as in the past.

TIJ

Tij, which falls on the third day of Sudi-Savan, marks the beginning of an important cycle of festivals concluding with Holi. A local proverb says: "Tij comes and sows the seeds of festivals; Holi comes and takes away the festivals in her shawl."

After the hot summer months the monsoon rains have finally come, and now the air is cool and everything is green. Millet has been planted, sugar cane cultivated, and the villagers are in good spirits. Tij is meant to express this mood. Villagers say that the festival was started by the daughters of the ancient ruler Vikramaditya, who inaugurated the custom of swinging, the most characteristic aspect of Tij.

On the evening before Tij the young men go to the village common lands and look for trees on which to hang swings. Some place marks on their trees or separate branches of trees to claim them, while others keep watch all night to ward off rivals. Fights sometimes spring up in this competition over trees. The swings are set up early in the morning—sometimes at 1:00 A.M.—but the swinging does not begin until later in the day.

Some of the young men gain reputations for their skill in putting up swings and are sought out by their sisters, sisters-in-law, cousins, and daughters of neighbors, to hang swings for them. Tij provides more opportunities for flirtation than most festivals. If a young married woman asks her husband's younger brother or cousin to put up a swing, it shows her interest in him.

Children start to use the swings early in the morning while the men are working in the fields and the women are at home making small pancakes (*gulgula*), rice pudding, and other festive dishes. At about noon the men come home, and all the young women and children put on their good clothes. An hour later they are off to the groves where the swings have been hung, walking in family groups, singing as they go. One or two double swings are put up for each extended family. The swings are made so that two women, each sitting on a board 1½ feet long and 5 to 6 inches wide, face each other and place their feet on the opposite swing. Two other women stand behind them and push, while others are grouped about, singing songs. Here are some of the currently popular songs sung at Tij:

> The month of Savan is come. Get me a swing of yellow silk rope.
> O Daughter-in-law, we have no yellow silk rope. Get it from your father's.
> O Mother-in-law, my brother has come. Send me to my father's place.
> O Daughter-in-law, there is work to do in the fields. Go to your father's place in Katik.
> O Mother-in-law, my brother will be married in Katik. Then I shall go for the second time.

> When I took the first swing, O mother mine!
> It was as if someone thundered through the sky.
> There is a swing in the green garden.
> When I took the second swing, in the garden green, O mother mine!
> It was as if someone swung through the sky.
> There is a swing in the green garden.
> My head veil flew away, O mother mine!
> My seating-plank is made of black *candan* [sandalwood], O mother mine!
> The strings are as if made of fine silk.
> There is a swing in the green garden.
> O mother mine!

Toward evening, at about 5:00, all the women go home, while the men and children stay to watch wrestling matches between the young men of the adjoining four villages. These matches are over by sunset, and then everyone goes home to eat the festive meal. Formerly, food was given to the lower castes in the village on Tij, but now only the Bhangis are given gifts, since they are the only ones who still work regularly for the Jats.

Tij is the time when young brides receive gifts of clothing from their fathers-in-law, especially in the case of recent brides who are still living at their parents' home on the first Tij after the wedding. Such a girl receives from her father-in-law a shirt, a veil, a skirt, some bangles, a colored rope and wooden board for a swing, 8 to 10 *sirs* of sweets, and some henna to stain the palms of her hands and the soles of her feet. The bride may give some of the sweets to her brothers and sisters, nephews and nieces, but not to her parents, uncles and aunts.

When a bride comes of age and lives at her husband's house, her father sends her *kothli,* gifts of clothing, on the first Tij. She receives a skirt, veil, and shirt; her husband and his father and brothers each receive a cotton sheet; her husband's unmarried sisters and mother receive a skirt and veil, while the mother is also sent about 5 *sirs* of special sweets, *suhalis.* In a well-to-do family all the children of the husband's brother are given shirts and caps. On every subsequent Tij, a skirt, veil, and shirt are sent to the married daughter by her father, as well as sweets, and a shirt and cap for each of her children. The responsibility for sending this annual gift passes to the sons and grandsons at the father's death. The general practice now, however, is to send gifts of clothing for the first consecutive three or four years. After that they are sent only occasionally, especially if a man has two or three married daughters. The Nai who used to deliver the gift of clothing to the married daughters no longer performs this role. Now the girl's brother takes the gifts to her. Some send money or money orders of 2 to 5 rupees, since money is more useful and more convenient to send. In the past the sweets were often stale upon arrival and had to be thrown away. In Rampur the cost of the annual gift of clothing for a married daughter or the *sindhara* (ceremonial gifts) for a daughter-in-law is about 30 rupees.

One of the songs sung at Tij reflects the custom of *kothli:*

> The whistle bird sings in the garden.
> I know someone will come, someone will come, will come.
> My *patmal* [dear] brother will come.
> He will bring a dress for my brother, another for my sister,
> And bangles for my sister-in-law.

SILONO

Silono falls on the full-moon day of the month of Bhadon (August-September), eleven days after Tij. It coincides with Rakhi Bandhan ("Charm Tying") and has merged with it, as McKim Marriott has noted for village Kishan Garhi:

This all-Indian festival ["Charm Tying"] coincides and blends in Kishan Garhi with the festival known regionally as *Saluno* . . . a festival which marks the end of that annual fortnight during which most young wives return for a visit with their parents and siblings. On *Saluno* day, many husbands arrive at their wives' villages, ready to carry them off again to their villages of marriage. But, before going off with their husbands, the wives as well as their unmarried village sisters express their concern for and devotion to their brothers by placing young shoots of barley, the locally sacred grain, on the heads and ears of their brothers. Since brothers should accept nothing from their sisters as a free gift, they reciprocate with small coins. . . . Parallels between the familial festival of *Saluno* and the specialized Brahmanical festival of Charm Tying—between the role of the sister and the role of the priest—are obvious.[15]

The "charm-tying" procedures at Rampur are as follows: A Brahman ties a *ponchi*, or wrist band of colored thread, around the wrist of the head of the family. In return he is given a handful of grain, or sometimes as much as a *sir* of grain. Girls also tie *ponchis*, more elaborate ones, around the wrists of their brothers or cousins and their brothers' or cousins' wives and sons, receiving from a few annas to 5 rupees in exchange. (When unmarried girls receive money, they give it to their mothers.) A girl receives a scarf or a shirt from her sisters-in-law. Some families give her a calf.

Two different explanations of the festival's origin trace it back to Paras Ram, a Brahman who is said to have lived some one hundred thousand years ago. According to the Brahmans of the village, Paras Ram, after fighting twenty-one battles against the Rakshasas, called in the rulers who had asked him for help in this campaign, and tied *ponchis* to their wrists to symbolize *dharma*, or duty. According to the local Jats, Paras Ram tied *ponchis* around the wrists of subjects who did not pay their taxes and made them pay. There were also different explanations for the girls' custom of tying bands on their brothers' wrists. One traces it back to Abhimanyu, a warrior in the Mahabharata who was given a *ponchi* by his grandmother; he was invulnerable while wearing it, but was overpowered when it broke in battle. Another explanation for the custom is that Brahmans and girls are held equally sacred. Brahman girls used to give *ponchis* to their fathers on Silono, and the custom later spread to other castes.

15 Marriott, 1955a:198.

According to Mukerji, Brahmans take advantage of this festival occasion to exploit the public.[16] But the Brahmans of Rampur are not guilty of this offense. In fact, they have not tied *ponchis* for the villagers for the past thirty years, since they consider the gifts of grain a degrading form of charity. But there is a Brahman from another village who performs this function at Rampur and receives the grain offerings. Despite their abstention from this custom, the Brahmans still celebrate Silono more than do the members of other castes. The Jats consider it a minor festival, but they prepare special foods, such as rice pudding and pancakes, on this day, and sometimes give some food to the Bhangis who work for them. A fair is held on Silono at Bahadurgarh, about 3 miles from Rampur, and about forty or fifty men from Rampur go there every year to attend the wrestling matches and visit the markets.[17]

JANAM ASTAMI

The anniversary of Lord Krsna's birth falls on the eighth lunar day in the dark fortnight of the month of Bhadon. The festival of Janam Astami

[16] His amusing description is worth quoting: "Raksha Bandhan, popularly called 'Salono,' is the full moon of Sravana, and this occurs exactly ten days after Nag Pachami. 'Salono' is a corruption of the Persian term *Sal-i-nau*, 'the new year'; and it is a name given to the full moon of Sravana, because it marks the point of transition between the old and the new Fasli, or agricultural year. . . . It is treated as a great harvest-day by Brahmans of the priestly order, and the mendicant class, who wander about the town all day from sunrise to sunset, carrying a bundle of 'Rakshas,' visiting the houses of the well-to-do, tying a 'Raksha' round the wrist, whenever they can, hanging on until they have received a cash present, and then departing to repeat the same performance, in as many more places as they can go to. If they happen to meet any of their clientele on the road, they waylay him there, and insist on tying a 'Raksha' round his wrist, however unwilling he may be to be manacled in this manner in the public streets. The merest chance of an acquaintance, the most casual contact, the remotest connection is enough to establish a bond of relationship between you and a Brahman of this class; entitling him to the privilege of tying a 'Raksha' round your arm, wherever he may happen to catch you on this day. Discharged cooks, whether of your own house or that of a friend at whose place you have once dined; post and telegraph peons, who happen to be Brahmans by caste; Brahman constables attached to the Police Station under whose jurisdiction you live now or ever lived in the past; nephews of a former Chaukidar or Chaprasi [office boy] of your office; not to speak of *all* Brahman members of your present domestic and office establishment—all these have a strong claim upon your wrist and your purse." Mukerji, 1918:91-94.

[17] Wiser gives a brief account of this festival: "On this date, the bard places the coloured cotton bracelet on the wrists of his jajmans, for which he receives 11 ounces of grain and from 2 to 4 pice. The florist supplies henna for staining the feet of the ladies of the jajman's family and receives 11 ounces of grain. All of the employees receive a handful of *Simai* [a small millet], cooked with raw sugar, one or two *puris* and 1 or 2 *Dal ki kachoris* [*puris* made with *dal*]." Wiser, 1936:87. Here the *bhat*, or bard, ties the bracelet rather than the Brahman.

("Eighth Day of Birth") is observed by Hindus all over India. The story told in Rampur about its origin agrees in general with the legend of the Great Tradition, to use Redfield's phrase. The demon King Kansa determined to kill all the children born to his sister Devaki, because his Brahman advisers had told him that he would be killed by one of them. Kansa imprisoned his sister and brother-in-law and killed each child as it was born; but just before the birth of Krsna, the eighth child, Devaki persuaded her sister to exchange babies. Krsna was smuggled out to safety and lived to kill King Kansa.

Fasting is observed on this day throughout India, commemorating the fast of those who were anxious for Krsna's safety. In Rampur at least two or three people in each family fast on Janam Astami, especially women and girls over thirteen. Schoolboys are apt to fast too, because they are told about Janam Astami in school. During the day no food or water is consumed by those observing the fast. No pipes are smoked. Around 4:00 P.M. people take some sweetened water, but food is eaten only on the appearance of the moon. Those who are fasting face the moon and pour some water out of a pot onto the floor. Then everyone is given some *charnamrit*, made of milk, sugar, and *tulsi* leaves, and the meal begins. The special dish is usually *corma*, made of baked *capatis* torn into bits and pounded with sugar and *ghi*. Rice pudding and pancakes are made by those who can afford them; those who cannot eat *lapsi*. No food is given away, since it is a fasting day. During the evening the people sit on the housetops, tell stories about Lord Krsna, and sing songs. At the end of each song the women repeat, "Victory to Lord Krsna!"

GUGA NAUMI

On the ninth day of Badi(first part)-Bhadon (August-September) there is a festival in honor of Guga *pir*, who, according to Crooke, is also known as Zahir Pir, "the Saint Apparent," or Zahir Diwan, "the Minister Apparent," or, in the Punjab, as Bagarwala.[18] According to Rose, his cult is widespread in the Punjab. "His worship extends throughout the province, except perhaps on the frontier itself. It is probably weakest in the Western Plains; but all over the eastern districts his shrines, of a peculiar shape and name, may be seen in almost every large village, and he is universally worshipped throughout the sub-montane tract and the Kangra Hills. . . . He flourished about the middle of the 12th century. He is really a Hindu, and his proper name is Guga Bir or Guga, the Hero. . . . But Musulmans also flock to his shrine, and his name has been altered to Guga Pir or Saint Guga, while he

---

[18] Crooke, 1896, *1*:211.

himself has become a Muhammadan in the opinion of the people." [19] His grave is in Bikaner, near Dadrewa. Crooke says that it is in his function as a snake king that Guga is specially worshipped.

When he is duly propitiated he can save from snake bite and cause those who neglect him to be bitten. His shrine is often found in association with that of Nara Sinha, the man-lion incarnation of Vishnu, and of Goraknath, the famous ascetic, whose disciple he is said to have been. He is adored by Hindus and Muhammadans alike and by all castes, by Rajputs and Jats, as well as by Chamars and Chuhras. Even the Brahman looks on him with respect. "Which is the greater," says the proverb, "Rama or Guga?" and the reply is, "Be who may the greater, shall I get myself bitten by a snake?" in other words, "Though Rama may be the greater, between ourselves, I dare not say so for fear of offending Guga." He is represented on horseback, with his mother trying to detain him as he descends to the infernal regions. He holds as a mark of dignity a long staff in his hands, and over him two snakes meet, one being coiled round his staff. Both the Hindu and Muhammadan Faquirs take the offerings devoted to him, and carry his chhari or standard, covered with peacocks' feathers, from house to house in the month of August. . . . According to the last census Guga had 25,000 worshippers in the Panjab and 123,000 in the North-Western Provinces.

Legends about Guga may be found in the works of Rose and of Temple.[20] The following story, which accounts for the festival's origin, is the one popularly told in Rampur:

There were two sisters, Bachal and Kachal, who served a holy man. Bachal was devoted, but Kachal was lax in her attentions to the *pir*. One day the *pir* opened his eyes from a trance, and on seeing Kachal in attendance, blessed her with a gift of two sons. Later, when Bachal came and asked the holy man for a favor, he said that he had already bestowed one. Bachal then complained that her sister had served him very little, whereupon the *pir* said that Bachal would give birth to a son who would kill Kachal's two sons. This son became known as Guga, a brave fighter, who eventually fulfilled the prophecy. When his mother refused to look at him after the murder, Guga had himself buried alive with his horse. Many years later a prisoner had a dream in which Guga appeared, asking him to build a shrine above the place where he had buried himself. The prisoner escaped from jail and managed to reach the spot but was recaptured and returned to his cell before he could carry out the commission. Once more, however, the prisoner made his escape and this time succeeded in building a monument above the grave, dedicated to Guga *pir*. It is said that Guga appeared to other living persons as well, principally his wife, whom he used to visit

---

[19] Rose, 1919, *1*:171.

[20] Rose, 1919, *1*:172-92; Temple, 1900.

every night after his death. But he stopped these visits when his mother hid herself in the room to get a glimpse of him. Some people say that his grave still shakes every night at midnight, when Guga leaves it.

Somehow, the cult of this hero has become mixed with snake worship. The snake is said to be Guga's brother, and the two are worshipped together during the festival, which comes at a time when snakes are rather abundant in Rampur, frequently turning up in people's homes. It is said that those who do not offer worship on this day will be visited by snakes— which may perhaps help to keep the cult alive.

On Guga Naumi the women of the household take the black soot from their iron griddles and draw figures on the wall representing a snake and a man on horseback. An earthen lamp is lit and placed before the drawing, together with some pancakes and a little of everything else cooked that day. Some oil and *ghi* are poured over a hot ember to make it flare up and burn. Everyone says, "Guga has appeared." Then the worshippers fold hands and pray, "O Guga *pir,* please don't appear to us during the coming year."

There used to be a Muslim fakir in Rampur who received the food offered to Guga, but now that he is gone, the food is given to dogs or cattle. The fakir also used to receive offerings of brown sugar in Guga's name. This sugar was given by a family if a buffalo stopped giving milk, for Guga was believed to have power over buffalo milk, and brown sugar might therefore be vowed to him to restore the flow. Nowadays this offering is given to neighbors.

There used to be four *bhagats* or devotees of Guga *pir* in Rampur—three Jats and one Camar. To become such a *bhagat* it was necessary to go on foot to the grave of Guga *pir* in Bikaner. The pilgrim had to wear yellow robes and hang a wreath of yellow thread about his neck. Camars beating drums and carrying banners accompanied the devotee. At the monument a goat or a she-calf was sacrificed to the *pir.* On his return home the pilgrim gave a feast to all members of his caste.

It was the custom for each of the *bhagats* of Guga *pir* to burn a *ghi* lamp on a different day during the month of Bhadon, so that the *pir* would receive four days of worship. On these occasions the *bhagat* sat before his *ghi* lamp while a group of Bhangis and Camars beat small drums called *dorus* and sang songs about Guga. The *bhagat* was then considered to be possessed by Guga's spirit. After shivering and shaking, which indicated Guga's advent, the devotee would get up, jump about, and beat himself with an iron rod. People would then ask questions about future marriages, births, or the coming of rains. The *bhagat's* self-administered blows were supposed to cause no bruises, although he kept it up throughout the night. People who attended these sessions and received answers from the spirit gave small amounts of grain (¼ to ½ *sir*) to the drummers.

In the old days a Camar *bhagat* announced a session of this kind by parading about the village with a band of drummers and attendants carrying banners. Such a banner would have an emblem representing a horse and a man, and would be topped by a few peacock feathers. All the households in the village contributed grain to these entourages. On the day of Guga Naumi all the Camars of the villages and some from the adjoining four villages ate together at the home of the *bhagat*, who paid all the expenses of the feast beyond what was collected from the villagers.

These customs are no longer followed in Rampur. The last *bhagat*, a Camar, died fifteen years ago. During his lifetime this Camar became influenced by Arya Samaj doctrines, and for a while refrained from giving mediumistic sessions. But when his house became filled with snakes, he vowed to resume the performances again and to hold them every year until his death. After that time there were no more *bhagats* in the village, and no one in Rampur has made a pilgrimage to the Guga *pir* monument for the past twenty-five years. Yet almost all the families in the village still worship Guga *pir* and the snakes. There are only two or three Arya Samajist families in the village which do not. Guga Naumi is therefore still observed.

KANAGAT

Kanagat or Sraddha is the yearly ritual occasion for honoring the family dead through gifts of food to Brahmans. In this part of India these observances take place during the sixteen-day period between the full-moon day of Bhadon and Amavas (no-moon day) in the month of Asauj (September-October). A dead person is held in remembrance by his family (represented by the eldest son or grandson) on a particular day of this half-month, according to the day of the fortnight on which he died. Thus, if a man died on the third day of a month—any month—food is given in his name on the third day of Asauj. The dead family members who are honored at Kanagat may include the father, mother, grandfather, grandmother, and sons over eighteen. Sons below that age are not included. Daughters are considered members of another family through marriage. A girl cannot perform a *sraddha* in memory of her father and mother; only sons can do that. *Sraddhas* may also be celebrated for an uncle and aunt who died sonless and whose property has been inherited by the person concerned.

On the day before a *sraddha* a Brahman is asked to come and perform the ceremony. He arrives early the next morning and takes a bath at the family home; then he is given the raw materials for his meal—rice, milk, flour, and *ghi*—which he makes into rice-milk puddings and *capatis*. Meanwhile the eldest son or grandson of the family goes to bathe in the village pond. He must not wring out the wet *dhoti* which he is wearing. As he holds one hand over the other, the Brahman puts a few leaves of *dub* grass into his hand and pours water over it. Then he reads aloud some *mantras*.

The son or grandson of the household then gets up and pours water from a pot onto the floor. As he does so he faces the sun, which is said to be carrying the water, through its rays, up to the family ancestors. Then the Brahman takes two *capatis* and a little pudding and gives the former to a cow, the latter to the crows flying about the house. (The cow is considered sacred; the crows, which are common in the village, are believed to be descendants of a Hindu sage.) This done, the Brahman eats. The dead man who is being honored on this day receives the benefit of this food in the process and will be helped on the road to salvation. It is said that this custom was started by a good king called Karan, who always gave gold in charity. When Karan died and went to heaven, he in turn was given only gold, since that is what he had given away in his lifetime. He couldn't get anything to eat. Karan arranged to return to life for sixteen days, during which time he gave away as much food in charity as he was able. Thus the sixteen-day period of Kanagat was initiated.

The Brahman who eats the food may take some of it home to his wife. He also accepts some *daksina,* or ritual remuneration, the amount of which varies in different families. Some give ½ to 1 *sir* of grain; Kumhars or Camars may give from 2 to 8 annas. If a Brahman cannot come when summoned, he may delegate his powers to his wife or to another Brahman. In the latter case, the first Brahman is the one who gets the fees; he may turn over about a quarter of the amount to his substitute.[21]

A well-to-do man sometimes gives a big *sraddha* called *battis,* to which thirty-two Brahmans are invited, as well as other guests, all of whom must be members of the host's caste. A feast of this kind costs between 50 and 100 rupees and is given only once or twice in a man's lifetime.

On the day of a *sraddha* one should not use the grindstone or make butter, but these taboos are giving way and are often violated at present. Brahmans still follow the old customs, but the Jats and the lower castes are lax in their observance and have modified the ceremony in some ways. The main difference, which affects the whole performance, is that the serv-

---

[21] Wiser says that "In the case of the poor, Brahmans are fed only on the fifteenth day, which is Amawas." Wiser, 1936:88.

ices of a Brahman are sometimes dispensed with. Special foods are still cooked and given to the cow and the crows, and the son of the household faces the sun and throws water from the pot as usual. But the *mantras* are not recited, for nobody knows them. Ten of the fifteen Brahman families in the village attend *sraddha* ceremonies only in other Brahman households and not in those of other castes.

NIORTHA-DASAHRA

Niortha, which is the same as Marriott's Naurtha (from *nau ratri,* or nine nights) [22] is a nine-day period following the moonless Amavas day in Asauj (September-October). *Dasahra* means "tenth." The celebrations at this time are carried out by the women and children and take place after dark. They do not interfere with the intensive agricultural work in progress during the day—the harvesting of millet and maize. Sugar cane is now ready to be cut, and the sowing of gram has begun. All the men are busy in the fields.

There is no worship of tools or weapons at Dasahra, as in some other parts of India such as Rajputana and Maharastra. Nor do the local celebrations include such patterns as the burning of effigies of Ravana or the performance of Ram Lila plays which tell the story of the Ramayana. Some members of the village go to Delhi to see these celebrations. The story about Ravana does not seem to be well known in Rampur, although those who have been to school are familiar with it. A Ram Lila troupe performed in Rampur about twelve years ago, but none have done so since.

The principal object of worship during the nine days in Rampur is a local deity named Sanjhi, who was once the wife of a Camar. It is said that the Camar came to the village to weave cloth, but the villagers hesitated to give him thread, because other weavers had run away with their yarn. The Camar, however, promised not to leave without letting them know beforehand. After he had collected a lot of yarn from the villagers, the Camar sent Sanjhi and their son to another village. The next day the weaver wound the yarn about his waist and went around telling the people that Sanjhi and his son had gone and that he was leaving soon with the yarn. The villagers were working in the fields at the time, and when they heard the Camar's words they simply thought he was joking. Nobody took him seriously. But the man left the village just as he said he would, and nobody ever saw him or the yarn again. A year later some boys tending cattle came upon Sanjhi. They took some sticks and beat her until she died; then they threw her into a pond. This is the story behind the festival,

[22] Marriott, 1955a:192, 200, 202, 215.

but no one in the village could explain how or why Sanjhi came to be worshipped.

On Amavas day the women of seven or eight neighboring families belonging to the same caste join to make a representation of Sanjhi. A portion of the outer wall of one of the houses is plastered with mud and cow dung. On this are affixed some star-shaped pieces of earthenware to form the figure of a woman. Ornaments and bangles of limestone are placed on the image. Every evening for nine days the girls and young women of the families gather around the Sanjhi. The women hang a lighted earthen lamp on the wall, place some food at Sanjhi's mouth, and sit around singing songs for two or three hours. When the singing is over, one of the families distributes *bakli*, made of boiled gram and salt.

On the eighth evening of Niortha the figure of a man carrying a little bag is made beside Sanjhi. He represents her brother bringing her some gifts. On Dasahra, the tenth day, just before sunset, the figure of Sanjhi is removed from the wall and a coat of whitewash is applied to the spot where her image has been. The figure of a peacock is then drawn over it. Sanjhi's face is removed and her body is placed in a basket which is carried to the village pond by a few girls. There Sanjhi's body is broken up and thrown into the water. Later in the evening all the women go singing to the pond. Sanjhi's face is now placed, along with a lighted lamp, in the bottom of a broken earthenware pitcher, which is then set afloat on the pond. The boys of the village gather around and laughingly throw stones at the floating Sanjhis, eventually drowning them all, to the shrieks and cries of the women.

After the drowning of their Sanjhis, the different groups of women return to their homes, singing songs. They sing before the house of each family which participates in the Sanjhi group, and are given ½ to 1 *sir* of grain at each home. The women then take the collected wheat to the Baniya's shop and buy sugar cubes, brown sugar, or roasted rice, which are distributed among the contributing families. Sanjhi is honored by all the families in the village, although the Jat women apparently resent the idea that Sanjhi was a Camar. The Arya Samaj seems to have had no influence on this festival, primarily because it is celebrated only by the women, who have generally been resistant to Arya Samaj teachings.

The tenth day, Dasahra, marks the beginning of the sowing of barley. The barley seedlings planted by farmers in house plots on Amavas have sprouted by this time. On Dasahra day a Brahman presents the head of each household with a few barley seedlings called *niorthas*, in return for which he is given ½ to 1 *sir* of grain. A Brahman may have to cover many

villages, which makes it impossible to visit everyone at Dasahra. He therefore brings *niorthas* on any of the ten festival days. The Brahman who
does this at Rampur is from another village, since no local Brahmans will
perform this function any more.

Among the Brahman families themselves the daughter or sister of a
household gives *niorthas* to her father or brother and receives from them
1 or 2 rupees in return. Unmarried girls are given only 4 to 8 annas.

No one in the village harvests sugar cane before Dasahra. On this day
the first five sugar-cane stalks are given to a Brahman or to a cow.

On Dasahra day women make ten dung cakes with barley seedlings
placed in each. These are left to dry, to be burned on Devuthani Gias in the
following month. This is said to be a test, to see whether or not the dung
cakes will spoil, as they would have done during the rainy season just
passed.

KARVA CAUTH

Cauth means "fourth," referring to the day of the month, for this festival
comes on the fourth day of Badi-Katik (October-November).[23] A *karva* is
a small pitcher which figures prominently in the festival. The festival is
celebrated by married women of the Brahman, Baniya, and Kumhar castes
to honor their husbands. During this time most of the men are busy in the
fields sowing wheat, barley and peas; they play no part in the festival,
beyond being the objects of veneration.

On the day before Karva Cauth the women referred to above observe a
fast. The next morning they bathe and then fill a water pitcher around
which they tie a yellow thread. The pitcher is kept near the hearth until
needed. At about 4:00 in the afternoon the women of the neighborhood
gather about an elderly Brahman woman to hear her tell the story of Karva
Cauth, which runs as follows:

A king had seven sons and one daughter. All the boys loved their sister
very much. When she fasted on Karva Cauth everyone else in the family
fasted too. In the evening one of her brothers set up a tent, another cooked
food, and another brought water. One of the brothers asked her to eat.
In the first morsel of food the princess found a hair, in the second a fly, and
at the third she learned of her husband's death. The princess left her food
at once and started to travel toward her husband's home, bowing to every

---

[23] McKim Marriott notes in a personal communication, "That's what the name seems
to imply, but in Kishan Garhi and in Wiser's village, the festival actually occurs on the
third day." In Ram Ratan's report on the Bhangis of Delhi, the fourth day is given
(1955:261).

woman whom she passed. On the way she met Parvati, Lord Siva's wife, and bowed to her too. Parvati blessed her with happiness and the recovery of her dead husband. She told the princess to take some blood from her little finger and to put it on the corpse. The princess did so, and her husband came back to life.

After they have heard this story, the women of the village pour water to the sun from their pitchers. Each gives ¼ to ½ *sir* of wheat to the storyteller; on the following day they present their pitchers to her too. There are some variations in this celebration. The Kumhars offer the water to the moon rather than to the sun, and they do not break their fast until that time. The Brahman women break their fast at sunset. The women of Jat, Camar, and other castes do not observe the festival at all. The reason given by Brahmans is that Jat women remarry on the death of a husband, while Brahman women do not.

A Brahman, Baniya, or Kumhar bride, who is staying at her parents' home at the time of Karva Cauth, keeps a fast and worships some *patasas* (sugar cakes), which she sends to her husband. He eats some of them and distributes the others to children.

This festival seems to have a fairly broad local distribution, having been described by Crooke for Hardoi, by Wiser for Mainpuri, and by McKim Marriott for Kishan Garhi. Marriott gives some alternative (but basically similar) versions of the legend and describes some aspects of the festival which are not paralleled in our data from Rampur:

Wives of all castes but the *Jat* caste fast by abstaining from bread during the day. While they are fasting, each wife completes a mural picture showing two "moons" and depicting the events of the Pitcher Fourth story. The story is told before each picture by one of several elderly ladies, mostly Brahmans, who make a specialty of story-telling. . . . The fast continues until the real moon rises in the evening. Then each wife goes to where she can see the moon, sketches a sacred crossroads at her feet, and pours water onto the crossroads out of a spouted earthenware pitcher as an offering to the moon. She next worships the moons of her mural picture by pressing food against their "mouths"—a few wives also make mud figurines of a goddess at this point—and then breaks her fast after serving food to the men of the family.[24]

HOI

Hoi comes three days after Karva Cauth, on the seventh day of Badi-Katik. As in Karva Cauth, the festival is celebrated by women who fast and come together to hear an edifying story told. The men are still busy work-

[24] Marriott, 1955a:203-4.

ing in the fields, sowing wheat, barley, and peas, while the seed stocks of millet are being removed. Karva Cauth was in honor of husbands; Hoi is in honor of children. Only the women who have children fast on this day; others do not.

In the morning the women bathe and fill two small pitchers with water. Some fill one with grain. As in Karva Cauth, the pitchers are kept near the hearth. The fast is broken at about 4:00 in the afternoon, when the women of an extended family gather together. Then one of the women, usually a member of the family, tells the following story:

Once upon a time there was a king who had seven married sons and one daughter. One day the princess and her seven sisters-in-law had to go and dig some mud from a pond. The sisters-in-law all made excuses; they had to go and ease themselves. So the princess was left alone. She began to dig and filled up all the others' buckets. But in the process she unwittingly killed Hoi's children, who lived in the earth. Then Hoi came. In revenge he took away her womb.

When the seven sisters-in-law came back, the princess told them of how Hoi had stolen her womb. They were sorry to think that she could not bear children now. One of them, the eldest, asked Hoi to take her own womb in exchange for the princess'. So Hoi returned the princess' womb and took the other instead. Then the eight girls came home.

The eldest girl told her mother-in-law that she had given her womb to Hoi. The mother-in-law was furious and turned her out of the house, saying that she was of no use any more.

In her wanderings the outcast girl came upon a cow all covered with insects. She took care of the cow and looked after it for twelve years. Then she gave birth to a child. When she distributed pancakes to relatives, announcing the birth, the news reached the ears of her mother-in-law. The mother-in-law asked the barber's wife, who had brought the pancakes, to take her to see the baby. So she found her daughter-in-law with her little son. When the old woman asked how this had happened, the daughter-in-law told about how she had looked after the cow for twelve years.

While telling this story, the narrator puts a few grains in a tumbler of water at the end of every sentence. Then, when the story is finished, she throws the contents toward the sun. Then all the women go home and eat the food they have prepared. Sometimes the storyteller is given a few handfuls of grain by each of the women present. The water in the small pitchers filled that day is kept for later use at the Gobardhan festival. If the grains are kept, they are given to children who go and buy sweets from the Baniya.

Fig. 37.   An elderly Jat woman in her native attire.

The purpose of the fast, it is said, is to protect children. Only some of the families prepare special foods at Hoi—*halva* or rice cooked with brown sugar. The Kumhars get a little profit from the small pitchers used on this day. They receive ¼ *sir* of millet or maize for each pitcher. All the women in Rampur observe these customs. They are not likely to die out soon. It is said that formerly Brahman women were called in to tell the Hoi story in different families, but nowadays one of the older women of the family tells the story instead, and Brahman women are no longer summoned.

Hoi seems to have a very limited regional distribution. It is not mentioned by either Wiser or Marriott in their lists of festivals. However, an account of Hoi appears in Ram Ratan's study of the Bhangis of Delhi:

On this festival women first plaster some space on some wall of the home in the evening with a mixture of cow-dung and water and clay and on it draw a woman-like figurine. Then one nail is fixed in the wall near the figurine, and it is by this nail that a silver necklace consisting of as many silver beads as the number of sons in the house, is hung. The necklace also has a flat piece of silver, with engraved figures of a cow with its calf. The following articles are put before the figurine: Four pots full of water, an earthen lamp full of ghee which is lit on that very spot, some cooked rice, "Sivian" (a kind of dish) and some "patasha" (a kind of sweet). The women sit before the "Hoi" figurine and an old woman tells a story to them. This story is never told to any male—adult or child for, in the opinion of the women, it brings bad luck to the males.[25]

GIRDI-DIVALI-GOBARDHAN

Divali, the festival of lights, which is popular all over India, is one of the four main festivals of the village. It falls on Amavas day in Katik. Girdi comes the day before, Gobardhan comes on the following day. By this time there is less activity in the fields. Ploughing is nearly over, although the sowing of wheat and barley are in progress. The weather is cooler, and people are beginning to wear warmer clothing.

On Amavas day the cattle are not yoked but are decorated with a reddish paste made of red oxide and oil. Spots are daubed on the animals' sides and faces; their horns are painted red, green, or blue, and peacock feathers may be attached to their heads, while their necks are hung about with bead necklaces and leather bands clinking with little bells. There is much competition in decorating the cattle. While the Jats are bedaubing their cows and oxen, the Kumhars do the same with the asses used for carrying clay. Domestic animals may be given brown sugar to eat on this day.

[25] Ratan, 1955.

The houses are refurbished too. Few people go to work in the fields now, for every family is busy with house cleaning. A new coat of plaster or whitewash may be applied to the walls, while oil is administered to door hinges and wagon axles. Everything in the house is cleaned and polished. Some people draw flower-shaped figures on their doors. Most of the women prepare special foods—*halva,* rice pudding, *puris,* etc.

The Brahmans who celebrate Girdi light five small lamps and one big lamp on that day, but most of the other castes do not do so, preferring to combine Girdi and Divali in one celebration. It is on the day of Divali, then, that the lamps are lit all over the village. Little earthen lamps line the tops of the houses, while others are placed on carts, yokes, and implements used by the household. More lamps appear in cattlesheds. Children from every family in the village go to place lamps at the shrines for Bhuiyan, Gurgaon-wali Mata, Kainthi-wali Mata, and other village godlings and local *pirs.* Children enjoy Divali. They get toys and candies and they enjoy going about looking at other people's houses in the evening, with all the lights and excitement about. By 9:00 P.M., however, everyone in the family is at home for the worship of Laksmi, goddess of wealth. The head of the family puts money and ornaments in a big metal dish and places it near an oil lamp, applies turmeric marks to the money and ornaments, and repeats some Sanskrit *mantras,* if he knows them, or else says, "Goddess Laksmi, come to me once again during the coming year." Among the Kumhars a silver rupee is placed near the lamp, with a turmeric mark on it. Sometimes the head of the family prefers to worship Laksmi alone, in order to hide from other members of the family how much money he has.

It is the custom to leave a light burning all night in the house, and to leave the doors open, so that Laksmi can come in to bless the household. (It is believed that Laksmi will not enter an untidy of poorly lit home.) But since there is a possibility that thieves may enter as well, some people now lock the front door.

Sidha, consisting of rice, brown sugar, and *ghi,* is sent to daughters or sisters at this time. Shirts or veils may also be sent for their children. The expenses differ for different families, some preferring to send cash amounting to from 2 to 5 rupees. The Baniya in the village sends sweets to his neighbors on Divali and starts new account books. Of the various castes, the Kumhars seem to benefit the most. They make earthen lamps for the families in the village and receive 4 or 5 *sirs* of grain from each. However, they are not satisfied with this amount and believe that they should receive 8 *sirs.*

Local "explanations" for the celebration of Divali correspond with those given elsewhere in India and are related to the Hindu Great Tradition. One is the yearly coming of Laksmi; another refers to the kindling of lights by Raja Bali, and a third attributes it to the return of Rama from the conquest of Lanka (Ceylon). The Arya Samaj supports still another rationale for the festival: they say that on this day their leader Swami Dayanand achieved enlightenment. But this interpretation was not offered by even the most staunch Arya Samajist families in the village.

The Gobardhan festival comes on the day after Amavas. On this morning the pitchers set aside at Hoi are brought out, and the water from them is used to clean a place in the family courtyard. Here a mound of cow dung is accumulated and shaped into the crude figure of a man. A cot is placed over it to protect it during the day. At about sunset the head of the family takes a metal plate on which he places a rupee or a silver ornament, a few roasted rice grains, and some turmeric. He lights a lamp placed in the middle of the cow-dung man and pours some buttermilk into the creature's mouth. Then the family head walks around the figure seven times followed by the male members of the family. He pours some water and places some roasted rice on each of the four corners of the figure. After the last round, he sets the plate down near the legs of the cow-dung man and puts a turmeric mark on it. Then roasted rice grains are distributed among all the family members.

A Brahman usually announces the proper time to make cow dung into dung cakes. Nine to eleven cakes are usually made on this day; it must be an odd number (except for thirteen, which is unlucky), for even numbers suggest an end, while odd numbers indicate progress. Then the dung cakes are placed for storage in a *bitaura*. Formerly, dung cakes were not made between Jaith-ka Dasahra (May-June) and Asauj (September-October). But after Partition dung cakes sold at high prices in Delhi, and people began to make them throughout the year.

The Great Tradition "explanation" for this festival is known only to one or two Brahmans in Rampur. This is the story about the locking up of cattle by Indra and their release by Lord Krsna. Indra, in revenge, poured rain in torrents, but Krsna protected the world by holding up a mountain over it. Later the cattle dung was collected and the Gobardhan festival initiated. The reason given by the villagers for celebrating this festival is simply that cow dung (*gobar*) is wealth (*dhan*), for it is used as fuel, manure, and for other purposes.

McKim Marriott, who describes this festival as given at Kishan Garhi, translates Gobardhan as "Cow-Nourisher" (*gow + vardhana*), later transformed by village etymology to *gobar + dhan.* In his account of the Krsna legend he refers to a hill named Gobardhan, about 40 miles from Kishan Garhi, as being the hill which Krsna is said to have lifted up as an umbrella to protect the people and their cows. Marriott's description of this festival is worth quoting:

The sacred hill of the *Purana* has become in each household yard a literal pile of cowdung, shaped into a rough homunculus with four embracing walls appended to its neck, and decorated on top with "trees" of straw and cotton. Within these walls are crowded rude loaves representing all of the cows, bullocks and buffaloes that the family owns or would like to own. To secure any possible benefit to the family's milk and fodder supply, feeding troughs, milking vessels, churns, etc., are also represented in fecal model. The family cowboy is there, too, modelled in dung—the real family cowboy gets a rupee on this day—and so is a model tank to which the cowboy can take the animals for water. The women and children of each family finish this dung construction by day; in the evening all of the agnates of each family worship it jointly by placing a lamp on its navel, winding a thread around its trees, and shouting in solemn procession, "Long live Grandfather Cowdung Wealth!" Members of the Weaver caste of Kishan Garhi add their bit, too, for on the next morning they must be paid to sing a Cowdung Wealth awakening song before the dung image can be broken up for use as daily fuel. But a portion of the cowdung remaining from the celebration must be set aside; this portion is re-shaped and scored into the form of an enormous cracker; the cracker is dried and preserved as sacred until it can be contributed to the great annual all-village bonfire at the *Holi* festival six months later.[26]

Mukerji says that Gobardhan is purely a cattle feast, observed almost exclusively by the Ahir (herder) caste, but this does not agree with our data or with Marriott's. He also states that Gobardhan has died out except in remote villages: "Except in such parts of the United Provinces as are not yet traversed by a railway line, this old festival may be said to have become altogether defunct."[27] However, it is still observed in some of the villages which have been studied in the area—in Rampur, Kishan Garhi, and Wiser's village of Karimpur, and—far from being limited to marginal areas remote from the railway lines—it is celebrated by the Bhangis of Delhi.[28]

DEVUTHANI GIAS

Devuthani is derived from *dev*—god, and *uthana*—to wake, and refers to the awakening of the gods who have been asleep between Bhadalia

---

[26] Marriott, 1955a:200. See also the similar account in Briggs, 1920:119; Crooke, 1896, 2:296.

[27] Mukerji, 1918:174, 175.

[28] Ratan, 1955:263.

Naumi in Sadh (June-July) and Devuthani Gias, which falls on the eleventh (gias) day of Sudi-Katik. Marriages cannot take place while the gods are asleep, for they are invoked at weddings. The marriage season begins, therefore, after Devuthani Gias. This is a woman's festival in which men play no part. Boys are warned to stay away and are told that they will get eczema if they come near the women. The men are apt to be working in the fields as usual, although the sowing of wheat and barley is nearly over, and the Savan crop has been harvested. Winter is on the way.

The women prepare corma, semian (sweet burned needles), and other delicacies on this day, but fast until evening. In the afternoon a group of small girls who generally belong to the same extended family go around to the component family households, singing songs. They are given ½ to 1 sir of grain by each family, which they sell to buy roasted rice grains for distribution among themselves. In the evening all the women of one or two neighboring extended families get together, bringing with them the corma they have made. They set up a pile of ten dung cakes which were prepared at the last Dasahra festival. Then the oldest lady present sets fire to the heap. The women sit around the fire, eat their corma, and sing songs about the awakening of the gods. Unmarried girls sing a refrain, "Harnarain teri puchri; Desodah tera biyah" ("O Harnarain, your tail; God grant your marriage"), while burning the tips of the strings of their skirts. One informant interpreted this song to express relief that the period of waiting for marriage was over. The singing continues until the fire burns out. Then the women go home, eat what they have prepared, and set aside some of the food for the gods. This food was formerly given to a Brahman, but is now presented to a daughter or sister of a neighboring family.

On Devuthani Gias the women draw foot-shaped figures made with red earth and water on the walls of their homes. One explanation for these figures (which always outnumber the members of the family) is that they are a magical device for making the family grow. Another interpretation is that they represent the gods who have awakened and are walking about.

Ram Ratan describes the festival as observed by the Bhangis of Delhi: "In the morning, the women plaster with clay and cow-dung some space on the wall and on the ground, in a corner of their house, where they draw a female figurine with long lines called 'Harnarain ki Poochdi,' and as many footprints in number as there are persons, animals, and birds in the house. Sweetmeats, pudding, fried bread (puri), 'Khir,' and a lighted lamp are kept there, and are covered with a big vessel 'parant.' The women and girls keep fast. At about nine in the evening, women gather and beat the big vessels 'parants,' and sing songs for awakening the gods 'devtas' who are supposed to be in sleep." One of these songs is translated as follows:

> Gods go to sleep in the month of Mas [Magh].
> Gods get up in the month of Katak.
> I make them rise.
> My hand is put in a hanging basket.
> There are four breads in the hanging basket.
> Should I give them to the Brahmin or should I eat them?
> I give a cow with a broken horn to the Brahmin.
> The cow urinates in the house and makes water in front of the house.[29]

GANGA-JUMNA NAHAN

Fifteen days after Divali, on the full-moon day, it is customary to go and bathe in the Jumna River at Delhi or in the Ganges River at Garh. The sowing is now finished, and work in the fields has slowed down. So it is generally possible for about twenty or thirty families from Rampur to leave for Garh (about 50 miles away) in their bullock carts. They leave five or six days before Nahan, with the members of one extended family sharing a cart. (A well-to-do family may take along a servant as well.) All of the carts travel together and halt together for lunch, evening meals, and sleep. Sexual joking is tabooed, for this is a pilgrimage to a sacred place. Hymns in praise of Rama are sung along the way.

On reaching Garh the pilgrims fix up mat tents on the river bank. It is believed that bathing washes away the sins incurred during harvesting—the beating of cattle, etc.; besides, it is part of one's religious duty to bathe on this occasion. After an early-morning dip in the stream, the bathers give food to a Brahman or to a *sadhu* (holy man). The latter may also be given clothes by a woman who had formerly vowed to do so if blessed with a child. Everyone goes to the big fair at Garh, which is attended by about a hundred thousand people. Clothes, ornaments, ploughs, etc., may be bought and religious discourses listened to.

On the same evening or the following morning the people return home, taking with them some Ganges water and a few candy balls and roasted rice grains for distribution among the neighbors. Returning pilgrims also present food to a Brahman who, in return, gives 8 annas or a rupee to the daughter or sister of the household. It is only members of the agricultural castes who use bullock carts for transport; others, like the Camars, go by train.

---

[29] Ratan, 1955:267. See also a brief account of this festival in Crooke, 1896, 2:300.

Katik (October-November) is considered to be a sacred month for taking baths. Childless women and unmarried girls of more than ten years of age take a bath every day throughout the month. On every Sunday during the month they light little earthenware lamps near the place where they bathe, and also leave a handful of grain for birds and animals. On the full-moon day those who can afford it go to the Ganges or the Jumna for a dip, while those who stay at home take a bath at the local well or pond and give something in charity to a Brahman or a beggar. Elderly people and young girls keep a fast from the afternoon before Nahan until the rising of the moon. Those who go to the Ganges or the Jumna eat only after bathing in the river.

MAKAR SANKRANT

"The first few days of Pausa are unlucky," writes Mrs. Sinclair Stevenson, "but on Sankranti the sun ceases to travel towards the inauspicious south, where is the abode of death, and begins to move towards the north, and this changes everything." She goes on to add that Sankranti is followed by two months fortunate for marriages. It is the great day of the year for alms giving.[30] We are told by Gupte that the festival, which marks the transit of the sun at the Tropic of Capricorn, is the beginning of the day of the gods and the night of the demons.[31] Makar Sankrant may fall either in the month of Poh (December-January) or Magh (January-February). It comes at a time when there is little work being done in the village, beyond the preparation of brown sugar. Although the weather is cold, everyone must take a bath and wash one's hair to avoid getting "heat in the brain." A less arduous custom at Sankrant is the eating of rice pudding, pancakes, *halva, ghi,* and brown sugar. Charity is no longer given to the Brahmans at Rampur, except by a few families in the village; but the cattle are still fed, every family putting a little fodder near the village pond where the cows gather. There are protests about this custom, however, and the amount of grain given has been diminishing. *Sidha* is given to the daughters and sisters of a family, together with some bangles and clothes for the children.

It is also customary to patch up quarrels at Makar Sankrant, particularly those between a married girl and her in-laws. The girl, accompanied by other women of the household, goes singing to meet her parents-in-law, who have gone out to the fields early in the morning to wait at an appointed

[30] Stevenson, 1920:272 ff.
[31] Gupte, 1919.

place. They enact a hypothetical quarrel in which the in-laws have supposedly left the house; the bride begs pardon and brings them back home
with gifts. She may give a shawl or a blanket to her father-in-law and a veil
or a shirt to her mother-in-law—clothes which she originally brought from
her parents' home. The girl may also put some sugar into her mother-in-
law's mouth—no doubt to sweeten it. The parents-in-law give nothing in return except their blessings. Gifts may also be given to the husband's older
brothers and their wives, who reciprocate with a small gift. These customs,
however, are maintained for only the first two or three years after marriage.

BASANT PANCAMI

Basant Pancami, which means "Yellow Fifth Day," or "Spring Fifth Day,"
falls on the fifth day of Sudi-Magh, at a time when the fields are full of
mustard seed and yellow flowers. It is a pleasant spring-like time of year,
when there is little work to be done in the fields. It used to be the custom
to wear yellow clothing on Basant Pancami. This is still done by the local
Baniya family and a few others in the village. Starting on Basant Pancami
wood is collected for Holi, particularly a pole or "foundation stick" for the
bonfire. A fast is observed by some women at Rampur, and some cook
special foods, but in general little attention is paid to Basant Pancami. It is
not mentioned by McKim Marriott in his list of festivals at Kishan Garhi,
but he informs us that it is observed there on a small scale.[32] No fairs are
held in the neighborhood of Rampur on this occasion.

SIV RATRI

Siv Ratri, or Bholai-ka Barat (Bholai being one of Siva's names), is a
festival in honor of Siva which falls on the thirteenth day of Badi-Phagun
(February-March). After an early-morning bath, the villagers fast until
about 2:00 P.M. No cereals are eaten then, but *lapsi*, berries, and *cholai* (a
small millet)-seed sweets may be consumed. At about 1:00 P.M. the women
of Rampur gather in extended family groups and walk together, singing, to
Siva's temple at Rasulpur. Each woman carries a metal dish with a little
earthen *ghi* lamp, a few berries, some flour, and a pot of water. She pours
the water on the cylindrical stone *linga* which represents Siva and places
her *ghi* lamp there, together with the berries and other things she has
brought along. These offerings are taken by the Gosain, who lights a lamp

---

[32] "Near Kishan Garhi observances were much more extensive in towns and cities.
It is a major holiday of Arya Samajists and of other sects such as Sikhs and Siva Nara-
yanis." Personal communication.

in the Siva temple every day. This office is said to have formerly been held by a Brahman, but nowadays a Gosain has been hired by the Baniya who built the temple.[33]

After bathing Siva's *linga*, the women come home again, singing songs. Their fast is broken by drinking whey, prepared by adding fresh water to milk. No cereals are eaten until the following day. About three-fourths of the women in Rampur observe this fast—ill or pregnant women being required to abstain from it. Only about a dozen men observe the fast, however. Those who do so go to the temple early in the morning, so as not to be laughed at by others. (This, at least, is what some of the villagers say.) Some of the local schoolboys, who are told about the festival by their teachers, fast on Siv Ratri. The fast is observed mainly by Brahmans, Jats, Baniyas, and Kumhars, but not by Camars, Bhangis, and Dhobis. Untouchables are not admitted to the temple to see Siva's *linga*.

The Siva temple at Rasulpur attracts women from the three adjoining villages, including Rampur. But there are larger temples, with inns for pilgrims, at Madipur (5 miles from Rampur), Kundal (9 miles), and Seoli (12 miles), where there are big fairs, with wrestling matches, etc., on Siv Ratri. About twenty people from Rampur go to one of these temples and attend the fair.

HOLI-DULHENDI

Holi, which comes on the fifteenth day of Sudi-Phagun (February-March) and lasts through the first day of Cait, is one of the most popular and widespread Hindu festivals, having a particular appeal for the lower castes and younger age groups. A month of preparation leads up to Holi. At the time of Basant Pancami the main pole for the Holi bonfire is selected, and boys start to collect wood for the fire. (Wood is scarce in this region, so the boys keep close watch on their firewood.) During this time, too, the women of Rampur gather in extended family groups in the evening to sing songs. Young girls do the singing during the earlier half of Phagun, but they are joined by the older women after Amavas. Some women throw water on others, not just on the day of Holi, but throughout the month of Phagun.

---

[33] According to Ibbetson, Brahmans should not be temple priests at Siva temples. "No Brahmans can partake of the offerings to Shiv, or be priest in his temple, though they will worship him and sometimes assist in the ceremonies, thus deviating from the strict rule of the original cult. On the Sheoratri, on the thirteenth of Sawan and Phagan, such people as have fasted will go to the Shivala; but it is seldom entered on any other days." Ibbetson, 1883:147. Ibbetson states (1883:146) that Siva temples are built without exception by Baniyas and their priests are Gosains.

Fig. 38. Some of the village children at play.

On Holi day itself the women fast until late afternoon, but they keep themselves busy in the morning by collecting color pots and by preparing food—rice, pancakes, brown sugar, and *halva*. In the afternoon, at around 2:00, the women walk in extended family groups, singing songs, as they approach the Holi pyre, all dressed in their best clothes and ornaments. Every woman carries a metal dish laden with cow-dung wreaths, cotton strings, turmeric, brown sugar, and a pot of water. Some also have small *ghi* lamps made of flour. The women's palms and soles are stained with henna, applied the night before. On reaching the Holi pyre, each woman takes off her shoes and walks around the pyre once, twice, or three times, pouring water from her pot and placing cow-dung wreaths on each of the corners. She ties some yarn around the pyre, and if she has brought a lamp with her, lights it there. Turmeric marks are placed on the pyre and on her children as well, and flour and brown sugar are given to the Brahman from Rasulpur who sits there, accepting offerings. After this worship the women return, singing, to their homes and break their fast.

In the evening both men and women go to the Holi pyre, but not in their best clothing. They wear clothes which are clean, but which they do not mind dirtying. In former days a Brahman fixed the proper time for lighting the pyre, and was the one who started the fire. (As soon as he had done so, he used to run with a burning dung cake toward the pond, which signified the sea.) But nowadays any boy may start the fire. As it begins to burn, children set off firecrackers, while the women continue singing songs. But as the fire mounts higher, the people start to throw water on each other and rub *gulal* (red oxide) into each other's faces. This may develop into a conflict between the sexes, with much shrieking and laughter, as young girls throw red powder at their husbands' younger brothers, and vice versa. Older people are not so actively involved as the young in this horseplay, which may go on for two or three hours. As it finally dies down, people go back to their homes to sing and dance until late at night.

Sometimes people put barley stems into the Holi fire, to test the ripeness of the crop; they also watch the direction of the flames, for it is believed that this shows which part of the country will be benefited.[34]

[34] Mrs. Stevenson reports the same traditions: "Directly the fire is lit, the wise old people of the village watch the direction of the flames with the keenest interest, for the land over which they and the smoke blow will be specially fertile during the year. In the same way, after the fire is out, and when all is over save the shouting, they dig up the pot of grain. . . . If all the grain is well cooked, there will be no fear of famine; if it is well cooked in one part, say the part of the pot facing north, and uncooked towards the southern part of the pot, then the lands to the south of the village will be unfertile, and even famine-stricken, whilst the northern fields will yield a bumper crop." Stevenson, 1920:284.

The Great Tradition legend of Holika is told at Rampur to account for the festival. The legend seems to have variations in different parts of India, but these generally agree in having a hero (Prahlad) who is not burned while he is held in the lap of his aunt, Holika, as she sits in a blazing pyre. In the Rampur version Prahlad is a devotee of Rama; the villain of the story is his father, who tries to make Prahlad abandon the worship of Rama. The father makes several attempts to murder his son, but fails and is finally killed in the end.

On Dulhendi, the day after Holi, the celebrations continue, with some interesting modifications. The women are now forbidden to throw water at the men, while the men may continue to throw water at the women. But the women have the significant privilege of using sticks to beat up the men, including those of higher castes. Brother-in-law—sister-in-law rivalry continues, but now a girl may give a drubbing to her husband's younger brother. One young man was given seventeen strokes of the stick (until it broke) by his sister-in-law one year, after he threw some cow urine at her. A woman may also beat her husband's older brother, but not her father-in-law. Incidentally, the women keep their faces respectfully covered with veils while beating their menfolk. Girls do not beat their brothers, only brothers-in-law and those outside the family.

Some lower-caste women hold up people passing through the streets and demand money from them. If the man pays, he is allowed to pass; otherwise he is given a drubbing. A few years ago a subinspector was held up in this way, but he saved himself with a 5-rupee note. (A rupee is the usual tariff.) A Brahman from Rampur, on the other hand, was struck so severely across the legs that they ached a month later. Cases of this kind are not taken to the courts, and no doubt some people take advantage of this immunity, beating being sometimes administered at the instigation of a woman's husband. Most of the horseplay at Holi, however, takes place among the members of a few joint families who play together.[35]

The women enjoy the advantages they possess on Dulhendi. Of about twenty women interviewed in five different groups, all expressed unanimous enthusiasm for the custom. They said that men beat women on all the other days of the year; why shouldn't there be a day when the situation is reversed? Not all the women wield sticks on Dulhendi, but those who do not can look on as spectators and get at least vicarious satisfaction.

The villagers claim that the use of sticks is an innovation, introduced

[35] McKim Marriott informs us that this is not the case at Kishan Garhi or in its neighboring villages, "where sometimes all castes and groups pitch in, Bhangi women beating and joking with Brahmen men, etc." Personal communication.

only about five years ago. Formerly, women beat their husbands symbolically with their veils. Then the veils gave way to little sticks, and the little sticks to larger sticks. Now 2½-yard sticks are used for beatings. However this may be, the custom seems to be widespread in India and not very recent. Fuchs describes the festival of Jhenda, five days after Holi, in which the women of his untouchable group, the Balahis, wield sticks unmercifully: "The women do not spare the men, and many a man feels the pains of his sore and swollen back for days after. Some women have taken a glass of country liquor or a pinch of *bhang* (hemp) before the performance, to bolster up their courage. They are half-drunk and so excited by the noise and the fighting that at last they attack the whole crowd of village people who stand around shouting and laughing and enjoying the whole thing immensely. If the women can get hold of the *patel* [headman] and the *kotwal* [police officer], they beat them until these men buy themselves free by a small present." [36] Briggs also describes Camar women as carrying sticks on the days after Holi and demanding gifts from people.[37]

Holi is one of the four main festivals of the year at which *sidha* is sent to the daughters or sisters of a household. Some families provide only rice, brown sugar, and a rupee, while others send from 2 to 5 rupees in cash. A brother or nephew may take the presents to the girl a few days before Holi.

AMAVAS

An account of village festivals would be incomplete without mention of Amavas, the monthly moonless day. According to Mrs. Stevenson, it is an inauspicious day, on which one should not take more than one meal, and should not wash clothes or use soap when bathing. Women should not sew or grind grain, and men should not hunt or fish. Carpenters, coolies, and artisans do no work on Amavas.[38]

In Rampur these taboos are not closely observed. Everyone works on this day, although some people go to bathe in the Jumna River. Oxen are given a holiday, however, and are not put to the yoke. If Amavas falls on a Monday—a sacred occasion—about a dozen people from Rampur go to bathe in the Jumna. It used to be customary to feed Brahmans on Amavas, but this is no longer widely observed, partly due to the Jats' reluctance to feed the Brahmans, and partly because the Brahmans consider the charity beneath their dignity. Some people feed a *capati* to a cow instead.

[36] Fuchs, 1951:300-301.
[37] Briggs, 1920:118.
[38] Stevenson, 1920:260 ff.

DISCUSSION

We come now to a general consideration of the festivals. Before turning to the questions raised in our introduction, we may note some broad characteristics and general patterns. Eighteen of the twenty festivals celebrated in Rampur are religious festivals. Tij and Basant Pancami are the exceptions, but of these the latter is barely observed, although it is a national holiday.[39] Tij is thus the only secular festival of importance. National holidays such as Republic Day (January 20), Independence Day (August 15), and Gandhi's birthday are not celebrated in the village, nor are the holidays set aside for Muslim, Christian, and Sikh festivals. Bharata Milap and Baisakhi are other national holidays ignored at Rampur.

About half the Rampur festivals are widespread in Hindu India: Rakhi Bandhan (Silono), Janam Astami, Kanagat (Sraddha), Niortha-Dasahra, Divali, Devuthani Gias, Makar Sankrant, Holi, Siv Ratri, Basant Pancami, and the Devi festivals. Some have a fairly wide regional distribution: Tij, Karva Cauth, and Guga Naumi. Ghantal Deo and Hoi have a very limited distribution, although Hoi is found in the city of Delhi. These two festivals, as well as Guga Naumi, are not given in Marriott's list of the festivals at Kishan Garhi, nor do they appear in Wiser's list for Karimpur. Rampur, on the other hand, does not have two festivals mentioned by Marriott—Burho Babu-ki Puja ("Old Clerk's Worship"), and Kue-ka Devata-ka Mela ("Fair of the Well Godling"),[40] and it lacks some of those listed by Wiser, such as Nag Pancami, Khan Bahadur-ka Mela, Bhim Ekadasi, and Anant Chaudas.[41] All of these villages, then, although they are not far apart from one another, have certain local festivals in addition to the more familiar great Hindu festivals. At Rampur there are some deified human beings, such as Guga *pir* and Sanjhi, whose cults are regional, while other deities who are venerated elsewhere are given little recognition. Ganesa Caturthi in honor of Ganapati or Ganesa, the elephant-headed god, is not observed at Rampur; nor is Hanuman given homage as in the south.

According to Ibbetson, the people of the Karnal tract with which he was concerned (located close to Rampur and with a similar ethnic composition) are Vaishnavas. The name of Visnu is rarely mentioned there. "But under the name of Ram and Narain he is the great god of the country. . . .

[39] As noted in footnote 32, Basant Pancami is a religious holiday for some sects in other communities, and it is possible that Tij may have religious associations elsewhere. Both may have been religious festivals in the past but are not now at Rampur.

[40] Marriott, 1955a:192.

[41] Wiser, 1936:84 ff.

He is worshipped under the name of Ram by Rajputs only; under the name of Narain by other castes." [42] But the present inhabitants of Rampur could not well be called Vaishnavites. The latter term seems to have been used quite broadly by British administrators.[43] Elsewhere Ibbetson paints a rather different picture: "The student who, intimately acquainted with the Hindu pantheon as displayed in the sacred texts, should study the religion of the Hindus of the Tract, would find himself in strangely unfamiliar company. It is true that all men know of Shiv and of Vishnu;" [footnote: "Brahma is never mentioned save by a Brahman; and many of the villagers hardly know his name"] ". . . but his daily concerns in his work-a-day world are with the host of deities whose special business it is to regulate the matters by which he is most nearly affected." [44] Indeed, in this region of early Aryan settlement, where the local religion, as Marriott puts it, "must have been subjected to constant Sanskritization over a period of about three thousand years," [45] one is surprised to find so much that is outside of the Sanskritic Hindu Great Tradition—such as the worship of the Mata deities, Bhuiyan, Ghantal Deo, Guga *pir,* Sanjhi, and Hoi. For Kishan Garhi—about 100 miles from Rampur—Marriott points out that fifteen of the nineteen village festivals are sanctioned by one or more Sanskrit texts. These include: Ekadasi, Patthvari Puja, Pitar ki Puja, Tij, Rakhi Bandhan, Janam Astami, Kanagat, Naurtha, Dasahra, Divali, Gobardhan, Devuthan, Sakat, Siv Ratri, and Holi.[46] Twelve of these festivals are found in Rampur. But, as Marriott also points out, these festivals represent only a small selection out of the total annual cycle of festivals which find sanction in the Great Tradition, and the festivals contain much ritual which has no evident connection with the Great Tradition.[47]

In how many of the festivals of Rampur do the great deities of the Hindu tradition play an important part? We can point to only five with certainty: Siv Ratri, in which Siva is honored; Janam Astami and Gobardhan, in

[42] Ibbetson, 1883:146.

[43] In Rose's glossary (based partly on Ibbetson's material) we read that "The Hindu, generally speaking, is not a Shaiva but a Vaishnava, that is to say, he does not eat flesh, onions, or garlic, and does not drink spirits. The main features of the Hindu pantheon are revealed to him in Vishnu or the incarnations of Vishnu. . . . He is, in fact, the orthodox Hindu, and in our returns the word Vaishnav means, as a rule, little more than this. . . . The numbers returned at our census as Vaishnavas exceed greatly the numbers returned under any other sect." Rose, 1919, *1:* 366.

[44] Ibbetson, 1883:142.

[45] Marriott, 1955a:193.

[46] Marriott, 1955a:193.

[47] Marriott, 1955a:194.

which Krsna is given homage; Divali, in which Laksmi is worshipped; and Devuthani Gias, in which the gods are awakened.[48]

We had the general impression that the great Hindu deities were not well known to the villagers of Rampur.[49] The stories of the Ramayana and Mahabharata, for example, did not seem to be very familiar to the peasants. "The Ramayana is to the peasants of North India what the Bible" is to Englishmen, says O'Malley.[50] But many of the villagers do not know this Bible very well, as is evidenced by the replies to a part of our questionnaire in which they were asked to identify mythical figures drawn from the Ramayana and Mahabharata. The familiar tale of Ravana is not well known to the villagers. This story is usually enacted by Ram Lila troupes at the time of the Dasahra celebrations in North India, but no such performances have been held at Rampur for the past twelve years or more, and the younger villagers are not familiar with the legend, except for those who have learned it at school.

The general impression remains, then, that the Hindu Great Tradition is not so familiar to these villagers as one might have expected, whereas the worship of local godlings and disease goddesses, etc., is very important. This supports the statement by Rose quoted at the beginning of this chapter.

THEMES AND RECURRENT PATTERNS

To turn to another question, what are the themes and purposes of the festivals? Do they have any recurrent, common patterns, or is there much differentiation? To be sure, the "purpose" of festivals is not always clear-cut; they may serve multiple ends. With this proviso, the following rough grouping may serve: two festivals are for protection from sickness (Basora, Devi-ki Karahi), three are for purification (Jaith-ka Dasahra, Ganga-Jumna Nahan, Makar Sankrant), six are for the honoring of deities (Ghantal Deo, Janam Astami, Guga Naumi, Niortha-Dasahra, Devuthani Gias, Siv Ratri). The other festivals are not so easily grouped. Kanagat is for the honoring of ancestors, Karva Cauth for the honoring of husbands, and Hoi for the honoring and protection of children. Tij, Basant Pancami, and perhaps Holi may be described as festivals which celebrate the change of seasons.

In general, it does not seem that there is any major theme or emphasis

---

[48] According to Crooke (1896, 2:300) the purpose of the latter festival is to awaken Visnu, but in Rampur it is "the gods" in general who are summoned. The same appears in Ram Ratan's study of the Bhangis of Delhi.

[49] See Chapter 7 for a fuller discussion of this question.

[50] O'Malley, 1935:58.

running through all the festivals, such as some ethnologists have found in the ceremonial cycle of groups such as the Hopi or Navaho, in which a stress on fertility or health may be detected in most phases of ritualism. Rather, one gets an impression here of diversification, as if the festival cycle were trying to cover as much ground as possible, giving a due amount of homage to a variety of gods, spirits, and human relationships. Marriott has commented upon this diversification from a different though related angle in his discussion of Kishan Garhi: "There is no temple of the whole village, no one cremation ground, no sacred tank or well. Instead, dozens of different trees and stones and tiny shrines are made objects of worship separately by members of the many caste and lineage groups." [51]

If over-all common themes are not evident in the festivals, there are some ritual and social practices which do recur frequently. Food is offered at most festivals—to the gods, or to Brahmans, beggars, bystanders, cows, or crows; and sweets are frequently distributed. Mud is dug up from the river on some occasions (Devi-ki Karahi, Ghantal Deo); at both of the latter festivals a child's hair is cut for the first time. But perhaps the most interesting of the recurrent patterns is the custom of joint singing and worship by a group of women who are generally drawn from one, two, or three joint families (Basora, Ghantal Deo, Tij, Niortha-Dasahra, Devuthani Gias, Makar Sankrant, Siv Rati, Holi). At some of the women's festivals an image (usually of a female deity) is drawn or constructed and worshipped, and one of the women in the group tells a story (Niortha-Dasahra, Karva Cauth, Hoi, Devuthani Gias). Men are excluded on these occasions. This female solidarity—which reaches a climax at Dulhendi when women beat men with sticks—is a striking feature of the festival cycle.

This raises the question of whether the significance of the festival cycle may not be quite different for men and women. It may be noted that the men of Rampur have a more regular and active social life, with hookah groups forming every day in the male quarters of the household. Women, however, have fewer opportunities to get together; the festivals provide their big moments. Perhaps it is largely for this reason that the women are so much more conservative than the men in religious matters, for the perpetuation of the festival cycle seems to be largely in their hands. There are five festivals for women only; none for men only. Moreover, the women seem to play the major roles in some of the other festivals, such as Tij, Ghantal Deo, and Siv Ratri. To be sure, male participation is often essential; the head of the family must worship Laksmi on Divali and "cow-dung wealth" on Gobardhan, and only a male son can perform a *sraddha*

---

[51] Marriott, 1955a:175.

for the family dead. But most of the festival activities are carried out by the women. It is they who do all the cooking and cleaning on festival days, and it is they who are most assiduous in worshipping at shrines, lighting lamps, fasting, and taking vows. The men may sometimes scold them about honoring a particular godling, but this has little effect. As one woman, aged forty, remarked, "Our menfolk keep on telling us not to do this or that, but we go on worshipping our gods, goddesses, and godlings just the same."

Another point may be made about differential sex roles. The principal deities worshipped by the women seem to be female (the Matas, Devi, Sanjhi, and Laksmi) and the stories told at Hoi and Karva Cauth are about women. Male deities are also honored, of course (Ghantal Deo, Guga *pir*, Bhuiyan, Krsna, and Siva), but the deities most concerned with the vital personal matters of life—such as childbirth and the protection of children from sickness—are goddesses. This is such a widespread pattern in India that it may reflect an ancient pre-Vedic cult. Whitehead and Elmore have described the goddess worship of South India, in which one commonly finds a cult of seven sister deities, mostly concerned with diseases.[52] It is interesting that Rose has described the seven-sister theme for the Punjab: "Sitala, the smallpox goddess, also known as Mata or Devi, is the eldest of a band of seven sisters, by whom the pustular group of diseases is supposed to be caused, and who are the most dreaded of all the minor powers. The other six are Masani, Basanti, Maha Mai, Polamde, Lamkaria, and Agwani, whose small shrines generally cluster round the central one to Sitala."[53] Bloody animal sacrifices to the goddesses are not the rule in this region, as they are in the south, however.

Another recurrent element in the social aspect of festivals is their utilization for the strengthening or reaffirmation of family ties—especially in connection with married-out daughters or sisters. Every family tries to send gifts to its daughters at each of the four main festivals—Tij, Divali, Makar Sankrant, and Holi. On the first Tij after a marriage, a special gift is sent to a daughter-in-law, who may still be living with her parents. Another occasion for the offering of presents is Silono, when a girl ties a *ponchi* to her brother's wrist and receives a rupee or so in exchange. Gifts sent to daughters usually consist of rice, brown sugar, *ghi*, clothing, bangles, and henna. Well-to-do families send complete dresses to their daughters and their children; others send a shirt and a veil to the daughter and a shirt for

---

[52] Whitehead, 1921; Elmore, 1915. See Elmore's chapter on the seven sisters, p. 19 ff.

[53] Rose, 1919, *1*:350. For a similar description, from which Rose has probably drawn, see Ibbetson, 1882:149. The seven-sisters pattern also appears in West Bengal. See Bhattacharyya, 1955.

each child—presents for which all the brothers in an extended family are expected to contribute. The festival of Makar Sankrant is supposed to be an occasion for the patching up of quarrels, especially in the case of a girl and her in-laws, and she gives presents to them on this occasion. Family solidarity is also expressed at Kanagat, when the family dead are honored.

Other ties are affirmed at the festivals as well, village or clan solidarity being emphasized by the worship of Bhuiyan and Ghantal Deo. At least five of the twenty festivals celebrated at Rampur provide opportunities for the people of neighboring villages to meet (Ghantal Deo, Devi-ki Karahi, Tij, Ganga-Jumna Nahan, and Siv Ratri). Fairs also provide an occasion for social interaction in a larger regional setting. On Siv Ratri there are fairs at Madipur, Kundal, and Seoli, which attract a thousand people or more; there is also a large fair at Bahadurgarh on Silono. Some people from Rampur generally attend these fairs. Pilgrimages to Beri, to the Jumna and Ganges rivers, and to other sacred places also take people out of the village, while there are some festive occasions which bring outsiders into Rampur. People from other villages, for example, come to worship Ghantal Deo in Baisakh. And sometimes a Camar gives a big feast on Devi-ki Karahi, inviting the Camars from neighboring villages to attend.

CASTE PARTICIPATION

Sixteen of the twenty festivals are celebrated by all castes in the village. Ghantal Deo and Siv Ratri are not celebrated by the lowest castes—Camars, Bhangis, Dhobis, and Jhinvars. When Brahman priests officiate, they don't accept the offerings of untouchables. Nor are the latter admitted to Siva's temple to see the *linga*. The lower castes observe Devi-ki Karahi more than do the higher; only about half the Jats do so. Karva Cauth is observed only by Brahman, Baniya, and Kumhar women—not by Jats. On Basant Pancami only the single Baniya family in Rampur and a few Brahman families observe a fast. Some mingling of caste groups takes place at festivals such as Tij and Holi, but for the most part caste lines are carefully drawn. When the women sing Holi songs in the month of Phagun the women of one caste sing together. Brahmans, Baniyas, and Khatis may sit with the Jats, but the others sit separately. At Tij the same distinctions hold. A Brahman or Baniya woman may use the same swing as a Jat, but a lower-caste woman is not allowed to do so. When the women go to worship Mata or Devi, they go in extended family groups, and the different castes take turns in worshipping the goddess. One group waits until the other is through. In worshipping Sanjhi the women of one caste form groups to prepare Sanjhi figures. Women of another caste are never admitted. On Devuthani Gias the women of one, two, or three extended families sit together to burn cow-dung cakes and eat *corma;* these are always members of the same caste. The same is true of the women who meet to sing songs at Janam Astami, or to hear stories told at Hoi and Karva Cauth. Most of the horse-play at Holi takes place within the same caste. However, there are licensed exceptions to the rules at Dulhendi, when the lower-caste women may beat up a higher-caste man. While the festivals do bring people together, then, it cannot be said that they override caste lines. Social integration does not extend so far. Although the aggressive practices at Dulhendi may serve as a safety valve to some extent, they also draw attention to caste tensions and conflict.

THE FESTIVALS, ECONOMIC PRODUCTION, AND EXPENDITURES

May the festival cycle be said to inhibit economic production? Do the celebrations consume much-needed capital, and do they take up a disproportionate share of the villagers' time? To be sure, there is a rather hard-boiled value judgment underlying this question, which ignores the emotional and socially "functional" benefits of the festival cycle, and perhaps it could only be raised by a Westerner who comes from a secular civilization with rationalized production and a cult of efficiency. Nevertheless, the question does have significance in connection with the current efforts being made to raise India's agricultural productivity and standards of living.[54]

Let us first consider the amount of time consumed by the festivals at Rampur. Here we may note that sixteen of the twenty festivals are of one day's duration only. Divali lasts for three days and Holi for two. Dasahra is celebrated for only two days, although evening festivities take place over a ten-day period. Technically, Kanagat or Sraddha lasts for fifteen days, but in practice the observances are usually limited to four or five. This gives us about twenty-eight "workless" days, which is not much, considering that the villagers do not have free week ends in the Western sense. Eight of the twenty festivals coincide with holidays set aside by the Government of India or the Delhi State Government. But national holidays are often ignored by the villagers, as is Amavas, traditionally the monthly day of rest.

Actually, the festival days are not "workless" at all. Twelve of the festivals celebrated in Rampur fall during the four months from Savan to Katik. This is a busy season; yet no loss of manpower seems to result from the festivals, because some of them are limited to the women, and most of the

[54] See Moore, 1955; Anstey, 1939:55.

celebrations take place in the evenings. Three of the five festivals in Katik are for women only (Karva Cauth, Hoi, and Devuthani Gias). In Asauj most of the Niortha-Dasahra observances are carried out by women. Men's work in the fields therefore proceeds much as usual at these times.

Some of the other festivals come during slack seasons. At Tij, for example, ploughing cannot be done because of the heavy rains. Four festivals fall during the summer months between March and June, when work is relatively light. These festivals too, especially Basora, Devi-ki Karahi, and Ghantal Deo, are celebrated primarily by the women, who make their observances in the early mornings and evenings. At Kanagat or Janam Astami, when fasting takes place, there is generally only one man in a family who stays home to fast, while the others go out to the fields. Viewed in this light, it cannot be said that the festivals consume a disproportionate amount of the people's time in Rampur.

As for expenditures, the main expenses at festival times are for food and gifts. The gifts, itemized in a previous section, are primarily for daughters of the family, including the sisters and aunts of the family head as well as his daughters. Others who receive gifts at festival time are Brahmans and people who work for the family in a *jajmani* relationship. Brahmans may receive ½ to 1 *sir* of grain at each of the main festivals. A Brahman also receives some grain at Silono in exchange for the *ponchi* he leaves at a household. He is entitled to a handful of grain at Dasahra and a full meal at Makar Sankrant. The Brahmans who sit at the shrine of Ghantal Deo, at Siva's temple, or beside the Holi pyre, all receive offerings—usually flour and brown sugar with sometimes a few berries. People who have gone to bathe in the Ganges at Ganga-Jumna Nahan should give a meal to a Brahman on returning, and the Brahman who visits a household at Kanagat must similarly be fed.

However, in the case of the Brahmans these customs are now losing force, and cows or young girls are often substituted for them. The local Brahmans are not at all eager to fill their traditional roles and look on the receipt of charity as demeaning. Although Brahmans from nearby villages have been carrying out these functions in their place, it seems likely that the expenditures for Brahmans have been going down in recent years.

The same may be said of the expenditures to people who work for the family in a *jajmani* relationship. The *jajmani* system is weakening at Rampur. Some of the lower castes, like the Camars, no longer carry out their traditional obligations and services. Their former *jajmans* therefore give them fewer gifts at festival times. Some of the Bhangis, Dhobis, and Kumhars, however, have remained faithful to their *jajmans*, and receive

presents. The Bhangis and Kumhars at Rampur still get offerings of porridge, veils, etc., at the shrine of Mata on Basora day, although they no
longer care so much for this charity. The Kumhars also get some grain
for the pots used at Hoi, and gifts of grain may be given to the lower
castes informally on other festival occasions.

A few words may be said about the special foods prepared at festivals.
These are often considered the main feature of a festival, for one may then
eat things rarely prepared at other times in the year, such as vegetables,
or rice, which is not a staple food in these North Indian villages. Rice-
milk pudding or rice served with brown sugar are very popular. Other
festive dishes include *halva, lapsi,* and *puris.* The chief festivals involving
the preparation of foods are Tij, Divali, and Holi. The expenditure for these
festivals is nearly twice that of the others. Special sweets are included in
the *sidha* sent to a daughter at Tij. But everyone in the family enjoys the
good food prepared at festival times. This periodic supply of extra calories
must fill a real need and could hardly be termed an extravagance.

Data on expenditures at festivals were collected from four families at
Rampur, each representing a different socio-economic group. According
to our data, the lowest-income family spent half as much on food as the
others. The money spent on *sidha* (for a daughter) showed a great range
from 4 rupees to 32 rupees, 8 annas. The expenses for *kothli* at Tij showed
less variation, although the poorest family of the group spent one-sixth
as much as the richest. The poorest family gave about half as much as the
others to Brahmans, while the other three families spent about the same
amount. The sums given to sisters or daughters at *ponchi*-tying show the
same patterns, with the upper three families spending about the same
amount and the poorest family again spending about half as much.

STABILITY AND CHANGE

In about 1030 A.D. the Muslim scholar Alberuni, who passed through this
region of North India in the train of Mahmud of Ghazni, wrote an account
of India in which there are some descriptions of fasts and festivals so
similar to those current in present-day Rampur that the evidence for
cultural stability is remarkable. A few quotations will make this clear:

Devuthani Gias: "When in the month of Karttika the moon stands in
Revati, the last of her stations, it is a fast-day in commemoration of the
waking up of Vasudeva. It is called *deotthini,* i.e. the rising of the Deva." [55]

Divali: "The 1st Karttika, or new moon's day, when the sun marches in

---

[55] Sachau, 1910, 2:177.

Table 32

COMPARATIVE EXPENDITURES AMONG CASTES DURING FESTIVALS, RAMPUR [a]

Festival	Kumhar Ib (very low) (5 family members)	Jat Ib (high) (7 family members)	Jat II (higher) (12 family members)	Jat III (highest) (14 family members)
Basora	1–14–0	6–8–0	11–4–0	5–14–0
Devi-ki Karahi	3–0–0	8–8–0	15–5–0	15–8–0
Ghantal Deo	2–4–0	9–0–0	7–4–0	9–8–0
Jaith-ka Dasahra	—	—	—	—
Tij	9–8–0	15–14–0	16–12–0	13–4–0
kothli for one girl:	2–6–0	18–8–0	25–0–0	27–0–0
Silono	6–12–0	5–4–0	15–4–0	7–12–0
for one sister:	1–0–0	7–0–0	2–0–0	2–0–0
for Brahman:	0–4–0	1–0–0	0–8–0	1–0–0
Janam Astami and				
Guga Naumi	4–6–0	6–8–0	14–12–0	11–5–0
Kanagat (for one)	5–10–0	7–6–0	12–13–0	5–8–0
Niortha-Dasahra	0–11–0	2–0–0	3–8–0	3–8–0
for food:	1–0–0	11–9–0	12–13–0	12–4–0
Devi-ki Karahi	3–0–0	8–8–0	15–5–0	15–8–0
Karva Cauth	3–0–0	—	—	—
Hoi	3–0–0	3–6–0	6–8–0	9–0–0
for Brahman:	0–12–0	0–12–0	0–12–0	0–12–0
Divali	5–0–0	22–8–0	40–9–0	40–8–0
sidha for girls:	4–0–0	7–4–0	16–0–0	32–8–0
Devuthani Gias	4–2–0	6–8–0	10–0–0	8–8–0
Ganga-Jumna Nahan	1–0–0	6–8–0	14–12–0	15–8–0
Makar Sankrant	6–12–0	7–14–0	8–10–0	14–8–0
for Brahmans:	0–10–0	1–0–0	1–14–0	1–8–0
sidha for girls:	4–0–0	7–4–0	16–0–0	32–8–0
Basant Pancami	—	—	—	—
Siv Ratri	1–8–0	3–7–0	4–4–0	4–13–0
for Brahman:	0–3–0	0–5–0	0–5–0	0–7–0
Holi	5–0–0	8–14–0	19–0–0	23–8–0
sidha for girls:	3–0–0	7–4–0	16–0–0	32–8–0
Amavas	3–12–0	6–9–0	7–4–0	11–4–0

Summary

Total expenditures				
for food at festivals:	65–3–0	145–7–0	243–8–0	239–8–0
Money spent on *kothli*				
for a daughter:	2–6–0	18–8–0	25–0–0	27–0–0
Money spent on one *sidha*:	4–0–0	7–4–0	16–0–0	32–0–0
Money given to a				
sister for *ponchi*:	1–0–0	2–0–0	2–0–0	2–0–0
Money given to Brahmans:	1–12–0	3–1–6	3–7–6	3–9–0

[a] The sums are given in rupees, annas, and pice. The figures Ib, II, III refer to relative positions on our socio-economic scale.

Libra, is called Dibali. Then people bathe, dress festively, make presents to each other of betel-leaves and areca-nuts; they ride to the temples to give alms and play merrily with each other till noon. In the night they light a great number of lamps in every place so that the air is perfectly clear." [56]

Siv Ratri: "On the . . . night . . .of the 16th, called Sivaratri, they worship Mahadeva during the whole night; they remain awake, and do not lie down to sleep, and offer to him perfumes and flowers." [57]

Some of the festivals described by Alberuni must have been ancient before his visit to India. In the case of Divali, at least, P. K. Gode has traced the festival's existence back to about 100 A.D.[58] It may well be much older. Several of the festivals described by Alberuni are no longer current, but the persistence of some in all essential details is striking, as is the evidence that the general nature of the festival cycle has remained much the same since Alberuni's time.

This cultural stability is all the more remarkable in the light of Rampur's geographical location. This is an area which has been a battleground throughout much of its past history. The legendary battles of the Mahabharata were fought here, and through this territory came the invading Muslims who made Delhi their capital. Between 1760 and 1805, after the collapse of the Mughal empire, Sikhs and Marathas were engaged in a desperate and bloody conflict, until the superior power of the British was established. Ibbetson reports that at that time out of 221 villages in *pargana* (a local subdivision) Karnal (close to Rampur) the inhabitants of 178 had been wholly driven from their homes and fields. And for a long time thereafter the whole region was in a state of lawlessness and anarchy. The heavy exactions of revenue collectors led to a large-scale abandonment of villages and escape to Sikh territory.[59] Later uprisings at the time of the Mutiny of 1857 and the more recent upheavals of Independence and Partition have also affected the area. The past history of the general region, then, has been a turbulent one. It has also been the scene of conflict between different religions and political ideologies—of Hinduism, Islam, Sikhism, the Arya Samaj movement, and of political groups such as those of the Congress Party, the Socialists, etc. But perhaps in most cases these movements affected the cities more than the villages. The cultural stability, at any rate, is noteworthy in villages like Rampur.

---

[56] Sachau, 1910, 2:182.

[57] Sachau, 1910, 2:184. Alberuni also gives an account of the Gobardhan legend, p. 175.

[58] Gode, 1946.

[59] Ibbetson, 1883:33, 48.

Nevertheless, some changes may be noted in the festival cycle of present-day Rampur, particularly in the abandonment of former practices. Some festivals, such as Kaj, which were formerly observed at Rampur, have recently been dropped. There used to be regular ceremonies at a Muslim Saiyad (Musulman martyr) shrine, but in 1947 the shrine was destroyed by members of the R.S.S. (Rastriya Swayam Sevak Sangh), a Hindu extremist group, and the ceremonies are no longer held.

A variety of practices have lost currency in recent years, some of which may be itemized: Few lamps are now lit at Devi's shrine on Devi-ki Karahi; some lamps are lit at people's homes instead. There has been a falling off in the number of pilgrims who go to Beri or Gurgaon to worship Devi or Mata, and also in the number of men who go to bathe in the Jumna or Ganges, according to the villagers. Cocks are no longer held over children's heads at Basora. *Bhagats* no longer perform in honor of Guga *pir*. Butter is now made during Kanagat by most families, although this was formerly taboo. Oxen are yoked by some families on the afternoon of Amavas. A variety of factors are involved in these cases.

In another set of changes, however, we can discern a common element—the decline of the Brahman's role at Rampur. A Brahman is no longer called upon to fix the "foundation pole" of the Holi pyre. A Brahman woman is not asked to tell the story of Hoi at Karva Cauth, as she was in the past. This is usually done by one of the older women in the family. Local Brahmans do not usually accept food offerings at *sraddha* ceremonies or at Makar Sankrant, and they do not tie *ponchis* at Silono or present *niorthas* at Niortha-Dasahra. The offerings at the Siva temple are accepted by a Gosain instead of a Brahman; and only one Brahman—from another village—accepts offerings at the shrine of Ghantal Deo or at the Holi pyre. The local Brahmans are generally reluctant to accept offerings. There is also some reluctance to feed them—more, it is said, than in the past.[60]

This is partly due to the influence of the Arya Samaj and to the weakening of the *jajmani* system.[61] The latter has particularly affected the lower castes in Rampur. But it is not only the Bhangis, Kumhars, and Camars whose roles in the festival cycle have been affected. Also involved are the Nais and their wives, who no longer act as messengers at festival times. They do not carry gifts to the daughters of a family any more; instead a brother or nephew does so nowadays.

---

[60] Brahmans are weakly represented at Rampur and do not have the high status which the Brahmans enjoy, for example, in Karimpur, the village studied by the Wisers. One would expect to find a greater stress on Hindu orthodoxy there than in Rampur, where the Jats are the dominant landholding group.

[61] See pp. 78-79.

These are important social developments. But despite these significant changes one is struck, after all, by the relative stability of village life. The festival cycle, at least, remains as important as ever in the lives of the people of Rampur, and its essential structure is unchanged. Reformist doctrines and male skepticism have not shaken the women's faith; and the extended family women's groups are still active centers in the maintenance of festival traditions. While individual festivals may decline or disappear, the basic character of the festival cycle has remained remarkably stable at Rampur.

7

Concepts of Religion and Ethics

It is often asserted that the average Hindu is very religious. "The Indians," writes Sir Harcourt Butler, "are essentially religious as the Europeans are essentially secular. Religion is still the alpha and omega of Indian life." [1] Often associated with this assumption is another, to the effect that this religion is one which emphasizes detachment and otherworldliness. This view finds expression in a recent account of North Indian village life by the anthropologist Morris Opler: "The fact that the highest goal of the Hindu is to eliminate earthly concerns, desires, and personal existence itself introduces a large element of asceticism, intellectualism, detachment, and withdrawal into Hindu religious philosophy. In no other country have so many men renounced the world, and in no other place is there so much fasting and mortification of the flesh. The world is considered transitory and an appearance. Reality is escape from the world and from the forms which existence in the world makes necessary." [2]

[1] Quoted in O'Malley, 1935:45, where a number of other quotations to the same effect are assembled.

[2] Opler, 1950:314. Opler explains that his essay is intended as an "outline of village life in one part of India" (p. 279). ". . . we shall depict village life in the Ganges valley of north India. It will be understood, however, that most of the institutions and prac-

Fig. 39. Shrine of the ancestral god, Bhuiyan, founder of the village.

To what degree Indian peasants actually share views such as those set forth by Opler is questionable. The concepts under consideration are ancient Sanskritic doctrines, products of a sophisticated urban milieu. Do Indian peasants really hold them? A negative statement on this point has been made by another anthropologist, S. C. Dube: "Clearly, Hinduism as it is practiced in the village is not the Hinduism of the classical philosophical systems of India, for it possesses neither the metaphysical heights nor the abstract content of the latter. It is a religion of fasts, feasts, and festivals, in which prescribed rituals cover all the major crises of life. . . . Analysis of life-histories reveals that spiritualism cannot be said to be the keynote in the life of the community; far from it the religion appears to be a practical one." [3]

The general statements made by Opler and by Dube are offered with little, if any, supporting data to substantiate them. In the absence of published interview material or other such data, generalizations about the beliefs of Indian peasants must remain impressionistic.

The present chapter includes some quantitative data relating to the religious views of the people of Rampur. As far as we know there has been only one previously published questionnaire on religious topics given to Hindus, and that was for school children rather than peasant villagers.[4] Our questionnaire was given to twenty-five individuals. While the present study cannot be considered definitive, it does set forth a method of investigation which could be applied elsewhere for further research.

The purpose of the questionnaire was to obtain some notion of the basic ethical and methaphysical concepts shared by the villagers and to find out how familiar they were with the mythology and philosophy of the Sanskritic Hindu Great Tradition. We were interested in questions such as these: Are the major deities of the Hindu pantheon known in the village? Which are neglected? Do the villagers share the concepts of *karma* (doctrine of action determining one's destiny) and reincarnation? What differences, if any, appear in different caste groups or age groups with respect to religious beliefs?

The subjects were asked to identify the following gods and the powers they represent: Indra, Visnu, Siva, Brahma, Kali, Agni, Yama, Laksmi,

---

tices described are true of all sections of the country" (p. 280). In this context it seems fair to interpret the paragraph quoted in our text as a description of contemporary peasant beliefs. However, it may be that Opler had in mind a description of ideal rather than real patterns.

[3] Dube, 1955:93. See also O'Malley (1935:69) who writes: "The popular creed is but feebly influenced by and only dimly reflects higher ethical teaching."

[4] McGavran, 1936.

Sarasvati, Kabir. The informants were requested to name the different incarnations of Visnu. A list of thirty-three mythical figures, drawn principally from the Ramayana and Mahabharata, was presented for identification.[5] The subjects were also asked for their conceptions about Heaven *(svarga)*, Hell *(naraka* or *narakh)*, reincarnation *(punarjanman, avagavan)*, salvation or "release" *(mukti)*, God *(isvara)*, soul *(atman)*, illusion *(maya)*, the world or cosmos *(sansar)*, and life *(jivan)*. Finally, their opinions were solicited about the nature of sin, and they were asked to give examples of both good acts *(punya)* and evil ones *(papa)*. In the course of the interviews the investigator often posed further questions for the purposes of clarification, such as: "The actions you describe as virtuous can be undertaken only by a wealthy man. Tell me how a poor person can acquire *punya*."

The interviews were carried out during harvest time, when most of the able-bodied people were in the fields. The older and more conservative villagers are, therefore, largely represented in the sample. Since the interviewer was a male, it was difficult for him to interview women. Hence there is only one woman in the sample—a Jat, aged sixty. The sample includes equal proportions of literate and illiterate informants. Fifteen of the subjects were of the Jat caste, with the following age groups represented: seven in the 18-35 age group, three in the 35-55 age group, five in the 55 and over age group. Five subjects were Brahmans, with four coming from the 55 and over age group and one from the 18-35 age group. There were five lower-caste subjects (three Camars and two Kumhars) with ages ranging between thirty and sixty. The caste distribution here roughly follows the caste distribution in the village.

AGE DIFFERENCES

Analysis of the results of the questionnaire showed a decline down the age ladder with regard to the knowledge of Hindu mythology. Persons thirty-five years of age recalled an average of twenty-seven names in the list of thirty-three mythical figures, with the lowest score being twenty-four and the highest thirty-three. Persons in the youngest group (18-35) identified, on the average, seventeen names on the list, while those in the intermediate age group scored about the same. In the identification of deities, members of the oldest group averaged five correct answers out of ten, with Indra, Yama, Laksmi, and Sarasvati being identified by all.

---

[5] The list is as follows: Hariscandra, Prahlada, Druma, Dadhica, Karna, Bhima, Moradwaj, Laksmana, Rama, Bharata, Yudhisthira, Janaka, Nala, Hiranyakasipu, Ravana, Sakuni, Kamsa, Duryodhana, Jarasandha, Kumbhakarna, Sisupala, Sita, Anasuya, Kunti, Draupadi, Savitri, Radha, Ahalya, Kaikeyi, Surpanakha, Vasistha, Valmiki, Visvamitra.

Brahma and Visnu were identified by three each and Siva by two. Agni, Kabir, and Kali were not identified. The average of correct answers dropped from five to three in the lower age groups.

IDENTIFICATION OF GODS

It is hard to see why Siva and Visnu would not be more widely identified. One of the yearly festivals, Siv Ratri or Bholai-ka Barat, is in honor of Siva, while two (Janam Astami and Gobardhan) are in honor of Krsna, who is generally regarded as being one of Visnu's incarnations. The explanation may be that the rationale of the festivals is not well known to the villagers. (The women are more familiar with the supporting myths than are the men, and are more active in carrying out the religious observances associated with the festivals.) Or perhaps the difficulty is simply one of terminology. Siva is known locally as Bholai, while Kali is known as Devi. If the more common names had been given, there might have been a larger number of correct identifications. On this point McKim Marriott has commented: "In Kishan Garhi I was at first nonplussed by villagers' failure to respond to my questions about Siva; later I found I could elicit a great deal of information by asking the same questions about their name for him— Mahadev. Ultimately, I found villagers to be acquainted with quite esoteric lore of the same deity, and to know him also by many other names of uncommon sort, such as Bawa." [6]

If the apparent failures to identify some deities are surprising, so are the successes in the identification of Indra, a Vedic deity who is not celebrated in festivals or honored at shrines.

CASTE DIFFERENCES

Replies to the questions about ethics and life after death show different tendencies between the Jats and non-Jats, with a more "positivistic" this-worldly view represented by the Jats, as will be seen later. However, there was little difference between the castes in the identification of mythical figures. The performance of the Brahmans was almost exactly equal to that of the Jats, except in the identification of gods, where they averaged seven out of ten as against five out of ten for the Jats. In the list of thirty-three mythical figures the averages were just about the same (nineteen for Jats; twenty for Brahmans), with the highest score being thirty-one for both Brahmans and Jats. Interestingly enough, the highest score was made by a forty-year-old Camar, who identified all thirty-three of the mythical figures

---

[6] Personal communication.

and six of the gods. He also named five of the *avatars,* or incarnations, of Visnu, which hardly anyone else could do. (Most of the people who named Visnu's incarnations named only two, except in the oldest age group, in which some individuals gave four.) When asked for the sources of his knowledge, the Camar mentioned folk tales and rural plays. This does indicate the possibility of learning the Sanskritic Great Tradition at Rampur.

As far as the identification of mythical figures is concerned, no great differences appear among the various caste groups. But some interesting differences do emerge between the Jats and the members of the other castes in connection with the concepts of life after death discussed below.

LIFE AFTER DEATH

Only fourteen of our twenty-five subjects expressed belief in the doctrine of reincarnation. Of these fourteen only four were Jats—from the 60 and over age group. Seven of the eleven nonbelievers were Jats—from the 18-35 age group. Thus, while Brahman and lower-caste subjects tended to accept the concept, the Jats tended to reject it. Several Jats placed the emphasis upon life on earth, claiming that Heaven and Hell are to be found here. The operation of *karma* was similarly conceived to take place only within this life—not necessarily through a chain of lives. One's posthumous reputation on earth was sometimes equated with Heaven or Hell—an extreme development of what Riesman would call "other-direction." Here are the statements of some of our subjects:

"There is no question of going to Heaven or Hell after death. A person experiences Heaven and Hell in this life itself. Those who are blessed with health and wealth are in Heaven. Those who are in want are in Hell. For instance an old person who cannot enjoy peace and is forced to work and bear sorrows is in Hell. Everything is found in this life itself. There is no punishment after death. One who does good or evil deeds is rewarded or punished for them in this life." (A Jat woman, aged sixty.)

"After death the air in a man mixes with the air; his body turns to earth. I think one ends with death. Nobody knows what happens after that. A living being experiences Heaven and Hell in this very world. One who is destitute or unsatisfied is in Hell. One who does not have too much work to do and who has good clothes, a motor car, and so on, is in Heaven." (A Jat, aged sixty.)

"I think Heaven and Hell are here in this world. Everybody speaks well of a good man and ill of a bad man. But nobody knows what happens after death, or remembers his previous births." (A Jat, aged thirty-one.)

"What people say about you after death is your Hell or Heaven. The world is the touchstone. There is no Heaven or Hell after death. I don't believe in the next life. I've seen Hell here—when a man dies in agony, and there are worms in his body. When a man dies among comforts and wealth, he is in Heaven." (A Jat, aged thirty-two.)

Not only Jats, but some members of other castes spoke in this vein, as did a forty-year-old Camar: "Heaven and Hell are here. People call you good or bad according to your own actions, and that is Heaven or Hell. They say that there are gardens in Heaven where they swing you in a swing; in Hell there are pits where the worms eat your flesh. But nobody has seen it; we've only heard so. I think that when an old man has children and grandchildren to serve him, and when he has every type of comfort, he is in Heaven. But when the sons and grandsons do not serve him, the worms begin their work in his body; then he becomes blind and diseased and dies in great pain. That is Hell."

These views are so often expressed in similar terms that there seems to be evidence of a rather clear-cut ism or ideology here, which may, indeed, be rather widespread in India.

There is also another point of view which may be distinguished in some of the replies to our questionnaire. Since it is more in accord with the Hindu doctrines with which the Western world is familiar, this viewpoint will be called "traditional" here, although the views just cited may also represent an ancient tradition rather than a wave of latter-day skepticism. Some quotations will help to indicate how the "traditional" view differs from the more "positivistic" and this-worldly one which has just been discussed.

"Heaven is a place where man goes in the form of *atman*, after giving up his body. Not everyone gets there—only the *dharmatma*, the man of [good] character. The evildoer goes to Hell. Heaven and Hell are in this world too. According to your *karma*, so you go from one life to the next. The human form is reached with great difficulties. Good deeds bring about *mukti*—release from the cycle of reincarnation. Then the soul reaches God." (A Brahman, aged sixty-two.)

"A man who does good deeds, such as worshipping God or performing social services, is born into the home of a good person. Due to the good conduct of the father, the child also develops good conduct and is led to the worship of God, until he finally achieves release from the world [*mukti*] and finds a place in Heaven. Then he is never born again. Wicked people are born again and again and suffer all sorts of troubles. If you go against your duty, you will have to undergo God's punishment and be born as a Bhangi or a pig in your next incarnation." (A Brahman, aged thirty-nine.)

"Even at the time of death a man should wish to do good deeds and wish to be reborn in a place where he can do good deeds again. Then he will get enlightenment and come to know his past lives. After many lives a man attains *mukti;* he then controls God and is released from the chain of incarnations. When the world is in trouble, such a soul takes birth of his own free will to render service to others. If one does evil deeds, his form changes and he falls lower till he becomes a *jar,* an inanimate thing. They say that there are eighty-four *lakhs* [hundred thousands] of forms." (A Jat, an extreme Arya Samajist, aged thirty-one.)

To simplify the picture we may say that two basic concepts prevail regarding life after death: the "traditional" view on one hand, represented at Rampur primarily by the Brahmans and lower-caste groups, and a "positivistic" this-worldly view on the other hand, represented mainly by the Jats. Sometimes there is a blend of these two viewpoints, as in this statement by a twenty-year-old Jat: "You get Heaven in this world, when all your wishes are fulfilled—when you have a good character, money, etc. Hell is just the opposite—having a bad character, less money, a disfigured body, or blindness. Then a man experiences Hell in this world. One who performs good deeds is born in a good home." In such a predominantly this-worldly statement the last sentence introduces a "traditional" element. This kind of fusion is not uncommon. However, it is generally possible to group our subjects into one of these metaphysical camps or the other. It is rather surprising, then, to find how many of our subjects fall into the second camp.

In accordance with this dichotomy, the concept of *mukti* (or *moksa*)— release, liberation of the soul—was interpreted quite differently by our two groups. The Brahmans who have been quoted above expressed the "traditional" view—release from the cycle of incarnations and union with God. While all the Brahmans in our sample shared this concept, only five of the Jats did so. A more frequent interpretation of *mukti* among the Jats was "death without suffering"—the coming of death while one is in comfortable circumstances and well thought of by others. Eight individuals gave overlapping replies expressing both views. Our lower-caste subjects were about evenly divided between the two concepts.[7]

---

[7] McKim Marriott comments: "It is interesting that these villagers (like mine—except a few highly literate) use the word *mukti,* apparently a borrowing in Pali form, possibly from Buddhist texts, rather than the Sanskrit *moksa.*" Personal communication.

ETHICAL BELIEFS

In concepts of the *dharmatma*, or righteous man, and in the listing of sins and virtues, different emphases appear which parallel the contrasting views about life after death. Here again we note different tendencies among the Jats and non-Jats. When asked to list virtues or traits characteristic of the *dharmatma*, the Jats tended to emphasize practical humanistic virtues, while the Brahmans stressed piety and the worship of God. Four of our five Brahman subjects mentioned "Worship of God" as a characteristic of the *dharmatma*, but only one of our fifteen Jat subjects did so. Two Brahmans listed "Visiting holy places" as a meritorious act; no Jats did so. "Acting according to *dharma*" (religious duty) was mentioned by three Jats, five Brahmans, and two lower-caste members, showing that the more weakly represented non-Jats placed more emphasis upon this trait than did the Jats. The Jats, on the other hand, tended to specify practical acts of altruism, many of which were not mentioned by the members of other castes, such as "Contributes to schools"[8] (four Jats), "Helps repair a bad road" (two Jats), "Gets a pond dug" (two Jats), or "Gets a well dug" (three Jats). Four Jats and three Brahmans mentioned "Opens watering places" as a virtue. None of the five lower-caste members referred to these items in their lists of virtues. It is interesting to note, however, that all the lower-caste individuals singled out "Gives loans without interest" as a virtue, while none of the Jats or Brahmans mentioned this possibility.

Animals were included by the Jats as objects of charity. The following, at least, were cited as meritorious deeds by one individual each: "Feeding ants with sugar and flour," "Feeding monkeys with roasted wheat and *gur*," "Scattering grain for birds." Six Jats and one Brahman listed "Contributes to Gaushala," Gaushala being a society for the protection and feeding of cows. (This is three more than the number of individuals who mentioned contributions to schools.) The lower-caste members did not include any of the good deeds listed above in their replies.

The principal virtue emphasized by lower-caste individuals was generosity. Four of the five mentioned "Helps the helpless," and four cited "Gives food to the poor." It occurred to us that perhaps the lower-caste subjects were referring here to the virtues of others rather than to their own, for they are traditionally the recipients, not the donors, of charity. However, low-caste individuals do give charity, and some of the Camars are wealthier than some of the local Jats and Brahmans. Besides, all caste groups stressed the virtues of giving food to others; eight Jats and three

---

[8] All the members of the local school committee are Jats.

Brahmans did so. This was one of the largest categories. Four of the lower-caste men cited "Respecting the women of others" as a virtue. Again we wondered whether they might have had others in mind rather than themselves, for lower-caste women are more vulnerable than the women of other castes to the sexual advances of higher-caste men.

The lists of sins reflect similar differences between the Jats and non-Jats, corresponding with the lists of virtues. Four of the five Brahmans regarded disbelief in God as a sin. "Acts against *dharma*" was listed by three. None of the other castes included these items as sins. Other sins mentioned by the Brahmans were murder (4), causing pain or suffering (4), theft (4), seduction (3), lying (2), refusal of food to the hungry (2), rebellion against the government (1), and causing pain to an animal (1).

The sins most commonly mentioned among the Jats were murder (12), causing pain or suffering (11), stealing (12), lying (11). Other sins listed by them were seduction (6), deception (4), and looking at women with sensuous thoughts (3). Most of the other sins referred to were given by only one or two persons. Stealing and lying were usually mentioned together in a stock phrase, "*chori-jari*," which lumps the two together. They were generally cited after the other major sins. Four Jats, however, listed lying as the worst sin of all, claiming that it was an initial step, or a concomitant of all the other sins.

Only six sins were listed by the lower-caste subjects. These were refusal of food to the hungry (4), refusal of help (3), murder (3), theft (3), deception (2), and lying (2).

Perhaps a few quotations will give a better picture of our subjects' ethical attitudes.

"A *bhagat* (devotee of God) is also a *dharmatma*. Without being a devotee one cannot become a *dharmatma*, because it is only then that he understands that everyone is His creation and hence equal. A *dharmatma* is one who treats other men as equals, rich and poor alike, gives food to the hungry, doesn't quarrel, and is a good man. A false *bhagat* offers prayers here and goes and backbites there. That is no worship." (A Brahman, aged forty-four.)

"A *dharmatma* offers his worship through acts and by rituals, taking the name of God. Worship has power. But we don't do *bhajan* [worship]. Since taking to farming, we've given it up. We're not really Brahmans any more—just farmers. But we still try to worship." (A Brahman, aged sixty-two.)

"I have my own views. My family do not accept them. A *dharmatma* is one who earns his own living, looks after his children well, and receives guests hospitably. He maintains his family and serves the village, upholds his faith and aids society. But besides all this he should worship God. God is omnipresent. One should accept that, for only then can one have good conduct. A man must find time for worship. There should be a place for the worship of God, and these places should have teachers to guide the people, to help lead them away from orthodoxy toward the new ways of living." (A Brahman schoolteacher, aged thirty-nine.)

"A *dharmatma* is one who serves the world. Those who have money do this with money. But we won't call that *dharma*. One who does *dharma* with his *atman* will win the world." (A Jat, aged sixty.)

"In our village only one or two are known as *dharmatmas*. A real *dharmatma* is filled with pity at the sight of a man suffering, and he goes to help—gives him food, or warm clothing in winter; he takes an active part in opening up a watering place; he helps to repair bad roads, and collects food and fodder for the Gaushala." (A Jat, aged sixty.)

"A *dharmatma* is a man whose *atman* is clear, who helps others and his country, and who considers how his actions will affect others. He will never inflict pain or suffering on others, but will sacrifice his own self-interest for others—like Dayanand and Mahatma Gandhi." (A Jat, an Arya Samajist, aged thirty-two.)

"A *dharmatma* is a man who gives food and water to a hungry man, sympathizes with others, contributes to the Gaushala, arranges for watering places, and provides warm clothing for others. A true *dharmik [dharmatma]* never looks at the possessions of others. . . . This is our *bhajan*—that we do good deeds and remember God for one hour in the morning and one hour in the evening." (A Jat, aged thirty.)

"A *dharmatma* is one who gives loans without interest, gives without asking, and sympathizes with others." (A Kumhar, aged thirty-two.)

"A *dharmatma* is one who does good deeds, helps the poor, is pious, and gives food to the hungry." (A Camar, aged forty.)

INTERPRETATIONS

In considering the different tendencies in the Jat, Brahman, and lower-caste replies to our questionnaire, one is tempted to explain the differences in terms of the traditional expectations concerning caste behavior. Brahmans, that is, are supposed to be more concerned with religion than the other groups; judging from the replies to our questionnaire, this seems to hold true for Rampur, in spite of the fact that the local Brahmans do not fill priestly roles and are relatively ignorant of Hindu mythology. Our sample, of course, was very small, but the few Brahmans interviewed did express the more "traditional" views about life after death, *mukti,* and ethical behavior, while the Jats stressed a more practical this-worldly view of life.

However, another interpretation of these group differences is possible, although it need not conflict with that just given. The emphasis upon practical charity among the Jats might be explained by the fact that they are the wealthiest group, the landowners of the village, for many of the virtuous acts they specified can only be carried out by someone with sufficient means. Since the Jats are the dominant force in the village, their views are influential and are shared to some extent by the lower castes.

But the lower castes generally seem to follow the lead of the Brahmans in expressing "traditional" views. This is not only because they must look to the priestly caste for religious guidance; another factor to be considered is that adherence to orthodoxy is a recognized means of enhancing social status. Bernard Cohn has described how the Camars in an eastern Uttar Pradesh village have made efforts in recent years "to suppress their distinctive traditional religion, to Sanskritize their rituals still further, and to emulate the specific religious forms of the higher castes," [9] largely for the purpose of enhancing Camar prestige.

Harking back to the conflicting views of Opler and Dube quoted at the beginning of this chapter, we may say that the evidence from Rampur does not seem to support Opler's generalization. In the "traditional" views there is some reference to the goal of escape from the chain of rebirths, but this does not hold true of the characteristic Jat viewpoint. While our data incline more toward Dube's generalization, it must be said that some of the classical metaphysical concepts are known and shared by some of the villagers. It may also be noted that the views associated with the Jats have a kind of consistency which seems to mark them out as a distinctive ideology. They are not simply negative. Some of the quotations from our informants are impressively worded and have a spiritual flavor which seems quite unusual.

---

[9] Cohn, 1955:74-75.

8

Concepts of Disease
Causation and Cure

Great efforts are being made in the so-called underdeveloped countries of today to improve the health conditions of the people. In these areas there are two groups which, generally speaking, have adopted somewhat different approaches. Government administrators and medical technicians (doctors, sanitation experts, health educators, etc.) tend to see as the major problem the acquisition of sufficient supplies, equipment, and personnel to carry out their work. They generally assume that, just as a starving man is eager to accept food, so will the villagers be glad to accept their innovations, which have a self-evident value. The underlying assumption is that the villagers suffer from ignorance and need only to be educated.

But social scientists, and particularly anthropologists who live with the people they study, see the problem somewhat differently. They are more aware of the resistances and culture conflicts involved. Thus, one writes of the difficulty of persuading people in a Peruvian town to accept so simple an innovation as water boiling, while two others discuss the snags encountered in a program of diphtheria immunization in a Thai com-

Fig. 40.   Sixty-five years of experience.

munity.[1] These cases both deal with a single item of culture pattern; there must be much greater problems facing community projects like those in India, where efforts are made to improve the general health standards of the people.

Anthropologists see the problem here as being one of re-education rather than education. For all peoples, whether tribal, peasant, or urban, have their own beliefs and practices concerning health and disease. Nor are all these beliefs and practices bad.[2] Some are based on centuries of trial and error and have positive values, while others, it is true, may be either useless or downright dangerous. In any case there is an already existent body of doctrine concerning sickness and health in any area where health programs may be instituted—not simply a vacuum waiting to be filled by the community worker—and there is usually an already functioning group of curers who may have a stake in the perpetuation of the old system of beliefs. Awareness of these cultural and social factors has led anthropologists to emphasize the difficulties and resistances encountered in health programs. Some, indeed, may have overemphasized them in an effort to justify the practical significance of their profession.

Anthropologists have tried to alert administrators to three factors in works dealing with these problems: First, they have stressed the importance of understanding the community as a whole, its general culture patterns and its social and political structure.[3] Secondly, they have focused on the study of the roles played by native practitioners and the problems posed when a Western-trained doctor comes to a village where he has no clearly defined role.[4] Thirdly, they have stressed the importance of understanding native concepts of health and disease. The present discussion concerns this last point.

The knowledge of what people believe about health and disease can be helpful in a number of ways. First of all, it may be a great aid in establishing rapport between doctor and patient. Patients in all societies like to think that the doctor understands them. If he can couch his scientific advice

---

[1] Wellin, 1955; Hanks and Hanks, 1955.

[2] It is interesting to note that the Government of India is supporting research to test the value of indigenous remedies. "In the five year plan a provision of Rs. 37.5 lakhs has been made for research into indigenous and other systems. Government of India have sanctioned a central institute for research in indigenous systems of medicine at Jamnagar. It is considered necessary, however, to promote research at more than one such centre. . . . Provision has to be made specially for a comparative clinical study of different techniques." *The First Five Year Plan*, 1952:516.

[3] For example, Leighton and Leighton, 1945; Lewis, 1955b.

[4] Marriott, 1955b.

in terms which fit an already existing culture pattern, there is a greater chance that this advice will be followed. For example, in communities where diseases and medicines are classified as hot or cold, it might be helpful for the doctor not to challenge this belief openly. A mere statement to a patient that the medicine is "hot" and will help to cure a "cold" disease may make for increased confidence. Similarly, where it is customary to drink teas of all kinds, a prescription of boiled tea will be more effective, psychologically, than telling a diarrhea patient to boil his drinking water. Well-established number rituals (such as those which employ the number three or four) can be exploited in prescribing new medicines. ("Take this three times a day for three successive days.") In short, folk traditions have many superficial and formal analogies with modern medicine which can be utilized by doctors who are attempting to introduce modern medicine into peasant or folk societies.

A second advantage in learning the indigenous beliefs and practices of the community is the insight gained into the world-view of the people. While the doctor may make use of local beliefs in the ways just indicated, he must also, in the long run, be concerned with re-education. Concepts of disease causation are part of a society's total world-view, which is also reflected in other spheres such as agriculture, politics, and interpersonal relations. If there is much emphasis on magical belief concerning disease, it may be predicted that the people will not interpret agricultural innovations in a truly scientific spirit. In other words, if new practices in any field are not to be just new types of magic, community workers must begin to change the total world-view of the people, working on many fronts at once.

An interesting aspect of our interview data is the way in which traditional views about disease exist side by side with modern germ theories. This reflects the pragmatic bent of the villager, who is willing to try anything if it works. But it also highlights the superficial way in which new teachings have been assimilated, and demonstrates the great need for increased education in the field of health.

A great deal, clearly, needs to be done in the sphere of public health in India. Many diseases flourish through poor sanitation. Only 6 per cent of India's towns have protected water supplies, which serve only 6.15 per cent of the total population. Only about 3 per cent of the total population is served by sewerage systems, and latrines are a rarity.[5] The prevalence of illiteracy, poverty, and malnutrition are great obstacles to proper health education, and the living conditions of the people make sanitary precau-

[5] *The First Five Year Plan*, 1952:496-97.

tions difficult to institute. This is evident in an interview with a thirty-nine-year-old Camar informant at Rampur:

Q. "Why can't you wash your clothes, if, as you say, dirty clothes cause disease?"

A. "We are lucky if we have one complete set of clothes. We can't find time to wash them, but have to wear them twenty-four hours a day."

Q. "Why can't you keep your house clean, though, if an unclean house also causes sickness?"

A. "I have two rooms. In the back room the buffalo is kept at night all winter. She drops dung and passes urine there. It is impossible to keep the place really clean. There is one living room for us. I do my weaving there. The food is cooked there, and we all sleep there at night. During the day the other family members stay in that room. It is hard to keep it clean."

Another difficulty in connnection with India's health program is the shortage of doctors and nurses. According to official government figures, there is only one doctor to 6300 people in India, one nurse to 43,000, and one dentist to 300,000.[6] Moreover, 75 per cent of the doctors are in cities; their distribution in the rural areas—where the bulk of the people lives—is very sparse. Consequently, more than half of the total expenditure contemplated in the medical projects devised by the central and state governments will be spent on hospitals and dispensaries.[7]

India's villagers, however, are not always eager to make use of what hospitals and clinics there are. For example, there is a free civil dispensary at Nangloi, a few miles away from Rampur, but the villagers do not like to go there. This is partly because it is such a long way from the village; if a person is sick enough to need medical aid, he may also be too sick to travel to Nangloi, or to Delhi, where hospitals are available. Besides, the villagers are mistrustful and fearful of the clinic. Of six informants who expressed their views about it (four Jats, one Camar, and one Bhangi), only one (a Jat) claimed that the treatment was good. All the others said that a patient had to spend money there to get attended to properly, and that only well-to-do people are well treated, but not the poor. Three informants expressed a suspicion that real medicines are not given—just colored water. Two complained of the distance, and one of callous treatment by the personnel.[8]

---

[6] *The First Five Year Plan*, 1952:490.

[7] *The First Five Year Plan*, 1952:494.

[8] There is also a private dispensary at Kanjhawla School, a few miles from Rampur, where a compounder attends patients daily and a doctor visits twice a week, giving consultations free of charge; and there is a Khati at Rampur who gives medicines. But there are no medical facilities of the Western type in the village itself.

In general, the villagers prefer to resort to indigenous remedies. There used to be a man in Rampur who prepared medicines, of which the following may serve as an example. For a form of anemia common among children, a dried cotton plant was burnt and applied to the patient's body, and the patient was given pills in which some of the ingredients were part of a cow's head, the flesh of a tiger, and elephant's urine. There are also simple home remedies which can be applied by a housewife, some herbal, some magical. (For a headache, drop a heavy brick or stone into a well on Sunday.) Some of these local treatments have the virtue of being inexpensive, and they are familiar to the villagers, inspiring less fear and mistrust than the clinics. McKim Marriott has written, "In terms of numbers of patients, amount of expenditure, and frequency of use, patronage of indigenous medicine surpasses that of western medicine one hundredfold." [9]

There are many varieties of indigenous medical practitioners in India. There are, first of all, an estimated 200,000 curers known as *vaids* and *hakims*. These work in the ancient traditions of Ayurvedic medicine, which is popular among Hindus, and the Unani system, favored by Muslims. There are also numerous village medical specialists, religious exorcists, snake-bite curers, Brahman priests, *dais* (low-caste midwives), etc. Medical concepts associated with the practices of these various kinds of curers prevail among the majority of the people. Village-level workers and others who wish to bring about new concepts and practices should first become familiar with the actually existent beliefs and the nature of the community. As George Rosen has written, "A knowledge of the community and its people . . . is just as important for successful public health work as is a knowledge of epidemiology or medicine. . . ." [10]

With this idea in mind we present the following data concerning the beliefs about health and disease currently held by the inhabitants of Rampur village. Eight Rampur villagers were interviewed—five Jats (one of whom was a woman), one Brahman, one Camar, and one Bhangi. The interviews averaged about eight hours each. Three or four other Jats gave additional information, with less full coverage. The interviews dealt with beliefs concerning such diseases as malaria, smallpox, typhoid, cholera, dysentery, pneumonia, tuberculosis, rheumatism, puerperal fever, eye inflammation, and hysteria. Native terms or equivalents for these diseases were obtained from a few informants in a pre-test period, so that they could be used during the interviews.

[9] Marriott, 1955b:241.

[10] Quoted by Benjamin Paul in Paul, 1955:3.

MALARIA

Malaria causes more sickness than any other disease in India. There are
said to be 100,000,000 cases of malaria every year in India, and the annual
mortality is estimated at 1,000,000.[11] According to Marriott, one in five of
the villagers at Kishan Garhi, not very far from Rampur, suffers from it.[12]
In Rampur, however, the incidence has gone down in recent years, due to
the antimalaria campaigns. Health authorities come to the village in July
every year to spray DDT in the houses and spread oil on ponds and stag-
nant pools to kill the larvae of anopheles mosquitoes. Two months later
the same processes are repeated. One Jat informant estimated that the
incidence of malaria had thus been reduced by 90 per cent; another placed
the estimate at 50 per cent. It will be recalled that Rampur is situated in the
slightly raised *bangar* country, which, to some extent, cuts down on the
incidence of the disease. Communities at a lower elevation suffer more from
it.

Malaria, as scientists discovered before the turn of the century, is caused
by microscopic parasites which have passed a phase of their life cycle in
the bodies of anopheles mosquitoes. After a mosquito has bitten an infected
person, the parasites swallowed with the blood conjugate and produce off-
spring. In about eight to fourteen days the latter penetrate to the poison
glands of the mosquito. When the mosquito then bites a person, the parasites are injected into his body, where they multiply and generate fever-
producing poisons. This is the only way in which malaria can be conveyed
under natural conditions.[13]

Most of the Rampur villagers have learned that malaria is transmitted by
mosquitoes, but they also single out various other factors as causing the
disease, particularly overexertion and exposure to heat or cold. These are
often given as the primary cause. Of ten informants who discussed malaria
(seven Jats, one Brahman, one Camar, and one Bhangi), seven attributed
the sickness to mosquito bite, while two Jats and one Bhangi were ignorant
of the connection between mosquitoes and malaria. The Bhangi said that
he had no idea what caused the disease. One of the two Jats stated that
it might come from a weak heart and added that some people consider it
good to have malarial fever, for then one's system is cleaned up, and heat
goes out of the body. Seven of the informants attributed malaria to overexertion, three to getting wet, and four to hot or cold temperature. Four

[11] *The First Five Year Plan*, 1952:490.
[12] Marriott, 1955b:240.
[13] See Megaw, 1946:219-20.

thought that it came from eating certain kinds of food. One attributed it to worry. Many gave several of these explanations.

Some quotations from interviews will illustrate the range of beliefs:

A Camar: "In malaria the temperature of the body rises, and the body becomes very hot and begins to ache. The patient lies in bed under a heap of clothes. He begins to perspire and thus is relieved of the fever."

Q. "Why do people lie under a heap of clothes?"

A. "Because the heat kills the heat, and so the fever comes down."

Q. "How does one get malaria?"

A. "If a man does strenuous work, for which he does not have enough stamina, he may develop fever. A man may also get it from mosquito bite."

Q. "How do mosquito bites cause fever?"

A. "Mosquitoes carry poison with them, and when they bite somebody, they pass the poison into the body and cause fever."

Q. "If all the people living in the village were bitten by mosquitoes, would they all develop fever? If not, why not?"

A. "No. The people who are healthier may well escape. The persons who are weak in health and get wet in water are more liable to fall sick."

Q. "How may a man protect himself?"

A. "He should protect himself from mosquito bite. He should not let himself get wet in the rain. The body should be kept clean. One should not eat stale food or food with a sour taste. A person should protect himself from the heat of the sun while working."

A Jat: "Malarial fever is preceded by a fit of shivering. There are aches all over the body, and the man suffers from severe headache. Sometimes he vomits. If the vomiting increases, he feels unrest in his stomach too."

Q. "How do you get malaria?"

A. "In the rainy season the ponds are full of water, and the wells fill up. If people then drink water from the wells or from ponds, as they sometimes do when working in the fields, they may get malaria. Secondly, in the rainy season there are lots of mosquitoes, and their bite also causes malaria. Thirdly, in August and September, if a man works too hard or exposes himself to the heat of the sun for too long, he may get this fever. Fourthly, if curds are eaten in the month of August, that may cause fever."

Q. "Why does the pond water and the water from the wells cause malaria?"

A. "As a man may get dysentery or diarrhea when he changes from one grain to another, so he gets fever when he drinks new water all of a sudden. He has to get used to it."

Q. "Why does mosquito bite cause fever?"

A. "The doctors say that it does. Mosquitoes bear a poison and pour the poison into the person's body when they bite."

Q. "If the mosquitoes bite ten people, will they all get malaria?"

A. "No. It all depends upon the blood of the victims. Some blood can kill the poison; others cannot and lead to fever."

Q. "How can malaria be prevented?"

A. "A man should protect himself from mosquito bite by using mosquito nets or by covering his body with a sheet. He might also rub his body with mustard oil, which repels mosquitoes. Water from ponds and flooded wells should be avoided. Curds should not be eaten during the rainy season. Exposure to the sun should also be avoided."

A Brahman: "In malaria the patient runs a temperature. The cases are mostly in the months of August and September. It is preceded by a fit of shivering."

Q. "How does one get it?"

A. "If a man eats curds in the evening, especially after strenuous work, he might get malaria. Some get malaria from eating milk and rice preparations. If a man remains wet for a long time, he may get malaria. Mosquito bite also causes malaria."

Q. "Why do mosquito bites cause malaria?"

A. "Mosquitoes sit in dirty places and carry poison."

Q. "How is malaria treated?"

A. "Quinine tablets and quinine mixture are given. *Nim* leaves should be ground into a thin paste and given to the patient. *Tulsi* leaves, black pepper, and *patasas* should be boiled together, and given to the patient with water. As soon as a man is attacked by malaria, he should take hot milk with sugar. This tends to bring out perspiration, and the fever subsides. There is an herb called *sah dai,* bitter in taste, which is given to the patient after being ground into paste. This herb is found in the fields during the rainy season."

SMALLPOX

In 1944 and 1945 there were, respectively, 216,500 and 137,100 recorded deaths from smallpox in British India. Between 1932 and 1941 the average annual deaths from this disease were 69,500.[14] The means of preventing smallpox has long been known, although the microbe which causes it is not completely understood. "The infection of smallpox is spread by contact

---

[14] Davis, 1951:47.

with persons who are suffering from the disease or by contact with clothing which they have worn, and probably also by flies which have settled on the infected persons and afterwards on susceptible persons. Droplet infection probably plays a part in the spread of infection." [15] April-May is the worst season for smallpox in India.

As in the case of malaria, an official government campaign has helped to reduce the incidence of smallpox in Rampur. According to one informant, the last such case was eight or nine years ago. Authorities of the health department come to the village at least once a year to give vaccinations, particularly to school children and to all newborn infants. If adults have formerly been vaccinated, their vaccination is optional. But everyone is vaccinated if there has been an epidemic in the vicinity.

The traditional explanation for smallpox is that it is sent by the goddess Sitala, also known as Mata or Devi. This deity is particularly honored at the festival of Basora, held every year in Rampur.[16] She is specially worshipped by women of the lower castes. According to Marriott, vaccination annoys the goddess: "If vaccination or medication of the skin were applied to any child of the village at a time when Mata was also present in the body, the touchy goddess would be angered and would surely kill or maim those infants whom she had already seized." [17]

While the villagers at Rampur tend to know about vaccination, they may also have supernatural explanations for the disease. Of seven informants (five Jats, one Brahman, and one Camar) who discussed smallpox, four referred to vaccination as a preventive measure. Three of these were Jats; the fourth was the Camar. Three informants (two Jats and the Brahman) did not mention vaccination. The Camar and one of the Jats each cited both vaccination and supernatural causation in their comments. Analyzing the responses, it seems that the Jat informants tended to give nonsupernatural causes, while the Camar and the Brahman explained the cause or cure of smallpox in terms of gods, evil spirits, or "the stars." One Jat, however, described a magical cure.

The Brahman and two of the Jats gave certain kinds of food as a cause. One Jat said that children get smallpox when their mothers have worked in the fields and have become overheated. If the women suckle their children after exposure to the sun, the milk is too warm, and the children may get sick. This was also given as an explanation for various other ailments, including diarrhea.

---

[15] Megaw, 1946:238.

[16] See pp. 200-203.

[17] Marriott, 1955b:253.

One of the Jats said that a smallpox patient should be kept in a darkened room to protect his eyes; otherwise he might go blind. The same informant said that the disease gets worse if the shadow of a low-caste person—a Camar or Bhangi—falls across the patient. The consequence of this might be fatal. To protect the patient against such eventualities, a bunch of *nim* leaves is hung at the doorway, while a second bunch is placed beneath his cot. Another Jat said that the purpose of this custom was to keep flies away.

One or two informants expressed doubt about the efficacy of vaccination. In answer to the question, "How can you prevent smallpox?" one informant said, "I don't know." Q: "Haven't you heard of vaccination?" A: "Yes, the children in the school get it, but how will that help? Everything is God's will."

Here are some more excerpts from the interviews:

A Camar: "In smallpox there are blisters all over the body. The blisters contain water. The patient becomes very weak. The pain develops later on in blisters. It is accompanied by a slight temperature. At times the patient may be under the influence of an evil spirit. Even after the ghost is driven away through the help of a curer, there is an increased likelihood of his falling ill with smallpox."

Q. "What is the treatment?"

A. "Ashes are applied to the blisters after they have been screened through a cloth. Cow dung is plastered over the floor. Efforts are made to observe cleanliness near the patient. After he has recovered, the patient is taken to the village goddess. She is given offerings of *gulgulas, patasas,* and glass bangles. Some of the food is eaten by the dogs; the rest is given to the Bhangis."

Q. "Is the patient segregated?"

A. "No, we feel no particular fear."

Q. "If a man gets smallpox, are other people also apt to suffer during that period?"

A. "Yes, sometimes it spreads."

Q. "Why does it spread?"

A. "It is generally in summer. It spreads from some foul air from the disease. As long as the patient does not recover completely, he does not have his hair cut, a shave, or a bath. After his recovery, water from the Ganges is sprinkled over him, so that he may become pure. In the village the people who are more well-to-do have their children vaccinated, but the poor do not."

Q. "Do they have to pay for the vaccination?"

A. "Yes. And we cannot bear that expense."

Q. "Do you believe that it works?"

A. "Yes. When there is a smallpox epidemic, people who have been vaccinated usually escape."

A Jat: "In smallpox there are blisters all over the body. I can't say if the patient suffers with fever, as there have been few cases in the village. If the illness is light, the patient may recover after four to five days. It is said that only those people get it who have not been vaccinated. The patient may sometimes lose his eyesight. He feels a burning pain all over his body. If it attacks the tongue, the patient may become dumb for the rest of his life. I don't know what causes it."

Q. "What is vaccination?"

A. "I don't know about it. Some liquid from a file is applied on the arm, and a scratch is made with a knife, so that it may mix with the blood. If a patient gets the disease, he is made to lie on screened ashes, so that if a blister bursts, the matter won't come into contact with some other part of his body. Food which produces matter in the body is not given to the patient. Flies are not allowed to sit on him. A vow is taken by the patient's relatives that if he recovers they will offer *gehna* to the goddess Devi. *Gehna* consists of 5¼ *sirs* of wheat, one *gur* cake weighing about 4 *sirs*, and 4 annas. Some take a vow to go to Gurgaon and give an offering of 5 to 20 rupees' worth of sweets, or even more. Women sit together at night and sing songs in praise of the goddess of Gurgaon, and pray to her to give relief to the patient."

Q. "What will happen if matter from the blisters comes into contact with the body of a healthy man?"

A. "There is danger of the healthy man's contracting the disease."

Q. "How does smallpox spread?"

A. "Whoever comes into contact with the matter from the blisters will get it."

Q. "How does the first patient get it?"

A. "I cannot say, but I believe that only those who do not get themselves vaccinated get this disease."

Q. "How many incidents have there been of smallpox in the village?"

A. "I know of only two such cases in the village. The last case of smallpox was eight or nine years ago."

Q. "What is the general belief about taking vows to offer *gehna* to the village goddess, or to the goddess of Gurgaon?"

A. "It was believed that the patient could recover only if the goddess wished it. That is why they made vows to offer *gehna* to the goddess. The women still cling to this belief, but among the men it has been losing ground for some time because of the influence of the Arya Samaj. The Arya Samaj held meetings here. They said that there were only two Matas (mothers)—the mother who gives birth to a child and the mother earth. The Mata goddesses are false. Some women were influenced by the Arya Samaj, besides the men, but their number was not large; that is because they were not literate."

A Brahman: "When the patient has fever for two or three days and makes no effort to treat it, but instead takes a cold bath after working, this disease may develop inside his body. The heat comes out of the body in the shape of blisters. If, at such a time, the stars are also unfavorable, they also play a part in developing the fever into smallpox."

Q. "What is done to right the unfavorable influence of the stars?"

A. "When the blisters appear, people vow to offer *gehna* to Mata. So long as the patient does not recover, Mata is bathed daily in the morning and evening. If the pundit asks for an offering of sweets to be made to Mata during the illness, that is also done."

Q. "Is the disease caused by the anger or dissatisfaction of Mata?"

A. "No. But *gehna* is offered to get her help in driving the disease away."

Q. "If there is a case of smallpox, does it spread?"

A. "No."

A female Jat: "In smallpox there are blisters all over the body. The patient has fever. There is a burning pain all over the body. From the appearance of the blisters to recovery might take fifteen to twenty days."

Q. "How is it caused?"

A. "I don't know. But if a healthy person comes in contact with the patient, he can also get the disease. It can fly from one to the other."

Q. "How is it treated?"

A. "A small brick is heated in the fire, and cow's urine is dropped over it. The brick is brought near the patient, so that the vapors reach his body. This is supposed to bring relief."

Q. "Why is cow's urine used and not that of buffaloes?"

A. (The informant laughs.) "The cow is the most sacred animal, and only the cow's urine has curative value."

Q. "What other diseases are cured by cow's urine?"

A. "It is said that if a man suffers from liver trouble, some cow's urine should be given him with a little salt to drink, for a period of four or five days. When there is a vaccination, the place is exposed to the vapors of cow's urine. That is supposed to bring relief."

Q. "Why are vaccinations given?"

A. "It is said that they give protection against smallpox."

Q. "Does vaccination provide protection?"
A. "In most cases it does, but in others it does not."
Q. "Are there cases of vaccinated persons getting smallpox?"
A. "Yes, there have been many such cases."

A Jat: "No medicine of any kind is given for smallpox, but every day, early in the morning, as soon as the mother gets up, she takes some gram, wheat, or *haldi,* [different on different days], and goes to the outskirts of the village, where she places the grain in five groups—five handfuls. This is done for five days in this form:

❀   ❀

❀

❀   ❀

The grain is removed, a little at each time, with the hope that the smallpox will similarly go down."

TYPHOID

Enteric fever, or typhoid fever, is caused by a bacillus which usually enters the body through food or liquid. The infection is so widespread in India that many Indians suffer from it in childhood and then acquire an immunity which may be lifelong. Epidemics of the disease are therefore rare. A large percentage of Europeans visiting India formerly got the disease, but nowadays inoculation provides a generally effective artificial immunity.[18] Cases of typhoid occur fairly often in Rampur, but the mortality rate is low.

The traditional explanation for the disease is similar to that for smallpox. A goddess, Kainthi-wali Mata, or Kanti Mata, is held responsible, and offerings are made to her to release the patient from sickness. Another explanation may be that evil spirits cause the disease, and Kanti Mata drives them out. Of seven informants (five Jats, one Brahman, and one Camar), two gave such interpretations—the Camar and one of the Jats.

There did not seem to be much unanimity of opinion concerning this disease. Three informants (the Brahman and two Jats) attributed it to "heat in the body." One Jat said that the cause and cure depended upon God. Such factors as food, overexertion, flies, temperature, and "foul air" were cited by one person each. Two persons—the Camar and one of the Jats—referred to the dangerous effects of people's shadows. The Camar stated that the shadow of a strange person or that of someone in new clothes should not fall on the patient. This is reminiscent of the belief re-

---

[18] Megaw, 1946:235.

lating to the shadows of lower-caste persons in smallpox cases. Since the Camar is himself low-caste, he would not be apt to offer the latter version. In this case, as well as in that of smallpox, *nim* leaves are hung by the door to counteract the evil influences. Excerpts from the interviews follow:

A Camar: "In typhoid there are something like sand particles on the front portion of the neck and chest. The patient feels discomfort and at times loses consciousness. He begins to talk as if he were dreaming something. He has a slight temperature. There is sometimes pain in the ribs. There is a repellent smell from the patient. Mostly, it is due to the influence of evil spirits. The patient gets fever from them. Then the goddess, Kanti Mata, appears in the shape of sandy particles on the chest. It is believed that she comes to drive away the evil spirits."

Q. "Before the goddess appears, how do you know that the patient is suffering from typhoid?"

A. "If the patient's fever does not go down for two or three days, the people go to visit a pundit or a curer. He tells them that the patient is suffering from the influence of evil spirits. They set aside an offering to Kanti Mata consisting of *gulgulas, patasas,* and coconut. This is given to the goddess after the patient has recovered. No other treatment is followed. Cleanliness is observed, however, and fruits like grapes are given to the patient. After browning flour on the fire, sugar and some milk are added to it, and the mixture is given to the patient to eat. In seven or eight days the marks on the chest become black, and the patient recovers. Sometimes he may not recover for a month, if the shadow of a person in new clothes falls over him. *Nim* leaves are hung by the door to keep away evil influences. Some incense is burned. Such a shadow is very dangerous and may lead to the death of the patient. Therefore foreign people and men or women who may be wearing new clothes are not allowed to enter the patient's room."

Q. "What sort of cleanliness do you observe?"

A. "Cow dung and mud are applied to the floor of the patient's room. Water is kept for his use in a new earthen pot. Clean clothes are provided for him."

Q. "What is the use of cleanliness?"

A. "So that flies may not collect in swarms. Cleanliness is generally beneficial in this disease."

Q. "Why should flies be avoided?"

A. "Flies cause dirt. They also worry the patient through their bites."

A Jat: "The patient runs a high temperature. There is sometimes pain on the right side of the chest. The fever is continuous. The patient feels extremely thirsty. When these symptoms are present, the people suspect that the man is suffering from typhoid, and that there will soon be eruptions of minute spots on the chest. If the fever does not go down after three or four days, people who are expert in diagnosing typhoid are called in to examine the patient. He is taken out and his chest exposed to direct sunlight. When the eruption has taken place, there is a sort of sandy shine on his chest. If the patient cannot be taken out, torch-light is used, if available. No food is given to the patient. Milk is banned, since it causes loose motions; nor are *gur* and jaggery given. But if the patient feels hungry, he may have some millet porridge, or some wheat flour browned in the fire and prepared like a porridge with salt. Water is boiled and kept in a new earthen pot for the patient. If there is a delay in the eruptions, or if they have not fully erupted, pomegranate leaves are boiled in water, and the patient's chest is exposed to the vapors. The men don't raise any objections if the women want to take a vow to Kanti Mata, promising *gehna* to her if the patient recovers. Cleanliness is observed in the patient's room, and people who may be wearing dirty clothes are not allowed to enter. *Motia khamira,* a medicine prepared from real pearls, is obtained from Unani *hakims,* and may be given the patient."

Q. "Why is boiled water given?"

A. "The doctors say that there are germs in the water, and when the water is boiled, they are killed. These germs can cause disease."

Q. "If you believe in this theory, why don't you follow their treatment?"

A. "What we fear is that the doctor may give the patient a laxative. Loose motions can be very dangerous in this disease. Doctors often prescribe milk, which we think is a laxative."

Q. "Are any precautions taken during the convalescent period?"

A. "Light food is given to the patient. A hot bath of boiled *nim* leaves is given him. The body is not rubbed. Food containing tamarind and red chilies is not given to the patient, but milk and porridge may be eaten."

Q. "Why don't the men object to the women taking vows to Mata, when they don't believe in it?"

A. "We don't want to hurt the women's feelings, and it is thought good to give something to charity."

Q. "If a patient is suffering from typhoid, is there likelihood of its spreading?"

A. "No."

A Brahman: "If a patient runs a temperature, and it does not come down for three or four days, it is suspected that he has typhoid. He aches all over.

The temperature goes very high, and he may lose consciousness. After seven or eight days of continuous fever, there are some small eruptions on the chest. When the patient is taken out in the sun, they shine like sand particles. The patient also emits a peculiar smell. This shows clearly that he is suffering from typhoid. There are many cases of typhoid every year in the village, but I don't know the cause of it. I think that if a man works hard in the sun, he accumulates heat in the body which comes out in typhoid and in the eruptions on the chest."

Q. "What treatment is followed?"

A. "Millet porridge is given to the patient. He should not be given anything cold. Only a little milk should be taken and no *ghi*. There is a plant called *kondra*, from which small berry-like fruits are gathered at the end of the rainy season. These are ground into a paste in cow's urine or fresh water and given to the patient. A yeast made from pure pearls may be obtained from Unani *hakims* and given to the patient as well. *Gehna* may be kept for Devi. It consists of a cake (with 5¼ *sirs* of wheat), 1¼ yards of red cloth, and ten bangles. A rupee and a few annas are put into a bag and tied to a string around the patient's neck. After the patient has recovered, sweets are bought with this money. Some are given to Devi, the rest to children. The cloth and the bangles are given to a Brahman's daughter. If there is a typhoid case among the Brahmans, it [*gehna*] is given to some married girl in that caste."

Q. "How can one prevent falling ill from typhoid?"

A. "A man should try to keep himself healthy; that is the best prevention for every disease. He should not fatigue himself unnecessarily, and should work according to his capacity. He should not get overheated."

A Jat: "In typhoid the person has a high temperature, and there are eruptions on the chest and stomach. The person may get better in ten days, but sometimes he may have to lie in bed for a much longer period. I don't know what causes it. In the morning the person is all right, and in the evening he goes to bed with fever. A doctor or *hakim* is not usually consulted."

Q. "What sort of treatment is given?"

A. "We always try to do something which will make the eruptions come out soon. If this is done, the person feels relieved. For instance, gold jewelry can be washed in water, and the water given to the patient to drink."

Q. "How does this help?"

A. "It does, though I cannot say why. I only know it is good medicine."

Q. "What else is done?"

A. "A brick is heated and made red-hot. In the night, when the whole village is quiet, and there is nobody roaming about, the red-hot brick is removed, placed on a *thali,* and a little cow's urine is dropped on it. This *thali* with the red-hot brick and urine is placed in front of the patient, who is fully covered up. He is made to stay in this hot vapor for some time."

Q. "Why is this done?"

A. "It is done to drive away the effects of an unclean shadow. For this disease especially, the shadow of an unclean person has a very bad effect, and much care should be taken to see that no shadow falls on one. Besides this method, another is to smoke the dung of donkeys in the room."

Q. "What medicine is given to the patients?"

A. "*Kondra,* a wild herb, is mixed with *gangajal* [holy Ganges water], and the person drinks it."

Q. "What diet is given?"

A. "The patients are not able to eat anything. They are given only water, and milk in a diluted form. Sometimes *bajra* porridge, made very soft, is given, because this will help the eruptions to fall off soon."

Q. "Are there any steps taken by the doctors to prevent typhoid?"

A. "I don't know what is done in the case of typhoid; but I know that in smallpox, vaccination is given, and it has no good effect."

A Jat: "A person can only tell that he has typhoid after a few days. At first it looks as though he were suffering from excessive heat. After a while his temperature goes up, and he has a slight cough. Later, spots like prickly heat appear on his neck, chest, and stomach, and he feels dizzy and has a headache."

Q. "What causes it?"

A. "Who can say? A person is feeling all right; then suddenly he is down with fever."

Q. "Has it anything to do with food or water?"

A. "No."

Q. "Is a doctor consulted?"

A. "No."

Q. "Why not?"

A. "Because everything depends on the will of God, and who can help a dying man?"

Q. "But is nothing done to relieve the pain?"

A. "Yes, the patient is kept warm and looked after. If he is exposed to the cold, his body may become twisted and deformed. The mouth may become crooked. If that happens, the affected part is massaged."

Q. "If no doctor is called, how does one get well?"

A. "We leave it in the hands of God. We pray to God that if the patient recovers, sweets will be distributed. If a person is rich, he may buy sweets and distribute them to the children of the village. If one is poor and cannot afford to spend a lot, then a rupee and 4 annas are tied up in a cloth. This is either worn around the neck of the patient or set aside in a safe place until he recovers. Once the patient is all right, the money is spent for sweets, and they are distributed to some children."

Q. "Can typhoid be prevented?"

A. "No, I don't think so."

CHOLERA

During the last four decades the death rate for cholera has been two or three times the rate for smallpox.[19] It is apt to flourish in late summer, particularly when crowds gather at pilgrimage centers. "Cholera belongs to the group of diseases caused by special kinds of microbes which are swallowed and then multiply in the intestine. Everyone who gets cholera has recently swallowed food or drink contaminated by excreta coming from an infected person." [20] There seem to have been no cholera epidemics at Rampur. Only two of our Rampur informants discussed the disease, a Camar and a Jat. Their interviews follow:

A Camar: "In cholera cases the patient begins to vomit and starts passing loose motions. Their frequency becomes so great that a man loses consciousness and ultimately dies."

Q. "What is the color of the stools and vomit?"

A. "I have not seen a cholera patient and cannot say. Cholera is on the increase in May and June because of the extreme heat. If a man has an empty stomach in such a season, he may get cholera. If he drinks water on an empty stomach, he may also get cholera. The man's hands and feet become cold."

Q. "Why is there an increase of cholera in summer?"

A. "In the hot weather, the heat may affect the heart and lead to cholera. It is not due to the influence of evil spirits. A doctor's treatment should be followed. When there is a cholera epidemic, people who can afford to do so move away from the village until the epidemic subsides."

Q. "Why do people leave the village?"

A. "They are afraid that they may catch it from the patient."

Q. "Does it pass from the cholera patient to a healthy man? If so, why?"

A. "Yes. A man feels afraid of falling ill, and that nervousness makes him

[19] Davis, 1951:49.

[20] Megaw, 1946:231.

sick. There is also some foul air, which tends to make people sick. When there are such cases, people try to get away from the village."

Q. "Was there ever such an incident in your village?"

A. "No. There may have been some isolated cases, but never in epidemic form."

A Jat: "The patient runs a temperature. He passes loose motions and vomits. He feels thirsty."

Q. "What is the color of the stools?"

A. "Yellowish."

Q. "What is the cause of cholera?"

A. "It is due to eating stale and rotten vegetables. The sweetmeat sellers make some sweets with yeast, and if they use too much of it, the preparation may cause cholera."

Q. "How do stale and rotten vegetables cause different diseases?"

A. "They cause different diseases in different seasons. If taken in winter, they would cause another disease, but in May they cause cholera."

Q. "If some people eat some vegetables together, why do some people get it and others not?"

A. "The other people may have eaten some food which might have neutralized the bad effects of the rotten vegetables."

Q. "What is the treatment?"

A. "Unripe mangoes are baked in fire, and their juice is extracted and given to the patient after mixing in water. *Sada sindu*, an indigenous medicine, is a specific for cholera. A lot of cold water is given to the patient."

Q. "Do you use allopathic treatments also?"

A. "As this disease takes only a few hours, there is little time in which to take the patient to the hospital. If it can be arranged, every effort is made to get a doctor."

Q. "Does the disease spread?"

A. "No."

DIARRHEA

The average annual number of deaths in India due to diarrhea and dysentery in 1940-49 was 227,850.[21] These diseases are very widespread in India, and there are many chronic sufferers. Although diarrhea and dysentery cannot be clearly distinguished, they have been treated separately here. There are, of course, various causes of diarrhea.

---

[21] *The First Five Year Plan*, 1952:489.

Of eleven Rampur informants (eight Jats, one Brahman, one Camar, and one Bhangi), all mentioned food as a cause of diarrhea. Four cited exertion; four mentioned hot or cold temperature; two said that the trouble was sent by God; one said that it was brought on by worry. The concept of *dharan digna* was referred to several times; it will be discussed below under "Dysentery."

Opium is sometimes given to cure diarrhea, including that of infants. Various herbs are used in treatment, and supernatural devices may also be resorted to. A Brahman mendicant may advise a women to place cooked rice and jaggery powder at a crossroads or local shrine, as an offering to the goddess. Some excerpts from interviews follow:

A Camar: "Diarrhea is a disease of loose motions. One may go five times a day to pass stools. It may be twenty times. When the crops are harvested and new wheat comes in, people change from old wheat to the new wheat, and the change may cause loose motions. If somebody takes hot food and chilies, he may have loose motions too. Cane juice also causes it."

Q. "What are hot foods?"

A. "Potato and *bangain* [eggplant] are considered hot, among vegetables. So is *masur ki dal* [pulses]. Spicy food is also hot. Jumping or walking on uneven ground may also cause diarrhea."

Q. "How can you prevent diarrhea?"

A. "Hot food should not be taken in summer. *Pudina* [mint] and onions should be eaten. The patient should go to the *vaid* and the doctor for medicine."

Q. "Should a man go to a curer to find out if the patient is under the influence of ghosts?"

A. "Well, if the patient does not respond to the other treatment, he should go to the pundit and such curers as well."

A Jat: "Where there is heat, people suffer from diarrhea. It is also due to overexertion. *Dalda* [hydrogenated oil] also causes diarrhea."

Q. "Do all people, who may be exposed to the same amount of heat, get diarrhea?"

A. "No, the people with stout hearts will not get it. Only people with weak hearts, who might worry about the heat, get it."

Q. "Is it the people who worry most who get diarrhea?"

A. "Yes. People with stout hearts don't fall victim to it so easily. Children who eat lots of *gur* also suffer from it. So do suckling children, whose mothers have been overheated in the fields. The mothers pass the heat to their children through the milk. Sour milk, stale milk, and food also cause diarrhea. Fresh foods can be easily digested, but stale food becomes harder and cannot be digested."

Q. "What is the treatment?"

A. "A jam of *bel giri* fruit is given to the patient, and curds and rice. *Ganga-dhar churan* powder, costing about 4 to 6 annas, may be bought and given to the patient. If the loose motions were due to getting overheated, the patient is given a cold bath. For children there is an herb called *maror phali,* which is rubbed on a clean stone with a little water. The paste is given to infants and adults as well. There is also *kabuli gokhru,* which is first soaked for a few hours in water and then ground on a stone."

Q. "Do you follow allopathic treatment?"

A. "No."

Q. "Why not?"

A. "Only rich people can afford such treatment; the poor cannot."

Q. "If you had enough money, which treatment would you follow?"

A. "Allopathic treatment. I have no faith in the free civil dispensary."

Q. "If somebody in your family fell sick with diarrhea and you did not have to worry about money, how would you treat him?"

A. "First of all, I'd follow my own treatment, and if there were no relief, I'd go to the doctor."

Q. "What would you do if you had no money, and your own treatment failed?"

A. "I'd do nothing and would leave the person to his fate."

Q. "Wouldn't you try the civil dispensary?"

A. "No. I have no belief in their medicines. Even if I were to go there, they wouldn't give me genuine medicine, because I am poor. These days the doctor usually prescribes an injection in addition to his medicine, and I might have to pay as much as 5 rupees."

A Brahman: "A man can get diarrhea from exposure to cold or heat, or from overeating."

Q. "If five people get exposed to the same amount of heat or cold, why would only one get it?"

A. "It depends on the varying temperament and bodily health of the people. It is also sometimes due to eating laxative food. If a man eats stale bananas and too much fat, he may get loose motions. Green gram can cause it too. If a mother eats food carelessly and exposes herself to too much heat or cold, her baby can get it through his mother's milk."

DYSENTERY

There are two principal forms of dysentery: bacillary and amoebic. Both forms are widespread in India. According to J. E. Spencer, the number of cases ordinarily increases in the rainy season in some areas, though in regions with prolonged dry seasons and water shortages, the dry season may be the worst period of the year.[22] Eight Rampur informants discussed dysentery—five Jats, one Brahman, one Camar, and one Bhangi. Six gave food as a cause of dysentery, five cited physical exertion, three attributed it to constipation, two to God or Fate, and one to the working of the evil eye.

An interesting physiological explanation was given by five informants in discussing diarrhea or dysentery—the concept of *dharan* (a pulse under the navel) *digna* (displaced). According to our informants, over-exertion or a sudden jerk may throw the nerve off center. It is then necessary to bring the *dharan* back into line, so that it is in its proper place, equidistant from the two nipples. The stomach and legs are massaged with *ghi,* and then a lighted *ghi* lamp is placed on the patient's stomach. An inverted *lota* (brass jug) is placed over it. "The *lota* sucks the stomach and brings the pulse into the center," said one informant. This treatment is given once a day for three days. Rice and curds are given the patient to eat. Excerpts follow:

A Camar: "In dysentery there is sometimes blood in the stools. There is also *radh* [mucus]. The color is green or yellow."

Q. "How is it caused?"

A. "It is due to bad food. If we take vegetable oil, or if the bread is partially baked, it upsets the stomach. There are foods which are somewhat laxative, from which we may get dysentery. And if a man lifts a heavy load or jumps from some high place, he may get cramps in his stomach, which may cause dysentery. Weak diet or watermelons in summer may bring it on. Also, if somebody looks with envious eyes at a person because of his physical beauty, he may get dysentery, or some other disease."

Q. "How do you know that a person has fallen sick for such a reason?"

A. "When somebody is ill, a *vaid* or doctor should be able to diagnose the ailment and treat it. If he is not able to do so, we go to the pundit, and he, after calculating from his books, reveals the cause of the sickness."

Q. "What is the treatment followed?"

A. "Some incense is burned. The pundit may advise any treatment. The patient's ear may have to be bled slightly. In the case of animals, a piece of burnt human bone is brought from the cremation ground, and the animal is made to swallow it. Seven red chilies are waved over the head of the patient three times and then thrown into the fire."

---

[22] Spencer, 1954:109.

Q. "Who is the pundit who diagnoses such ailments?"

A. "Pundit Yad Ram of Karala village."

Q. "Does he charge anything?"

A. "No. The usual procedure is that when he opens his religious book, some cash offering of 1 to 2 annas is placed on the book. There is also Pundit Hardev in Rasulpur village. He also uses his powers in curing such ailments."

Q. "How does he do it?"

A. "He puts some incense before the patient in a broken earthen pot, together with two hairs and some *ghi*. He does not charge anything. He begs alms from the villagers."

A Brahman: "There are various causes of dysentery. If one eats food which is not compatible, one may get dysentery. It also comes from overeating. If a man eats his meals later than usual and gulps them down hurriedly when he is feeling very hungry, he may get it. And if a man takes food which tends to cause constipation, he may get dysentery. Also, if a man walks on uneven ground or lifts some heavy weight, it upsets the stomach and may lead to dysentery."

Q. "How are certain foods not compatible with a particular person?"

A. "Some foods upset one man, but may be harmless for another person. Incompatible foods, in my own case, are *urad*, among pulses, dry gram, *bathua sag* [a weed], and sweet porridge."

Q. "What foods cause constipation?"

A. "*Corma*, stale *prautha* [fried *capati*], *puris*, cooked potatoes without plenty of gravy, *jalebis* [fried pancakes], and *pera* [a sweet]."

A female Jat: "When it is suspected that a person has dysentery, a lamp is placed on the center of his stomach, and a *lota* is placed over it. It is kept there for a few minutes and then removed. This is supposed to cure the patient. If this does not work, the patient is made to stand, after he has had his meal, and some nerves at the back of the feet are vigorously rubbed. This is supposed to do good, but the treatment is very painful. Curds and rice are also given to the patient. No special treatment is given to infants, but curds may be given them. There is no way to prevent this disease. How can someone know that he is going to fall ill? And one cannot avoid lifting heavy weights, because that has to be done."

A Jat: "The main cause of diarrhea and dysentery is *dharan digna*. This comes when a certain pulse near the navel is shifted. The pulse should be in its correct position, because if it is shifted up, a person has constipation, and if it moves to the side or comes down lower, it causes diarrhea. A person's *dharan* moves if he happens to slip and fall, or when he lifts something heavy."

Q. "How does one know that the *dharan* has shifted?"

A. "One can make this out by holding the finger and thumb together and placing it in the navel and pressing in. After some time one can hear a tick-tick sound, but this is only possible if the *dharan* is in its normal condition; otherwise the finger has to be shifted to the side or lower down, to locate the sound. If it is found in a wrong place, it is known as *dharan digna*."

Q. "What is done then?"

A. "There are many ways of shifting the *dharan* back to its proper place. One simple way is to make the person lie down straight and jerk his limbs with a good shake. Rubbing the nerve near the ankle helps. Another way is to make a small dish-like thing with *atta* [wheat flour] and light a wick in it. This is known as *diva chun*. It is lighted, placed on the navel, and covered up by a *lota* with a big opening. When it is allowed to remain in this fashion for some time, the *dharan* comes back into place. Another method which is popular is to place the round part of the hookah in the navel and twist it around tight."

Q. "Does the person become perfectly all right again, once the *dharan* is shifted back to its place?"

A. "Yes."

Q. "How do little babies get this sickness?"

A. "If the mother works in the fields and gets overheated, her milk gets hot, and the baby gets it from the hot milk. She should first have a bath and wait for some time, so that her body gets a chance to cool off."

RESPIRATORY DISEASES: PNEUMONIA

The average annual number of deaths due to respiratory diseases in India in 1940-49 was 415,345.[23] Sir John Megaw states:

Pneumonia, bronchitis, and other respiratory diseases are responsible for a large part of the total mortality in India, and many of the millions of deaths attributed to "fevers" are really due to them. The official returns of causes of death do not throw much light on the relative frequency of pneumonia and other infections of the respiratory system, but it is certain that taken together they cause more deaths than cholera, small-pox, or any of the other dramatic diseases. The problem of these diseases is twofold: on the one hand, they are caused by microbes which enter the respiratory tract by droplet infection . . . on the other hand these

---

[23] *The First Five Year Plan*, 1952:489.

microbes are effective causes of disease and death in direct proportion to the degree of malnutrition in the community.[24]

The influenza epidemic of 1918 more than doubled the regular mortality rate in India and probably took about 20,000,000 lives.[25]

Many people suffer from coughs in Rampur, and informants were questioned for their explanation of this. A Brahman said: "There are more cases in winter. Changes of diet and changes of season are partly responsible. People chew sugar cane in the beginning of the season, when the juice is not fully matured, and this causes coughing. If water is drunk immediately after eating fatty food, coughing results. If food is touched by a dog or a cat, it may make a man cough."

Of six informants who spoke about cough (three Jats, a Brahman, a Camar, and a Bhangi), all mentioned food and water as causative factors. Three referred to tobacco smoke, two to temperature, and one to change of season. One mentioned dust, one overexertion, and one suggested that it was due to infection from another person. One person said that a baby gets cough through its mother's milk. It was formerly assumed that Mata was responsible for coughing attacks. A Jat informant said that two small coins (pice) were consequently buried in front of Mata's shrine, and some dogs were fed with *capatis*, in order to get rid of the cough.

Seven informants were also questioned about pneumonia. Here all seven were unanimous in singling out exposure to cold weather as the chief causative factor. Only one person mentioned food, and one Fate. One Jat described a cure formerly followed in the village. The ribs of a pneumonia patient were touched by a sickle which had been heated until it was red-hot. Even now many villagers have burns and scars on their bodies as a result of this treatment. Some excerpts from the interviews follow:

A Jat: "When a pneumonia patient breathes, he not only has difficulty in breathing, but also experiences pain in the ribs. He has a temperature. If the fever goes high, the patient may lose consciousness and begin to chatter. He may try to get up from the bed and run away. It becomes difficult to restrain him. When a man inhales some cold air, the blood may freeze in some part of the chest and cause pain there and lead to fever. Sometimes the man may fall sick due to exposure of his chest to cold air."

Q. "If a group of people breathe cold air, why does only one of them get pneumonia?"

A. "The others may be of hot type, while the one who got the attack may

---

[24] Megaw, 1946:231.

[25] Davis, 1951:41.

be of cold type. The former can withstand the cold; the latter cannot, and his blood freezes."

Q. "How does a man become of hot type or cold type?"

A. "It is his nature. Some people are born with a hot constitution, others with a cold one. The latter people can fall ill if they eat cold food."

Q. "How many types of food are there?"

A. "Cold food, hot food, and hot-wet food. Cold foods include wheat, rice, oranges, bananas, some vegetables, curd and *mung* among the pulses. Hot foods include millet, grams, hot milk, some vegetables including *karela*, *urad* and *masur* among pulses. If there is a combination of cold and hot foods, it is hot-wet food."

Q. "What would happen to a man of hot constitution who ate hot food?"

A. "He might have diarrhea or suffer from headache. He might have a slight temperature."

Q. "Would a hot man never get pneumonia?"

A. "No, he might get pneumonia, if the cold exceeded the heat of his constitution."

Q. "How is pneumonia treated?"

A. "The patient is given some liquor to drink. Raw eggs are also given to him, and if the patient refuses to take such nourishment on religious grounds, attempts are made to make him swallow it in the guise of medicine. A baked brick of small size is heated in the fire, and after dropping it in water, it is immediately taken out and wrapped in a piece of cloth. It is then applied to the part of the chest where the patient experiences pain. A small charcoal fire or a fire made of cow-dung cakes is placed below the patient's cot. Eight or nine people out of ten will survive with this treatment. If the illness persists more than twenty-four hours, in spite of these measures, we go for medical aid."

Q. "Do you think that allopathic treatment is effective in pneumonia?"

A. "Yes."

Q. "Has anybody in the village taken penicillin injections?"

A. "About nine or ten months ago a man came to the village and said that he was a doctor and owned a shop in Khera Khural. Dharma Jat was suffering from a slight fever in those days. His heart had also become weak. The doctor examined him and said that he would cure him with a penicillin injection. He gave the injection and charged 2 rupees, saying that he would collect another rupee on his next trip after Dharma was cured. When he got the injection, Dharma said that some heat had been generated in him. They gave the doctor his meals. After four or five hours Dharma said that he was feeling better, but that was only temporary relief, and his trouble continued as before. The doctor has not yet returned to the village to collect his extra rupee.

"Some people say that doctors have been giving penicillin injections for every kind of sickness, and that it has not been successful in curing various diseases."

Q. "How may pneumonia be prevented?"

A. "After a man has worked hard, he should not expose himself to cold all of a sudden. If he is thirsty, he should not drink cold water right after exertion, but should take it only after ten to fifteen minutes' rest. In winter he should guard against the cold. He should not sleep in a cold, drafty room. A man should also avoid cold food in the cold season."

A Brahman: "If a man exposes himself to extreme cold, he may get pneumonia. If he is warm, after doing strenuous work, and exposes himself to cold all of a sudden and breathes cold air, he may get pneumonia. The cold air abruptly slows down the circulation, and the shock may cause some injury and lead to pneumonia. To treat a patient, he should be well covered up, so that his body is warm. A bottle should be filled with hot water and applied to the place where the patient feels pain. Cotton is warmed on an iron plate and is also applied there. A small brick is heated in the fire, and then it is wrapped in a cloth and applied to the chest. Mustard seed is ground into a paste and applied to the chest as well. Betel leaf may also be placed on his chest, as well as boiled millet. Liquor may be given the patient. If none of these measures works, an allopathic doctor may be sent for."

Q. "Have you heard about penicillin injections?"

A. "No, I haven't heard of them."

TUBERCULOSIS

J. E. Spencer states that the mortality rate of tuberculosis in the Orient is five to ten times that of the United States.[26] The incidence of tuberculosis in India is hard to estimate. For the period 1932-41 estimates of deaths from tuberculosis in British India ranged from 450,000 to 820,000 per year, or from, roughly, 7 to 13 per cent of all deaths.[27] *The First Five Year Plan* estimates that there are 500,000 deaths from tuberculosis every year in India, while 2,500,000 people suffer from the active disease.[28] The incidence is believed to be increasing as the infection spreads from the cities to rural

[26] Spencer, 1954:109.

[27] Davis, 1951:55.

[28] *The First Five Year Plan*, 1952:502.

districts. In the West the disease is quickly being overcome, but in India it is increasing "in an alarming manner." [29]

Tuberculosis may attack any part of the body, but in most cases the lungs or bowels are affected. The bacillus usually enters the body by inhalation into the lungs, but the infection may also be started by swallowing food contaminated by the sputum of a t.b. patient. Very few persons escape infection with the bacilli, but a good state of general health may suffice to overcome the germs. Hence the seriousness of India's widespread poverty and malnutrition in the face of the spread of this disease.[30]

Rampur, being situated close to Delhi, is in a vulnerable position with regard to tuberculosis. Our informants seemed to be familiar with the chief symptoms and expressed fear of the disease. One Jat informant said that a man suspected of having t.b. should be avoided. Nobody uses his utensils, plate, or glass "because the person has sputum in his mouth, and it touches the utensils. And sputum is dirty and may have all sorts of germs in it." The same informant added, "The definite sign that one has tuberculosis is that the person becomes terribly thin and looks like a skeleton. No treatment is given, because nobody likes to tell others that one has that disease. The family members feel very sad, but nothing can be done. He either gets better, or he dies."

Of seven informants (three Jats, one Brahman, one Camar, and one Bhangi) who discussed tuberculosis, four attributed the disease to transmission of infection. The two lower-caste informants—the Camar and the Bhangi—did not. The Bhangi thought it came from having the heart attacked by worms. Two informants (both Jats) thought that t.b. came from too much sexual activity, or from having sexual relations during fever or after a meal. The Brahman attributed the disease to lust and worry on the part of the patient. One Jat said that it came from stale food, or food cooked in aluminum utensils. The Camar stated that it came from a wound in the lungs. Five informants mentioned the curative properties of goat's milk, and four said that a tubercular patient should be in the presence of goats, whose smell has a therapeutic effect. Goats are therefore tied to the beds of t.b. patients. Excerpts from the interviews follow:

A Camar: "In t.b. one has a slight temperature all the time. The patient coughs and spits out a lot of phlegm. Sometimes it is accompanied by blood as well. When a man has a slight temperature for some time, his lungs become weak. Perhaps some wounds develop in the lungs, and pus is formed

29 Megaw, 1946:228.
30 Megaw, 1946:228.

there. He spits out pus and blood. I do not know if some worms go into the lungs and cause wounds, or if the wounds are from some other cause. The appetite becomes weak. The patient cannot do any work. Young people up to the age of seventeen are more likely to get it. Both rich and poor people fall victim to it."

Q. "How is t.b. treated?"

A. "The patient's bed is placed where goats are kept. The smell of their urine and dung is supposed to have curative effects. Goat's milk is given to the patient. Otherwise, the treatment usually followed is that of the doctors in the government t.b. hospitals."

Q. "Do you know some cases of t.b. patients who were cured through smelling the urine and dung of goats?"

A. "No. Most of the people die. It is a terrible disease, and the man may live to suffer two or three years before he dies."

A Jat: "A t.b. patient has a fever. Sometimes he has diarrhea. Sometimes he feels hot, at other times cold. He has a dry cough. It is only when the patient exerts himself that he is able to spit out phlegm, which is sometimes accompanied by blood. Sometimes he has a pain in his chest when he coughs."

Q. "Why does the patient cough out blood?"

A. "I've heard that some wounds develop in the lungs; the blood comes from those wounds."

Q. "Have you ever seen the lungs of men or animals?"

A. "No. But I have seen a photo of human lungs in the hospital."

Q. "What are lungs used for?"

A. "I have heard that blood is made in them, and it is from there that it goes all over the body."

Q. "How is t.b. caused?"

A. "If either a man or woman has fever at the time of sexual relations, he or she may get t.b. When a person has fever, his blood boils because of the heat of the body. Again, when a healthy man and woman have sexual relations, their blood boils; after it has been churned, semen forms and is discharged. Now, if a man or woman has fever and they unite sexually, the one who had fever, and whose blood has already boiled over, has his blood boiled again; and the result is that the blood becomes thin and flows out of the lungs. At that moment he develops wounds in his lungs. Also, if a man has sexual relations with a woman right after taking food, he may get t.b."

Q. "Have you taken precautions against having sexual relations when either you or your wife had fever?"

A. "Yes."

Q. "Can you tell me how one gets t.b. if one has sexual relations after eating?"

A. "When one eats food, it takes a few hours to digest. If there is sexual union right after eating, the food is still undigested, and if the blood boils at such a moment to form semen, a wound may develop in the lungs. I have also heard that this disease can fly from one person to another. If a healthy man brings his face near to that of a t.b. patient, and inhales the air breathed out by him, he may get t.b. Also, if a man eats food in aluminum utensils, he may get t.b."

Q. "How does the disease fly from one person to another?"

A. "There are wounds inside the lungs, and when the patient breathes out, he expels foul air. If a healthy man inhales it, he may get wounds in his lungs."

Q. "If a healthy man looks at a body wound and inhales that air, will it cause wounds in his lungs?"

A. "No."

Q. "Then why would the air breathed out by a t.b. patient cause such wounds?"

A. "The doctors say that there are small germs inside the lungs of t.b. patients; they are so minute that they cannot be seen by the naked eye, but only through a machine. When a t.b. patient exhales, he lets out those germs which, if inhaled by a healthy person, would cause t.b."

Q. "Does a man who suffers from t.b. as a result of sexual union while in fever or right after eating have the same germs in his lungs?"

A. "Yes."

Q. "How do they come to be there?"

A. "They are produced when the wounds have developed there."

Q. "Why aren't there t.b. germs in body wounds?"

A. "Lungs and body wounds are exposed to different air, and t.b. germs may not live in outside wounds in the open air."

Q. "Do you believe in the germ theory of disease?"

A. "No. I believe in the reasons I have given—that if people have sexual relations when one of them is suffering from fever, or if they have sexual relations right after eating, they may get t.b. It is also due to eating food cooked in aluminum utensils."

Q. "How do you know that? Does anybody in the village use aluminum utensils?"

A. "No. Only some poor people use them, but even they have only a few. Unani *hakims* say that food cooked in aluminum utensils causes t.b."

Q. "Where can t.b. be treated?"

A. "This disease cannot be treated effectively in the village, but only in hospitals."

Q. "What treatment is followed in the village, if the patient doesn't go to a hospital?"

A. "He is fed a light diet. Tamarind and mustard-oil preparations are not given him. Efforts are made to suppress the name of the disease, so that the patient may not know that he has t.b., from which few people recover. The patient is given goat's milk to drink. He is kept clean, and his sputum is covered by ashes."

Q. "Why is that done?"

A. "So that flies will not sit on it."

Q. "Do flies carry disease? If so, how?"

A. "Flies usually sit on dirt, and when they also sit on food, they carry some dirty stuff and leave it on the food. When the food is eaten, the dirt is bound to upset the stomach."

Q. "Does goat's milk have any curative value in t.b.?"

A. "Yes, goat's milk is light, as well as cold in its value."

A Brahman: "The patient runs a temperature, and he suffers from a slight cough. He feels tired. He would not like cold or warm weather. When the fever doesn't respond to treatment for a month or two, and the patient begins to spit phlegm which sometimes has blood in it, it is presumed that he has t.b. A man who worries a lot and is always dreaming about getting this and that can fall victim of this disease. A man who is lusty and passionate can also get it. Even a healthy man can contract this disease from a t.b. patient."

Q. "How does a healthy man contract it?"

A. "If he breathes in diseased air exhaled by the patient, containing germs, he may get it that way."

Q. "What are germs?"

A. "The doctors say that they are so minute that they cannot be seen by the naked eye, and healthy people should be protected from them."

Q. "How does a man who worries a lot get these germs?"

A. "His heart becomes weak owing to illness, and the germs develop there by themselves."

Q. "Are the germs found in the heart?"

A. "I cannot say whether they are in the heart or in the lungs. I don't even know where the lungs are in the body, but it is said that they are in the chest."

Q. "How is t.b. treated?"

A. "Goat's milk must be given to the patient. The patient is kept as far as possible among goats. He should get clean, fresh air, which contains the smell of green trees and flowers. If he can't be kept among goats, at least one or two goats should be tied near his cot. Mustard-oil preparations should not be given to the patient. He should have plenty of fruits—apples, oranges, papayas. The patient should be treated by a doctor, *vaid,* or *hakim.*"

Q. "What benefit is obtained by keeping the patient near goats?"

A. "Goats eat all kinds of leaves and herbs in the jungle, and the vapors which they breathe out tend to destroy the germs."

Q. "Don't cows and buffaloes also eat those herbs?"

A. "No. They are not solely dependent for fodder on jungle grass, and they don't eat the same herbs."

Q. "How can t.b. be prevented?"

A. "However bad conditions may be, a man should not worry a lot. He should control his lust and passions. He should protect himself from t.b. patients, if he is atending them. A man should try to control his wants and avoid greed, and he should keep regular habits."

RHEUMATISM

Of six informants who discussed rheumatism (four Jats, one Brahman, and one Camar), five attributed the disease to some kind of food. Three Jats and one Brahman singled out temperature as a causative factor, while two Jats cited overexertion. Quotations from two informants are given here.

A Camar: "In rheumatism there is pain all over the joints. The patient has difficulty in moving about and suffers pain. People mainly get it in winter. If a man takes cold medicine in winter, he may develop pain in the joints. Cold medicines include almonds and some herbs which the *vaid* gives. Doctors and *vaids* give treatments. They give medicine and some medicated oil to rub on the joints. In winter one should avoid cold medicines, but should have plenty of milk and *ghi.*"

A Jat: "In rheumatism there is pain in the joints, which can't be moved freely. There is some swelling in the joints. If a man works strenuously and becomes overheated, and then goes suddenly into a cool place, he may get this trouble. Also, if a man of cool temperament eats some cold food, he may get it. For treatment, a pit is dug in which a fire of cow-dung cakes is made. After the pit has become sufficiently hot, something is put on the floor of the pit, so that when the patient lowers himself into it, his feet will not burn. The patient is made to sit in the heated pit for about five minutes, after which he comes out and is immediately covered with clothing. The patient is naked except for his loincloth when he enters the pit. This treatment is followed in the village, but I haven't seen it with my own eyes. There was a Camar many years ago who suffered from this trouble. He was lowered into the pit, but he didn't stay long in it and started shouting that he was getting burned. The people had to take him out. Since he came out too soon, he did not fully recover, but only the pain in the knee joints remained. I have heard that this treatment is very effective if the patient can manage to stay inside the pit for the prescribed period."

POSTPARTUM PUERPERAL FEVER

Maternal mortality in India has recently been estimated to be twenty per thousand live births. About 200,000 maternal deaths take place every year, while the morbidity resulting from causes associated with childbearing is believed to be around 4,000,000.[31] Puerperal fever is one of the causes of maternal mortality and morbidity.

Only four informants discussed postpartum puerperal fever—three Jats and one Brahman. All attributed it to the weakness of the mother and to the taking of indigestible or "unbalanced" food, except for one Jat, who did not specifically refer to the weakness of the mother. One Jat mentioned exposure to the cold as a factor. Excerpts from the interviews follow:

A Jat: "A woman gets this disease if she takes diluted milk. No milk should be taken within ten days after delivery. It should be given only after the mother has had a good bath [a purificatory bath], and all the dirty clothes have been discarded and the house swept and cleaned. If the mother takes milk before this time, she will get ill."

Q. "Why does drinking diluted milk have this effect?"

A. "I don't know, but that is how women get the disease. The disease can be prevented by not drinking diluted milk for nearly two months."

Q. "Is this the only precaution?"

A. "Yes, as far as I know; but I do not know much about this disease."

A Camar: "After delivery the woman's body becomes very delicate. Great care has to be taken that she gets food which can be easily digested, and that the food is properly cooked. If she is careless about this, she may get the fever. It may also be due to exposure to cold. Our own treatments are followed, but if the woman has once got the fever, there is little hope for her. Allopathic medicine may be tried, but few women are cured. Food which can easily be digested is best in the woman's delicate state of health.

[31] *The First Five Year Plan,* 1952:489.

No solid food should be given. After delivery the woman should take every precaution against exposing herself to cold."

A Brahman: "The woman becomes very weak after delivery. Sometimes she suffers from fever before delivery. The woman thinks that she has got rid of the fever, but it continues. Balanced food should be given her. If there is too much of one thing or too little of another, that might cause the fever."

EYE INFLAMMATION

Many villagers suffer from eye inflammation, for which their most common—and probably correct—explanation was dust or dirt in the eye. Of seven informants (four Jats, one Brahman, one Camar, and one Bhangi), all gave the latter explanation. There were, however, additional interpretations. Three informants ascribed eye inflammation to the effects of sun and heat, two to the change of season, two to some kinds of food, two to fear or anxiety, one to overexertion, one (the Camar) to ghosts, and one to work in poor light.

A belief that eye inflammation is "catching" through psychological causes was expressed by one informant as follows: "If a person who is well sees a person with sore eyes, he feels bad and sick. As soon as he feels that way, he catches the disease. Those who can stand seeing people with sore eyes won't catch it." A Jat informant, who expressed the same view, said that skin irritation and vomiting may be caused the same way. Some excerpts from the interviews follow.

A Camar: "The eyeballs become red, and water flows from the eye. Dirt also begins to accumulate. The patient's eyes hurt. There is sometimes a swelling over the eyes. It is difficult to open them. In summer, if sweat gets into the eyes, they become sore. If red chilies touch the eyes, or if, while washing the face, soap gets into the eyes, one may have sore eyes. It may also be due to the shades of ghosts. Dust can also cause it. Drops of alum water may be put into the eyes. If the treatment by the *vaid* or doctor doesn't help, the pundit or curer may be consulted."

A Jat: "The eyes become red, and sometimes there is a swelling over them. The patient suffers unbearable pain. It is due to the change of season from winter to summer. It is also due to dust getting into the eyes, or flies carrying dirt. Children suffer from it because the women are no longer careful to wash their children's eyes and do not put soot from the mustard-oil lamp into them regularly."

Q. "Why don't all people suffer from sore eyes when the season changes from winter to summer?"

A. "I don't know why. But most of the cases of eye inflammation occur then."

Q. "Flies carrying dirt can cause various different diseases. How is that? Why don't they just cause one particular disease?"

A. "It is like this: if sand enters into one's eyes, one will have irritation in the eyes. If it goes along with food into the stomach, there will be irritation there. Wherever the sand enters, there will be irritation. Wherever the flies leave the dirt, there will be disease. If it goes into the food, the stomach will be upset; if into the eyes, one will get eye inflammation."

A Brahman: "There is unbearable pain in the eyes, and they become red and swollen. If the trouble is prolonged, the patient may lose his eyesight. My own son, when he was eight months old, lost an eye owing to this trouble. He was operated on at Bahadurgarh Hospital. The cases of eye inflammation are found mostly in the months of March-April and August-September. The season changes during these months, and this change of season causes eye inflammation. There is also dust and heat during these months. That also causes it."

Q. "Does this disease spread from one person to another?"

A. "No, it does not spread through contact or air, but if a man has an obsession that he will catch it, the fear may speed up the inflammation."

Q. "What is the treatment?"

A. "Soot, prepared by burning a mustard-oil lamp, is put into the eyes. Another concoction is made by the women—by putting some other medicine in the soot. There is some yellow medicine available in the hospitals that is also put into the eyes. In cases of swelling of the eyes, bamboo, *jamun*, or *nim* leaves are placed on the eyes with a piece of cloth. The eyes should occasionally be washed with boiled water containing salt or alum, and cold water baths should be taken daily as a precaution, so that the brain may remain cool. The eyes should be washed twice a day with fresh water."

Q. "Why should the water be boiled?"

A. "Warm water cleans the eyes thoroughly."

HYSTERIA

The term "hysteria" is here applied to a condition called *ghot*, which the villagers traditionally associate with spirit possession. Natural causes may also be invoked. Of six informants (four Jats, one Brahman, and one Camar), one Jat and the two non-Jats cited the influence of evil spirits.

The other three Jats all gave "heat in the body" as an explanation. One Jat offered other explanatory factors, such as delay in the menses, the eating of some kinds of food, and the breathing in of gas or germs. The Brahman cited overexertion, worry or shock, and "evil air," in addition to the influence of evil spirits.

Various stories were told about cases of spirit possession in Rampur. There is a Bhangi woman, aged thirty-five, who used to lie unconscious for hours. She was finally cured by a man who offered worship to the goddesses Kanti Mata and Kali. The treatment was described as follows: The earth is first plastered with cow dung, and the patient then sits before the curer face to face. After offering worship, the curer invokes the powers of the goddess, whereupon the evil spirit speaks through the voice of the patient. The curer then asks the spirit who it is. In this case the spirit belonged to the wife of a Camar woman who had been drowned in the canal—allegedly by her own husband. The curer asked this spirit to leave the woman and got her to promise not to return.

Excerpts from the interviews follow:

A Jat: "A person who is said to be suffering from *ghot* is one who has been possessed by the spirit of a dead person. If it is still roaming about the village, the spirit can get hold of a person at any time—usually if the person goes out in midday or in the night. It is easy to tell when a person is possessed, because he is not in his normal senses. He talks a lot, laughs, or just remains quiet. It is not the man himself who is doing that, but it is the spirit in him."

Q. "How does one drive away the spirit?"

A. "We throw chilies into the fire, bring smoke near the person and make him chew pepper. Then the spirit starts to speak and says, 'I will go away. Don't do this and don't do that.' Sometimes the spirit can tell a lot of things. After the person is all right again, the people make a *roti* as big as the palm of your hand, smear it with oil, take it around the person three times, and then throw it away outside the village. If the spirit can't be driven out by a layman, a *siyana* [healer] is called. He chants *mantras*. Sometimes he plucks a single hair from the person's head and bottles it up. The hair becomes as thick as a finger. This is the spirit which has been caught and bottled up; now it cannot escape. Then it is buried. After that the person will no longer be tortured. Sometimes a man who is possessed is difficult to control."

Q. "Is there any way of protecting oneself from possession?"

A. "You should try to please the spirits of the dead and not go near burial places or walk about in the night after eating a sweet dish."

Q. "How can one please the spirits of the dead?"

A. "By giving something in their names to the poor."

Q. "Do many get *ghot*?"

A. "No, very few. And they can often be cured just by slapping, and having the smoke of chili powder in the room. That frightens the spirit, and once he leaves the person, the man becomes normal again."

A Camar: "Both men and women may fall under the influence of spirits. The patient may lie senseless, or start vomiting, or he may talk like a lunatic. Doctors, *vaids*, pundits, and curers, who have goddesses in their power, will each give a different explanation. The pundit would say that it is due to the influence of bad stars, while the curer would say that the person is under the influence of evil spirits."

Q. "Can you tell me about the case of someone who was under the influence of an evil spirit?"

A. "Yes. There was a man named Harphul from our community. He was a young boy of eighteen. About three months ago he was working at the cane crusher. Just after sunset one day he took some fresh jaggery from the cane crusher and went toward the pond, eating it. There he got fever. Somehow, he walked back to the cane crusher but could not move after that. He was carried back to his house. His temperature went up. Later he had diarrhea. He was made to lie down under a heap of clothes, and they made him drink hot tea now and then. When he didn't get better after three days, they consulted a curer who was supposed to have the power of diagnosing such ailments. He said that Harphul had fallen victim to an evil spirit. So they sent for a man from Rohtak who could drive evil spirits away. This man gave him black pepper to eat, after he had recited some *mantras* over it. Then he burned a *ghi* lamp and offered worship to it. Then he asked the spirit to reveal his identity. The patient spoke out, and it was found that he was actually under the influence of two spirits.

"About ten or twelve years ago there was a lame Bhangi who had a very miserable life; he committed suicide at sixty by jumping into a well. At about the same time there was also a Jhinvar who worked black magic; he also died. These were the two spirits who had entered Harphul's body. The curer forced them to speak out through the voice of the boy. They said that they had been sitting by the pond, when Harphul came by, eating sugar cane. He did not offer a piece to them. Then they complained that Harphul had trampled over them, and that they felt very annoyed with him. The curer played a small drum, waved a broom of peacock feathers over the head of the patient, and recited something to call up powers to aid him in driving the spirits away. The curer threatened the spirits, saying that if they did not leave immediately, he would take them along with him and would not release them. He asked them to name the price at which they would agree to release the boy. They said that if some sweets, sugar drops, and cooked rice were placed in the fields to the north of the village, they would let him go. The boy's relatives sent the provisions to the proper place, and then the spirits went out from the boy. The curer left after taking *gur,* flour, and *ghi,* and a cash offering of a rupee and 4 annas to give to the goddess 25 miles away. He had sought her power in driving away the spirits, and he had promised to give her an offering if he succeeded. At the end of the ceremony the boy admitted before everyone that he was no longer under the influence of the spirits, but after the curer had left, he said that the spirits were still there and wanted to drag him along with them. He was sick for seven days, and then, two days after the curer left, he died."

A Jat: "In *ghot* the patient loses consciousness. The fit may last only ten or fifteen minutes. The pulse becomes weak. The patient must have breathed some bad air. I don't know any particular cause for it."

Q. "What kind of air causes such a fit?"

A. "It must be air with some germs or some gas in it, which, when inhaled, cause the blood circulation to stop."

Q. "Does a man or woman get this fit only once in life, or do they recur at certain times?"

A. "Men may have it only once, while women may have it many times. The latter get it due to a different cause. Heat accumulates in the woman's body if there has been a delay in the menses. That leads to periodic fits."

Q. "How is it treated?"

A. "When a man has a fit, he is covered with clothes, so that he will sweat profusely. If he doesn't sweat, some *ajwayan* [a spice] is boiled in water and given to the patient. He is kept in a closed room, as long as he does not regain consciousness."

Q. "Does a man mutter things when he is unconscious?"

A. "No. When a woman has a fit, honey is given to her. No effort is made to provide heat in her case, as her body is already hot from inside. There used to be a belief that this was due to the influence of evil spirits, but now this belief is no longer held, and medical aid is sought instead. If a woman has a delay in the menses, she should find out the cause of it and make every effort to keep it from happening again."

A Brahman: "Sometimes a man receives such a shock that he loses consciousness. If he is worried and in a weak state of health, and he performs some strenuous work, he might lose consciousness. Or if a man is hungry for a long time, or if a woman is affected by some evil air, they might lose consciousness. Women think that it is due to the influence of an evil spirit. Sometimes the woman suffers from no mental worry at all and has not received a shock, yet she loses consciousness. It has to be considered, then, that something evil, or some evil spirit, may be the cause. Water should be put into the mouth of an unconscious person, to bring him to. About fifteen or twenty minutes after he has regained consciousness, the patient should be given some warm milk to drink, and should have a bath about an hour or so later, so that he may feel light and fresh. If a woman suffers from the influence of an evil spirit, black pepper is burned before her. There is a Jhinvar in Rasulpur who drives away spirits. The curer has some charms with which he drives them out. Some believe in this theory, while others think that it is due to some disease. I think it may be due to different causes. Sometimes it responds to medical treatment. Sometimes it doesn't, and the curer's charms work. About a month ago Ram Gopal Jat's wife, aged twenty-two, used to lose consciousness at times. She also had fever. In her unconscious state she used to mutter that she was this or that. She was treated by some doctor, but was not cured. Then the curer from Rasulpur came and made her well with his treatment. People should try to keep their minds at peace. They should not worry unnecessarily, and when some calamity comes, they should try to withstand it without thinking too much about it. Some people believe that if a person goes out at an untimely part of the day—at noon or an hour or two after dusk—to the pond, well, or crossroad, he may annoy some wandering spirit, and the spirit may enter into the person's body. Sometimes the spirit announces who he is and says, 'I am so-and-so's ghost.' The curer then asks the spirit how it came to occupy the body, and the spirit says that it was at the pond, well, or crossroad when the person trampled on it, spat at it, or insulted it in some way. Thus the people know about the haunts of such spirits and the hours when they are present there."

DISCUSSION

Despite the introduction of Western concepts about germs and other aspects of modern medicine, traditional belief is still strong in Rampur. Propitiation of Mata and evil spirits coexists with a faith in vaccination. A great variety of concepts prevails concerning the different diseases; unanimity of opinion is rare.

Although the beliefs concerning disease causation are often unscientific, to say the least, the informants frequently showed acuteness in their descriptions of particular diseases. Cases of such diseases were evidently frequent enough so that the informants had become familiar with their chief symptoms and with the progress of different ailments. Some informants showed a good knowledge of the etiology or treatment required in particular diseases. The role of mosquitoes in malaria, for example, was understood to some extent, although the informants generally cited additional factors as causing the disease. The value of a bland diet during sickness was often realized by the informants, and some knowledge of germs was indicated by their answers.

The single item most frequently mentioned in connection with disease causation was food. This was the case with regard to diarrhea and dysentery, where the choice is warranted, but food was also the most frequently cited item with regard to rheumatism and puerperal fever, and was a close second or third in the case of smallpox, malaria, and eye inflammation. Food was not, however, mentioned prominently in connection with typhoid, where it should have been; and it was referred to by only one of the two informants who discussed cholera. The villagers are right in believing that certain foods may cause sickness, but they are not right in picking out the diseases which are so caused. The distinction between hot and cold foods was considered important, and the proper balance between them was believed necessary for good health.

Overexertion was another factor that was frequently cited—especially in connection with diarrhea, dysentery, rheumatism, and malaria. Exposure to hot or cold temperature was cited most prominently for pneumonia (by all informants), but was also mentioned in connection with rheumatism, diarrhea, malaria, eye inflammation, and cough.

God or gods, Fate, evil spirits, or the evil eye figured in responses concerning smallpox, typhoid, diarrhea, dysentery, hysteria, and eye inflammation, but these were generally the views of a minority, representing only one or two individuals. The Camar informant singled out spirits in connection with typhoid and eye inflammation, and mentioned the evil eye in the case of dysentery. The Brahman informant, as well as the Camar, spoke of supernatural agencies in connection with smallpox, while the Jats all invoked natural causes in this connection. The Brahman, the Camar, and one of the Jats singled out evil spirits as a causative factor in *ghot* or hysteria. The latter Jat also invoked Fate in connection with pneumonia. With the exception of this Jat, the eight or nine Jats who answered questions in this survey favored mundane and natural (but not necessarily scientific) explanations for disease. One suspects that a higher percentage of supernatural and magical interpretations would have been given if more low-caste informants and female informants had been interviewed. The sample, however, is sufficient to show the range of beliefs and the kinds of explanations most commonly resorted to.

As one reads through this material, it becomes evident that there is an important problem of communication here. The causes and cures of most of the diseases discussed above are well known to Western medicine. The problem is how to bring this knowledge to the vast population of India's villages, whose death rate is among the highest in the world. There seem to be communication blocks even within the village of Rampur itself, as is indicated by the somewhat greater sophistication of the Jats, the land-owning caste, as compared with the poorer and less educated lower-caste Bhangis and Camars. Evidently the medical information imparted in school does not diffuse readily through all the caste groups.

It is hoped that the data in this chapter will be of some practical use to people concerned with Community Development Projects; for, as we have argued above, a knowledge of local beliefs should be of help both in treating particular ailments and in learning to understand the basic concepts of the village people.

9

A Comparative Analysis

In this chapter I want to compare, briefly but systematically, some of the similarities and differences between the North Indian village of Rampur and the Mexican village of Tepoztlan. The major purpose of this comparison is to contribute toward our general understanding of peasantry. It is recognized that there is something about being a peasant which makes peasantry seem similar all over the world, even in the most different historical and cultural settings. On the other hand, it is also true that the cultural setting and the general nature of the larger society of which peasantry is a part must undoubtedly influence the forms of peasant life and the very nature of the people.

Since most discussions of peasantry have emphasized the common elements, I have chosen in this chapter to elaborate more fully upon the differences in order to illustrate the wide range of cultural forms possible under the rubric of peasant society and thereby indicate the need for a typology of peasantry. At the same time, I recognize the crucial importance, especially for theoretical purposes, of discerning and documenting the similarity

Fig. 41. Tepoztlan in its mountain setting.

within diversity. Moreover, I suspect that this similarity will probably be greater in the field of values, a field only touched upon in this chapter.[1]

Two additional and secondary aspects of this chapter, bearing primarily upon methodological considerations, may now be mentioned. This study represents one of the relatively few examples of firsthand comparative field research by the same investigator in peasant society in different parts of the world. It seems to me that this kind of research enables one to make more detailed and refined comparisons than is generally possible by the traditional library methods, since the investigator carries with him a common frame of reference, similar methods of work, and a similar sense of problem. From a more personal point of view this kind of research pays double dividends. Not only did it provide me with firsthand knowledge of a new culture but it also sharpened and somewhat altered my earlier understanding of Tepoztlan and of Mexico.

Second, this chapter raises the question of the degree to which a single

---

[1] I am grateful to Robert Redfield for his kind and stimulating discussion of this and other points. His paper "The Peasant's View of the Good Life" (mimeographed version of a lecture delivered at the University of Chicago, May 14, 1954) is a pioneer effort toward getting at some of the common elements in peasant value systems.

Fig. 42.   The village pond and flat surroundings of Rampur.

village, selected more or less at random in terms of our problem, can tell us something about the nation of which it is a part. It is my own belief that almost any village in a predominantly agricultural nation reflects some distinctive aspects of the nation, its culture, and its problems. It is my hope that this chapter will convey to the reader some feeling for the differences not only between Rampur and Tepoztlan but also between India and Mexico.

At the outset, I would like to point to a few difficulties in making comparisons between the two villages. In dealing with two villages in distant and contrasting culture areas of the world the question arises whether the village is a meaningful and proper unit for comparison, especially since the Indian village differs so markedly in its structure and functions from the Mexican village. Despite these differences, I believe that the two villages are sufficiently similar, isolable, and well-defined units for comparative study. However, to acknowledge that the village is an isolable unit does not mean that we should treat it as an isolate. To do so could lead only to a limited understanding. Neither Tepoztlan nor Rampur is an isolated entity. Each, in its own distinctive way, is part of a larger sociocultural system, a larger whole—the region and the nation—through which it must be understood.[2]

Comparison between a Mexican and an Indian village presents problems over and above those encountered in comparing villages within a single country or a single great tradition. Items which exist in one and not in the other are simply not comparable. For example, Tepoztlan has no caste system, and Rampur has no *compadre* system. In Tepoztlan the *municipio* is the landholding unit (for communal lands); in Rampur the village is the landholding unit. How are we to weight the influence of such items on

---

[2] The discussion of this point in my study of Tepoztlan applies with double force to the study of peasant villages in India: ". . . anthropological studies in Mexico . . . have been characterized by what might be called an ideological localism whereby each little community is treated as self-sufficient and isolated. Undoubtedly, this is a carry-over from an older anthropological tradition which was concerned with salvaging cultural data from rapidly disappearing primitive peoples. While such an approach might still have some justification in dealing with an isolated tribe in the jungles of New Guinea, it has little justification in studies of modern Mexico.

"In studying communities in Mexico [or India] it is important that the anthropologist become a student not merely of the single community but of the region and the nation as well. The anthropologist must be sufficiently versed in the more important historical, geographical, economic, and cultural characteristics of the region and nation to be able to place his community in relation to each of them, and to indicate just what the community is representative of in the larger scene . . . the anthropologist must know what is unique to his community and what it shares with broader areas, what is new and what is old, what is primitive and what is modern." Lewis, 1951:xx, xxi.

the total culture pattern of the community? Both the caste system and the *compadre* system are cohesive forces in social life, but can we equate them? The answer is probably "No," but the matter of weighting is not so easy.

The difference in size of communities may also be important. Tepoztlan is over three times as large as Rampur, and it may be that some of the matters to be discussed are related to size of population. Then there is the difference in topography and climate. Tepoztlan is in a hilly, mountainous area, while Rampur is on a level, almost treeless plain. However, this difference reflects national differences and to this extent our choice may inadvertently have been advantageous. We generally think of Mexico as a mountainous country and of India in terms of its vast plains.

In regard to climate, both are relatively dry areas. But the average annual rainfall in Tepoztlan is approximately 60 inches, while that of Rampur is less than 30. This difference is less important than it seems, because in both cases the rains come within the four-month rainy season, and there is practically no rain for seven or eight months of the year. Both communities feel the greatest need is for more water for irrigation.

Finally, there is the difference in the intensity with which each community was studied. I spent about two and a half years in five separate visits in Tepoztlan. I spent only seven months in Rampur and only a portion of this on a full-time basis, relying much more heavily upon my Indian research assistants. In short, I know Tepoztlan much better than Rampur, and what follows is subject to this limitation.

TEPOZTLAN AND RAMPUR COMPARED

Tepoztlan is a Catholic village of about 3500 people, 15 miles from Cuernavaca, the state capital, and 60 miles south of Mexico City. It is an ancient highland village which has been continuously inhabited since the Archaic period, or for at least two thousand years. Two languages are spoken in Tepoztlan: Spanish and the indigenous Nahuatl. About half the population is bilingual, the other half speaks only Spanish.

Rampur is a Hindu village of 1100 people, about 15 miles from New Delhi, the national capital. It is only 2 miles from a major highway which runs to Delhi. It is an old village which was conquered about 750 years ago by the Jats, an ethnic group which is now the dominant caste in the village. The language spoken is a local dialect of Hindi mixed with a sprinkling of Punjabi. Only a few people speak English.

Both villages may be designated as peasant societies in the sense that both are old and stable populations with a great love of the land, both depend upon agriculture, both are integrated into larger political units such as the state and the nation and are subject to their laws, both exist side by side with cities and have been exposed to urban influences for long periods of time, and both have borrowed from other rural areas as well as from urban centers but have managed to integrate the new traits into a relatively stable culture pattern. Moreover, both communities exist by a relatively primitive technology and depend upon hoe culture as well as plow and oxen in agriculture; both produce primarily for subsistence but also participate in a money economy and use barter; both are relatively poor, have a high incidence of illiteracy, a high birth rate and a high death rate; and, finally, both communities have lived under foreign domination for long periods in their history and have developed that peculiar combination of dependence and hostility toward government which is so characteristic of colonial peoples.

Settlement Pattern

So much for the broad similarities. Now let us examine some differences. One of the first things that impressed me about Rampur and other Indian villages, as compared to Tepoztlan, was the village settlement pattern (or rather the absence of pattern), the greater density of population, the

Fig. 43.   The Tepoztlan plaza.

greater crowding, the housing shortage, the shortage of space for animals, and, in general, an atmosphere of much greater poverty.

Unlike Tepoztlan (and other Mexican highland villages), with its relatively well-ordered grid pattern of streets at right angles, its plaza and market place, its *palacio*, or government building, and its central church, in Rampur there is no orderly arrangement of streets, many of which are narrow dead-end alleys, there is no village center, no government or public building for the village as a whole.[3]

In Tepoztlan the houses are spread out, and most house sites have their own patio, corral, and orchard; in Rampur the houses are crowded together, and, unlike Tepoztlan, which has many vacant houses, there was not a single available house for our field workers in Rampur.

Another thing which stood out in Rampur because of its contrast with Tepoztlan was the much greater separation of the sexes. The preferred

[3] That some of the elements here desecribed may apply to India as a whole is suggested by the description by Spate, who writes of the settlement pattern as follows: "There is in general very little that looks like a 'plan,' other than that dictated by such site factors as alignment along bluffs or levees, grouping around a fort or a tank; but within the seemingly chaotic agglomeration there is, as a rule, a strong internal differentiation, that of the separate quarters for various castes." Spate, 1954:172.

Fig. 44.   A street in Camar quarters, Rampur. Indian villages have no plazas.

arrangement for family living is to have two residences, one for the women and children, another for the men and the cattle. There are also two *caupals*, or men's houses, one for each division of the village, which are used for male smoking groups and other social gatherings.

Land and Economy

I have said that agriculture is important in both villages. But here the similarity ends. In Rampur agriculture is much more intensive than in Tepoztlan. Of the 784 acres of Rampur, 721, or well over 90 per cent of the total area, is under cultivation, as compared with only 15 per cent in Tepoztlan. Moreover, Tepoztlan depends almost entirely on a single crop, corn, with beans and squash of minor importance, whereas Rampur has a diversity of crops which include, in order of importance, wheat, millets (*juar* and *bajra*), gram, sugar cane, and hemp. Unlike Tepoztlan, which has no irrigation and produces only one crop a year, Rampur grows two crops a year on about one-fifth of its lands which are under canal and well irrigation.

The apparently greater agricultural resources of Rampur are tempered by serious limiting factors. Rampur has practically no grazing lands and no forest resources. This makes for a crucial fuel shortage so that the valuable cow dung has to be used for fuel instead of fertilizer, and the cattle have to be stall-fed rather than pastured. By contrast, Tepoztlan has very rich forest resources (almost 50 per cent of the total area), and these provide ample firewood and charcoal both for domestic consumption and for sale.

Still other differences in the village economy need to be mentioned. In Tepoztlan over 90 per cent of the 853 families engage directly in agriculture as cultivators, and until recently even the shopkeepers and artisans would close shop to plant corn when the rains came. In Rampur only 53 per cent of the 150 families engage directly in agriculture, that is, are cultivators, and most of these belong to a single caste, the Jats.

The importance of this difference goes beyond the matter of the relative proportion in the community of what in the United States would be called the "farm" and "non-farm" populations. It is related to a fundamental difference in the social and economic structure of the two villages. In Tepoztlan the family is much more of a self-sufficient unit, free to engage in a variety of activities and occupations, and it cherishes this self-sufficiency and independence from others. In Rampur the specialization of occupations along caste lines makes for a greater dependence of the villagers upon each other.

But it is a dependence organized along hierarchical lines, institutionalized in the traditional, semifeudal *jajmani* system of reciprocal obligations in economic and ceremonial affairs among the various castes. In the past the potential contradictions between the interests of the farm and non-farm populations in the village were held in check by the power of the land-holders and by the lack of alternatives for the untouchables and other low-caste people. Now that the system is weakening, primarily because of the increased opportunities for employment in munitions factories, the non-farm population in the village is beginning to take on aspects of a rural proletariat with its own special problems and its own sense of growing power.

If, on the basis of other studies, one could generalize these differences on a national level, it would be possible to say that in India there is a much greater landless rural proletariat than in Mexico and that this may well have important implications in the respective political developments in the two countries. And I might add that the Five Year Plan of the Government of India, with its emphasis upon increased agricultural production, has relatively little to offer to the rural nonagricultural portions of the population.

Returning again to the agricultural economy, we find that in both villages there are privately owned and communally owned lands. The communal lands of Tepoztlan are truly communal in the sense that any member of the *municipio* of Tepoztlan has equal rights to their use. However, the communal lands of Rampur are held by the Jats on a share basis, and the rights of the Jat families in the communal, or *samilat*, lands are proportionate to the size of their holdings of private land.

In Tepoztlan about 80 per cent of all the land is communally held either as municipal lands or, since the Mexican Revolution, as *ejidal* (common) lands. In Rampur about 7 per cent of the lands are communally owned, and most of these consist of the village house sites, the village pond, roads, and some uncultivable areas. Traditionally, the communal lands in North India were intended to serve as pasture and woodland. In both Rampur and Tepoztlan the communal lands have been a source of constant strife, but for different reasons. In the former it was between families within the village who attempted to appropriate communal lands for themselves. In the latter it was between villages, concerning the rights of villages to the communal lands. It is important to note that in both cases the communal lands are not subject to taxation. In the case of Tepoztlan this means that about 80 per cent of its total area is tax free.

Population pressure on the land is considerable in both communities. But whereas Tepoztlan has 1.5 acres of cultivable land per capita, Rampur has only .75 of an acre. The advantage for Tepoztlan is even greater than is indicated by these figures, for, whereas Rampur has practically no other land, Tepoztlan has an additional 8 acres per capita of forest and grazing lands, and about 10 per cent of this area can be used for growing corn by the primitive method of cutting and burning the forest to make temporary clearings.

In Tepoztlan only about 36 per cent of the families had private landholdings, as compared to 52 per cent of the families in Rampur.[4] But, while the landless families of Tepoztlan have access to the rich resources of the communal lands, the landless of Rampur have to depend primarily upon nonagricultural occupations. It may be noted that in both communities hoe culture is looked down upon as a last resort of the poor. In Rampur about fifteen low-caste families raise vegetables as a part-time occupation on land rented from the Jats. Some Jat families have also taken to raising vegetables.

The size of private landholdings shows fundamental similarities in both communities. Holdings are very small. In both cases 50 per cent of the holdings are less than 5 acres, 70 per cent are less than 10 acres, and 90 per cent are less than 20 acres. The range in size of holdings is also remarkably similar: from less than a half acre, of which there are many, to 50 acres, of which there is one in each community. It is noteworthy that in both Tepoztlan and Rampur the peasants independently suggested the same figure of about 10 acres as a desirable minimum-sized holding for a "decent" standard of living for a family of five. This figure is apparently based upon the acreage that can be worked economically with a single team of oxen.

As might be expected, there is a striking difference between the two communities in regard to the respective role of livestock in the economy and the attitude toward livestock. In India there is an ancient cattle complex, and most people are vegetarians. In Mexico domesticated cattle are relatively recent, dating back to the Spanish Conquest. The cattle industry was never very important and never became well integrated with the economy. In Tepoztlan there is relatively little livestock, and most of it is of poor quality. Investment in cattle is viewed as precarious. By contrast, the little village of Rampur supports a remarkably large number of livestock and this with practically no grazing resources. Whereas 85 per cent

---

[4] Again the difference is somewhat offset because almost 20 per cent of Tepoztecan families have *ejido* holdings. During the course of the Spanish Conquest and domination of Mexico, from 1519 to 1810, Tepoztlan lost a portion of its best lands, which were converted into sugar plantations. After the Mexican Revolution of 1910-20 and as part of the national *ejido* program Tepoztlan recovered many of its lost lands, and these were divided among the landless villagers into small holdings.

of the cultivators in plow agriculture own at least one ox in Rampur, only 45 per cent own oxen in Tepoztlan.

Social Organization

It is in the field of social organization that we find the most remarkable differences between these two peasant societies. Indeed, they seem like separate worlds, and I might add that by comparison with Rampur, Tepoztlan in retrospect seems much less complicated and much more familiar, very Western-like, and almost North American. Undoubtedly one of the reasons for this is the fact that the Spanish Conquest left its indelible mark on Mexican culture. Spain, for all its cultural idiosyncrasies in sixteenth-century Europe, was part of the Western European culture pattern.

The distinctive aspects of the social organization of Rampur as compared to Tepoztlan can be discussed in terms of (1) the more pervasive role of kinship, (2) the presence of a caste system, (3) the existence of multiple factions based on kinship, and (4) the differences in the role of the village as a community.

1. *The role of kinship.* In Rampur kinship plays a major role in the ordering of human relations and is the basis of most social and political groupings such as the *thollas* and *panas*, the clans, the smoking groups, the factions, the castes, the panchayats, and the intervillage networks. The extended family is strong and forms a basic unit for individual identification. The caste system acts as an integrating and cohesive factor in village life, primarily within the castes and to some extent between castes. Caste members are bound by kinship, by common traditions, interests, and social interaction. The castes in turn are bound by economic interdependence resulting from the specialization of occupations, and this is formalized by the *jajmani* system of reciprocal obligations.

In Tepoztlan kinship is a much less pervasive force: the nuclear family predominates, the extended family is weak (the elaborate *compadre* system seems designed to make up for this), and social relations and social solidarity are organized around religious, political, and other non-kinship bases. The independence and individualism of the nuclear or biological family in Tepoztlan make for an atomistic quality in social relations. And while these discrete family units are organized into larger units such as the barrio, the village, and the *municipio,* these organizational forms are relatively impersonal and do not impinge so directly upon the lives of the individuals as does the extended family, the faction, and the caste in Rampur. In Rampur the extended family, the faction, and the caste are the units which demand one's loyalties and channelize most of one's life-activities. But by the same token they provide the individual with a much greater degree of psychological security than is present in Tepoztlan, and this in turn affects the quality of community life.

The role of kinship organization on the political level is also markedly different in the two villages. In Tepoztlan the connection between the village and the state and federal government is in terms of elected officials who vote as members of their *demarcacion,* an arbitrary division of the village for secular purposes. The officials do not represent kinship units or even the barrios. But in Rampur the political organization and the kinship organization are more closely intertwined. Each of the two headmen of the village represents a *pana,* which is essentially a kinship unit consisting of related patrilineages.

Rampur, like other villages in North India, is fundamentally a part of a larger intervillage network based upon kinship ties. Other villagers are very often relatives, and entire villages are classified by the kinship terminology as mother's brother villages, grandfather villages, grandmother villages, etc. As we have seen, Rampur is a member of a four-village unit known as a *caugama* and of a twenty-village unit known as a *bisagama.* These are known as Dabas villages, that is, they are descended from a common ancestor, Dabas. These twenty-village units in turn are members of larger intervillage networks which culminate in a 360-village unit, whose inhabitants' ancestors were all related in the distant past. The four- and twenty-village units are still active in this area, although less so than in the past. Within them there is a traditional division of labor for ceremonial and panchayat purposes, and each village performs special functions at panchayat meetings.

2. *The caste system.* In Rampur the caste system organizes life in terms of hierarchical principles and plays up the status differences between groups. The Jats are by tradition agriculturalists and own all the land of the village, including the house sites, that is, the land upon which the houses of the other castes are built. In a sense, then, the other castes, even the Brahmans, are in the village at the sufferance of the Jats. The village is officially known as a Jat village, and clearly the Jats dominate village life. Even the formal organization of the village into two *panas,* each with its headman, is solely in terms of the Jats. The lower castes tend to live on the outskirts of the village and are not part of this formal organization despite the fact that some of the lower-caste families are ancient inhabitants.

In Tepoztlan there is no caste system, and the society is much more democratically organized. No one group dominates the life of the village. Each family, whether rich or poor, owns its house site and house, has

recognized status, and can proudly say, "This is my village." The quality
of interpersonal relations among Tepoztecans is comparable with what
exists within the single caste of Jats, that is, status differences are played
down at least on a verbal level, and wealthy individuals are careful not
to "pull rank."

In Rampur the caste system divides the village and weakens the sense of
village solidarity. The caste generally represents a distinct ethnic group
with its own history, traditions, and identifications, and each caste lives in
more or less separate quarters of the village. There are separate wells for
the Harijans, or untouchables; dining and smoking between higher and
lower castes are still taboo; low-caste persons (this does not include Baniya,
Khati, or Nai) will not sit together on the same *carpai*, or cot, with a Jat or
Brahman; and when government officials come to the village and call meetings to explain the new Community Development Projects, the Harijans
may attend, but they stay off to one side in the audience and "know their
place." In a sense, then, each caste, or at least those with larger representation in the village, forms a separate little community. The social structure
of the village therefore has somewhat the quality of our urban communities
with their variety of ethnic and minority groups and a high degree of
division of labor.

In Tepoztlan the population and the tradition are much more homogeneous, and there is nothing comparable to the divisive effects of the caste
system. Perhaps the nearest approximation to segmentation in the village
results from the organization of separate barrios, each with its own chapel,
patron saint, and *esprit de corps*. The barrios, like the castes, can be thought
of as subcommunities within the village. This was truer thirty years ago,
when barrio localism in Tepoztlan was stronger than it is today. But of
course the barrio and the caste are very different in nature. The barrio is
primarily a religious and social unit rather than a kinship unit. It does not
control marriage, and there is no tradition of barrio members having a
common origin. And while the physical limits of the barrios have remained
remarkably stable over the past few hundred years, barrio membership is
changeable, and one can belong to two barrios at the same time, provided
the barrio house-site tax is paid. Moreover, the barrio organization is strictly
within the village and is unified on a village-wide basis by the central village church.[5] But the castes cut across villages and have their cross-village
organizations.

---

[5] It seems clear that Catholicism and the Church, embracing the principle of hier-
archy and centralization, play a much more decisive role in the formal organization of
Tepoztlan and other Mexican villages than does Hinduism in Rampur and other North
Indian villages. That the Mexican pattern applies over even wider areas is shown by

The caste system in Rampur is undergoing changes and in some ways may even be said to be breaking down. The proximity to Delhi, the Gandhian movement against untouchability, the preaching of the Arya Samaj, and increased off-farm employment opportunities as a result of the past two world wars have all had some effect.

Perhaps the greatest change in the caste system has occurred in relation to the occupational structure, that is, caste and occupation are now less synonymous than formerly. Some of the Jat families no longer cultivate their land, and their children have become schoolteachers or have taken miscellaneous jobs in Delhi. The Brahmans no longer carry on their priestly functions. Most of them are occupancy tenants of the Jats, but only four are cultivators; one family sells milk, another does tailoring, and the remainder are employed in jobs outside the village. Though the Camars are leatherworkers by caste, only two are now shoemakers, and they no longer skin the dead cattle. The substitution of Persian wheels for the earlier system of drawing water with leather buckets threw some of the Camars out of work; three families are weavers, four rent land from the Jats for vegetable gardening, four are employed outside the village, and the remainder earn a living in the village by combining part-time agricultural labor with cattle raising. Of all the castes, the Bhangis, or sweepers, seem to have shown the least change in occupation.

There have been other changes. Children of all castes now attend the village school, and there is no discrimination or segregation in the seating arrangements. And since 1949 a Camar has been elected to the new four-village council. However, despite all these trends the caste system is still very strong in the village.

3. *Factions.* In both villages there are factions, but their structure, functions, and role in village life differ greatly. As we have shown in Chapter 4, factions in Rampur are an old, ingrained pattern in village life and must be considered as a basic structural aspect of traditional village organization, along with lineages, castes, *thollas, panas,* and other groupings. The factions in Rampur are small and relatively cohesive groups of varied lineage and clan composition which act as units in social, economic, and ceremonial undertakings. The quarrels between factions center around wealth, women, and land.

In Tepoztlan factions are political groupings rather than kinship group-

Redfield and Tax, who write of Mesoamerican Indian society as follows: "The community consists of a village, a group of hamlets or a rural region, but in any case its residents look toward a common civic and religious center, where is housed the image of a saint that is patron to them all. The community tends to be endogamous. . . ." Redfield and Tax, 1953:31.

ings and reflect diverse social and economic interests. The factions are fewer in number, only two as a rule, and are larger and more loosely organized. Faction membership is less stable and faction loyalty more tenuous. In Tepoztlan, unlike Rampur, brothers may be members of hostile and opposed factions. In Rampur, first, second, and even third cousins are generally members of the same faction.

One of the major cleavages in Tepoztlan was between the *Bolsheviki* and the *Centrales*. These groups became clearly delineated in the early twenties when two socialistically oriented Tepoztecans from Mexico City, who were members of the Confederacion Regional de Obreros Mexicanos, returned to the village to organize the peasants in defense of the communal lands against the sons of the ex-*caciques* (political bosses) who controlled the local government and allegedly were exploiting the forest resources of the *municipio* in their own interests. The *Bolsheviki* had their greatest strength in the smaller and poorer barrios of the upper part of the village, while the *Centrales* were strongest in the larger central barrios. To some extent this grouping corresponded to class distinctions, since, in the days before the Mexican Revolution of 1910-20, most of the *caciques* and well-to-do merchants lived in the center of the village.

In contrast to the predominantly private familial objectives of factions in Rampur, the objectives of the factions in Tepoztlan were broadly social and political. The aim was to dominate the local government and to appeal to the voters in terms of broad public issues. In the twenties the slogan was "Conserve the Communal Forests," and in the thirties the new organization known as the *Fraternales* had the slogan "Union, Justice and Civilization."

Since the middle thirties the factional groupings have more and more become political groupings which align themselves for or against the government in power. The establishment by Tepoztecans of two competing bus lines from Tepoztlan to Cuernavaca has led to bitter quarrels and violence and has again split the village into hostile groupings.

4. *The village as a community.* The comparative consideration of the question, "Is the village a community?" is more complex than it seems, for there are numerous dimensions of "community," such as the ecological, physical, social, economic, political, religious, and psychological. To what extent do the physical limits of the village define the limits for these dimensions? Or to what extent do these aspects of community spill over into other villages so that the community might better be defined in terms of units larger than the single village? As we might expect, not all aspects of community have the same spatial distribution, so that a village may be a clearly self-contained unit for some purposes and not for others.

There is yet another aspect of the problem, namely, what is the quality of social relations, of mutual interdependence of persons or social groups within each village? We must be ready to deal with the possibility that although Village A does not define the physical area of social, economic, and other relations as clearly as does Village B, the quality of such relations in A or subgroups within it may be so much more cohesive that we are justified in saying that there is more community within A (as well as the villages into which this spills over) than there is in B. With these observations in mind, let us first consider those aspects of community which Rampur and Tepoztlan share and then go on to consider some of the more important differences.

Both Tepoztlan and Rampur are corporate bodies which enjoy legal status and can take suits to law courts. Both are units of taxation for the respective revenue departments. In both cases the greater part of the social, economic, and religious activities takes place within the village. The village is home and there is relatively little out-migration, but more in Tepoztlan than in Rampur. Of Tepoztlan it can be said that most villagers are born there, live and work there, and die there. This cannot be said of Rampur, for the married women were not born there, and the daughters of the village will not die there. Yet the very designation "daughter of the village" speaks eloquently for the sense of village consciousness.

In both villages, despite the existence of schisms and factions, there are occasions when the villagers act together as a unit for some common goal such as the building of a road or a school, drainage of a pond, or the defense of the village against attack from the outside. In the case of Tepoztlan the defense of the village last occurred in the twenties, when it was attacked by the *Cristeros.* In the case of Rampur one must go back almost a hundred years for a comparable occasion.

One of the important differences between our two villages is related to the contrast in settlement pattern between highland Mexico and the Indo-Gangetic plain. The Mexican pattern is that of relatively self-contained nuclear groupings or pockets of a small number of villages centrally located within *municipios,* so that the density of population decreases almost to zero as one moves from the center or seat of the community to the periphery. In North India, on the other hand, there is an almost even and continuous scattering of large numbers of villages, so that no distinct pattern of groupings emerges. Thus in Mexico the physical groupings of villages practically define and encompass the social and political groupings, whereas in India the physical pattern gives much less of a clue, and one must trace out the specific kinship and other alignments which organize villages into units. This contrast between the centripetal settlement pattern of Mexican villages and the amorphous pattern of India applies also to the internal settlement pattern of the villages, so that the Mexican village stands out more clearly as a centrally organized unit.

From an economic point of view, the village of Rampur is a more clearly isolable and self-contained community than the village of Tepoztlan. Village boundaries are clearly fixed and contain within them the land resources upon which the villagers depend for their livelihood. In Tepoztlan the larger *municipio* is the functional resource unit. Village boundaries are ill-defined and are essentially moral boundaries, whereas the municipal boundaries are clearly demarcated. It is within the bounds of the *municipio* that the everyday world of the Tepoztecan exists. Here the farmers work the communal lands, cut and burn communal forests, graze their cattle, and hunt for medicinal herbs.

From the point of view of village government Tepoztlan stands out as a more clearly organized and centralized community. When I first studied Tepoztlan, local government seemed very weak indeed, but by comparison with Rampur and North India in general it now seems extremely well developed, what with elected village presidents, councils, judges, the collection of taxes for public works, police powers, and the obligations of villagers to give twelve days a year for cooperative village works. The traditional local government in Rampur is much more informal and consists of caste panchayats which cut across village lines. Only recently has the government established a new statutory local panchayat with taxation powers, which, however, has not been effective so far.

Village-wide leadership in Tepoztlan is formally expressed by the local government. In Rampur it does not yet exist, and the idea of positive constructive leadership in the public interest is only now beginning, particularly in connection with the establishment of public schools. As yet there are no village heroes or outstanding citizens who are popular for their contribution to village welfare as a whole.

In Rampur leadership is limited to faction leadership and is primarily of a protective and defensive nature in which each faction or combination of factions defends its family interests. The "leader" is essentially a spokesman for a family or a group of related families and has little authority to make independent decisions or to exercise power over the group.

In Tepoztlan there is more verbalization about village community spirit. Candidates for political office always speak in terms of "*mi pueblo*" and promise to improve their village. The fact that officials may in fact do very little and may even steal public funds is another matter. But at least the sense of village identification and loyalty exists as a potential ideological force. Village solidarity is also reflected, albeit in a negative sense, by Tepoztecan characterizations of the surrounding villages of the *municipio* as "assassins," "dullheads," "primitive," and "backward." Moreover, the bogeyman used to frighten children is often a man from a neighboring village. In Rampur there were no comparable designations of neighboring villages, most of which contain related lineages.

The difference in the role of the village as a community can also be appreciated if we examine marriage in both cases. In Tepoztlan over 90 per cent of the marriages take place within the village, and, lest this be thought a function of the larger size of the village, we can point out that 42 per cent of the marriages were within the same barrio within the village. The single important rule in marriage is not to marry close relatives, and this generally means eliminating first, second, and third cousins.

In Rampur the question of whom one can marry is much more complicated. Marriage is controlled by a combination of factors, namely, caste endogamy, village exogamy, limited territorial exogamy, and clan exogamy. As a result of all these regulations fathers or go-betweens must go long

Fig. 45. A typical poor peasant home in Tepoztlan.

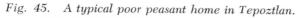

distances to find eligible mates for their daughters, and for months before the marriage season they scour the countryside for husbands.

Our study of Rampur showed that the 266 married women living in the village came from about two hundred separate villages at distances of up to 40 miles. We found also that the average distance between spouses' villages varied considerably by caste, with the lower castes, who are less numerous, having to go much longer distances. If we now examine the other side of the picture, that is, the daughters who married out of the village, we find that over 220 daughters of Rampur married out into about two hundred villages. Thus, this relatively small village of 150 households becomes the locus of affinal kinship ties with over four hundred other villages. This makes for a kind of rural cosmopolitanism which is in sharpest contrast to the village isolationism in Mexico.

The People

Finally we come to a brief comparison of the people in both villages. I have noted elsewhere that Tepoztecans are a reserved, constricted people who tend to view other human beings as dangerous and the world in general as hostile. Children are required to be obedient, quiet, and unobtrusive,

Fig. 46.   A poor home in Rampur.

and parents play upon children's fears to maintain control. There is a certain pervading air of tension and fearfulness among Tepoztecans; the individual and the small biological family seem to stand alone against the world.

Despite the much smaller size of Rampur, one has the impression that there are more people there. One rarely sees a solitary figure: children play in groups, men talk and smoke in groups, women go to the well or collect cow dung in groups, and a visitor is always surrounded and followed about by crowds of people. The low value placed upon privacy in Rampur is in marked contrast with Tepoztlan, where privacy is so valued that one gets the feeling of an apartment-house psychology in this ancient village.

Faces are different in the two villages. In Tepoztlan, outside the home, faces are generally unsmiling, unrevealing masks. In Rampur faces seem more secure. Children are more open-faced and laughing, old men are bland and peaceful, young men restless but unrebellious, women straight and proud. Here too there is individual reserve and formalized behavior, but it does not seem to mask so much of an undercurrent of hostility and fear as in Tepoztlan.

The women of Rampur work even harder than the women of Tepoztlan, but they appear less drab and bemeaned. They seem strong, bold, gay, and sharp-tongued. Their skirts and head scarves are brilliantly colored and spangled with rhinestones and mirrors. Heavy silver jewelry on their ankles, wrists, and necks seems to validate their worth as women. Even with their faces modestly covered, the women of Rampur seem more independent than Tepoztecan women and have less of a martyr complex.[6]

It must be remembered that these observations on the people of Rampur are highly impressionistic and deserve more careful study.

---

[6] David G. Mandelbaum, in his article "The World and the World View of the Kota" in *Village India*, has suggested that some of our findings on Rampur are not only local or regional but reflect a basic Indic quality and are found in most villages in India. Among these traits he mentions ranked groupings, concern with pollution, the wide contractual and informal relations with other villagers and other groups, a reluctance to delegate authority to leaders, and a jealous guarding of traditional functions by each village (p. 251). Mandelbaum also raises the interesting question of how to explain the greater psychological security of the villagers of Rampur as compared to Tepoztlan, especially in the face of the reported quarrels and factional disputes in Rampur. He writes, "Can it be that the quarrels, the status competition, the defensive machinations, add up to a world which is generally more rewarding than another which may be as well endowed physically but not as well provided with societal extensions of the self? In [Rampur] . . . the individual sees himself as always identified with a large range of people, as part of a main. In Tepoztlan the individual evidently more often sees himself as an island, or perhaps as part of an archipelago" (p. 252).

CONCLUSIONS

In conclusion, I believe our comparative data from these two villages demonstrate the wide range of culture that can exist in peasant societies. When I left India in 1952, I expected to find many similarities between Indian and Mexican peasant communities, this despite my earlier critique of the folk-society concept. I did find similarities, but on the whole I was more impressed by the differences. The similarities are greatest in material culture, level of technology, and economics, and the differences are greatest in social organization, value systems, and personality. In terms of raising the standard of living the problems seem much the same, for the bulk of the population in both villages is poor, illiterate, landless, and lives so close to the survival margin that it cannot afford to experiment with new things and ideas. However, the poverty of the Indian people seems so much greater and the agrarian problems so overwhelming and complex as to defy any easy solution even on the theoretical level.

In making comparisons between Mexico and India, we must remember that they are in different stages of evolution in terms of nationhood. Mexico has had its political independence for almost 150 years and has lived through the great Revolution of 1910-20, while India has only recently gained its freedom and has not had the equivalent of the Mexican agrarian revolution. These broad differences are reflected in many ways in our two villages.

In stressing the range of variation possible under the rubric of peasant society, I do not intend to suggest that the concept "peasant society" is not meaningful or useful as a classification for comparative research. However, it is not sufficiently predictive in regard to cultural content and structure to take the place of knowledge of concrete reality situations, especially in planning programs of culture change. For both applied and theoretical anthropology we need typologies of peasantry for the major culture areas of the world, such as Latin America, India, Africa, etc. Moreover, within each area we need more refined subclassifications. Only after such studies are available will we be in a position to formulate broad generalizations about the dynamics of peasant culture as a whole. The difficulties encountered in this paper suggest that a typology of peasant societies for Mexico or Latin America would hardly serve for North India. However, once we had adequate typologies for both areas, meaningful comparisons could more readily be made.

One of the most striking findings in our study of Rampur, especially when compared with the report of Beals (1953) on a South Indian village, is the remarkable stability of local village life and institutions, despite the proximity of Rampur to Delhi and the many urban influences to which it has been subject, such as Arya Samaj, the Congress and other political movements, and increased opportunities for education and jobs. The stability is particularly evident in the agricultural economy. The Jats still love the land; in the last fifty years there have been only two families who sold their land and left the village. The land-tenure system continues as of old, with the Jats still in control. The caste system still remains strong and dominates the thinking of the villagers, despite the many reformist movements and the coming of independence. But the *jajmani* system has weakened, and this has increased intercaste tensions, particularly in the case of the Camars.

Rampur and Tepoztlan face many common problems. In both villages population has increased rapidly in the last thirty years, means of communication have been improved, there is greater dependence upon a cash economy, education is increasingly valued, and the general aspiration level of the people is going up. But there have been no comparable changes in agricultural production.

We have seen that both villages are meaningful units for comparative study. However, our analysis has shown the complexities involved in evaluating the extent to which each village is a community. From some points of view it would seem that Tepoztlan is more of an organized and centralized village community, that is, in terms of the internal settlement pattern, the greater ethnic homogeneity of the population, the formal organization of village government with elected and paid village officials, the religious organization with a central church, the village market and plaza, and the absence of multiple intervillage networks based on kinship.

From the point of view of ecology Rampur is a more clearly defined and self-contained community than Tepoztlan. Moreover, if we define community in terms of the degree and intensity of interaction and interdependence of people, then we might conclude that, despite the divisive effects of castes and multiple factions within castes, there is more community within Rampur than within Tepoztlan. Villagers in Rampur seem psychologically more secure and relate better to each other. There is a greater readiness to engage in cooperative activities within kinship and caste. The villager spends a greater proportion of his time in some group activity, in smoking groups, in the extended family, in cooperative economic undertakings, and in the caste councils. There is more frequent visiting and more sociability. It is tempting to view the greater verbalization about village identification and solidarity in Tepoztlan as a psychological compensation for the actual atomistic nature of social relations. And by the same token the absence of such verbalization in Rampur may reflect the greater cohesiveness of social relations.

Our data on social organization from North India call attention to aspects of village organization, both in its internal and in its external relations, which either have been neglected or have not been given sufficient weight in earlier considerations of peasantry and in the formulations of models for the peasant society. It will be recalled that in Redfield's model the peasant society is intermediate between the folk society and civilization. It differs from the folk society in that it has developed economic and political relations with the city, but in its relations with other villages it still retains a good deal of the folk quality of isolation and "looking in." [7]

This formulation applies better to Tepoztlan and other Mexican villages than to Rampur and other North Indian villages. It does not adequately provide for situations like Rampur, where the village is part of multiple intervillage networks and where a single village is related by affinal and lineage ties with over four hundred other villages, thereby making for a kind of rural cosmopolitanism.

The widespread affinal and lineage relationships of Rampur find their closest parallel in reports of tribal societies rather than of peasant societies. And indeed there is a tribal flavor in the Jat social organization which recalls the description by Evans-Pritchard of the Nuer, a people of the Anglo-Egyptian Sudan numbering over 200,000 and consisting of many tribes, some of which have populations of over 40,000. In both cases we find patrilineal clans, maximal and minimal lineages, the dominance of a single lineage within villages, and local exogamy.[8] Evans-Pritchard writes:

. . . Nuer people see themselves as a unique community and their culture as a unique culture. . . . All Nuer live in a continuous stretch of country. There are no isolated sections. However, their feeling of community goes deeper than recognition of cultural identity. Between Nuer, wherever they hail from, and though they be strangers to one another, friendly relations are at once established when they meet outside their country, for a Nuer is never a foreigner to another as he is to a Dinka or Shilluk. [9]

Their members, individuals and families, move often and freely. . . . Wherever they go they are easily incorporated into the new commuity through one or more kinship links . . . Nuer frequently visit all the villages in their neighborhood, and in all of them they have kinsfolk . . . the different local communities of a whole tribe could be presented on a single genealogical chart. Given unlimited time and patience, the entire population of Nuerland could be so presented. *There are no closed communities.*[10]

---

[7] Redfield, 1953a:33.

[8] Evans-Pritchard, 1947:123-24; 1951:1-48.

[9] Evans-Pritchard, 1947:123.

[10] Evans-Pritchard, 1951:29.

The contrast is striking between this and the picture of small localized hamlets of the mountainous areas of the Philippines in which groups in the next valley are fair game for head-hunting.

Our data suggest that it may be helpful to re-examine a good deal of the literature on the social structure of folk and peasant societies in terms of our well-known and traditional concepts of endogamy and exogamy, but from a somewhat different point of view than in the past. I believe most discussions of exogamy and endogamy have been in terms of rules applying to some unit, generally a clan or lineage within a local community. But when the entire local group is exogamous or endogamous very important consequences follow—indeed so important that it might be useful to add endogamy and exogamy as crucial universal variables in our models of the folk society and peasant society. Moreover, these two variables seem to be quite independent of some of the other variables, such as size and homogeneity. The world-view of a small, homogeneous, and endogamous village or local group will necessarily be more "isolationist" and "inward-looking" than that of a small, homogeneous, but exogamous village or local group. Furthermore, the difference between exogamy and endogamy sets up processes which in themselves accentuate localism or play it down. When half the total adult population (i.e., the women of the patrilocal exogamous village) goes out of the village generation after generation, and new women from other villages come in, there is the basis for a type of intervillage relation which differs considerably from that of endogamous villages or communities. In the former case there is a natural development of a "one-world" concept in terms of a region whose limits are determined by kinship bonds. Also, in the case of exogamic villages the children are reared by parents from different villages, so that in a sense village differences are bred out over the generations. Murdock has recently demonstrated this last point with American Indian data.

The difference between the "inward-looking" and the "outward-looking" peasant village is of course a relative mater. All tribal and peasant societies have some relations with the outside. It might therefore be more profitable to compare the nature, occasions, and quality of these relations. In the case of Tepoztlan and Rampur the differences are striking. In the former, trade is the primary bond between Tepoztlan and the outlying villages, with religious pilgrimages ranking second, and kinship ties a very low third. By contrast, in Rampur intervillage relations result primarily from affinal and consanguineal ties, with religious pilgrimages ranking a low second, and trade a very low third. The type of impersonality in intervillage relations based on trade, reported by Redfield [11] for Guatemala and applicable also

---

[11] Redfield, 1939:53.

to Tepoztlan, would be unthinkable in the case of North Indian villages where relations are more intimate and personal because they are primarily familial and not trade relations.

While the distinction between relatively inward-looking and outward-looking communities may be one of the differentiating characteristics between a tribal society and a peasant society, the distinction also has meaning both *within* the tribal level and *within* the peasant level. It may be argued that kinship ties, no matter how far-flung, still represent an inward-looking orientation. We believe, however, that there is a significant social and psychological difference between relations confined within a small area and to relatively few people and relations which, though still based on kinship, are spread out over vast areas and encompass thousands of people who are personally unknown, yet are potentially accessible and part of the in-group.

A typology of peasant societies must also include as a variable the role of kinship, that is, the extent to which the society is organized on a kinship basis. Where the kinship basis is pervasive, as in Rampur, we can say that the society is more primitive or tribal. As Kroeber writes: "It is generally accepted that among primitive peoples society is structured primarily on the basis of kinship and in more civilized nations largely in terms of economic and political factors. The function of kinship is relatively less in higher civilization, and may be absolutely less. But kinship considerations always persist." [12]

On the basis of our comparative findings and in line with the generally accepted position as stated by Kroeber, we might go on to classify modern nations with predominantly peasant populations in terms of the role of kinship in the social organization of village life and intervillage relations. If our findings for Tepoztlan and Rampur could be generalized for Mexico and India as nations, and this is an empirical question, then we would have to conclude that, insofar as the role of kinship is concerned, India is much more "primitive" than Mexico and represents a different stage of socio-cultural evolution.[13] However, in terms of other variables, such as the ethnic composition of the population, we have seen that Tepoztlan is more homo-

---

[12] Kroeber, 1952:219.

[13] The manifold implications of such a finding cannot be treated here. However, this finding suggests that the introduction of a modern Western democratic process, based upon voting, elections, and the spirit of individuality implicit in this system, is more foreign to contemporary Indian culture than to contemporary Mexican culture. Perhaps this is what Gandhi had in mind when he suggested many years ago that India would have to work out forms of representation which would be more in keeping with India's special tradition.

geneous than Rampur. Similarly, the communal land system of Tepoztlan seems to be more primitive than that of Rampur.

One conclusion to be drawn from these facts is that separate institutions or aspects of culture develop at different rates, within limits, in accord with particular historical circumstance. It is this factor which creates serious difficulties in the construction of holistic societal or cultural typologies which are not historically and regionally defined. This would also help explain how Tepoztlan and Rampur can be so similar in terms of economics and so different in terms of social organization.

Appendix

Analysis of *Patvari* Records

To the student of comparative culture who has worked in other parts of the world where land records are meager or nonexistent, the rich *patvari* records of India serve as a most welcome asset to the study of village life. They contain a mass of useful data on many aspects of village economics and social organization, including such items as land tenure, land types, size and distribution of holdings, land sales, mortgages, inheritance patterns, crops sown, village subdivisions, kinship groupings, the castes of the agriculturists, and the customary relations between agriculturists and nonagriculturists in regard to the use of village lands. In many areas the records go back more than one hundred years and thereby give us a picture of economic development. The records are of particular value in providing the field worker with background data and an initial orientation to the village without the need to work through informants.

However, there are a number of obstacles in the use of the records. *Patvari* records are numerous and complicated and not without their esoteric and baffling aspects. The *patvari* system is old and has its own distinctive tradition, terminology, and special techniques which have changed relatively little in the past 400 years. Despite the many modifications and improvements by the British, it still reflects many pre-British survivals such as Persian terminology, Arabic numerals, the use of Hindu months and eras, and the use of local units of measurement which vary from region to region. But in addition to these obstacles the accounting system, with its elaborate cross references and duplications of data, is quite complicated for the uninitiated. Indeed, in some respects *patvari* entries are like the Latin prescriptions of the doctor, unintelligible to all but the specialists.

Under these circumstances most students who want data from village records are, like the villagers themselves, utterly dependent upon the *patvari*. Moreover, they are unable to guide the *patvari*, since they do not know the range of data available, the reliability of the various registers, or the short cuts by which to get what they want.

It is our purpose to provide a preliminary guide to the use of *patvari* records by describing a complete set of *patvari* records found in the village of Rampur, explaining some of the key concepts in the record system and evaluating the reliability of the various types of data. The records found in Rampur are quite typical of records in Delhi State and the Punjab and are not too different from those of Uttar Pradesh. It will be recalled that the settlement system of the Punjab was derived from the earlier settlement experience of the northwest territories. It is difficult to say to what extent the record system examined here is similar to those of other parts of India. Further comparative studies are necessary.

The materials here will be presented in four parts:

1. A account of the social role of the *patvari*.

2. An examination and summary description of the various records found with the *patvari*.

3. A brief discussion of some key concepts in the organization of *patvari* records.

4. A summary of the uses of the data along with some comments on their strengths and weaknesses.

THE SOCIAL ROLE OF THE *PATVARI*

Baden-Powell has defined the *patvari's* position as follows: "The patwari is, in effect, the *accountant of the village*, both as regards the revenue-payments due from the various co-sharers, the distribution of the profits of the joint-estate, and the accounts of rent payment between landlord and tenant; he is also the *registrar of changes in ownership* due to succession and transfer: he is also the recorder of statistics of the village." [1]

The *patvari* system seems to have been established at the time of Akbar in the sixteenth century. In former times *patvaris* were servants of the village and were paid by the *zamindars*. The standard equipment of a *patvari* reflects the old conservative tradition behind his office. The bespectacled accountant sits on a carpet on the ground and writes on a low slanting desk, using the required black India ink and a pen of his own manufacture. The bag in which he carries his books is of an old Indian type which consists of an unsewn piece of cloth

---

[1] Baden-Powell, 1892, 2:278.

wrapped around the books and tied at the corners *(basta)*. The numerous books which the *patvari* keeps are, for the most part, patterned after ancient models.

In the collection of revenue, a *patvari* helps the subdivisional officer in those parts of India where the *ryotwari* (land tenure) system of revenue collection prevails. (In other areas the *zamindars* pay the revenue to the state treasury.) [2] As the key governmental representative in his village, the *patvari* has long enjoyed a power and income far above that of his official status and salary. There is a Punjab saying, "As the Deputy Commissioner is in the district, the *patvari* is in the village." However, in the minds of some, the *patvari* even outranks the Deputy Commissioner. Once a Deputy Commissioner who had aided several villages came to Rampur, and a grateful peasant blessed him and said, "May God make you and your son *patvaris.*"

The British began to make use of *patvaris* in 1817 and developed the system of *patvari* circles in 1860. Until 1873 *patvaris* continued to draw wages from the *zamindars*, but after that date they were paid by the government. Cohn informs us that in the area where he worked the payment by *zamindars* continued until May, 1953, when the Senapur *patvari* still collected 10 *sirs* of grain for each plow in each Thakur household.[3]

[2] Joardar, 1952:1.
[3] Cohn, 1954:61.

Fig. 47.   The village patvari.

Recently, since India's achievement of independence, the *patvari's* position has become less secure. But he still has power and influence in the local village. As recorder of all land records, including such items as land tenure, land types, size and distribution of holdings, land sales, mortgages, inheritances, crops sown and harvested, and land evaluation, the *patvari* is in a unique position to exercise this power. In this he is facilitated by the following conditons:

1. The *patvari* has control over all the land records. Not only is he the sole recorder of all land negotiations but the *patvari* is generally the sole interpreter of the records and the only one who can read them. Because of the esoteric nature of the records even literate peasants and outside government officials must rely entirely upon a *patvari* for the information contained in his books. For the ordinary villager there is no way of checking on the accuracy of the *patvari,* either in recording or reading out information. It is necessary to go to the High Court to challenge any record in the *patvari* books. In practice it is very difficult, if not impossible, to challenge the *patvari's* statements. It is a simple matter for a *patvari* to work mischief without being discovered. A *patvari* seldom finds himself in a vulnerable position. Changes made in his records become legal if unchallenged for a fixed period—about seven years. If the villagers do not hear about a given transaction during this period, it becomes legal when the period is up. However, it is the general opinion in the village that abuses on the part of the *patvari* are not so common as in the past. *Patvaris* who overstep themselves are in danger of being killed by disgruntled groups. Nevertheless, fear of the *patvari* persists, particularly among illiterate peasants.

The *patvari* is able, by delays and manipulation of records, to force the peasants to pay his fees and bribes. If anyone wishes to see his records or ask for an accounting, in order to fight a case in court or to get information about one's own lands, the *patvari* can delay it for a long time without giving a clear refusal, putting pressure on the person to pay the consulting fee. Those who have not gained the good will of the *patvari* in the past may then suffer. Fees vary at the discretion of the *patvari,* but they can be officially charged for each book consulted.

In cases of transfer of land, either through mortgage or sale, the *patvari* can delay the *intkal,* or registration of mutation, until he receives his unofficial fee, which ranges from 2 to 5 rupees per 100, depending upon the *patvari.* Since the *intkal* is supposed to be signed by the *tehsildar* (court officer), the *patvari* can legally refuse to do it himself, thus causing persons the expense of going to the *tehsildar* or to court to get it done. The *patvari* does so only if he wants to be uncooperative; in practice he generally makes out the *intkal* and has the *tehsildar* sign the papers on his next visit to the village.

The common practice of recording in the mutation register a larger sum than the purchaser or mortgager actually pays for land or for a mortgage also requires the cooperation of the *patvari;* hence another bribe. This practice stems from the need to protect the purchaser of land from later claims by the original owner's relatives, who, after the sons, have priority in the purchase of land. They can claim this right in court. However, they must buy back the land from the purchaser at the price recorded in the *patvari* book. By raising the price out of reach of the relatives, the purchaser safeguards himself against possible claims.

The land consolidation program places the *patvari* in an even more strategic position, at least during the period of resettlement of the land. It is the *patvari* who assesses the value of new plots and who can be of great service to his Jat friends by giving lower values to the land received. For example, if a new plot is made up of two or three old plots of different values, the new value is not arrived at by adding up the old values, but through approximation by the *patvari*. New plots are assigned in proportion to the amount and value of the old plots; by fixing new values low, the Jat is eligible to receive more land. In the large-scale reshuffling of the land, the *patvari* is in a position to allot to friends the more desirable plots and to harm his enemies. Members of the consolidation committee and the panchayat, who want to remain on good terms with the *patvari*, generally do not challenge him. As the village *patvari* said, "The panchayat members will mostly do what I tell them, for who among them knows all about plots and their value?"

Because of pressure for land redistribution, particularly to tenants, owners of rented-out land want to register their land as being owner-operated. Thus, through the cooperation of the *patvari*, much of the tenant-operated land in Rampur is now officially listed as owner-operated. Tenants are also shifted from one plot to another, so that they may not have claim to the land.

2. The *patvari* is the sole representative of the revenue department in the village. All cases coming up in connection with the revenue department must be first transacted through the *patvari*. A Jat who wants a loan from the government must get a list of plot numbers and all the details of his lands from the *patvari*, who is in a position to delay the procedure and to get money.

The *patvari*'s contacts with other revenue officers makes the peasant dependent upon him. There is generally unity among the revenue officers, who, rather than serving to check one another, cooperate to see that each receives his "just" rewards. The *patvari* says, "All our officers [i.e., the local *quanungo* and *tehsildar*] know from where we get money and can catch us at any moment they like, but they just ignore us, provided we don't cross our limits." The *quanungo* (official in charge of a group of *patvaris*) says, "We can just smell the *patvari*'s paper and can tell where he has taken money, but we think that his getting money during *intkal* and on other occasions is his reward for hard labor. Otherwise, how can he afford to live on such little pay?"

A *quanungo* related the following story, which well illustrates the degree of cooperation among the officials of the revenue department.

Once a man who had a distant relative in the revenue department refused point blank to give money for the *intkal* of a land mortgage. I continued delaying, and finally he got angry and started shouting at me, repeating that he was a relative of a revenue officer and was going to see him. Meanwhile I rang up the *tehsildar* and told him that

I had asked only 20 rupees, and that the man had refused to give even that. I told the *tehsildar* that the man was coming to see him, and the *tehsildar* in return hinted to me to get ready. So I tore off two papers of a register and went to a still senior revenue officer with the story. The thing became so serious that the man had to pay 220 rupees to the *tehsildar* and 50 rupees to me.

The *quanungo* added that in the revenue department no one shares bribes unless he is forced to, and that in judging income differentials among *patvaris* and other officials, the factor of honesty is not so much to be considered as opportunity.

3. The *patvari* is the main village contact with other government officials. All visiting officials, such as those of the revenue, police, health, and veterinary departments, as well as those connected with the census and district elections, meet and consult with the *patvari*. It is one of the *patvari's* functions to offer them hospitality and to maintain good relations with them. To rich Jats, therefore, the *patvari* is a useful contact. To poor Jats, and particularly to menials, among whom there is a strong fear of the police and other officials, the *patvari* becomes a more powerful figure. There was a time, under the now-defunct system of *begar* in which any government employee was authorized to get the services of Camars free of charge, as well as of the bullock carts and animals of the Jats, when the appearance of a single police constable or even a peon of the revenue department could terrify a whole village.

The *patvari* could use his contacts with these officers to intimidate or help the villagers, a circumstance which substantially increased his power over them. A *patvari* often depends heavily upon bribes. He is not apt to demand money directly but has a special way of hinting at what he wants. First, he begins to laugh a lot and talk in a friendly way. He laughingly tells stories about people who have helped him by giving him money and may say jokingly, "God helps those who help a saint like the *patvari*." Or, "These days of consolidations are coming near and because of all this hard work I need plenty of milk and *ghi* to eat; otherwise how can I work?" If hints are of no avail, the *patvari* asks some Jat friends of his to convince his client to bribe him. These agents generally do what the *patvari* asks—either for a cash reward or to keep his good will. Meanwhile the *patvari* delays the case until he is paid.

The extortionate habits of *patvaris* are well known in India and have been commented on by some Western observers. Ibbetson recognized the *patvari's* exploitative role but did not consider it particularly harmful or reprehensible. "I believe that only exceptionally scrupulous patwaris ever pay their bill with the village Banya, the great majority living free at the expense of the village. But I do not think that a patwari who does so is necessarily corrupt or extortionate. The custom is in consonance with the habits of the people. . . . So long as the patwari is impartial and not too luxurious in his style of living, the people are well content to secure at the price the good offices of one who has very much in his hands, and are, perhaps, not sorry to have little entries in Banya's account books which can be brought up against him in case of need." [4]

---

[4] Ibbetson, 1883:115.

In a book dealing principally with South India, T. B. Pandian gives a more acid and indignant picture of the *patvari*'s methods:

In the Zamindari villages the accountant has endowments of lands, the revenue of which goes towards his support. And this sum is not all; every village accountant can demand from each villager a certain quantity of grain at the time of harvest. Besides this, he gets from them a considerable supply of vegetables, fruits, and other produce. The accountant is always bent upon making money by fair means or foul. In every dispute and quarrel of the villagers the accountant has a hand. He has power to do and undo things in the village. He thinks that to allow a village to be in peace is to injure his own interests. So "Divide, and rule, and gain" is his motto. A careful investigation will lead to the conclusion that the accountant is at the bottom of almost all the troubles and difficulties rising in the villages. . . . The great time of harvest for the wily accountant is the distribution of annual *pattaw* [land leases]. . . . this bloodsucker of the village—the accountant—will leave no one without getting some harvest from him. If a man fails to get the money, the accountant will put off giving his *pattaw*, and make him wander up and down, or else he will make some wilful mistakes in the *pattaw*. And he will go so far even as to give one man's *pattaw* to another, and thus he will make a delightful muddle. The accountant is noted for his document writing, for he is the only man who is able to write with pen and ink in the village. He gets money for every document he writes. Besides this, he will write false documents, in order to bring his enemy or his friends' enemy into trouble.[5]

A more recent picture of the *patvari* appears in Bernard Cohn's thesis on the Camars:

. . . the *patvari* in Senapur had been given six *bighas* of land by one of the biggest *zamindars*. The *patvari* received, in addition to his ten seers per plow, a salary of 36 rupees a month. This remuneration was not sufficient to keep him honest and he was always open to bribes which were freely offered. In most cases, the *patvari* sided with the Thakur-landlord against the low caste tenant and would enter the Thakur as cultivator as well as owner of the fields which a Camar or other low caste person actually was cultivating. With the aid of the *patvari*, the *zamindars* were able to eject and harass their tenants. There was little recourse for the tenants, who were neither rich nor powerful enough to seek redress in the courts.[6]

In a typical case, one man tries to evict another from a piece of land, the *patvari* is bribed to enter a person's name in the land records, the *patvari* may be bribed again by the other side, the records become a muddle, and then both men try to cultivate the field or both try to harvest the field.[7]

The *patvari* more than any other government official affects the lives and fortunes of the Camars. With the enactment of land reform laws, the *patvari*'s power temporarily increased. . . . In numerous cases, the *patvari* has falsified records in favor of the landlord, entering the landlord rather than the Camar tenant as the cultivator of a field. Not only have the tenants been affected by the dishonesty of the *patvari*, but many of the land disputes among the Thakurs have their basis in his activities.[8]

In the area around Rampur there has been a decline in prestige among *patvaris* in recent years. The *patvari* strike in Uttar Pradesh and the threat of strikes in the Punjab reflect a new situation. The period of prosperity for Jats which began

[5] Pandian, 1898:168-69.

[6] Cohn, 1954:62.

[7] Cohn, 1954:142.

[8] Cohn, 1954:256.

in 1944 was an economic blow to the *patvari*. The major source of the *patvari's* income is from land sales and mortgages. According to the *patvari* records in the *lal kitab* (book of statistical analysis) at Rampur, the amount of mortgaged area was 57 acres in 1931, 77 acres in 1935, 81 acres in 1939, and only 35 acres in 1943. In 1944, 77 acres of mortgaged land were reclaimed by the owners. After 1944 the mortgaging of land continued to decline. In 1947 there were only 13 mortgaged acres, and in 1953 there were only seven people who mortgaged their land.

The present *patvari* of Rampur has worked in the village for two years. During this period he has earned nothing from mortgages, sales, or exchanges, and only about 8 rupees from three cases of *fards* (transcripts of land records). "This is all my personal income in this unlucky village," said the *patvari*, "except for milk, grain, *gur*, and fuel, which I get free sometimes." The *patvari* related that just before he had come to the village, there was a sale of land for which the *quanungo* took 200 rupees. Part of this was to be given to the previous *patvari*, but since the *quanungo* knew that the *patvari* was to be transferred, he pocketed the entire amount.

The decrease in income of the *patvari* has made for much bitterness on his part. The official salary received by the Rampur *patvari* (30 rupees per month, with 40 rupees additional allowance, 8 rupees as stationery allowance, and 4 rupees as *basta* allowance) is too low to be relied upon alone. During the pre-war years of nation-wide depression, when the income of the *patvari* was good, the official salary was of little importance. *Patvaris* used to get free fodder, grain, and fuel, in addition to frequent gifts of *gur, ghi,* and other food. Animals were also given as gifts to *patvaris,* and most *patvaris* had from one to three buffaloes and a horse. The *patvari* generally lived in a *pakka* house, and some retired *patvaris* were able to build bungalows worth thousands of rupees. The *patvari* of Rampur maintains that if it were not for the consolidation of lands now going on in the village, he would not be receiving gifts of milk, fuel, grain, etc. "In this village no one would even give the *patvari* accommodations. The greedy *lambardar* has given me a house only because he hopes to get some help from me in the consolidation." However, four or five Jats have been offering the *patvari* 100 to 311 rupees for his help, so the *patvari* is looking forward to increasing his income in the future.

The economic decline of the *patvari*, coupled with a parallel rise in income and standard of living on the part of the Jats, has lowered the social standing of the *patvari*. Formerly, he was perhaps the only man in the village who was literate, who sent his sons to schools and universities, who dressed well, entertained well, lived in a *pakka* house, and received a regular monthly income. After 1940, however, when Jats and other villagers began to find jobs outside the village and started to enjoy higher cash incomes, they felt less inferior to the *patvari*. Their sons were also learning to read and write, and they were building better houses for themselves and making contacts outside the village. Even more important, since it lessened their dependence upon the *patvari,* is the fact that Jats now invest their money in ways not connected with land. Several Jats have taken to transporting goods and to trading, in addition to farming. Money, which formerly was almost always used for buying land or animals, is now spent on education, clothing, and improving housing—all to the direct loss of the *patvari.*

The achievement of independence and the work of the Congress Party have brought a new group of bureaucrats into the area, and Congress workers have now taken precedence over the old-time government officials. The *patvari* of Rampur clearly preferred to work under the British than under the present government. He said, "The British were intelligent enough to understand the usefulness of *patvaris.* But the foolish Congress government fails to understand that the *patvari* is the most trustworthy and useful part of any government."

DESCRIPTION OF THE *PATVARI* RECORDS

In Rampur there are nineteen separate books and registers with the *patvari.* Two additional *patvari* registers are with the *patvari mal* or permanent *patvari,* who resides in the nearby village of Madanpur. In the following pages each document is briefly described. The order of presentation roughly agrees with the order of preparation of the respective document by the *patvari.*

Shajrah Kistwar (plot map)

The *shajrah kistwar* is a map prepared by a *patvari* showing all the plots with their numbers. The *patvari* of Rampur has two such maps on hand. One is of cloth for daily use, approximately 6 feet by 4 feet, drawn to the scale of 1 inch for 40 *gathas* (1 *gatha* is equal to 8¼ feet) with descriptive data and numerals written in Urdu script. This is the map the *patvari* must carry with him during his field inspections. If changes are necessary they must be recorded in red ink. The second map is made of fine silk and is approximately 5 feet by 2½ feet. No scale is given. This map distinguishes between cultivated *(mazroha)* and uncultivated land *(gair mazroha).* The latter is classified into three subtypes: *banjar jadid* or new fallow, that is, fallow for four to eight successive crop seasons; *banjar kadim,* old fallow, that is, fallow for more than eight successive crop seasons; and finally *gair mumkin* or uncultivable land, which includes the village habitation area, roads, footpaths, ponds, temples, schools, houses built outside of the traditional habitation area, graveyards, bridges, canals, subcanals, and wells. (Note that the *samilat* or various types of collectively owned land is not shown as such on this map.)

Because consolidation of holdings is going on in the village a special consolidation map has been prepared. This is of cardboard, in two parts, one for canal-irrigated land, the other for the nonirrigated and well-irrigated land. The scale is 1 inch to 40 *gathas.* This map shows the new plots prepared for consolidation grouped within squares of twenty-five 1-acre plots or *mustatils*. Each 1-acre square is called a *kilah*, from which the term *kilabundi* is derived.

The original *shajrah kistwar*, prepared at the time of settlement, is kept up to date by the *patvari's* regular field inspections, which are always done just before harvest operations begin. A copy of the original settlement map is kept on hand to provide a base line for later changes. All permanent changes in field boundaries are noted in red ink. Temporary changes in field boundaries are noted in the *khasra* book (register of plots) only. When a field is subdivided into two or more more plots the *patvari* gives a separate number to each, writing the original number as the denominator and the new number as the numerator. For example, if the highest plot number on the map is 1200 and plot number 39 is to be subdivided, he will write the subdivisions as $^{1201}/_{39}$, $^{1202}/_{39}$, $^{1203}/_{39}$, etc. If fields bearing fractional numbers are again united to reconstitute an earlier holding, the fractional numbers are omitted and the original field number is restored. It should be noted that fields with distinct numbers at the time of settlement cannot be united unless a new settlement or consolidation is made.

Every eight years the *patvari* is supposed to prepare a new map. However, we have no data on the extent to which this is carried out.

Field Books

There are three field books, an original prepared at the time of settlement, a supplementary one or *tatima* containing the record of all changes in plot numbers since the earlier settlement, and a recently prepared field book for purposes of consolidation. The field books are of rectangular shape bound at the top, and open like a pad. The pages are old and broken. The paper is lined vertically to form columns in which the following entries are made, from right to left: 1. Present field number; 2. Number in old field book; 3. *Khatouni* (group of landholdings) number; 4. Peripheral plot measurements direction-wise, that is, north, south, east, and west; 5. Area of each field in *bighas* and *bisvas* and type of irrigation, if any; 6. Remarks of *patvari* (generally vacant).

The field books are work books in which the *patvari* makes his spot entries of plot measurements and types of land. At the end of each page a total is given summarizing the total number of plots and total area by land and irrigation type. At the end of the book a grand total is given.

The supplementary field book is titled as follows: "Supplementary Field Book of Village Rampur; 4 yearly measurement from 1911-12 to the present." Entries in the supplementary field book are made once every four years as a preliminary to preparation of the *jamabandi* (record of rights). The paper is lined vertically and the following entries are shown for each plot: 1. Old plot number and new number, if any; 2. *Khatouni* number (generally vacant, because of carelessness of *patvari*); 3. Peripheral plot measurements direction-wise; 4. Area and type of land; 5. Remarks. Here are found the signature of the *quanungo* or *patvari* inspector.

Khatouni Asthamal (register of owners and cultivators)

The *khatouni* is prepared along with the maps and field book at the time of the settlement. A new *khatouni* has just been prepared in Rampur in connection with the consolidation, which is considered a new settlement. It is with the help of the *khatouni* and field book that the *khasra* and *jamabandi* are prepared. After preparation of the *jamabandi*, the *khatouni* is deposited at the *tehsil* office and is prepared.

The title of the book appears as "*Khatouni Asthamal* of village of Rampur, Patwari Circle No. 116, Chak Bangar, Tehsil and District Delhi, 1951/1952." The book has no cover, the pages are unnumbered, and are held together by a thread in the upper right-hand corner. They are in good condition.

Eleven columns are shown with the following headings: 1. *Khewat* (a land-holding unit) number (1-72); 2. *Khatouni* number (1-279); 3. Name of *tarif* or *patti* (these are the traditional social subdivisions accepted by the revenue department). The order of names is from right to left according to the original genealogical table and is listed *tholla*-wise; 4. Name of owner, giving the name of *khewat* owners and the share of each; 5. Name of cultivator;[9] 6. Types of land and irrigation (for example, *chahi* [well-irrigated], *nehri* [canal-irrigated], *barani* [unirrigated], etc.); 7. *Khasra* or plot number; 8. Area; 9. Value (according to consolidation scheme); 10. Revenue (*mamla* or *lagan* [land rent]); 11. Remarks.

At the end of each *khewat*, total areas of land types and their respective values are summarized. Similarly, totals are given for each *tholla, pana,* and the whole village.

Khasra Girdawri (inspection of plot: numbers)

This is a register of plots listed serially by number showing the owner and cultivator, area (in *bighas*), type of land, crops sown in each of two harvests for four years, the condition of each crop, that is, success or failure,[10] the number of wells, and village boundaries.[11] This register contains data collected in twelve field inspections per year. A new book is prepared every four years, with the help of the *jamabandi* or *khatouni*. The *khasra* book is preserved by the *patvari* for twelve years, after which he sends it to the *tehsil* headquarters where it is destroyed.

It is a large book of 196 pages full of data, with a thick paper cover that is well worn. The earlier *khasra* are well bound and in good condition.

---

[9] See section on reliability for discussion of defects of this item.

[10] To aid the *patvari* in judging success or failure of crops the revenue department supplies him with a list of the over-all yield per *bigha* of the main crops of *kharif* and *rabi* which can be used as a base line. This list generally appears on the first page of the *khasra girdawri*.

[11] The position of six stones called *sag-hadha* which indicate where three village boundaries meet.

The data on each page is given in eleven columns as follows: 1. *Khasra* number; 2. Name of owner as given in *jamabandi;* 3. Name of cultivator as given in *khatouni* and amount of revenue; 4. Area; 5. Type of land; 6. *Kharif* crop, 1944-45; 7. *Rabi* crop, 1944-45; 8. Name of actual cultivator, 1944-45; 9-11. Same as 6-8 but for 1945-46; 12-14. Same as 6-8 but for 1946-47; 15-17. Same as 6-8 but for 1947-48.

At the end of each page the totals are given for cultivated and uncultivated land, the various crops in all types of land, and the success or failure of the crops.

At the end of the register there is a crop chart known as the *goshwara* which sums up the page totals into a grand total. This crop chart is prepared for each *kharif* and *rabi* harvest and thus there are eight crop charts in a single *khasra* book. As a rule, all are given on a single page. It is with the help of this *goshwara* that the *naksha jinswar* of the *lal kitab* is prepared. The only difference between the *goshwara* and *naksha jinswar* is that in the former the area of each crop is given in *bighas* and *bisvas* while in the latter it is changed into acres and given in round numbers, omitting fractions.

Mislah Hakiat (record of rights)

This is the original record of rights prepared only during a land settlement. Unlike later *jamabandis*, it contains the *wajib-ul'-arz* or record of customs and the *tarika bacha* or revenue assessments. It is the first *jamabandi* and serves as the basis for the preparation of later ones. It is a well-preserved, carefully written document in which no changes can be made by the *patvari*. The *shajrah* or map discussed earlier forms part of the *mislah hakiat*.

The *mislah hakiat* of 1908-9, which we examined, contains the following data in order of sequence. 1. *Robkar hiza* or guide to the genealogical chart showing symbols used and their meanings (p. 1); 2. *Shajrah nasib:* genealogical chart showing the major village subdivisions such as *panas, thollas, hals,* the caste and *gotra* of the landowners, the kinship composition of each village subdivision, the landowners grouped in *khewats,* the local units of land measurement (*hals* in this case, of approximately 150 *bighas* each) in terms of which the holdings are grouped (pp. 2-9); 3. Index of *khasra* or plots showing plot numbers serially and the corresponding *khatouni* number and page number within this volume (pp. 17-28); 4. Index *radifvar:* an alphabetical index showing name of owners, privileged tenants, and tenants at will, with their corresponding *khatouni* number and page number within this volume (pp. 17-28); 5. *Mafasl jamabandi* or detailed *jamabandi* (the *jamabandi* will be described separately later); 6. List of *mofiat* (tax-exempted) and pension holders, giving names of persons exempted from revenue, type of exemption, the pension holders and the amount of pension; 7. *Hakuk chahat:* record of rights in wells; 8. *Shart wajib-ul'-arz* or village administration paper stating customs and conditions affecting the management of the village and including a discussion of the following items: the *samilat* land and its cultivation, management and use of derived income, grazing rights on *samilat* land, customs about manure, irrigation, canals, and tanks; 9. Signatures of the settlement officers certifying the validity and reliability of the records; 10. *Hakuk tarika bach* or revenue assessment scale.

Register *Intkal* (register of mutations)

This is an important record of land transfer showing changes due to sales, mortgages, exchanges, death and succession, and gifts. All transfers from the time of settlement are recorded serially, so that one can readily see the total incidence of land transfers. Eight registers were on hand with the *patvari* since the *intkal* register is never destroyed. No entries are to be made by the *patvari* without the approval of the *tehsildar* and of the parties concerned.

The data of this register is given in fifteen columns under the following heads: 1. Mutation number; 2. *Khewat* number according to last *jamabandi;* 3. Name of *pana* or *tholla;* 4. Names of persons involved in land transfer; 5. Name of cultivator; 6. Plot number, area, and type of land; 7. Revenue assessment; 8. Number of *khewat* to be given in the new *jamabandi;* 9. Name of owner; 10. Name of cultivator (presumably new cultivator); 11. Plot number, area and type of land; 12. Revenue; 13. Type of transfer (sale, mortgage, etc.) and date; 14. Mutation fee or *dakhil charij;* 15. Remarks.

At the end of each year a table is prepared which differentiates and classifies all transfers into four categories as follows: 1. *Tabadela* or exchange; 2. *Fah-ul-rahan* or return of mortgaged land to owner after payment of mortgage. Here is given the serial number of all such cases, the type of land and area, amount of money and the mutation fee for each transfer. This data is further summarized in red ink by total number of cases, total area involved, and total value of mortgages. 3. *Va-kiyat-te-rahan* or mortgaging out land. Totals are given as in number 2 above. 4. *Bah* or changes in ownership through inheritance or sale of land. This table is used in the preparation of one of the tables of the *lal kitab.*

Mafasl Jamabandi (permanent record of rights)

This is a permanent record of rights par excellence, prepared every four years [12] after the initial preparation of the *mislah hakiat* described above. Ten *jamabandis* were with the *patvari,* the last one being of 1947-48. Because of consolidation the preparation of the *jamabandi* for 1951-52 has been delayed. The *jamabandi* of 1947-48, described below, has 135 pages and is in good condition.

The first few pages contain the *shajrah nasib* or genealogical table and the *khasra* index. The remaining pages contain data listed under the following thirteen columns from right to left: 1. *Khewat* number; 2. *Khatouni* number; 3. Superior owner; 4. Names of *patti, tholla,* and *lambardar;* 5. Name of owner. This column shows the names of co-sharers and the share of each in the holding; 6. Name of cultivator; 7. Types of land; 8. *Khasra* number; 9. Area of each

---

[12] In areas under a temporary revenue system the *jamabandi* is prepared annually.

plot in each *khewat;* 10. Rental paid by tenant; 11. Total area of *khewat* in *hals;* 12. Revenue and cesses; 13. Remarks (by *patvari*).

A number of summaries of this data are given at various points as the record progresses—at the end of each *khewat, tholla, pana,* and finally for the whole village. These summaries are known as *milan raqba.* The summaries are given in terms of total area, cultivated area by various types of land, and uncultivated area. (For details see earlier discussion of the *khasra* book.) Items 6 and 7 described above under the *mislah hakiat* are also found in the *jamabandi.*

The *patvari* is not authorized to make any changes in the *jamabandi,* even if he is aware of errors therein. Only the *tehsildar* has authority to make changes. These appear in red ink at the end of the book.

Lal Kitab (red book)

The *lal kitab,* also known as Register *Hai Halgugari,* is a book of statistical analysis which summarizes data from most of the *patvari* records. It is intended for revenue officers and so no Arabic numerals are used. Moreover, the areas are given in acres rather than in the local units. The register contains nine tables which conveniently summarize the data from the other *patvari* records on a village-wide basis. The *lal kitab* is generally used by the revenue officials in building up total statistical reports for a region. The data summarized includes cultivated and uncultivated area, irrigated and unirrigated; name and extent of crops sown each year; revenue, its remission and postponements; land transfers through inheritance, sale, mortgage, gift, or exchange; type of land tenure; land owned by agricultural and nonagricultural castes and the incidences of mortgages on their lands; total area cultivated by tenants and owners; and a five-year animal census and a ten-year population census.

Roznamcha Karguzari (diary of daily activity)

This contains entries of daily official duties written in duplicate. At the end of each month the duplicate forms are sent to the *quanungo* office.

Roznamcha Hada-e-ti (diary of suggestions)

This contains notes of all suggestions made to the *patvari* by visiting revenue officials.

Roznamcha Vaki-a-ti (diary of events)

This is a most important diary. The title page shows the total number of pages (thirty-six), validated by the *quanungo's* signature to guarantee against loss of any pages. Each page carries a stamped official seal of the *tehsildar* and at the end of the entries for a given day a special symbol is affixed after which no changes can be made in the entries for that day.

There are twenty-four items required to be entered in this diary. Some of the more important items are as follows: mortgage, exchange, or sale of land; death or disappearance of a landowner, *mafidar* (one exempt from revenue) pensioner, or village headman; each time the *patvari* leaves the village; natural calamities such as famine, flood, hail, disease; instructions received from superior officers; legal disputes concerning revenue; the signatures of all visiting revenue officials; an entry at the end of each month remarking on the condition of crops and animals in the *quanungo's patvari* circle.

Roznamcha Fard Partal (inspection notebook)

This book is intended for the period during which a settlement is in progress. The book examined is dated January 23, 1951, to January 23, 1953, and contains the inspection notes by visiting revenue officers on the work of village consolidation.

Register *Chahat* (register of wells)

This register, cloth-covered and in good condition, contains a list of all village wells used for irrigation purposes, their local names, date and cost of construction, date use began, total depth and water depth, and shareholders.

Register *Abiana Tain Mufiat* (register of remission of additional revenue on well-irrigated land)

No entries are shown because no such tax has ever been levied in this village.

Register *Ujerat Fardat* (register of fees received)

Gives total number, amount, and kind of fees received by the *patvari* for copies of village records and other certifications.

Receipt Book

This is a book of receipts with duplicates showing the name of person, purpose, and fee charged.

Fard Bach (list of revenue assessment by holdings)

This is a list of families with their revenue obligations. It is the only *patvari* record in which there is some attempt at listing the landowners not only by their *khewat* numbers but also as family units. This document is meant to facilitate the work of the *lambardar*. The families are listed *tholla*-wise and *pana*-wise. Occupancy tenants are indicated in red ink and the rentals paid to the landowners *(malikana)* are given.

The total revenue for *kharif* and *rabi* crops is given for each *pana*. The cesses for *lambardar* and the "local rate" are also given. This register is prepared yearly. It is interesting to note that Arabic numerals are used throughout this document.

Khatouni Abiana Naher

This shows canal revenue paid by families.

Register *Barbardori* (register of movements)

An ancient register intended for entries on movements of armies. The register is kept by the *patvari mal* and is no longer used.

Register *Jagn* (register of war)

A register of war kept by the *patvari mal*.

Minute Book of Consolidation

Contains entries on all meetings on consolidation beginning with the first meeting on December 14, 1951, when the consolidation committee was formed. It gives all the resolutions of the committee meetings and serves as a convenient local history of the consolidation process. There are about one hundred pages in this record.

Naksha Haqdar (register of rights of owners)

This record was prepared for consolidation purposes. It gives the estimated value in rupees and annas of the landholding of each family by *khewats*. It also indicates the persons who have applied for the separation of *khewats* and the types of land a person owns in each *khewat*.

SOME KEY CONCEPTS OF THE RECORD SYSTEM

Three terms, *khewat*, *khatouni*, and *khasra*, must be clearly understood if one is to make intelligent use of the *patvari* records.

The *Khewat*

The *khewat* number is for many purposes the key to the record system. The *khewat* refers to a landholding unit which may consist of a single parcel or a group of scattered parcels. One or more persons may have ownership rights in a single *khewat* or in a few *khewats*. The assignment of *khewat* numbers to landholdings simplifies the complicated task of record keeping and is useful for purposes of cross reference in different registers. The *khewat* numbers are fairly stable over long periods of time, that is, the owners of particular landholdings may change but the *khewat* number remains the same. From 1909 to 1948 the *khewat* numbers in Rampur increased only by twelve from number 60 to number 72. When sons inherit land from their father they generally take the same *khewat* number, unless they make special application for a separation of holdings. As a rule this is done only when there is a serious quarrel among them. The point is that very often brothers will live in separate households and work the land separately and yet will retain a single *khewat* number. The same *khewat* number may persist for two or three generations.

If all the land under a single *khewat* number is sold, the *khewat* number remains the same. However, if only one portion is sold a new *khewat* number is assigned to that portion. *Khewat* numbers may also be consolidated, thereby reducing the total number. For example, when an owner dies childless his *khewat* holdings may be taken over by relatives and his *khewat* absorbed in theirs. Similarly, if the owners of *khewat* number 1 buy out *khewat* number 2, number 2 may be eliminated at the preparation of a new *jamabandi*.

The data on size of landholdings by *khewats* do not give a functional picture of the size of landholdings operated by family or household units. This is a serious problem in the use of *patvari* data, for if one wants to analyze the community in terms of family or household units it becomes necessary to reclassify the data. If the size of landholdings were calculated on a *khewat* basis the distortion would be in the direction of exaggerating the size of holdings. On the other hand, if the sizes of holdings of individual owners are taken the distortion is in the opposite direction, minimizing the size of holdings. For example, in Rampur there are sixty-five privately owned *khewats* [13] but 108 landowners. In our own study of Rampur we have used the family as our basic unit of analysis.

The *patvari* records, as a rule, do not tell us whether the co-sharers in a single *khewat* live together or separately, work their land individually or jointly. This must be learned by interviews with the cultivators. However, the persons listed under a single *khewat* number are, as a rule, close relatives and most often live in one compound or in adjoining or nearby houses. The *khewat* groupings can therefore be used as a guide in establishing the spatial distribution of house sites in a village. By examining the *khewat* numbers and the genealogical table in the *jamabandi* one can readily discern the spatial distribution of kinship groupings in the village.

The *Khatouni*

The *khatouni* is generally defined as a tenant holding. However, in practice the *khatouni* refers to a grouping of landholdings in terms of cultivating units within a *khewat*, irrespective of whether the cultivator is a tenant or an owner. The meaning of the term can be illustrated by an example. A *khewat* of 100 *bighas* with three co-sharers, A, B, and C, may have five *khatouni* numbers. A, B, and C may cultivate some land jointly, thereby forming *khatouni* number 1. In addition, A, B, and C may each cultivate some land separately, thereby forming *khatouni* numbers 2, 3, and 4 respectively. Finally, part of the land of the *khewat* owners may be cultivated by a renter, thereby forming *khatouni* number 5.

The *khatouni* numbers are assigned only once at the time of settlement and do not change thereafter. In this respect they differ from both the *khasra* and *khewat* numbers. The *khatouni* numbers are useful primarily as an aid to the *patvari* in locating specific plot numbers within the *khewats*, but are not helpful for social or economic analysis.

---

[13] There are seven additional *khewat* numbers which refer to various types of ownership. Four refer to *samilat* land, one to *mahazi malkan*, or area covered by canals, one to habitation area, and one to government-owned land.

The *Khasra*

Each plot of land in the village has a *khasra* or plot number. With the aid of the *khasra* number and *khatouni* number one can readily obtain for each plot of land the names of the owner, the cultivator, and the crop sown. However, the data on cultivators as shown in the *khasra* book is not always reliable. Land which is rented out is often found listed under the owner's name and plots which are self-cultivated are sometimes listed as tenant-cultivated. The *khasra* book is prepared once every four years and there is considerable lag in keeping entries up to date. Moreover, due to the fear of land reforms which might involve tenant occupancy claims, much rented land is listed by landowners as self-cultivated, with the tenants often shifted from one plot to another, and brothers with separate households listed as self-cultivators though only one may be actually working the land.

The degree of unreliability of the data on cultivation can be seen by a comparison of the *patvari* data on rentals with our data based on interviews of landowners and tenants. According to the *patvari* records, in 1952 there were only seven landowners renting out a total of 135 *bighas*, 15 *bisvas* of land. This was the figure recently given to the Community Projects in their survey. But our data showed there were thirty-three families renting out 484 *bighas* of land. Moreover, this did not include 55 *bighas* of land rented out by two residents of the village who own land in other villages. It is apparent that the *patvari* records showed only about one-third of the total rentals.

CONCLUSIONS

In the preceding pages we have had a glimpse of the role of the *patvari* in village life, the great variety of data found in the *patvari* records, the complexity of the record system, and some of the strong and weak points of the data. Some of the major findings can now be summarized as follows:

1. The records are on the whole reliable and of great value for getting background information on the agricultural economy as well as on some elementary aspects of village social organization.

2. Much time can be saved by an investigator who has some previous knowledge of the context and organization of the *patvari* records. It is hoped that with the aid of this guide a field worker can get the necessary data in two or three days of work instead of two or three weeks.

3. Three key concepts for understanding the organization of the records are the *khewat*, the *khatouni*, and the *khasra* numbers. The *khewat* number refers to a landholding unit which may consist of a single parcel or a group of scattered parcels. The *khatouni* number refers to a grouping of landholdings in terms of cultivation units within a *khewat*, irrespective of whether the cultivator is a tenant or owner. The *khasra* number refers to a specific plot of land. Each plot of land in the village has its plot number.

4. Of all the many records with the *patvari*, the following five are the most useful for our purposes: (1) *mislah hakiat*, (2) *jamabandi*, (3) *lal kitab*, (4) *khasra* register, and (5) *intkal* register. The diaries may also be useful in providing some record of the nature and frequency of contacts between the government, especially the revenue officers, and the village.

5. The data in the records can be classified under two broad headings as follows:

I

Agricultural Economics
1. Land use and land types
2. Land tenure
3. Landownership
4. Size of holdings
5. Tenancy
6. Fragmentation of plots
7. Land turnover
8. Crops and crop yields
9. Number and types of wells
10. Animal census
11. Miscellaneous census on agricultural equipment

II

Social Organization
1. Village subdivisions into *panas* and *thollas*
2. Kinship groupings under each
3. Castes of agriculturists
4. Inheritance patterns
5. Customary relations between agriculturists and nonagriculturists in regard to village land use

6. The major shortcomings of the records for community analysis are:

a) The data is limited to the agricultural families. We are told practically nothing about the lower castes who generally constitute a significant percentage of all village families—in the case of Rampur about 50 per cent.

b) The data on number of tenants and area cultivated by tenants proved unreliable, particularly since 1948. It can be assumed that this will be true for most regions in India where actual or pending land reform legislation has encouraged landowners to list tenant-cultivated areas as self-cultivated. Moreover, the data suggests that the *patvari* is more responsible to the interests of the landowners, particularly the landowners with larger holdings, than to those of the tenants. Other factors which may operate to reduce the reliability of *patvari* data on this score include the frequent shifting of tenants from plot to plot and the lag in *patvari* recording of it; the tendency to list all brothers who are co-sharers in ownership as self-cultivators.

c) The data on percentage of total land irrigated and nonirrigated has lagged far behind changes in the villages. As we have seen earlier only about one-sixth of the land is actually receiving sufficient water for irrigation but the records show about 50 per cent of the land as irrigated.

d) The data on crop yields is hardly accurate. However, it serves to distinguish between famine years and bumper-crop years.

e) The *patvari* data is not organized on a family or household basis. For an intensive village study it is necessary to reclassify the *patvari* data on a family basis.

A Glossary of Native Terms

abādī dhe—village habitation site

abiānā tain mufiat—remission of additional revenue on well-irrigated land

ajwayan—a spice

ākta—ceremony at mass cattle burial during epidemic

āngi, angiyā—bodice

āratī—ceremony of worship or means of honoring someone by rotating before him a tray bearing lights and incense

āṣrama—four traditional stages of Hindu's life

ātmā, ātmān—soul, spirit

āttā—wheat flour

āvāgavan—transmigration

āvatār—vehicle, incarnation

bah—change of landownership

baiṭhak—men's quarters or sitting room

bājrā—a kind of millet

bakli—boiled gram with salt

bān—ceremonial oil bath and massage given to both bride and groom before wedding

bangain—eggplant

bāṇgar—upland region, high ground

banjar—wasteland, land left fallow

barābhāt—big *bhāt*

bārānī—unirrigated

bārāt—marriage procession of groom's party to bride's village; wedding party

bārāt lena—ceremony in which groom is honored by Brahman of bride's family

barauthi—ceremony in which groom is honored by members of bride's family

barbardori—(army) movements

bāsī—stale

bastā—cloth wrapping around *paṭvārī* records
bathuā sag—a weed, *chenopodium album*
battis—big *srāddha* feast
begār—obligatory labor without pay
bel girī—a local fruit
bhābhī—elder brother's wife
bhagat—devotee, shaman
bhāī, bhāīyā—brother
bhajan—adoration, worship
bhāng—hemp
bhānjā—sister's son
bhāt—gifts given to bride or groom by mother's brother; bard
bhāyacāra—brotherhood, a type of land tenure
bhikṣu—fourth stage of *āṣrama* in which individual is wandering mendicant
bidā—leave-taking, permission to depart
bidāgi—adjective of *bidā*
bīgha—a unit of land. In Rampur 4.8 *bīghas* equal 1 acre
bīsagāma—twenty-village unit
bisvā—1/20 of a *bīgha*
biṭaurā—a heap of dried cow-dung cakes
biyāh—marriage
boonga—a structure for storing wheat and barley chaff for animal feed
brahmacaryā—first stage of *āṣrama* during which individual maintains strict chastity

cādar—sheet or covering
cak—a land unit
canā—a kind of pulse, black gram
candan—sandalwood
capātī—a thin wheat cake of unleavened flour
cāprasī—office boy

carā (karā)—wristlet
caras—leather bag used at wells and for irrigation purposes
cārpāī—cot
catnī—a kind of sauce, chutney
caudhar—leader (adj.)
caudharī—headman, leader
caugāma—four-village unit
cauk—a square
caukā—cooking place
caukidār—watchman
caupāl—men's meeting house
cauth—fourth
chāhat—wells
chāhī—well-irrigated
challā—small ring
chari—standard
charnamrit—a food made of milk, sugar, and *tulsī* leaves
chokain khelnā—"playing with sticks"—ceremonial stick-beatings during visit by bride and groom to Ghantal Deo's shrine after wedding
cholai—a small millet
chorī-jārī—stealing-lying
chulah neotā—an invitation to feed an entire family for a day
chūnrī—head shawl; presentation of gifts to bride's family
corma, curma—a concoction of bread, sugar, and *ghī*
cūmnā—to kiss

dādā—paternal grandfather
dādī—paternal grandmother
dahī—curds
dāī—midwife
dākhil chārij—mutation (transfer) fee
dakṣinā—ritual remuneration to Brahman
dāl—a split-pea preparation
dāl kī kachori—a *pūrī* made with *dāl*

dālda—hydrogenated oil

darinah—same as *kabzā kādim*

daṣahrā—tenth

deṣodah—God grant

dev, devtā—god

dēvar—husband's younger brother

dhan—wealth

dhanglā—a kind of pulse

dhaṛ—faction; upper part of body

dharan—a pulse under the navel

dharma—(religious) duty

dharmātmā, dharmik—righteous man

ḍhenkalī—a hand-lever well with a long beam having a weight at one end to raise the bucket at the other

dhotī—full, draped trousers

dhū̃ṛhi—a ball of parched rice with sugar syrup

ḍignā—displaced

dīvā chūn—procedure for reshifting the *dharan* whereby a wick in an *āttā* "dish" is lighted and placed on the *dharan* under a brass bowl

dorū—small drum

dūb—a fine, soft grass

dūgāma—two-village unit

fah-ul-rahan — return of mortgaged land to owner after payment of mortgage

fard—transcript of a land record

fard bach—list of revenue assessment by holdings

gair mazroha—uncultivated

gair mūmkin—uncultivable, waste and grazing (land)

gangā-dhar chūran—a powder used by natives in treating diarrhea

gangājal—holy Ganges water

garbha sanskāra—ceremony at pregnancy

garkhi—jacket

gathā—8¼ feet

gaunā, gāvanā—ceremony at puberty for bride, leading to consummation of marriage

gavār—a legume

gehnā—a gift given as a pledge to a deity in return for favors

ghaghri—skirt

ghar—house, women's quarters

ghī—oil of butter

ghī būrā—sugar with *ghī*

ghoṛā charhī—"horse riding"—same as *ghuṛ charhī*

ghot—ailment brought about by spirit possession; hysteria

ghuṛ charhī—groom's horseback ride in his village before wedding

giās—eleventh

gow—cow

gobar—cow dung

goshwara—crop chart, with area of each crop in *bīghas* and *bisvās*

gotra—nonlocalized patrilineal clan

gṛhastha—second stage of *āśrama* in which individual is householder and family man

gulāl—red oxide powder, thrown at Holī

gulgulā—a sweet cake made of flour, oil, and *guṛ*

guṛ—a crude brown sugar which includes molasses

gurū—teacher

hai halgugari—same as *lāl kitāb*

hākīkī—claimant to an inheritance

hakīm—curer

hakūk chāhat—record of rights in wells

hakūk tarika bach—revenue assessment scale

hal—plough; piece of land; team of oxen

haladhāt—"red hand"—day of first *bān*

halāī—a strip of land

haldī—turmeric

hālī—ploughman

hālvā—a delicacy made of wheat flour, syrup, and *ghī*

hanslī—neckpiece made of one piece of silver

hāvan—fire hole

hāvana—fire

hebah—charity

intkal—registration in *patvārī* records of transfer of land

īsvar, īsvara—God

jadīd—new

jagn—war

jajmān—patron

jajmānī—patronage, adjective describing the system of economic exchanges characteristic of rural India

jalebī—a fried ringed pancake made of fine wheat flour, syrup, and *ghī*

jamabandi—record of rights

jamūn—a native tree

jar—an inanimate thing

jeth—husband's elder brother

jhar phūnā—common-law marriage

jholī—apron receptacle, sack, beggar's bag

jīvan—life

johari—ritual at marriage period, involving ceremonial sucking of his mother's breast by groom

jovār, juār—a kind of millet or sorghum

kābulī gokhrū—an herb used by natives in treating diarrhea

kabzā kādim—"old possession" occupancy of land whereby no revenue is paid to owner by tenant

kaccā — raw, uncooked; unfinished; built of mud

kādim—old

kājal—lamp-black, soot

kalān—large, big

kamīn, kam karnē-wāla—menial servant, worker

kamiz—blouse, shirt

kangnā—a thread tied around the wrist, involved in the games played when a bride visits the groom's village

kangnā khelnā—playing of games at bridal reception in groom's village

kannyā dān—part of wedding ceremony involving bestowal of bride and dowry by father of bride

kārelā—a vegetable, a bitter gourd

karma—doctrine of action determining one's destiny

karvā—small pitcher

kharīf—rainy-season crop

khasrā—a specific plot

khasrā girdawrī—inspection of plot (numbers)

khatounī—a group of landholdings

khatounī abiānā naher—register showing canal revenue paid by families

khatounī āsthamal—register of owners and cultivators

khewat—a landholding unit

khīr—a pudding made of rice and milk

khurd—small, little

khurpā—weeding blade

kilabundi—fixing boundaries of plots

kilah—a 1-acre plot

kolhārī—a roller used for crushing lumps of mud

kondrā—a plant whose berries are used by natives in treating typhoid

kothlī—gifts; bag, purse

kotwal—police officer

kudhī-tarīf—house tax

kunbā—extended family
kurtā—collarless shirt

lā, lāo—jute rope
laḍḍū—a sweetmeat
lagan—formal reminder of wedding day
lagān—land rent
lāgi—embassy
lakh—a hundred thousand
lāl kitāb—"red book"—book of statistical analysis summarizing data from most of *patvārī* records
lambardār—headman of a *panā* responsible for government revenue
lambardārī—office or position of *lambardār*
lapsī—a glutinous delicacy made of toasted flour, brown sugar, and water
linga—cylindrical stone representing Śiva
loṭā—brass jug

mā—mother
mafasl jamabandi—detailed *jamabandi*
mafidar—one exempt from revenue
mahazi malkan — area covered by canals
maij—rectangular-shaped log used in farming
mālik kabzā—modified or incomplete ownership without any rights in the common
mālik kāmil — perfect or complete ownership entailing possession of rights in the common
mālikāna—tenancy fee
māmā—mother's brother
mamlā—land rent
mandap, maṇḍhā—a structure built for marriage ceremony
mantrā—spell, charm, incantation

maror phali—an herb used by natives in treating diarrhea
mārūsi—occupancy tenancy whereby occupancy fees must be paid to owner of land
masūr—a pulse, lentil
masūr kī dāl—a combination of pulses
maund—a unit of weight containing 40 *sīrs*
maur—crown; upper part of bridegroom's turban
māyā—illusion
mazrohā, mazrū'ā—cultivable, cultivated, tilled
mehṇdī—henna stain; myrtle
milān raqbā—summaries of land data appearing at intervals in *mafasl jamabandi*
milnī—greeting, reception of wedding party
mislāh hakiat—(original) record of rights
mofiat—tax-free holdings
mokṣa—same as *muktī*
motia khamīrā—a medication made from pearls and used by natives in treating typhoid
mūdhā—a village chair or stool
mūkh dikhānā—viewing of bride's face by groom's relatives
muktī—release, deliverance, salvation
mūng—a kind of pulse, green gram
muṛ khulai—joking between groom and bride's female relatives after *pherā*
mustatīl—a group of twenty-five 1-acre plots

nakshā haqdār—register of rights of owners
nakshā jinswār—crop chart, with area of each crop in acres
nālā—colored cotton skein

nānad, nānand—husband's sister

naraka, narakh—Hell

nau—nine

neg jog—presents made on a festive occasion, as in the conclusion of marriage arrangements

nehrī—canal-irrigated

neotā—contribution to a wedding or birth ceremony

nīm—a native tree

niorthā—barley seedling

orhnā—shawl

ori—sowing season

pagrī—turban

pakkā—cooked, boiled; perfect; strong; finished; made of brick (house)

pālī—cowherd

paltā—iron spoon

panā—subdivision of a village, revenue-paying group

pāp, pāpa—evil, sinful, evil deeds

parānt, parāt—big vessel

parcaran—ceremonial touching of the feet

parganā—a district subdivision

parjan—same as kamīn

patāsā—a sweet made of sugar and coconut

pātel—headman

patkā—sash, piece of cloth

patmal—a term of affection

patrā—ceremonial sitting-board

patrā pher—exchange of the sitting-boards

pattāw—land lease

pattī—same as panā

pattidārī—lands held by ancestral right

patvārī—village accountant, land recorder

patvārī mal—permanent patvārī

perā—a small, round sweet or cookie made with milk evaporated by slow boiling and sugar

pherā—circumambulation of fire or beam by bride and groom (high point of wedding ceremony)

pīr—saint (usually Muslim), spiritual guide

pīsna—grain, to grind

pīth—a long piece of cloth

ponchi—wristlet, arm band

prauthā—fried capātī

pūchrī—tail

pudina—mint

punarjanman—reincarnation

punya—good, good deeds

pūrī—a thin cake fried in ghī or oil

quanūngo—official in charge of a group of patvārīs

rabi—wintry-season crop

rabrī—thickened milk, a preparation made of churned curds and flour

rādh—mucus

radīfvar—index of tenants and landowners in mislāh hakiat

rākrī, raksā, rakshā—a thread used as an armlet, worn at time of weddings and at the Silono festival

rātri—night

robkar hiza — guide to genealogical chart in mislāh hakiat

rotī—cake or bread, like a capātī

roznāmchā fard partāl—inspection notebook

roznāmchā hada-e-tī—diary of suggestions

roznāmchā kārguzāri—diary of daily activity

roznāmchā vaki-ā-tī—diary of events

ryotwārī—land tenure

sada sindu—an indigenous medicine for treating cholera

sādhū—holy man
sagāī—engagement
sag-hadha—six stones indicating meeting of three village boundaries
sah dai—an herb used by natives in treating malaria
sainak — cooked rice and jaggery powder
sāmilāt—land held in common
sāmilāt dhe—village common
sāmnū—autumn or wet-season crop, sown in late June and harvested in September and December
sansār—the world, universe
sanskāra—ceremony marking stage in life cycle of individual
saptami—seventh
sārhi—spring or dry-season crop, sown in November and harvested in March
satain—seven
satī—suicide
sāvanī—same as *sāmnū*
semian—sweet burned noodles
sewal—ceremony of honor performed by mother of bride or groom and consisting of touching body of person honored all over with petticoat
shajrāh kistwār—plot map
shajrāh nasib — genealogical chart showing village subdivisions
shart wājib-ul'-arz—list of customs and conditions affecting management of village
sidhā—a food offering made of rice, brown sugar, and *ghī*
sidhi—cold
silvār—baggy trousers worn by women
simai—a small millet
sindhārā—ceremonial gifts; custom of giving gifts to certain relatives on various festival days

sīr—a weight of about 2 pounds
sīt—a kind of buttermilk
sivian—a food
siyana—healer
sohāg—glass wristlets or bangles and gold nosering—symbols of married woman donned on day of first *bān*
sohāgan, suhāgan—a woman whose husband is alive
srāddha—ceremonies in honor of the dead
suhali—a sweet *pūrī*
svarga—Heaven

tabadelā—exchange
tarif—a village social subdivision
tarika bacha—revenue assessments
tatima—supplementary field book
tāvū—father's elder brother
tehsil—administrative unit of a district; county
tehsildār—officer of a *tehsil*
tel chadhānā—annointment with oil
tera, terī—your
thālī—small brass tray
thāpā—handprint
thāpā lāna—to make handprints on a wall
thollā—subdivision of a *pana*
tīel—dress, woman's clothing
tīgāma—three-village unit
ṭīkā—a mark made on the forehead
tonga—two-wheeled passenger cart
tulsī—a local herb

ubṭan—an oil made with perfume, turmeric, and flour, used for massaging body of bride or groom at *bān* ceremonies
ujerat fardat—fees received
urad—a pulse
uṭhanā—to wake

vaid—curer
va-kiyat-te-rahan—mortgaging out land
vardhana—nourisher
vazīr—minister

wājib-ul'-arz — regulations concerning village administration

zamīndār—landlord, property owner
zamīndārī—body of landowners; land-ownership

Bibliography

Ahmad, Enayat
   1952.   "Rural Resettlement Types in the Uttar Pradesh (United Provinces of Agra and Oudh)," *Annals of the Association of American Geographers, 42,* 3:223-46.
"An Alphabetical List of the Feasts and Holidays of the Hindus and Muhammadans."
   1914.   Calcutta: Imperial Record Department.
Anstey, Vera
   1939.   *The Economic Development of India.* New York: Longmans, Green & Co., Inc.
Arensberg, Conrad
   1954.   "The Community-Study Method," *American Journal of Sociology, 60,* 2:109-24.
Baden-Powell, B. H.
   1892.   *The Land Systems of British India.* Oxford: Clarendon Press.
   1899.   *Village Communities in India.* New York: Charles Scribner's Sons.
Beals, Alan Robin
   1953.   "Change in the Leadership of a Mysore Village," *Economic Weekly* (Bombay), 5:487-92.

1955.   "Interplay Among Factors of Change in a Mysore Village," in *Village India*, ed. by McKim Marriott. American Anthropological Association, Memoir 83, June:78-101.

Bhattacharyya, Asutosh
1955.   "The Cult of the Village Gods of West Bengal," *Man in India*, 35, 1.

Bose, Nirmal Kumar (ed.)
1948.   *Selections from Gandhi*. Ahmedabad: Navajivan.

Briggs, George
1920.   *The Chamars*. London: Oxford University Press.

Cohn, Bernard S.
1954.   "The Camars of Senapur." Unpublished Ph.D. dissertation, Cornell University. Typescript.
1955.   "The Changing Status of a Depressed Caste," based on reports by Bernard S. Cohn, in *Village India*, ed. by McKim Marriott. American Anthropological Association, Memoir 83, June:53-77.

Cox, Oliver Cromwell
1948.   *Caste, Class, and Race*. New York: Doubleday & Co., Inc.

Crooke, William
1896.   *The Popular Religion and Folklore of Northern India*. London: Constable.

Darling, Malcolm Lyall
1925.   *The Punjab Peasant in Prosperity and Debt*. London: Oxford University Press.
1934.   *Wisdom and Waste in the Punjab Village*. London: Oxford University Press.
1949.   *At Freedom's Door*. Toronto: Oxford University Press.

Davis, Kingsley
1951.   *The Population of India and Pakistan*. Princeton: Princeton University Press.

Dhillon, Harvant
1955.   *Leadership and Groups in a South Indian Village*. New Delhi: Planning Commission, Programme Evaluation Organization, Government of India.

Dube, S. C.
1955.   *Indian Village*. Ithaca: Cornell University Press.

Dubois, J. A.
1947.   *Hindu Manners, Customs, and Ceremonies*, tr. by Henry K. Beauchamp. Oxford: Clarendon Press.

Eames, Edwin
1954.   "Some Aspects of Urban Migration from a Village in North Central India," *Eastern Anthropologist*, 8, Sept.-Nov.:13-26.
1955.   "Population and Economic Structure of an Indian Rural Community," *Eastern Anthropologist*, 8, March-Aug.:173-81.

Elmore, Wilber Theodore
  1915.   *Dravidian Gods in Modern Hinduism.* Originally Ph.D. dissertation,
           University of Nebraska; reprinted from the University of Nebraska
           Studies, *15*, 1.
Emerson, Gertrude
  1944.   *Voiceless India.* New York: John Day Company.
Encyclopaedia Brittanica
  1954.   "The Jats." *12*:970-71.
Evans-Pritchard, E. E.
  1947.   *The Nuer.* Oxford: Clarendon Press.
  1951.   *Kinship and Marriage Among the Nuer.* Oxford: Clarendon Press.
Foster, George M.
  1953.   "What Is Folk Culture?" *American Anthropologist,* 55:159-73.
Fuchs, Stephen
  1951.   *The Children of Hari.* New York: Frederick A. Praeger, Inc.
Gadgil, D. R.
  1952.   *Poona, a Socio-Economic Survey.* Poona: Gokhale Institute.
Gist, Noel P.
  1954.   "Caste Differentials in South India," *American Sociological Review,*
           19, 2:126-37.
Gode, P. K.
  1946.   "Studies in the History of Hindu Festivals: Some Notes on the
           History of Divali," *Annals of the Bhandarkaer Oriental Research In-
           stitute* (Poona), pp. 216-62.
Goshal, Kumar
  1944.   *The People of India.* New York: Sheridan House, Inc.
Gough, E. Kathleen
  1955.   "The Social Structure of a Tanjore Village," in *Village India,* ed. by
           McKim Marriott. American Anthropological Association, Memoir 83,
           June:36-52.
Gupte, Rai Bahadur B. A.
  1919.   *Hindu Holidays and Ceremonials.* Calcutta: Thacker, Spink.
Hanks, L. M., and Jane R. Hanks
  1955.   "Diphtheria Immunization in a Thai Community," in *Health, Culture,
           and Community,* ed. by Benjamin D. Paul, pp. 155-85. New York:
           Russell Sage Foundation.
Hazari (pseudonym)
  1951.   *An Indian Outcaste.* London: Bannisdale Press.
Hutton, J. H.
  1951.   *Caste in India.* New York: Oxford University Press.
Ibbetson, Denzil Charles Jelf
  1882.   *Census Report for the Punjab for 1881,* Part 1. Lahore: Superin-
           tendent of Government Printing.

1883.   *Report on the Revision of Settlement of the Panipat Tahsil and Karnal Parganah of the Karnal District, 1872-1880.* Allahabad: Pioneer Press.

1903.   "Jats," *The Census of India, 1901, Ethnographic Appendices,* pp. 74-80. Calcutta: Superintendent of Government Printing.

1916.   *Punjab Castes.* Lahore: Superintendent of Government Printing.

Jathar, G. B., and S. G. Beri
1949.   *Indian Economics,* Vol. 2. London: Oxford University Press.

Joardar, N. G. D.
1952.   "Village Administration in India." Paper presented at the Meetings of the Far Eastern Association in Boston. Mimeographed.

Karve, Irawati
1953.   *Kinship Organization in India.* Poona: Deccan College Research Institute.

Kroeber, Alfred L.
1952.   "The Societies of Primitive Man," in *The Nature of Culture,* by Alfred L. Kroeber, pp. 219-25. Chicago: University of Chicago Press.

Leighton, Alexander, and Dorothea C. Leighton
1945.   *The Navaho Door.* Cambridge: Harvard University Press.

Lewis, Oscar
1951.   *Life in a Mexican Village: Tepoztlan Restudied.* Urbana: University of Illinois Press.

1953.   "Preliminary Guide to the Use of Patwari Records." Mimeographed.

1954.   "Group Dynamics in a North Indian Village: A Study of Factions," *Economic Weekly* (Bombay), 6:423-25, 445-51, 477-82, 501-6.

1955a. "Peasant Culture in India and Mexico: A Comparative Analysis," in *Village India,* ed. by McKim Marriott. American Anthropological Association, Memoir 83, June:145-70.

1955b. "Medicine and Politics in a Mexican Village," in *Health, Culture, and Community,* ed. by Benjamin D. Paul, pp. 404-34. New York: Russell Sage Foundation.

1956a. "Aspects of Land Tenure and Economics in a North Indian Village," *Economic Development and Cultural Change, 4,* 3:279-302.

1956b. "The Festival Cycle in a North Indian Jat Village," *Proceedings of the American Philosophical Society, 100:*168-96.

Lewis, Oscar, and Victor Barnouw
1956.   "Caste and the *Jajmani* System in a North Indian Village," *Scientific Monthly,* 83:66-81.

Madan, B. K. (ed.)
1953.   *Economic Problems of Underdeveloped Countries in Asia.* London: Oxford University Press.

Majumdar, D. N., M. C. Pradhan, C. Sen, and S. Misra
1955.   "Intercaste Relations in Cohanakallan, a Village Near Lucknow," *Eastern Anthropologist, 8,* March-Aug.:191-214.

Marriott, McKim
1955a.   "Little Communities in an Indigenous Civilization," in *Village India*, ed. by McKim Marriott. American Anthropological Association, Memoir 83, June:171-222.
1955b.   "Western Medicine in a Village of North India," in *Health, Culture, and Community*, ed. by Benjamin D. Paul, pp. 239-68. New York: Russell Sage Foundation.

McGavran, Donald Anderson
1936.   "Education and the Beliefs of Popular Hinduism." Ph.D. dissertation, Columbia University.

Megaw, John
1946.   "Public Health. The Great Diseases of India," in *Social Service in India*, ed. by Edward Blunt. London: His Majesty's Stationery Office.

Miller, Eric J.
1952.   "Village Structure in North Kerala," *Economic Weekly* (Bombay), Feb. 9:159-64.

Miner, Horace
1952.   "The Folk-Urban Continuum," *American Sociological Review, 17*: 529-37.

Mintz, Sidney
1953.   "The Folk-Urban Continuum and the Rural Proletarian Community," *American Journal of Sociology, 55*:136-43.

Misra, Shridhar
1951.   "Caste Survey in Two Modal Villages with Stereotyped Discriminations," in *Intercaste Tensions*, ed. by Radhakamal Mukerjee. University of Lucknow. Mimeographed.

Moore, Frank J.
1955.   "Land Reform and Social Justice in India," *Far Eastern Survey, 24*, Aug.:124-28.

Mukerjee, Radhakamal (ed.), and others.
1951.   *Intercaste Tensions*. University of Lucknow. Mimeographed.

Mukerji, A. B.
1934.   "Jats: A Study in Human Geography," *Geographical Review of India* (Calcutta), *16*, 2:12-31.

Mukerji, Abhay Charan
1918.   *Hindu Fasts and Feasts*. Allahabad: Indian Press.

Nehru, S. S.
1932.   *Caste and Credit in the Rural Area*. Calcutta: Longmans, Green & Co., Inc.

O'Malley, L. S. S.
1932.   *Indian Caste Customs*. New York: Cambridge University Press.
1935.   *Popular Hinduism*. New York: Cambridge University Press.

Opler, Morris E.
1950.   "Village Life in North India." Reprinted from *Patterns for Modern Living*, Division 3, Cultural Patterns. Chicago: The Delphian Society.

Opler, Morris E., and Rudra Datt Singh
1948.   "The Division of Labor in an Indian Village," in *A Reader in General Anthropology*, ed. by C. S. Coon. New York: Henry Holt and Co., Inc.
1952.   "Two Villages of Eastern Uttar Pradesh," *American Anthropologist, 54,* 2, pt. 1:179-90.

Pandian, T. B.
1898.   *Indian Village Folk.* London: Elliot Stock.

Paul, Benjamin D. (ed.)
1955.   *Health, Culture, and Community.* New York: Russell Sage Foundation.

Planalp, Jack
1955.   "Life Cycle and Life Cycle Rites." Preliminary chapter of Ph.D. dissertation, Cornell University. Typescript.

Purser, W. E., and H. C. Fanshawe
1880.   *Report on the Revised Land Revenue Settlement of the Rohtak District of the Hissar Division.* Lahore: Superintendent of Government Printing.

Ratan, Ram
1955.   "Socio-Ethnic Studies of the Bhangis of Delhi." Ph.D. dissertation, University of Delhi. Typescript.

Reddy, N. S.
1955.   "Functional Relations of Lohars in a North Indian Village," *Eastern Anthropologist, 8,* March-Aug.:129-40.

Redfield, Robert
1939.   "Primitive Merchants of Guatemala," *Quarterly Journal of Inter-American Affairs, 1:*42-56.
1953a.   *The Primitive World and Its Transformations.* Ithaca: Cornell University Press.
1953b.   "The Natural History of the Folk Society," *Social Forces, 31:*224-28.
1956.   *Peasant Society and Cultures.* Chicago: University of Chicago Press.

Redfield, Robert, and Sol Tax
1953.   "General Characteristics of Present Day Mesoamerican Indian Society," in *Heritage of Conquest*, ed. by Sol Tax, pp. 31-39. Glencoe, Illinois: Free Press.

Rose, H. A.
1919.   *A Glossary of the Tribes and Castes of the Punjab and the North-West Frontier Provinces.* Lahore: Superintendent of Government Printing.

Russell, R. V., and Rai Bahadur Hira Lal
   1916.   *The Tribes and Castes of the Central Provinces of India.* London:
             Macmillan and Co., Ltd.
Ryan, Bryce
   1953.   *Caste in Modern Ceylon.* New Brunswick: Rutgers University Press.
Sachau, Edward C. (ed.)
   1910.   *Alberuni's India.* London: Kegan Paul, Trench, Trubner.
Sarker, Jadunath
   1937.   "Aurangzib," in *The Mughal Empire,* Vol. 4 of *The Cambridge
             History of India,* ed. by Richard Burn. New York: Cambridge Uni-
             versity Press.
Singh, Mohinder
   1947.   *The Depressed Classes.* Bombay: Hind Kitabs.
Spate, O. H. K.
   1954.   *India and Pakistan: A General and Regional Geography.* London:
             Methuen.
Spencer, J. E.
   1954.   *Asia East by South:A Cultural Geography.* New York: John Wiley &
             Sons, Inc.
Srinivas, M. N.
   1955a.   "The Social System of a Mysore Village," in *Village India,* ed. by
             McKim Marriott. American Anthropological Association, Memoir 83,
             June:1-35.
   1955b.   "Castes: Can They Exist in India of Tomorrow?" *Economic Weekly*
             (Bombay), 7, 42:1230-32.
Steed, Gittel
   1953.   Lecture notes. Hectographed.
Stevenson, Mrs. Sinclair
   1920.   *Rites of the Twice Born.* London: Oxford University Press.
Temple, Richard C.
   1900.   *The Legends of the Panjab.* Bombay: Education Society's Press.
The First Five Year Plan
   1952.   New Delhi: Planning Commission, Government of India.
Thorner, Daniel
   1953a.   "The Village Panchayat as a Vehicle of Change." *Economic Develop-
             ment and Cultural Change, 2,* 3:209-15.
   1953b.   "Land Reforms in India," *Economic Weekly* (Bombay), 5, Nov. 5:
             1217-20.
Underhill, M. M.
   1921.   *The Hindu Religious Year.* London: Oxford University Press.
Wellin, Edward
   1955.   "Water Boiling in a Peruvian Town," in *Health, Culture, and Com-
             munity,* ed. by Benjamin D. Paul, pp. 71-103. New York: Russell Sage
             Foundation.

Whitehead, Henry
    1921.   *The Village Gods of South India,* 2nd ed. New York: Crown Pub-
             lishers, Inc.
Wiser, William Henricks
    1936.   *The Hindu Jajmani System.* Lucknow: Lucknow Publishing House.
Wiser, William Henricks, and Charlotte Viall Wiser
    1951.   *Behind Mud Walls.* New York: Agricultural Missions.
Wolf, Eric R.
    1955.   "Types of Latin American Peasantry: A Preliminary Discussion,"
             American Anthropologist, 57, 3, pt. 1:452-71.
Wood, Oswald, and R. Maconachi
    1882.   *Final Report of the Settlement of Land Revenue in the Delhi District,
             1872-1880.* Lahore: Superintendent of Government Printing.
Young, Miriam
    1931.   *Seen and Heard in a Punjab Village.* London: Student Christian
             Movement Press.
Zimmer, Heinrich
    1951.   *Philosophies of India,* ed. by Joseph Campbell. Bollingen Founda-
             tion Series 26. New York: Pantheon Books Inc.

Index

Incarnation, 252, 253

Income, outside, 63, 64, 77, 88-91, 108, 110, 148, 336; by faction, 121-22; and landholdings, 89-91. *See also* Occupations; Revenue

Independence, 15, 74, 75, 82, 115n, 244, 322, 332, 337

Independence Day, 234

India: age distribution of, 16; *bans* in, 173; Camars in, 71-78; caste system in, 79, 81; and community development program, 153-54; disease in, 262, 263, 264, 266, 268-69, 273, 278, 279, 281-82, 284-85, 287-88, 293, 301; education for girls in, 42-43; festival distribution in, 234-36; Government of, 240, 262n, 264, 269; *jajmani* system in, 56-57; land reform in, 110; medical practitioners of, 265; and Program Evaluation Organization, xii; religion in, 249-50, 254; settlement pattern in, 308n

Indo-Gangetic Divide, 4

Indo-Gangetic plain, 317

Indra, 223, 250, 251, 252

Infanticide, female, 16

Influenza, 285

Inheritance, 91, 93, 94, 105-6, 107, 135, 139, 145, 148, 175, 213, 344, 347

intkal, 332, 333, 341, 347

Intervillage networks. *See* Social organization

Intervillage relations. *See* Social organization

Irrigation, 31-33; canal, 6, 9, 94, 97n, 98, 103, 106, 110, 116, 136, 296, 309; compared to Tepoztlan, 306, 309; effects on Jats, 6; and ethics, 256, 258; and factions, 116, 135, 136, 138; need for, 110, 306; in *patvari* records, 347; of rented land, 103; well, 6, 8-9, 35-36, 39, 40n, 72n, 88, 98, 103, 106, 309, 315

Islam, 3, 198, 244

isvara. See God

Jaimel, 23, 24, 99-100, 103, 108, 120, 144-46. *See also tholla*

Jaith-ka Dasahra, 199, 205, 236, 243

jajmani system, 38, 47-48, 55-84, 88, 89, 184, 219, 309-10, 312, 323; and factions, 115, 137, 138, 139, 141-42, 149; and festivals, 77, 78, 200, 201, 202, 207, 208, 209, 241-42, 245; and marriage customs, 60-61, 62, 64, 65, 66-67, 68, 70, 73, 77-78, 163-64, 169, 174, 177, 179, 185, 187

jamabandi, 338, 339, 340, 341-42, 345, 347

Jamnagar, 262n

Janaka, 251n

Janam Astami, 199, 209-10, 234, 235, 236, 240, 241, 243, 252

jar, 255

Jarasandha, 251n

Jat: age at marriage, 159; in agriculture, 6, 7, 32, 39, 88, 101, 309, 313, 323; and burial of dead livestock, 75; and ceremonies, 49, 139, 204, 205; clans, 22-26; common land, 92, 94, 310; and disease, 264-99; disputes, 27, 63, 66-67, 71, 74, 81, 95-97, 134-37, 139, 141, 144-47; education, 42-45, 121, 127-28, 256n, 315, 336-37; factions, 114-54; and festivals, 200, 203, 204, 205, 209, 214, 216, 218, 221, 229, 233, 234, 243; history, 4-5, 306; household size, 16, 17-19, 243; household types, 17-18; housing, 19n, 21, 121, 336-37; in *jajmani* system, 38, 60-84, 88, 137, 138, 139, 141; and land sale, 96, 108; land-ownership, 5, 24, 27, 79-80, 81, 87-91, 92, 96, 97, 100, 103, 121, 245n, 259, 301, 315, 323; location in Rampur, 19; longevity, 17; and marriage customs, 4, 157-95, 218; and mortgages, 107, 108, 122, 128; occupations, 4, 39, 63, 88-90, 107, 111, 311, 315, 336-37; outside income, 88, 89, 90-91, 108, 121-22, 336; ownership of oxen, 101-2; *panas* and *thollas*, 22-26; and panchayats, 23, 27, 29, 63, 74-75, 95, 114, 128; and *patvari*, 333, 334, 335-37, 347; personal characteristics, 5, 6, 7; population in northwestern India, 4; population in

Sexes, separation of, 52, 188, 308-9

Sexual relations: and beliefs on disease, 288, 289-90, 291, 292; after birth, 49; and caste system, 257; extramarital, 128, 136, 148, 189, 193, 194; during pregnancy, 47

Shadows, 270, 273-74

Shaiva, 235n

Shamirpet, 198, 201n

Sheoratri. *See* Siv Ratri

Shiv. *See* Siv

Shiva. *See* Siva

Shivala, 229n

Shoemaker. *See* Camar

Shoemaking, 72, 76, 77

Shrines, 12-14, 49, 178, 187, 198, 200, 201n, 203-5, 210-11, 222, 237-38, 241-42, 245, 252, 280, 285

sidha, 222, 227, 233, 242, 243

Sidhi Satain. *See* Basora

Sikh, 4, 6, 228n, 234, 244

Sikh path-ki-wali Mata, 167

Silono, 199, 208-9, 234, 238, 239, 241, 243, 245

Silversmith, 170

Sin, 251, 256, 257. *See also* Evil

sindhara, 207

Singing, 48, 50, 162, 180, 182, 204, 228, 237. *See also* Songs

Sirhind. *See* Hariana

Sisupala, 251n

Sita, 251n

Sitala. *See* Gurgaon-wali Mata

Sitting-board, ceremonial. *See patra*

Siv, 235

Siv Ratri, 199, 228-29, 234, 235, 236, 237, 239, 243, 244, 252

Siva, 198, 201n, 218, 228-29, 235, 238, 241, 245, 250, 252

Siva Narayani, 228n

siyana, 296

Smallpox, 203, 265, 268-73, 274, 284, 300; goddess of, 198, 200-203, 222, 238, 269, 271-72

Snakes: curers of bites of, 265; god of, 210-13

Social organization, 148-49, 154; clans, 22-26, 166; compared to Tepoztlan, 305-6, 312-20, 322, 323, 325-27; couples by caste and house site, 18; education influence on, 45, 76-77, 83, 315; exogamy, 10, 23, 160-62, 319-20, 325; family types by caste, 17; household size by caste, 16, 17-18; household types by caste, 18, 19; intervillage networks, 23, 29-31, 58, 77, 149, 312, 313, 314, 318, 324; intervillage relations, 116, 125, 127, 129, 130, 137, 142, 145n, 153, 161, 163, 167n, 189, 204, 205, 207, 213, 229, 239; kinship units and village subdivisions, 22-26, 339, 347; reflected in *patvari* records, 329-47; solidarity, 238-39, 246, 317, 321n, 323; stability, 322-23. *See also* Faction; Family; Kinship

Socialists, 244

Socio-economic positions, 88, 89, 90-91, 120-23, 127, 137-38, 243, 256, 259, 270, 301

Soil, 7-8, 32-33

Songs: in festivals, 191, 200, 206, 207, 210, 212, 216, 224, 225, 226, 228-29, 231, 239, 240; and marriage customs, 169, 171, 174-75, 176, 178, 180, 181, 183, 184, 186, 188, 189, 192, 193, 194, 195

Soul. *See atman*

Spain, viii, 312

Spanish, 306

Spanish Conquest, 311, 312

Spinning wheels, 14

sraddha, 213-15, 234, 236, 245. *See also* Kanagat

Stealing, 257

Stool, ceremonial. *See patra*

Streets, 10-12, 26, 95, 256, 258, 308, 310, 317

Sudan, 324

Sugar-cane crusher. *See* Agriculture tools and equipment

Suicide, 5n, 297

Sukhma, 195

Sultanpur Dabas, 30

vaid, 265, 280, 282, 292, 294, 297
Vaishnava, 234-35
Vaisya, 78
Valmiki, 251n
Vasistha, 251n
Vasudeva, 242
vazir, 30
Vedas, 72, 238, 252
Vidya, 195
Vikramaditya, 205
Village, characteristics of, 6, 10-14, 305-7, 316-20
Virtue. *See* Good
Vishnu. *See* Visnu
Visnu, 211, 234, 235, 250-51, 252, 253
Visvamitra, 251n

wajib-ul'-arz, 60, 74, 75, 163, 340
Washerman. *See* Dhobi
Wasteland. *See* Land
Watchman. *See caukidar*
Water carrier. *See* Jhinvar
Water resources, 6, 7, 8, 9, 98n, 110, 263; compared to Tepoztlan, 306. *See also* Irrigation; Pond; Rainfall; Wells
Wealth, 87-111; cow dung as, 223-24, 237; and disease, 264, 277-78, 281, 289; distribution of at ceremonies, 47, 48, 50; distribution of at festivals, 200, 207, 208, 209n, 214, 217, 222, 224, 226, 233, 243; distribution of at marriage, 60, 62, 65, 66, 68, 70, 73, 162-63, 164, 168-69, 175-77, 178, 179, 180, 183, 188; and factions, 115, 121-23, 124, 127, 137-38, 150, 315; goddess of, 222, 223, 236, 237, 238, 250, 251; as *kamin* prestige factor, 58; livestock as, 39-40, 64, 68, 71, 77, 89, 101-2, 107, 108, 111, 315; and religion and ethics, 251, 253-55, 256-58, 259

Weapons, worship of, 215
Weaver. *See* Kurmi
Weddings. *See* Marriage
Wells: building of, 116, 256; by caste, 8; in disease, 265, 267, 268, 299; drinking, 8-9, 51, 184, 189, 192, 314, 321; drowning in, 193, 297; in festivals, 227; god of, 234; hand-lever, 8; irrigation, 6, 8-9, 98, 103, 106, 309; *la-caras*, 35-36, 40n; and marriage customs, 179n; in *patvari* records, 347; Persian, 8, 9, 35-36, 39, 40n, 72n, 315; pit, 88; sacred, 237
Widowers, 18, 159, 190
Widows, 4-5, 18, 171, 189-90, 218
Women: in agriculture, 6, 37, 51; compared to Tepoztecans, 321; Dabas Jat, 5n; and disease, 265, 271-73, 275, 280, 283, 289, 293-94, 295, 296, 298-99, 300; eating habits of, 42; and factions, 116, 135, 315; and festivals, 202-3, 206, 207, 210, 215-21, 224, 225, 227, 228-33, 237-38, 239-41, 246, 252, 269, 271; and leadership, 129, 150; pre- and post-delivery care of, 47-49; and religion and ethics, 251, 252, 253, 257, 269, 271-72, 275, 280; work of, 49-52, 59, 166, 167, 184, 189, 191, 192, 321
Wood. *See* Trees
World. *See sansar*
World War I, 9, 108, 142, 147, 315
World War II, 74, 77, 108, 315
Wrestling matches, 204, 207, 209, 229

Yama, 250, 251
Yudhisthira, 251n

Zahir Diwan. *See* Guga *pir*
Zahir Pir. *See* Guga *pir*
zamindar, 80, 82, 93, 109, 330, 331, 335